Yogic Flying

According to Yoga Vasishtha

A translation of seven chapters from the Yoga Vasishtha, with a commentary written in the light of the teaching of the Transcendental Meditation® technique, the TM-Sidhi® program and Yogic Flying® around the world by Maharishi Mahesh Yogi

by
Peter F. Freund, Ph.D.

Golden Meteor Press—Fairfield, Iowa

ISBN-9781790917334

Cover design by Elinor Wolfe

Hyper-links for the digital edition at
http://peterffreund.com/books/yogavasishtha.html

Printed by Golden Meteor Press, Fairfield, Iowa, U.S.A. First 2019 printing.

Table of Contents

THE SANSKRIT ALPHABET

अ a	आ ā	इ i	ई ī	उ u
ऊ ū	ऋ ṛ	ॠ ṝ	ऌ lṛ	
ए e	ऐ ai	ओ o	औ au	
अं aṁ	अः aḥ			
क ka	ख kha	ग ga	घ gha	ङ ṅa
च ca	छ cha	ज ja	झ jha	ञ ña
ट ṭa	ठ ṭha	ड ḍa	ढ ḍha	ण ṇa
त ta	थ tha	द da	ध dha	न na
प pa	फ pha	ब ba	भ bha	म ma
य ya	र ra	ल la	व va	
श śa	ष ṣa	स sa	ह ha	

Introduction to Yoga Vasishtha

The Yoga Vasishtha is an authentic text of the ancient Vedic Literature, written by the great sage Vasishtha, one of the greatest minds of all time. The Yoga Vasishtha is one of a circle of texts which together recount the history of the noble and righteous king Rām, who ruled the world from Ayodhya, many thousands of years ago. The story of Rām is the greatest epic of world literature, and the Yoga Vasishtha tells one small part of that history, namely the detailed exposition of Rām's education under the tutelage of the sage Vasishtha. As recounted by the more modern poet Tulsidass, Rām, studying at the feet of Vasishtha, gained total knowledge in a short time. The Yoga Vasishtha chronicles what may be called the greatest education that any man has ever received. Vasishtha had encyclopedic knowledge of the ancient Vedic Science, a comprehensive vision of the natural laws governing creation, and exhaustive knowledge of the higher states of consciousness of man, based on his own supreme realization. He imparted total knowledge to Rām through a series of stories, some mythical, some factual, each brimming with profound insights into life, and all together orienting the young child Rām to the principles and practices of the Golden Age of human civilization on earth, the halcyon days of the solar dynasty of kings of Ayodhya.

The setting of the Rāmāyaṇa, the Indian epic that tells the life story of Rām, is in the distant prehistoric past. It is history, not mythology, as the long stone bridge between India and Śrī Lanka, discovered by NASA through aerial photography may confirm, but it was a far distant age, when sea levels were fifty feet lower than they are today.

The sage Vasishtha, renowned even then for his great wisdom, was an adviser in the court of Rām's father King Daśaratha. He was a sage of great personal presence and extraordinary spiritual radiance. He is described in the Vāsiṣṭha Laiṅgyam[1] as follows:

> The holy sage Vasishtha, having performed great austerity, virtuous, possessed of inner fulfillment, his senses fully under control, Divine, 1000 years old, living on air [as his only sustenance], the constant companion of *Agni* [through his long meditations,] was resplendent with the brilliance of the 5 syllable mantra; he moved about in the company of the hundred names (of Rudra in the Śatarudriya portion of Yajur Veda) made [manifest as forms] visible to the senses [through his constant performance of Rudra-abhisheka]. Having cleared away all stress and become pure by the repetition of Praṇava, consisting of six syllables, he [Vasiṣhṭha,] was the most virtuous of sages.

This was an age in which the spiritual knowledge gained through the subjective investigations into the nature of the Self, the nature of consciousness, was greater, more powerful than the destructive power of natural law harnessed by the military of those ages. Therefore the great sages who had realized the Self and gained spiritual power were profoundly revered and respected by even the most powerful kings of that era. Vasishtha himself participated in one such trial of strength and power between an enlightened sage and a king with an entire army. This is the story of Vasishtha and Viśvamitra, erstwhile enemies who later became friends, and cooperated in the education of Rām.

Viśvamitra was a provincial king who enjoyed hunting. One day, on his way home from a hunting expedition with his army, he came across the hermitage of the sage Vasishtha. He greatly appreciated the opportunity to have an audience with this great sage, and after receiving the sage's blessings, he begged permission for him and his army to depart. Vasishtha, however, wanted them to stay and spend the night and offered to feed them. After they had bathed in a nearby river, he lavishly fed and entertained the entire army. Viśvamitra asked how the resources of a small *Āśram* were able to feed an entire army. He was told that Vasishtha had a cow named Śabala who provided all the food and entertainment for the soldiers. He immediately wanted to have this wish-fulfilling cow for himself, but Vasishtha would not part with it. Not being able to acquire the cow amicably, Viśvamitra resolved to take it by force. But when he set his army the task of bringing home the cow, the cow defended herself by creating an army that completely destroyed Viśvamitra's army. Viśvamitra retreated to the Himālayas, where he practiced severe austerities and gained the favor of Īśvara, who granted him many divine weapons and the knowledge of how to use them. He returned to Vasishtha's Āśram and fired all of his mantra-charged arrows at Vasishtha, but the power of Vasishtha's Brahma-daṇḍa, his staff of righteousness, neutralized all the weapons. Utterly defeated by Vasishtha, he recognized that it was useless for a king to challenge the superior strength of an enlightened sage. He then abdicated his throne and devoted himself to purificatory practices in order to become a powerful Ṛṣi in his own right, like Vasishtha. As he advanced towards the status of a Brahma-ṛṣi, he grew in the ability to fulfill his own desires, so that he no longer had need for Vasishtha's cow of plenty.

This story establishes the superiority of Vedic knowledge and makes plausible that King Daśaratha would entrust the education of his son to this holy sage. Under the tutelage of Vasishtha, Rām became a perfect man, knowledgeable, cultured, refined, noble in his thoughts and demeanor, respectful of others, and always acting rightly in every circumstance.

The story of Rām's education at the feet of the great sage Vasishtha is called the *Yoga Vasishtha*, because the central teaching of the entire book is the unification and full integration of life through Yogic practices. The core story dealing directly with Yoga and Yogic practices in the Yoga Vasishtha is the story of Śikhidhvaja and his queen Cūḍālā. Here Vasishtha shows his mastery of the knowledge of Patañjali's Yoga and the attainment of the state of *Kaivalya* through these practices.

In this story, Cūḍālā learns to practice meditation, and through her meditation practice she gains enlightenment. The descriptions of her meditation practice indicate that it was in all respects similar to the practice of the Transcendental Meditation® technique, introduced to the world by Maharishi Mahesh Yogi more than half a century ago. Cūḍālā's meditation appears to be what modern scientists classify as "automatic self-transcending,"[2] in order to uniquely distinguish it from other meditation practices available in the world today. In referring to Cūḍālā's meditation, we have used variously transcendental deep meditation, effortless transcending, and automatic self-transcending as names to refer to the technique that she was practicing. The Transcendental Meditation technique has been shown to develop the same kinds of experiences, and have similar societal effects, so it is appropriate to place her technique parallel to the modern technique taught by Maharishi, although we cannot verify that it was identical.

Vasishtha describes Cūḍālā's practice of Yogic Flying in great detail also, and it appears to follow the parameters and guidelines of practice laid down by Patañjali. It is, of course, difficult to know whether Patañjali actually predated the story of the Rāmāyaṇa, or whether the principles of Yoga were known to Vasishtha and much later formalized by Patañjali in the textbook called *Yoga Darśanam*. Vasishtha's knowledge in any event is comprehensive, flawless and authentic. Vasishtha's teaching of the Siddhis and Yogic Flying, and his presentation of the higher states of consciousness, is completely in accord with the teaching of Patañjali in the *Yoga Darśanam*. The teaching of Yoga by Patañjali, and the teaching of Yoga by Vasishtha are both the same one universal, eternal teaching of Yoga, valid for all men in all ages.

The story of Cūḍālā's mastery of Yogic Flying has been dismissed by translators as mythical. In the Vedic Tradition of Masters, the most recent master to have publicly displayed his mastery of Yogic Flying was

Ādi Śaṅkarācārya, who lived 2500 years ago. Śaṅkara used Yogic Flying to travel from city to city and thereby bring his revival of knowledge of the Vedic tradition throughout India. Historical accounts of individuals flying are rare and generally poorly corroborated. A great exception is the story of Saint Joseph of Cupertino (1603-1663), who was seen flying through the air by thousands of people in over 300 recorded instances of aerial flights, some of them lasting for hours.[3] But it is not these isolated instances of individuals in more recent times who have mastered flying which give credence to this ancient story of Yogic Flying. More significant is the revival in modern times of Patañjali's procedure of Yogic Flying, and the teaching of Yogic Flying all over the world by Maharishi Mahesh Yogi. Many tens of thousands of people have learned the practice of Yogic Flying, and there are many who have been practicing more than 40 years. In the light of Maharishi's teaching of Yogic Flying, and his thousands of hours of lectures about the significance and import of the growing experiences of Flying, and in light of the worldwide availability of Maharishi's TM-Sidhi® program including Yogic Flying, it is now possible to revisit the words of Vasishtha, and gain deeper insights into the upper reaches of human potential. Yogic Flying is not mythological, it is the greatest gift to man from the ancient Vedic Tradition of Masters.

Endnotes

1 Vasiṣṭha Laiṅgyam, Government Oriental Manuscript Library Madras, D15664, Telugu script, unpublished manuscript, translation by author

2 Travis, F. and Parim, N. (2017) Default Mode Network Activation and Transcendental Meditation Practice: Focused Attention or Automatic Self-Transcending? *Brain and Cognition*, 111:86-94.

3 Pastrovicchi, Angelo; Laing, Francis S., tr., *St. Joseph of Cupertino*, B. Herder: St. Louis, 1918.

Translator's Preface

"Only a new seed will produce a new crop," is Maharishi Mahesh Yogi's rallying cry for revival of life in this generation from an age of suffering, disease, wars and natural calamities. The same principle applies to the field of hermeneutics, the field of interpretation of ancient texts: Only a new angle of vision will allow us to see the fullness of knowledge lively in the ancient Vedic civilization, the civilization that created a Golden Age of life, in which men moved about on earth, in affluence, joy and fulfillment, as if they were living in heaven.[1] Maharishi Mahesh Yogi's approach to Vedic interpretation is radically new, and the outlines of this approach to the interpretation of Vedic Literature were developed in great detail during a Ph.D. program in Vedic Studies offered at Maharishi European Research University in Switzerland, 1974-1976. The principles which he developed in lectures during this period were summarized at his request and presented in the author's Masters Thesis (1980). Maharishi's unique perspective is that there are universal principles of structure which apply to the Vedic Literature, and these principles determine the pattern of sequential unfoldment of knowledge in every package.

In the author's development of a regime of interpretation based on Maharishi's teaching, he has found that there are three principles that are paramount, which must be applied for the systematic interpretation of any Vedic text. The first principle is that the total knowledge is delivered in its completeness in the first expression. The first expression of any package of knowledge contains in seed form the total knowledge that will be unfolded in the entire package. Maharishi gives the example of the first word of Ṛg Veda, "*Agnim*," which he identifies as a complete and perfect package of total knowledge of Veda, the source of Ṛg Veda and the Vedic Literature.

This principle that the first expression contains the total knowledge of the text can even be taken to the level of syllables, where the first syllable of Ṛg Veda, "Ak," described as "the collapse of "A" into "Ka,"[2] is the seed of total knowledge of Veda. And even the first alphabet, "A" by itself, can be taken as the seed of total knowledge of Ṛg Veda and the whole of Vedic Literature.[3]

The practical application of this principle that the first expression of a package of knowledge contains the total knowledge of the text is that the first verse of any chapter in the whole of Vedic Literature must be construed as containing in seed form the total knowledge of the chapter. This is a challenge and a test for the translator to verify his understanding. The translator must be able to grasp the total knowledge of the chapter in its first verse and must similarly see that each verse in the entire chapter is a commentary on that initial verse.

The second principle in Maharishi's formulation of principles of Vedic structure that informs every moment of understanding of a text of Vedic Literature, is that each verse is a commentary or elaboration built upon the previous. This means that the verses in any text in the whole of Vedic Literature are not collections of independent verses that have been thrown together, but rather that there is a sequential unfoldment where each verse is elaborating on the previous, taking the knowledge contained in that previous verse one step further. This principle is true even on the level of the *Sūktas* or collections of verses in the *Maṇḍalas* or books of the Veda. Subsequent *Sūktas* may be by different authors, different Ṛṣis, but nevertheless, each following *Sūkta* is a commentary on the previous, in a perfectly ordered sequence of total knowledge.

This principle of the paramount importance of sequential unfoldment is so deeply embedded in the structure of every text in the whole of Vedic Literature, that Maharishi says that the commentary of any text is contained in the text itself. That means that one does not have to search outside a text for some handle or understanding in order to understand a text; one does not need to depend on the commentaries that have been written on a text in order to understand the text: The perfect commentary on any expression in any package of the whole of Vedic Literature is already there at your fingertips: You only need to follow the sequence.

This is stated explicitly in the Sūtra of Maharishi's Apaurusheya Bhāṣya, "Vedasya Bhāṣya Vede eva—ānupūrvikrameṇa." "The commentary of the Veda is in the Veda itself: Follow the sequence."[4]

Both of these principles, that the first expression is a seed for all that follows, and that each verse is a commentary on the previous, are idealized, consummate principles of good writing. One should always start by telling the reader what one is going to say, right at the outset. Similarly, in terms of sequential unfoldment, writers should always use "close connections and stern logic." This Maharishi teaches as a principle of good writing. These are principles that can be taught in the classroom. Maharishi's vision is that these are spontaneous characteristics of *Arsha Vākya*, the speech of the enlightened.

In the texts of Vedic Literature, the tree always emerges from the seed, and the growth of each part is perfectly sequential. These principles provide yardsticks to analyze and evaluate any understanding or translation of any text of Vedic Literature. Until one has seen the entire tree within the seed from which the tree emerges, one has not yet understood the whole. Similarly, until one has seen how a verse is commenting on the preceding verse, one has not captured the role of that particular verse in unfolding the knowledge of the whole.

The overall structure of a text, that means its division into discrete packages, provides a framework for systematic understanding of the knowledge of the text. These are ordering principles applicable to every text of Vedic Literature. One can learn a great deal about the overall survey of knowledge in the text even without entering onto the level of words. Maharishi has brought a new dimension, the analysis of structure, to the interpretation of the ancient Vedic Literature.

A third principle which is essential for the interpretation of any text in the Vedic Literature, is the principle that there is an inherent connection between the name and the form in the ancient Vedic language. That means that words have intrinsic meaning based on the vibrations of the sounds. Those vibrations give rise to the form spontaneously on the ground of pure consciousness. This theory of the form or meaning arising automatically from the sound or name gives life to the Vedic Literature: This means that the text will mean the same to anyone in any age if they can have their awareness open to that level where the sound gives rise to the form.

In practical terms, every word in the Vedic language is derived from verbal roots. Each root has specific defined tendencies that are known from grammar. These abstract tendencies of the sound of the word are collapsed into the form or meaning according to the structure of the text. Based on where in the sequence of unfoldment of the chapter the word appears and based on what primal seed of knowledge is being unfolded in that chapter, the inherent tendencies of the word take shape, and participate in the flow of knowledge.

If a text is written in the ancient Vedic language, then one needs to know the verbal roots of each word, and the development of the text from its initial seed formulation. One does not need to know the meaning of individual words in the common parlance of the time. The text stands outside of time as an eternal and perfect formulation of knowledge, based on clear and precise principles of Vedic grammar and sequential unfoldment.

This discipline of interpretation, called structural hermeneutics by the author, is based on Maharishi's Apaurusheya Bhâshya of Ṛg Veda, and has been used to good advantage in the translation of these chapters from the Yoga Vasishtha. In the commentary the author has endeavored to explain to the reader how the integrity of sequential unfoldment of knowledge is embodied in each successive verse, and how the text unfolds from its seed expression in the first verse of each chapter.

The author's unfoldment of Vasishtha's presentation of the knowledge of Yogic Flying® has been profoundly influenced by the teachings of Maharishi Mahesh Yogi. Maharishi introduced the practice of Yogic Flying to the world in 1977. In thirty years of lectures after the launch of Yogic Flying, Maharishi described in detail, and from every angle, the experience and implications of Yogic flying. The author, having been immersed in Maharishi's lectures on a daily basis for more than thirty years, has unavoidably imbibed that knowledge. This translation of Vasishtha's presentation of Yogic Flying is deeply informed by Maharishi's teaching, and by the author's thirty years' practice of Yogic Flying in the Golden Domes of Fairfield, Iowa.

Maharishi's teaching of Yogic Flying is a modern exposition of the eternal knowledge contained in the Veda and Vedic Literature. This translation, based on Maharishi's principles of interpretation, has found only that the modern presentation of Yogic Flying by Maharishi, and the ancient presentation of Yogic Flying by Vasishtha, are the same one voice of the eternal Vedic tradition of masters.

Endnotes

1 It is said that in Rām Rāj, the rule of King Rām, रामराज्य दुख काहु न व्यापा noone suffered.

2 "Ka" becomes "Ga" through internal Sandhi in the formation of the word, in order to better accommodate the voiced quality of the subsequent letter, "Na."

3 "akāro vai sarvā vāk," "The letter 'A' indeed is all speech." This is a traditional aphorism, quoted for example by Śaṁkara in his commentary on Chāndogya Upaniṣad, 2, 23.3.

4 The Sūtra of Maharishi's Apauruṣeya Bhāṣya was presented in a lecture, "Maharishi's Apaurusheya Bhāṣya of Ṛg Veda," 1978. The principles of sequential unfoldment of his Apaurusheya Bhāṣya are presented in *Celebrating Perfection in Education*, MERU, 1990, Vlodrop, Holland.

Synopsis of the Story of Śikhidhvaja and Cūḍālā

Śikhidhvaja was born the son of a king in ancient India. At the tender age of 16 his father passed away. Although he was heir to the throne, others wanted the power and prestige of ruling the kingdom, and he needed to assert his authority by force against these opponents, in order to become king. Successfully rising to the throne, he then used the resources of the kingdom to conquer the whole world and become universal monarch.

With his ministers, he ruled the world fairly, and justice, peace and prosperity prevailed everywhere. After a few years, Śikhidhvaja began to feel that he should enjoy the power of his office in play, in sport, in entertainment. He began to search everywhere for fulfillment through the senses. Now distracted from his initial single-minded focus on politics, his ministers noticed what was happening to him, and arranged for him a marriage with the daughter of a king in a neighboring province.

Cūḍālā was the perfect wife for Śikhidhvaja, and they became soul-mates, and shared everything together. More and more, Śikhidhvaja left the administration of the kingdom to his able ministers, and he engaged himself in royal sports and amusements with his wife Cūḍālā. The whole world was at his feet, and all the joys of the relative were his playground. In this way, many happy years passed for the royal couple.

As the years flashed by, Śikhidhvaja and Cūḍālā soon noticed the onset of aging, and the inevitable decline of their faculties. They began to realize that all their sports and amusements were fleeting joys, and their happiness was not based on anything substantial or permanent. So, they began together a search for fulfillment of a lasting sort, true spiritual fulfillment. They attended lectures and began various spiritual practices. Finally, they were instructed in the Yogic practice of effortless transcending, a technique similar in all respects to Maharishi Mahesh Yogi's Transcendental Meditation® technique, taught throughout the world today. They had an excellent start in the practice, with clear experiences of transcendental consciousness, and quickly lost their surface anxieties and stresses, and gained some measure of inner peace. Of the two of them, Cūḍālā alone persisted with the practice over many years.

With many years of practice, Cūḍālā gained enlightenment, Cosmic Consciousness. Then continuing in the practice, she rose to God Consciousness and eventually Unity Consciousness, the supreme state of integration of life. Now one day, coming upon her in the inner apartments of the palace, the king, Śikhidhvaja happened to notice the transformation that had come over his wife in her state of enlightenment: He noticed that she had retained the beautiful figure of her youth, and that her personal beauty was greatly enhanced by the advancing years, rather than declining with the wrinkles of aging. He asked her to tell him the secret of her youthfulness. His expectation was that she had found the nectar of immortality, and since they had always shared everything, she would now share it with him. But there was no magic elixir, there was only her experience of infinite fulfillment in the state of enlightenment that was responsible for her radiance of youthful vitality and great beauty. She described her state of enlightenment to him.

Even though they had long since taught each other all the sciences and arts which they had learned in their youth, and were skilled at teaching and learning new concepts, he did not understand what she was saying. Higher states of consciousness are not concepts, they are not moods of the mind, and there is nothing in the waking state of consciousness which can capture or even designate the essential nature of Unity Consciousness. Śikhidhvaja was not able to understand a single point of Cūḍālā's presentation of her experience of higher consciousness. He heard only gibberish and thought that she was amusing him with philosophical speculations. He refuted all her arguments, laughed heartily and left the room.

Cūḍālā realized that she needed to be able to show something that was practically useful in the state of enlightenment, and that the mere description of the state would not suffice. She then decided to learn Yogic Flying. She practiced Yogic Flying for long periods of time with discipline and determination, and in time mastered the ability to fly through the air. She gained all the Siddhis and became a complete master of total natural law. She also gained some wisdom and perspective and realized that flaunting her Siddhis would not be useful. So, she continued quietly in her role as the queen, anticipating and fulfilling the needs and desires of her husband, and using her Siddhi powers to explore the universe, and to be at the same time, the perfect wife. She continued from time to time to try to teach her husband about enlightenment, but always to no avail.

After some time, Śikhidhvaja tired of his royal responsibilities and amusements, gave the kingdom over to his wife, and went to the forest to practice austerities. Living the life of a mendicant, in a cave at the far outskirts of his kingdom, far away from civilized life, he lived in utter simplicity, renouncing all worldly joys for twenty years. At some point, Cūḍālā, who was closely monitoring the situation with her special powers, decided that Śikhidhvaja had matured in his practice of renunciation, and was now ready for the knowledge of enlightenment. She then flew through the air to his cave, and disguising herself as an enlightened man, presented herself to the former king, and became his guru. Under her tutelage he eventually gained full enlightenment.

Now that Śikhidhvaja was enlightened, her goal was achieved, and there was no need for the disguise. She revealed herself to the king, who was now delighted to be at long last reunited with his wife. She then convinced him that his renunciation of the throne and life in the forest was a mistake, and that there was no need to undergo such deprivations for the sake of enlightenment. She then conjured up an entire army, and sitting on the backs of elephants, they marched into the capital city to the great acclaim of their subjects and took over the kingdom once again. Together they ruled the kingdom in peace and prosperity for 50,000 years.

There is a story within the story, which comes at the

conclusion of the seven chapters that chronicle Cūḍālā's growth to enlightenment and mastery of the Siddhi powers. It is a story of a miserly merchant, who is well off financially, and lives with his family in the forest. One day, not far from his home, as he was coming home from his business affairs after a day's work, he happened to drop a small coin into the grass. Alarmed at the loss of the coin, he began to search through all the grass in the meadow to find that lost coin. That penny, he thought, through business could become two, then four, and then ten. Thousands, he imagined, even untold wealth could be gleaned from that single coin through business. He searched through the meadow looking behind every blade of grass for three days. At the end of the third day, he happened to find a philosopher's stone, which was capable of fulfilling all his needs for wealth. By making use of that stone, his wealth would never be depleted through business, and his wealth would only increase. Satisfied with that gain, he returned home and forgetting the lost penny, lived happily ever after.

The story of the merchant serves to show that the goal for which one seeks is not the same as what one finds. The goal of enlightenment that is attained is not the same as what one sought, because one cannot conceive of the grandeur of the state of enlightenment, it cannot be communicated in words. Some small boundary of peace of mind, or perhaps the hope of happiness captures the mind, and one searches for that diligently. Instead, one attains the infinite unbounded bliss of enlightenment. The enlightenment cannot be gained without the searching. One has to engage in the search. But there is no real connection between the small goal one holds in one's mind, and the great huge achievement of the wholeness, totality of life in Brahman Consciousness which one achieves.

This was Śikhidhvaja's experience of searching also. He was searching for a wife with great ardor, and he had in mind a great ideal of beauty, perfection of figure, charm and playfulness. But what he got was not anything he could have imagined in his wildest dreams: A wife who would devote her life to guiding him to the supreme state of enlightenment.

Vasishtha uses this beautiful love story to show that the goal of enlightenment is far greater, more valuable, richer in every way, than the Siddhis for which the seeker practices his technologies of consciousness. The rising Siddha wants to fly but gains instead not merely the ability to fly through the air, but mastery of total natural law, eternal bliss consciousness, every thought and action spontaneously fulfilled by natural law: life in perfection, for himself, his community and his world, life in enlightenment, heavenly life lived on earth. This is Vasishtha's presentation of Yogic Flying.

CHAPTER 1: THE MARRIAGE OF ŚIKHIDHVAJA

Verse 1:

वसिष्ठ उवाच
एतामवष्टभ्यौ दृशं भगीरथधिया धृताम्
समः स्वस्थो यथाप्राप्तं कार्यमाहर शान्तधीः १

The example is seen of two people taking recourse to the knowledge of the path to enlightenment upheld since ancient times by the kings in the dynasty of Bhagīratha.

[In this tradition] there is a technique to be practiced, producing a state of infinite silence in the midst of infinite dynamism, by which the permanent unwavering state of Self-realization—the highest plane of perfection of human existence—is attained.

Verse 2:

इदं पूर्वं परित्यज्य क्रोडीकृत्य मनःखगम्
शान्तमात्मनि तिष्ठ त्वं शिखिध्वज इवाचलः २

Gaining mastery of the ability to move [the body] through the air by the [mere] impulse of the mind, they achieved this [highest plane of perfection of human existence] long before the passing away of the physical body.

Do thou [O Rāma] establish eternal peace and contentment in the Self, that is unchanging, stable and ever the same, as did Śikhidhvaja [in olden times].

Verse 3:

श्रीराम उवाच
कोऽसौ शिखिध्वजो नाम कथं वा लब्धवान्पदम्
एतन्मे कथय ब्रह्मन्भूयो बोधविवृद्धये ३

Śrī Rām said:

Who was this man named Śikhidhvaja, and how did he gain enlightenment?

Please tell me the story of his attainment of Brahman consciousness, in order to expand my understanding of higher states of consciousness.

Verse 4:

वसिष्ठ उवाच
द्वापारे भवतां पूर्वमिदानीं च भविष्यतः
तेनैव संनिवेशेन दंपती स्निग्धतां गतौ ४

Vasishtha said:

There were two lovers who shared one life together, in the past, in the present, and in the future.

They were always married and lived together as husband and wife, having fallen deeply in love with each other.

Verse 5:

श्रीराम उवाच
यत्पूर्वमासीद्भगवंस्तदिदानीं तथैव हि
भविष्यति किमर्थं वै वद मे वदतां वर ५

Śrī Rāma said:

Whatever has happened in the past gives rise to the destiny that one enjoys in the present; in the same way, the future depends on the present.

What is the purpose of the same thing recurring in past, present and future times? Please explain this to me, O best of speakers.

Verse 6:

वसिष्ठ उवाच
जगन्निर्माणनियतेरस्या ब्रह्मादिसंविदः
ईदृश्यवस्थितिर्नित्यमनिवार्यस्वभावजा ६

Vasishtha said:

Because the path of evolution of all the beings in the universe is fixed for all time by the cosmic law established by Brahmā at the dawn of creation,

Both together having such [similar] qualities that they always follow the same path, irresistibly [they are] born together repeatedly because [of the similarity] of the innate nature within each of them.

Verse 7:

यदन्यद्बहुशो भूत्वा पुनर्भवति भूरिशः
अभूत्वैव भवत्यन्यः पुनश्च न भवत्यलम् ७

Whatever has repeatedly come into being on separate paths, again comes to be, variously.

Having been different in the past, [it] comes to be different again and doesn't become the equal [of the other].

Verse 8:

अन्यत्प्राक्संनिवेशाढ्यं सादृश्येन विवल्गति
सदृशा विषमाश्चैव यथा सरसि वीचयः ८

[However,] Always living for the other, living together in affluence and fulfillment, one experiences everything alike,

[Then] Similarities and dissimilarities are always there like waves on the ocean [not challenging the underlying unity].

Verse 9:

ता एवान्याश्च दृश्यन्ते व्यवस्थाः संसृतौ तथा
तस्माद्राजेव भूयोऽपि वक्ष्यमाणकथेश्वरः ९

Their differences continue on eternally [on the basis of the strength of their union:] they see their respective differences continuing in the same way through successive states of existence,

From the strength of that union the sovereignty of the ruler expands, becoming greater and greater, that is the story of the king being told now.

Verse 10:

भविष्यति महातेजास्तद्वृत्तान्तमिमं शृणु
द्वापरे पूर्वमभवदतीते सप्तमे मनौ १०

There will be very great powers [developed], that is how it works out in the end: Listen to this story.

Long ago in the previous Dvāpar age in the seventh Manvantara,

Verse 11:

चतुर्युगे चतुर्थे तु सर्गेऽस्मिन्कुरुणां कुले
जम्बुद्वीपे प्रसिद्धस्य विन्ध्यस्यादूरसंस्थिते ११

In the fourth cycle of the four Yugas in this creation, in the family of the Kurus,

Brought forth on the Indian subcontinent, in a settlement not far from the Vindhya mountains—

Verse 12:

मालवानां पुरे श्रीमाञ्छिखिध्वज इतीश्वरः
धैर्यौदार्यदशायुक्तः क्षमाशमदमान्वितः १२

In a city of the Mālava empire, [there was an] illustrious king named Śikhidhvaja.

Possessed of courage from birth, he was endowed with patience, calm, and self-control.

Verse 13:

शूरः शुभसमाचारो मौनी गुणगणाकरः
आहर्ता सर्वयज्ञानां जेता सर्वधनुष्मताम् १३

A valiant hero, virtuous in his actions, silent, he was liberally endowed with many excellent qualities.

The performer of all the prescribed yagyas, he [also] prevailed in all archery contests.

Verse 14:

कर्ता सकलकार्याणां भर्ता पूर्ववपुर्भुवः
पेशलस्निग्धमधुरो विदग्धः प्रीतिसागरः १४

He performed great charitable acts for the benefit of the whole society, and he was the upholder of the pristine beauty of nature and the environment.

Charming, loving and sweet, cultured and refined, he was an ocean of kindness.

Verse 15:

सुन्दरः शान्तसुभगः प्रतापी धर्मवत्सलः
वदिता विनयार्थानां दाता सकलसंपदाम् १५

Handsome, gentle and liked by all, he was the scorcher of enemies, and he fulfilled his duties and responsibilities with grace and kindness.

An eloquent teacher in every field of knowledge, he was the giver of fulfillment to those who approached him with desires.

Verse 16:

भोक्ता सत्सङ्गसहितः सुश्रोता सकलश्रुतेः
वेदासौ माननाशून्यः स्त्रैणं तृणवदस्पृशन् १६

He enjoyed the company of pure and virtuous people and enjoyed listening to the teaching of the scriptures.

He was knowledgeable but unpretentious; he showed no interest in women and had no contact with them.

Verse 17:

पितरि स्वर्गमापन्ने बाल एवोत्तमौजसा
कृत्वा षोडशवर्षाणि स्वयं दिग्विजयं वशी १७

When his father went to heaven, the boy of excellent valor, having reached the age of sixteen years, overcame his enemies and gained for himself control of the kingdom.

Verse 18:

नूनं साम्राज्यसंपत्त्या भूमण्डलमयोजयत्
अतिष्ठद्विगताशङ्कं पालयन्धर्मतः प्रजाः १८

Now, using all the means available to him, he attained universal sovereignty, uniting the whole world under his rule.

In his dominion, all his subjects were free from fear, protected [from the encroachment of neighbors,] and ruled with justice.

Verse 19:

स धीमान्मन्त्रिभिः सार्धं यशसा शुक्लयन्दिशः
अथ गच्छत्सु वर्षेषु वसन्ते प्रोल्लसत्यलम् १९

His brilliant intelligence, [sitting in court] surrounded by his ministers on all sides, shone with splendor, radiating light in all directions.

Now with the passage of years, entering into the spring of his life, he wanted the rewards of his station, the joy of living that reality [in play, dance, sport and entertainment].

Verse 20:

पुष्पेषु जृम्भमाणेषु स्फुरत्सु शशिरश्मिषु
मञ्जरीजालदोलासु विटपान्तःपुरान्तरे २०

Surrounded by flowers blossoming, [a new reality in his life was] zooming forth under the bright moon-beams,

Then the magic [the finest value of relativity] within the cluster of blossoms began to vibrate and be lively, what was hidden deep inside the surface of the growing creeper came to the fore.

Verse 21:

रजःकर्पूरधवले वलद्दलकपाटके
आमोदविलसत्पुष्पगुलुच्छकवितानके २१

Deep within the petal, in that celestial brilliance, the dazzling white color of camphor, something was unfolding that was intensely beautiful and attractive.

Within the supremely fascinating character of the finest level of existence glittering in the cluster of blossoms of the flower, there was something immensely attractive, gladdening the heart.

> These verses give a sense that the love that was blossoming in the heart of Śikhidhvaja was not directed toward something outside himself but was directed towards something deep within his own heart which was becoming visible as a sense of wonder, a sense of magic captured in the physical beauty of the object of perception. Bṛhadāraṇyaka Upaniṣad, IV.v.6.[1] "He [Yajñavalkya] said, It is not for the sake of the husband, my dear, that

he is loved, but for one's own sake that he is loved. It is not for the sake of the wife, my dear, that she is loved, but for one's own sake that she is loved. It is not for the sake of the sons, my dear, that they are loved, but for one's own sake that they are loved. It is not for the sake of wealth, my dear, that they are loved, but for one's own sake that they are loved. It is not for the sake of wealth, my dear, that it is loved, but for one's own sake that it is loved. It is not for the sake of the animals, my dear, that they are loved, but for one's own sake that they are loved. It is not for the sake of the Brāhmaṇa, my dear, that he is loved, but for one's own sake that he is loved. It is not for the sake of the Kṣatriya, my dear, that he is loved, but for one's own sake that he is loved. It is not for the sake of the worlds, my dear, that they are loved, but for one's own sake that they are loved. It is not for the sake of the gods, my dear, that they are loved, but for one's own sake that they are loved. It is not for the sake of the Vedas, my dear, that they are loved, but for one's own sake that they are loved. It is not for the sake of the beings, my dear, that they are loved, but for one's own sake that they are loved. It is not for the sake of all, my dear, that all is loved, but for one's own sake that all are loved. The Self, my dear Maitreyi, should be realized—should be heard of, reflected on and meditated upon. When the Self, my dear, is realized by being heard of, reflected on and meditated upon, all this is known."

Verse 22:

गायत्सु गहनेषूच्चैर्मिथुनेष्वलिनां मिथः
आवाति मधुरे वायौ शशिशीकरशीतले २२

High above in the flower-laden bushes the pairs of bees were humming to each other,

As the sweet scent of honey wafted through the air, it [as if] turned into cooling showers of *Soma*.

Verse 23:

कदलीकन्दलीकच्छतलपल्लवलासिनि
कान्तां प्रति बभूवास्य वसच्चेतः समुत्सुकम् २३

The banana tree on the river bank, covered with [male and female] flowers blossoming in the shade underneath its broad leaves, moving to and fro [in the breeze],

Excited his yearning for the manifest expression of the object of his desire that was dwelling in his heart.

Verse 24:

क्षीबं कुसुमसंभारसौगन्ध्यमधुरासवैः
मनो नान्यास्पदं चक्रे स वसन्तमिवोदितम् २४

He was intoxicated by the liquor of the honey-like sweet fragrance of the multitude of blossoms.

His mind had no other resort: Wherever he went, spring was in the air.

Verse 25:

उद्यानवनदोलासु लीलाकमलिनीषु च
कदा प्रणयिनीं मुग्धां हेमाब्जमुकुलस्तनीम् २५

"When will the beautiful young lady of my desires come to view, having breasts like golden lotus buds, swinging in the swings of the royal gardens and forest groves, and sporting in the lotus pools?"

Verse 26:

करिष्ये कामिनीमङ्के पर्यङ्के कुङ्कुमाङ्क्तिताम्
कदा कमलवल्लीनां दोलास्वलिरिवालिनीम् २६

"When shall I embrace my love on my couch, besmeared with saffron?

When shall we swing back and forth [in a swing] like so many bees on the blossoms of lotus stalks, drinking nectar from the flowers?"

Verse 27:

आलोलां तां निवेक्ष्यामि बालां भुजलतानुगाम्
मृणालहारकुन्देन्दुवृन्दवल्यभिलाषिणी २७

"In my heart I see her gently rocking to and fro, a young girl, with long slender arms, the perfect companion,

Charming and beautiful as a lotus, having the fragrance of jasmine, shining like the moon, richly ornamented, and having a beautiful voice."

Verse 28:

मत्कृते मदनातप्ता कदा स्यादिन्दुसुन्दरी
इति चिन्तापरो भूत्वा कुसुमावचयोन्मुखः २८

"When will my intense love be put to practice, when will the pure intelligence of my mind find material expression in the form of all surpassing beauty?"

Thus, absorbed in the possibility of the materialization of the object of his supreme devotion, he went about gathering flowers, looking to each flower one after the other.

Verse 29:

विजहार वनान्तेषु कुसुमोपवनेषु च
वनोपवनलेखासु लीलाकमलिनीषु च २९

He wandered here and there on the outskirts of forests and in flower groves,

Among the cultivated orchards and flower gardens and around the lovely pools full of lotus flowers.

Verse 30:

वल्लीवलयगेहेषु विविधोद्यानभूमिषु
वनोपवनविन्यासवर्णनावलितासु च ३०

He sought his ideal of perfect beauty among diverse royal gardens and in the cultivated gardens and grounds encircling homes.

Wherever he went, in forest after forest and garden after garden, he carried with him the mental image of his ideal of beauty.

Verse 31:

शृङ्गाररसगर्भासु कथास्वरमतोन्मनाः
हृदि हारलसत्कायविलोलालकवल्लरीः ३१

He constantly took delight in his own distracted musings about love,

Carrying in his heart the shapely figure of a maiden dancing amorously.

Life progresses on the steps of increasing fulfillment. The desire for more happiness, more love, more unity, more togetherness with the whole of one's environment, togetherness with the whole of life, is completely natural. Indeed, it is a universal feature of human life. Everyone wants more happiness and more love. Fulfillment in life lies in increasing steps of achievement towards the goal. Desire is not opposed to evolution, it is the touchstone of progress: With desire and hope for more and more, one engages in action for more and more, and thus alone one can achieve greater and greater levels of fulfillment. The notion of cutting down desires in order to enjoy fulfillment is a wrong notion. What is needed is the knowledge and guidance to not only achieve small steps of progress, but to continue on until the supreme goal of gaining more than the most is accomplished. That guidance Śikhidhvaja was fortunate to receive, and how knowledge guided him on the path to fulfillment forms the substance of the story. Here at this stage, we are rejoicing in his desire for more happiness and more love because this is the universal starting point for any quest, and for any achievement whatsoever.

The theme of search permeates this chapter, and the same theme is revisited in the last of this group of seven chapters, in the story of the miserly merchant. The merchant lost a small coin and dreaming of the great wealth that he would make in business starting with that one coin, he continued searching for the coin for three days. In both cases, the fulfillment that is attained lies far beyond the narrow and limited boundaries in which the hope for more and more is framed. The quest is a universal, epic theme. In this story, the fulfillment that is gained after many, many years, is far beyond the original conception, far surpassing Śikhidhvaja's highest aspirations.

Verse 32:

कुमारीः पूजयामास सुवर्णकलशस्तनीः
एतन्मन्ये विदुर्भव्या मन्त्रिणो नृपनिश्चयम् ३२

Young girls, beautiful and voluptuous, were the idols of his worship.

This desperate state of affairs, the one-pointed focus of the king [on love] was observed in his appearance by his ministers.

Verse 33:

इङ्गिताकारवेदित्वमेव मन्त्रिपदं परम्
अथ तस्य विवाहाय मन्त्रिवर्गो विचारयन् ३३

It is always the duty of the ministers to understand from signs in the king's outward behavior what are his true inner intentions.

Now the council of ministers deliberated on arranging a marriage for him.

Verse 34:

सुराष्ट्राधिपतेः कन्यां ययाचे यौवतान्विताम्
नवयौवनसंपन्नां भार्यात्वे विधिनोत्तमाम् ३४

They proposed the youthful daughter of the king of Surāṣṭra who assented to the proposition.

Having just attained marriageable age, she was considered the best match, according to their judgment.

Verse 35:

उपयेभे स तामात्मसदृशीं प्रतिमामिव
चूडालेति भुवि ख्याता नाम्ना नृपतिसुन्दरी ३५

In this marriage, she was the picture of the perfect soulmate for him.

The beautiful wife of the king became known across the land by the name Cūḍālā.

Verse 36:

सा तं भर्तारमासाद्य रेजे फुल्लेव पद्मिनी
नीलनीरजनेत्रां तां चूडालां स शिखिध्वजः ३६
स्नेहाद्विकासयामास सूर्यो देवो यथाब्जिनीम्

She was as joyous in having him as her lord and master as a newly bloomed white lotus at the rising sun;

And he, Śikhidhvaja, through his tender love made the innocent black-eyed girl, Cūḍālā, bloom like the sun god causing the bud of the lotus to open.

Verse 37:

अवर्धत तयोः प्रीतिरन्योन्यार्पितचेतसोः ३७

Their mutual affection and love for each other grew until each became emblazoned in the heart of the other.

Verse 38:

हावभावविलासाढ्यैरङ्गैर्नवलतेव सा
सुमन्त्र्यर्पितसर्वार्थः स सुखी सुस्थितप्रजाः ३८

She delighted him by her youthful playfulness and dalliance and her amorous gestures that were like a twining creeper.

He happily entrusted all the affairs of state to his ministers, to wisely promote the welfare and prosperity of the people.

Verse 39:

राजहंस इवाब्जिन्या रेमे दयितया तया
अन्तःपुरेषु दोलासु लीलाकमलिनीषु च ३९

Like a royal swan sporting in a lake filled with lotuses, he sported with his beloved In the swinging cradles and lotus-filled pleasure ponds in the inner apartments.

Verse 40:

उद्यानेषु विहारेषु लतापुष्पग्रहेषु च
कदम्बवनलेखासु चन्दनागुरुवीथिषु ४०

They amused themselves with walks in the gardens and flower arboretums,

In the forests of Kadamba trees and architectural gardens, and along the less-traveled paths through sandalwood trees.

Verse 41:

मन्दारदामलोलासु कदलीकन्दलीषु च
पुरान्तेषु वनान्तेषु दिगन्तेषु सरस्सु च ४१

They sported in the forests of coral trees, among the banana trees, and among the trees covered with *Kandalī* flowers;

On the outskirts of cities, at the edges of forests, in faraway remote places, and in lakes and ponds;

Verse 42:

जंगलेषु जनान्तेषु जम्बूजम्बीरजातिषु
बभूवाह्लादकं सर्वं तयोरन्योन्यचेष्टितम् ४२

In desert regions, and in places where rose-apples, and citrons grow;

Wherever they went they enjoyed everything together, each living for the other, moving together as one.

Verse 43:

सद्वर्षयोर्धुरवरैर्द्युभूम्योरिव कान्तयोः
नित्यमेव वियुक्तत्वात्प्रियत्वाच्चेष्टितस्य च ४३

The true love of the two lovers brought together heaven and earth, and made the rains fall from on high onto the fields below, by their amorous dalliance.

Because of being separate individuals, yet moving together as one, by their love for one another they became a powerful force in nature.

Verse 44:

मिथः कलाकलापस्य कोविदौ तौ बभूवतुः
स्वरूपमेकमेवैतौ दधतुर्मित्रतां गतौ ४४

Those two together [by virtue of their perfect love for one another] became masters of unity and diversity—the whole and its constituent parts, pure knowledge and organizing power, abstract theory and applied practice, the sciences and the arts.

These two were so closely united, they appeared as two people with one soul; so intimate was their friendship, that whatever knowledge one had they gave it to the other, so that by their union they each had the total knowledge [of all the sciences and arts].

Verse 45:

अन्योन्यहृदयस्थत्वादिव संक्रान्तमक्षतम्
सर्वशास्त्रार्थवैदग्ध्यं चित्राद्यपि मुखात्प्रभोः ४५

Because of each being seated in the heart of the other, the knowledge of each was transferred to the other.

Each had the facility of practically applying—from first principles—all the scriptures in diverse fields of practical life, through their complete mastery of the whole field of knowledge.

Verse 46:

बालः कालाद्रिवागृह्य साऽसीत्सर्वार्थपरिडता
नृत्यवाद्यादि यावच्च चूडालावदनादसौ ४६

From the time of her childhood she was trained by pandits expert in all the fields of knowledge.

As much as she knew in all the arts such as dance, Cūḍālā spoke out to Śikhidhvaja.

Verse 47:

अशिक्षत बभूवाथ कलानामतिकोविदः
अमावास्यामिवेन्द्वर्कावन्योन्यविलसत्कलौ ४७

They now learned and became masters of all the fields of knowledge they had studied in the past.

As at the time of new moon, the sun and the moon play about and mutually exchange life with one another, Śikhidhvaja and Cūḍālā shared their knowledge of the arts and sciences with each other.

Verse 48:

मिथो हृदयसंस्थौ तौ द्वावप्यैक्यमुपागतौ
तौ संस्थितावेकरसावन्योन्यं दयितावुभौ ४८

They were a perfect couple, each deeply seated in the heart of the other: Those two, although remaining two, moved about behaving as one.

Those two became all the more dear to each other, as they shared the same tastes and inclinations, and both had the same deep love and affection for the other.

Verse 49:

पुष्पामोदाविवाभिन्नो भूतलस्थौ शिवाविव
वैदग्ध्यसुन्दरमती सर्वशास्त्रार्थपण्डितौ ४९

Just as it is not possible to separate the fragrances of different flowers that are mixed in the air, so also the two earthly lovers, Śikhidhvaja and Cūḍālā, were both as deeply fixed in unity as Śiva and Mother Divine in heaven.

The thoughts they shared with each other were steeped with intelligence, and always charming and beautiful; they spoke like two wise pandits, exchanging their knowledge of the true purport of all the scriptures.

Verse 50:

कार्यार्थं च भुवं प्राप्तौ कमलाकमलाधवौ
स्नेहात्प्रसन्नमधुरौ समविज्ञातवादिनौ ५०

Both achieved the purpose of being born on earth [through union with the other] like Lakṣmī and Viṣṇu [in heaven].

Due to their love for each other, they were both always kindly disposed towards the other and sweet; both speaking out their observations and understanding [of the moment] with balanced even voices [devoid of excitement or anger].

Verse 51:

अनुवृत्तिपरावास्तां लोकवृत्तान्ततद्विदौ
कलाकलापसंपन्नौ लसद्रसरसायनौ
शीतलस्निग्धमुग्धाङ्गौ शशाङ्कौ द्वाविवोदितौ ५१

Each behaved suitably [with all dignity and respect] towards the other, both knowing that the goal of peace, progress and orderliness of behavior among their constituents depended on their own peace [according to the principle *Yathā rājā tathā prajā,* "As the king is, so are the subjects"].

If the behavior of the rulers is orderly, then the actions of the people ruled will unfailingly turn out successful in every respect; the king and queen's natural action, action on the basis of all the laws of nature, gives support to all the actions and aspirations of the whole population.

The loving tenderness of the flow of their thought, speech and action in accordance with the perfect orderliness of the finest level of feeling, like two moons shining from on high with gentle rays, [brought nourishment and support of nature to the whole population].

Verse 52:

रेजे लसच्च रतिभोगविलासकान्तमन्तः पुरेषु मिथुनं तदनुत्तमश्रि ।
ब्रह्माराडखराडकुहरेष्विव राजहंसयुग्मं विकासिमदमन्मथमन्दचारि ५२

Enjoying the pleasure of playing about and expressing their love for each other in the inner apartments, the intensely shining light of their love became visible to all, as their love shone with unsurpassed brilliance.

The two royal swans moving gently, intoxicated with the fullness of their love for each other, blossomed like flowers opening, expanding and shining the light of love into all the caves and hollows in the infinite expanse of the universe.

> All this is the description of the height of normal human life: Individual life on the level of fulfillment. This state of fullness of relative waking state life is the starting point of the couple's quest for higher states of consciousness, which begins in the next chapter. This is one positive achievement. What more could there be? The Upanishads describe this state of perfection of human life in the relative, and the possibilities that remain for even greater happiness and bliss, as follows (Bṛhadāraṇyaka, Upaniṣad IV.3.33)[2]:
>
> "He who is perfect of physique and prosperous among men, the ruler of others, and most lavishly supplied with all human enjoyments, represents greatest joy among men. This human joy multiplied a hundred times makes one unit of joy for the manes (ancestors) who have won

that world of theirs. The joy of these manes who have won that world multiplied a hundred times makes one unit of joy in the world of the celestial minstrels. This joy in the world of the celestial minstrels multiplied a hundred times makes one unit of joy for the gods by action—those who have attained their godhead by their actions. This joy of the gods by action multiplied a hundred times makes one unit of joy for the gods by birth, as also of one who is versed in the Vedas, sinless and free from desire. This joy of the gods by birth multiplied a hundred times makes one unit of joy in the world of Prajāpati, as well as of one who is versed in the Vedas, sinless and free from desire. This joy in the world of Prajāpati multiplied a hundred times makes one unit of joy in the world of Brahman, as well as of one who is versed in the Vedas, sinless and free from desire. This indeed is the supreme bliss. This is the state of Brahman, O Emperor, said Yājñavalkya."

Colophon:

इत्यार्षे श्रीवासिष्ठमहारामायणे वाल्मीकीये मोक्षोपायेषु निर्वाणप्रकरणे चूडालोपाख्याने शिखिध्वजविलास-कथनं नाम सप्तसप्ततितमः सर्गः ७७

Endnotes

1 Swāmī Mādhavānanda, tr., *The Bṛhadāraṇyaka Upaniṣad with the commentary of Śaṅkarācārya*, Advaita Ashrama: Calcutta, 1988, pp. 537-539.

2 Ibid., pp. 476-478.

Chapter 2: Cosmic Consciousness

Verse 1:

वसिष्ठ उवाच
एवं बहूनि वर्षाणि मिथुनं निर्भरस्पृहम्
रेमे यौवनलीलाभिरमन्दाभिर्दिनेदिने १

1. In this way many years passed in joyful revelry as day after day, with unrestrained enthusiasm the royal couple indulged their ardent love and desire [for each other] with their many youthful sports.

This verse summarizes all that transpired in the previous chapter and serves as the seed for the dramatic transformation of awareness which is going to take place now in this chapter. To understand exactly how this verse is the seed for all that is to come in this chapter, we need to go more deeply into one word of the verse, the word *Nirbhara-spṛham*. *Nirbhara-spṛham*, ardent desire, could also be construed as desire to be weightless, (*Nir*, without; *Bhara*, weight; *Spṛham*, desire, hence desire to be weightless, desire to fly). The desire to fly, the desire to be so light that the body floats up in the air, is the desire for all the earthly desires, all the desires related to everything on earth to be completely fulfilled. As long as there are earthly desires, as long as consciousness is unfulfilled, seeking for fulfillment of desires, there is imbalance, and that imbalance means that there is a bondage to the objects in the world, a lack of freedom. The desire to fly is the desire for all these worldly desires to be completely fulfilled, so that the bondage is broken, and the body can go wherever it likes, without limitations. The desire to fly takes within its fold all the earthly desires in which the royal couple were so happily enmeshed, in the same way as the footprint of the elephant encompasses the footprints of all the animals in the animal kingdom. All these worldly desires are summed up in the desire to fly, and all these worldly desires are completely fulfilled in the experience of Yogic Flying.

In this chapter, that material of which the fulfillment of all earthly desires is made—infinite bliss consciousness, is going to be unfolded. Desires can be on any level of creation, so in order to bring fulfillment to all earthly desires, one must go completely beyond all relativity, one must open to something which is timeless, non-relative. The transcendental Being is said to be *Sat-Chit-Ānanda*, Absolute bliss consciousness, and that infinite bliss alone is the source and goal of all earthly desires. The desire to fly, or in other words, the fulfillment of all earthly desires can only be on that Absolute level, the level of Absolute Being, the level of Sat-Chit-Ānanda.

The technology of Yogic Flying will not be introduced in this chapter. Rather, this chapter chronicles the search for and discovery of that field of life where all relative desires find fulfillment. This chapter is vital for understanding how Yogic Flying comes about—it comes about on the basis of something that is beyond the relative. Control over gravity only comes on the level of the Unified Field, on the level of *supergravity* in the language of some Quantum Field Theories, the level where all the forces and fields are completely united and integrated. The royal couple's ardent desire and love for each other is being summed up in the desire to fly, and now, at this stage of the story, in this chapter, we are going to discover that field in which all these relative desires, and even the desire to fly find their complete fulfillment.

Verse 2:

अथ यातेषु बहुषु वर्षेष्वावृत्तिशालिषु
शनैर्गलिततारुण्ये भिन्नकुम्भादिवाम्भसि २

Now many happy years passed by in the enjoyment of the pleasures of their love,

And gradually their youthfulness faded away, like water dripping out of a leaky pot.

Verse 3:

तरङ्गविकराकारभङ्गुरव्यवहारिणि
पातः पक्वफलस्येव मरणं दुर्निवारणम् ३

[They said,] "Transient is youth; the body ages and becomes increasingly frail and weak, until in old age, the body is subject to decay and death.

"Like ripe fruits falling from the tree, death cannot be held back.

Verse 4:

हिमाशनिरिवाम्भोजे जरा निपतनोन्मुखी
आयुर्गलत्यविरतं जलं करतलादिव ४

"Like the winter snows bring an end to the day-blooming lotus, old age befalls everything living.

"Life is ever-dying, like water flowing out of the palm of the hand.

Verse 5:

प्रावृषीव लतातुम्बी तृष्णैका दीर्घतां गता
शैलनद्या रय इव संप्रयात्येव यौवनम् ५

"[While] our thirst for the unity of love grows stronger, like the creeper of the bottle gourd growing longer in the rainy season,

"Our youth proceeds inexorably [to old age], like a fast-moving stream along a riverbed.

Verse 6:

इन्द्रजालमिवासत्यं जीवनं जीर्णसंस्थिति
सुखानि प्रपलायन्ते शरा इव धनुश्च्युताः ६

"Life withers away and dies, it is unreal like a magician's trick.

"Joys and pleasures are fleeting, like arrows shot from a bow.

Verse 7:

पतन्ति चेतोदुःखानि तृष्णा गृध्र इवामिषम्
बुद्बुदः प्रावृषीवाप्सु शरीरं क्षणभङ्गुरम् ७

"The joys of life disappearing, [give rise to] the sufferings of the mind, and the individual is filled with thirst and longing for the object[s] of his desire.

"[Evanescent, like a soap] bubble, [fleeting] as the waters in the rainy season, the fragile body exists only for a moment.

Verse 8:

रम्भागर्भ इवासारो व्यवहारो विचारगः
सत्वरं युवता याति कान्तेवाप्रियकामिनः ८

"Like the suitor who [at the outset] sacrifices everything for love, life is a losing proposition.

"Speedily youth goes, and as the youthful beauty fades, the object of love [in the end] loses its attraction.

Verse 9:

बलादरतिरायाता वैरस्यमिव पादपम्
तदिह स्याच्छुभाकारं स्थिरं किमतिशोभनम् ९

"When youth is gone, one loses the taste for the fleeting joys of love.

"Youth being gone for us here, there should be some righteous, good action, [that we can perform] that produces lasting happiness and permanent good, and which is virtuous beyond reproach.

Verse 10:

यदासाद्य पुनश्चेतो दशासु न विदूयते
इति निर्णीय युग्मं तत्संसारव्याधिभेषजम् १०

"We should seek something that takes the mind back to a state of eternal peace and contentment, where the mind is not [constantly] agitated and distressed."

Thus, the royal couple determined to find that which is the remedy for the affliction of worldly existence.

Verse 11:

चिरं विचारयामास शास्त्रमध्यात्मसंमतम्
आत्मज्ञानैकमात्रेण संसृत्याख्या विषूचिका ११

[Thus, they began] inquiring into the eternal and never changing [aspect of life], celebrated in the scriptures as the knowledge of the Self (*Ātmā*).

[According to the scriptures:] Merely by knowing one thing, the knowledge of the Self, one goes beyond the whole field of relative existence.

Verse 12:

संशाम्यतीति निश्चित्य तावास्तां तत्परायणौ
तच्चित्तौ तद्गतप्राणौ तन्निष्ठौ तद्विदाश्रयौ १२

[As the fulfillment of their search] They found the age-old practice of transcendental deep meditation, giving the experience of the infinite peace of the Self, beyond thought:

Both began the practice of meditation and both entered onto the path of going beyond relativity to experience the reality of the Self.

They experienced the Self directly in consciousness [through meditation], their physiology became involved when their breath became suspended during the experience of the Self, their hearts enjoyed the bliss of the experience of the Self above all, and they took recourse at every opportunity to the intellectual understanding of the experience of the Self.

Verse 13:

तदा तदर्चनपरौ तदीहौ तौ विरेजतुः
तत्रैवातिघनाभ्यासौ बोधयन्तौ परस्परम् १३

Then each communicated their fervor for the Self to the other, both experienced the Self directly [through initiation into meditation practice], and both lost their agitated state of mind [immediately and gained inner peace].

In that experience of transcending alone was their practice successful, awakening in both [for the first time] the experience of the true Self.

Verse 14:

तत्प्रीतौ तत्समारम्भावन्योन्यं तौ बभूवतुः
अथ साविरतं राम रमणीयपदक्रमान् १४

Both were deeply satisfied with their [initial] experience of the Self, both undertook to stabilize the experience of the Self fully, [and with further experience] both became adept at transcending and coming out.

Now she continued the practice of meditation with perfect discipline and regularity, enjoying increasing charm with every step in the direction of the transcendent.

Verse 15:

श्रुत्वाध्यात्मविदां वक्त्राच्छास्त्रार्थांस्तारणक्षमान्
इत्थं विचारयामास स्वमात्मानमहर्निशम् १५

Having heard [the instructions in the practice of meditation] from the mouth of wise, realized knowers of the Self who knew the meaning of the scriptures and were competent to guide aspirants on the path to enlightenment,

Morning and evening [she] explored the [nature of the] Self, the [infinite, unbounded] *Ātmā* according to the [teachers'] instructions.

Verse 16:

अव्यापृता व्यापृता वा धिया धवलयेद्धया
प्रेक्षे तावत्स्वमात्मानं किमहं स्यामिति स्वयम् १६

[Cūḍālā thought:] Whether engaged in activity or not engaged, by the light of consciousness made pure by the practice, I see nought but the Self everywhere, and That I am, infinite and unbounded, that [universal consciousness] is my own self.

> This verse is a commentary on the previous verse: Morning and evening she practiced her transcendental deep meditation as she was taught, and now, after some passage of time, perhaps even a few years, the experience of transcending, the experience of the *Ātmā* or Self, the experience of pure consciousness, has become very clear. That transcendental consciousness which was at first experienced only during the practice of meditation, has

> become so familiar to the mind, that spontaneously the mind maintains that pure consciousness even in activity. This verse describes her experience, "I am That infinite and unbounded universal Self."

कस्यायमागतो मोहः कथमभ्युत्थितः क्व वा
देहस्तावज्जडो मूढो नाहमित्येव निश्चयः १७

Verse 17:

By whose power does this field of illusion come into being? How does it become visible, or in whom?

The body is nothing but ignorant insensate matter, I am not the body, consciousness is all that there is.

> Verses 17 to 23 represent an intellectual analysis of the structure of her experience. What is inside the Self, and what is outside the Self? The Self is infinite and unbounded universal consciousness, but the body is non-Self.

Verse 18:

आबालमेतत्संसिद्धं मतौ चैवानुभूयते
कर्मेन्द्रियगणश्चास्मादभिन्नावयवात्मकः १८

This mental delusion begins in childhood and continues till the end of life, and always holds us in its tight embrace.

All the different organs of action in the body move in accordance with this delusion, uninterruptedly playing their part in the collapse of the infinite fullness of the Self.

The Self is infinite and unbounded universal consciousness, but all the organs of action belong to the field of non-Self.

Verse 19:

अवयवावयविनोर्न भेदो जड एव च
बुद्धीन्द्रियगणोऽप्येवं जड एवेति दृश्यते १९

In ignorance, no distinction is made between the physical limb of the body, and the knower who is the owner of the limb; only objectivity is considered real.

All the different sense organs are made of inanimate matter, and thus only the objective world is seen, [and knowable].

The Self is infinite and unbounded universal consciousness, but all the senses and their objects belong to the field of non-Self.

Verse 20:

प्रेर्यते मनसा यस्माद्यष्ट्येव भुवि लोष्टकः
मनश्चैवं जडं मन्ये संकल्पात्मकशक्ति यत् २०

The objective world is set in motion by the mind like a bat driving a ball: the mind acts on the physical world, so it is a part of the objective reality.

The mind in this way is thought to be objective, [it is the organ] whose power is the innate capacity for action of all the organs together.

The Self is infinite and unbounded universal

consciousness, but the mind belongs to the field of non-Self.

Verse 21:

क्षेपणैरिव पाषाणः प्रेर्यते बुद्धिनिश्चयैः
बुद्धिर्निश्चयरूपैवं जडा सत्तैव निश्चयः २१

As by being thrown, a stone is set in motion by the intentions of the intellect,

In this way, the object that is deliberated by the intellect is purely objective, [and as such] the deliberation is always concerning some objectively existing thing.

The Self is infinite and unbounded universal consciousness, but the intellect belongs to the field of non-Self.

Verse 22:

स्वातेनेव सरिन्नूनं साहंकारेण वाह्यते
अहंकारोऽपि निःसारो जड एव शवात्मकः २२

With the individual ego, the individual makes effort, and by that effort of the self, the individual ego is known just as surely as a river [is known by its banks]:

The going forth of the individual ego is always with reference to an object, is always objective: the ego is nothing more than a dead body made of the collapse of the wholeness of the Self onto the object of perception.

The Self is infinite and unbounded universal consciousness, but the individual ego belongs to the field of non-Self.

Verse 23:

जीवेन जन्यते यक्षो बालेनेव भ्रमात्मकः
जीवश्च चेतनाकाशो वातात्मा हृदये स्थितः २३

By virtue of the individual soul, one is born into the world: the soul comes to be known by the special characteristics of the child; the soul is the rambling in the field of relativity of the Infinite Being.

The individual soul or "*Jīva*," is the spatial manifold (*Ākāśa*) created by consciousness, [that means] the universal soul (*Ātmā*) in terms of manifest time-space causality (*Vāta*), seated in the heart.

> The Self is infinite and unbounded universal consciousness, but the individual soul or "*Jīva*," expressed as the space-time manifold in which life is lived, belongs to the field of non-Self.

Verse 24:

सुकुमारोऽन्तरन्येन केनापि परिजीवति
अहो नु ज्ञातमेतेन चेत्योल्लेखकलङ्किना २४

Extremely subtle and delicate is the interior of life, different from the mind, intellect, ego and soul, by virtue of whom one lives and moves about [in birth after birth].

Ah, now [at last] by this [analysis] we have come to that which is to be known: By virtue of a single dot, [the otherwise unseen abstract canvas of life] comes into view, becomes perceptible.

> The Self is infinite and unbounded universal

consciousness, and by virtue of the apparent existence of relativity, we see what the Self is. We see what it is by virtue of the realization of what it is not—it is not the body, the organs of action, the senses, the mind, the intellect, the ego, or the soul, it is not anything relative, it is not anything bound or constrained or qualified in any way.

Verse 25:

जीवो जीवति जीर्णेन चिद्रूपेणात्मरूपिणा
चेत्यभ्रमवता जीवश्चिद्रूपेणैव जीवति २५

The individual soul lives by change [in accordance with the "extremely subtle and delicate interior of life"]: In the beginning the body changes by growing and assuming its native form; then the consciousness in the body changes as the personality develops [through education, culture and experience], and finally [the destructive aspect of] change overtakes the process of growth and development and the body ages and decays.

If there could be change without mistakes, without entropy, then the individual soul could continue on with the same form, [without taking on a new body], living perpetually.

In verses 2-9, the royal couple became aware of the ever-changing nature of relative life, and how their bodies were decaying and thus their potential for continued ever-increasing enjoyment of life was slipping away. In verse 10, they resolved to devote their lives to something that is non-changing. In this verse, Cūḍālā realizes through the intellectual analysis of her experience, that she has indeed found that field of life which she was seeking, which is beyond the reach of change, never subject to aging.

Everything in the relative is ever-changing. But the changing aspect of relativity is not in itself responsible for aging. Aging is due to a failure of intelligence. The infinite intelligence that created the body could continue to recreate a new body, a fresh body, fully restored and rejuvenated, but mistakes enter in, and the physiology forgets its source. The body loses its connection with the field of intelligence which gave rise to it, and so disorder creeps in. Gradually the vitality of the system slips away, and this is experienced as aging.

If the change could continue without loss of intelligence, without mistakes, without entropy, then life could continue indefinitely, maintaining life at the same age without aging.

Reversal of aging or elimination of aging becomes conceivable on the ground of a field of non-change, which is itself a field of infinite intelligence, a field of perfect order. The discovery of the Absolute level of life is—in principle, if not yet in practice—the fulfillment of the quest for immortality so eloquently expressed by the royal couple in verses 2-10. Making that absolute level of life functional, so that the body is revitalized from moment to moment in accordance with the infinite intelligence of the Self requires technologies of consciousness. Specifically, the practice of Yogic Flying makes the health of the body perfect, free from disease and decay. This verse is only presenting the principle of immortality as a response to the inquiry of verses 2-10. It is a huge awakening to the power of knowledge, the power of pure consciousness.

Verse 26:

आमोदः पवनेनेव खातेनेव सरिद्रयः
असत्यजडचेत्यांशचयनाच्चिद्वपुर्जडम् २६

That one thing [to be known, see v.24], the absolute basis of orderly change in physiology and consciousness is bliss, infinite happiness: By contacting the root of life, by change that is always in the direction of greater happiness, the physiology and consciousness is purified, [and thereby] the stream of life is [always] connected to the ocean of life, [eternal bliss consciousness][and so continues on eternally].

> The Upaniṣads proclaim, "In bliss are these beings born, in bliss they are sustained …."

Verse 27:

महाजलगतो ह्यग्निरिव रूपं स्वमुज्झति
सद्वासद्वा यदाभाति चित्समाधौ सति स्वतः २७

That is cosmic creative intelligence, "*Agni,*" total Veda, because to the degree the manifestation of life is in accordance with the sequential unfoldment of Veda, the Self rises up onto the surface of life.

Whether truth or untruth, whether sequential unfoldment of total natural law, or partial natural law is radiating in society at any time, when consciousness is in the state of *Samādhi*, then the self is in accordance with truth, in accordance with total natural law.

Verse 28:

स्वरूपमलमुत्सृज्य तदेव भवति क्षणात्
एवं चिद्रूपमप्येतच्चेत्योन्मुखतया स्वयम् २८

The fullness of the Self being set free to the necessary degree, it sustains itself forever, from that moment forward.

In this way, a higher state of consciousness is experienced, [called Cosmic Consciousness][in which] the inner wakefulness of the Self is permanently maintained.

Verse 29:

जडं शून्यमसत्कल्पं चैतन्येन प्रबोध्यते
इति संचिन्त्य चूडाला केनैषा चित्प्रचेतनी २९

[This Self in Cosmic Consciousness is] Devoid of objects, pure unmanifest dynamism characterized by wakeful intelligence.

Cūḍālā [thought] that collecting the mind in the state of *Samādhi* is how this level of consciousness could be awakened.

Verse 30:

इति संचिन्तयामास चिरायेत्थं व्यबुध्यत
अहो नु चिरकालेन ज्ञातं ज्ञेयमनामयम् ३०

Thus, she began to meditate for long periods in this manner, her awareness settled in the transcendent, beyond thought.

"Ah, now [at last] by practicing for a long time, we have realized that which is to be known, the nameless [field of pure Being]."

Verse 31:

यद्वै विज्ञेयतां कृत्वा न कश्चिद्धीयते पुनः
एते हि चिद्विलासान्ता मनोबुद्धीन्द्रियादयः ३१

That [Being] indeed is what is to be known, having accomplished which nothing further remains to be done.

These [boundaries now fading away] are verily the last outposts of the delusion of consciousness that began with the mind, intellect and senses [being absorbed in boundaries].

> As the nature of Being, pure consciousness, is infused into the mind more and more through the regular practice of transcending and gaining unbounded awareness, the abstract qualities of consciousness become more and more familiar, more and more tangible. In time these qualities and characteristics of the unmanifest Self begin to be maintained spontaneously outside of the practice of meditation. Thus, in the activities of the day, and even in the sleep of the night, the pure consciousness begins to shine. As pure consciousness grows, the quality of the witness, the uninvolved and unattached nature of infinite unbounded pure unmanifest consciousness may be experienced fleetingly, as the higher state of consciousness, Cosmic Consciousness is being stabilized. Cosmic Consciousness is that state of consciousness in which the unbounded fullness of transcendental consciousness is spontaneously maintained in the awareness at all times. On the way to that fully stabilized state of Cosmic Consciousness, the experience of the witness could come and go, depending on the changing conditions of the nervous system, as a natural consequence of the growth

and progressive transformation of the physical nervous system. In verse 16, Cūḍālā had infused sufficient pure consciousness into the nature of her mind to have a very clear glimpse of Cosmic Consciousness. Analyzing her experience in verses 17-28, she confirmed that this growing state of Cosmic Consciousness was the fulfillment of her quest. Then in verses 29-30, she redoubles her efforts to stabilize pure consciousness, and by continued practice the Self becomes stabilized and permanent. Now, in this verse, the last stresses are being released, and she begins to enjoy the exalted status of eternal liberation. The experience of the goal, the experience of the stabilized state of Cosmic Consciousness is different from the path, different from the temporary experiences of unboundedness in activity and sleep, and this new perspective is now being described in detail, concluding in verse 51, "The eternally shining Self, the form of Totality, Infinite Pure Existence, Cosmic Consciousness is fully established."

Verse 32:

असन्तः सर्व एवाहो द्वितीयेन्दुपदस्थिताः
महाचिदेकैवास्तीह महासत्तेति योच्यते ३२

All the manifest objects in creation are in truth unreal, all that appears to be a second [thing, other than the Self], are [nothing but] the creations of the mind.

Here there is only one [true reality] which is called Cosmic Consciousness, cosmic being.

Verse 33:

निष्कलङ्का समा शुद्धा निरहंकाररूपिणी
शुद्धसंवेदनाकारा शिवं सन्मात्रमच्युतम् ३३

Stainless, ever the same, pure, the actuality which is beyond the sense of "I" or "mine,"

The quintessence of pure knowingness, [Lord] Śiva, the wholeness of eternal truth, the imperishable.

Verse 34:

सकृद्विभाता विमला नित्योदयवती सदा
सा ब्रह्मपरमात्मादिनामभिः परिगीयते ३४

The forever shining light eternal, pure immutable potentiality, ever the same, She is celebrated with names like "Brahman," (Totality), "*Paramātmā*," (the Supreme Self), and so on.

Verse 35:

चेत्यचेतनचित्तादि नास्या भिन्नं न मानतः
तयैषा चेत्यते चिच्छ्रीः सैषाद्या चिदिति स्मृता ३५

The primordial division of the wholeness into knower, knowing, and known does not apply to her, She is not conceptualizable.

By means of Her, this [consciousness] becomes conscious, by means of Her, [This] consciousness becomes multiple knowers, and by means of Her this [consciousness] becomes innumerable objects of perception. [This] consciousness alone is, according to the knowledge handed down [in the Upaniṣads].

Verse 36:

अचेत्यं यदिदं चित्त्वं तत्तस्या रूपमक्षतम्
मनोबुद्धीन्द्रियाद्यर्थरूपैः सैव विजृम्भते ३६

That which cannot be known [with the mind, intellect or senses] is this [all]knowing-ness. Her form is unbroken, undivided wholeness.

The mind, intellect and senses are characterized by [the grasping of] physical objects, [objective, conceivable phenomena]. She is ever-expanding, ungraspable.

Verse 37:

तरङ्गकणकल्लोलकलनेयं चिदात्मनि
जगद्रूपपदार्थानां सत्ता स्फुरति मातरि ३७

Oscillating back and forth [with infinite speed] between abstract wave and concrete particle, the consciousness in the Self is indeterminate [encompassing all possibilities in a virtual state].

The existence of the blueprints of all the forms and phenomena in the manifest world is revealed in Mother Divine.

Verse 38

यदिदं तत्परं रूपं तस्याः खलु महाचितेः
शुद्धचिन्मणिवत्सा हि सेयं समसमोदिता ३८

This phenomenal appearance of Mother Divine, the expression in form of the unmanifest transcendental Being, definitely emerges from cosmic mind.

She is This [infinite treasure] born of the homogeneous wholeness, indeed, She is crystal clear pure consciousness filled with innumerable [bright sparkling] precious jewels.

Verse 39:

अनन्ययैव या शक्त्या जगज्जृम्भिकया स्थिता
सत्ता मायातिरेकेण नान्या संभवतीह हि ३९

She is eternally one without a second, She who is characterized by the infinite organizing power responsible for the expansion of the whole universe,

She is the totality of Being, extending far beyond the illusory limitations of time and space; there is no other creator than her, because she creates this whole universe [from her own nature].

Verse 40:

विचित्रतेव भाण्डानां ननु हेमतया यथा
सा तथोदेति तद्रूपमात्मानं चेतति स्वयम् ४०

Like the ability of the goldsmith to fashion gold into innumerable ornaments of different shapes and sizes,

Mother Divine in the same way rises up as the phenomenal form of that infinite Being, so that the infinite unbounded Self can perceive itself.

Verse 41:

स्वचित्तेन द्रवत्वेन तरङ्गादित्वमम्बुषु
महाचितौ जगच्चित्तादुदेतीवानुदेत्यपि ४१

With the Self taking on material qualities and becoming an object of consciousness, the same primordial waters of Being are on both sides of the gap [having become both knower and known].

In Cosmic Consciousness, because the whole universe has become an object for consciousness, the universe appears to be real, but it is not real, [it is only consciousness appearing as the object].

Verse 42:

तदात्मैव यथा यातो रूपवान् जलधौ द्रवात्
एवं चिन्मात्रमेवाहमनहंभावमाततम् ४२

In the state of Cosmic Consciousness, it is *Ātmā* alone that has somehow gotten into a state of being possessed of innumerable forms, when the one unbounded ocean of consciousness [is seen] in terms of the dynamism of material creation.

In this way, consciousness is all that there is, there is only the Self; the appearance of non-Self is merely the congealed form of the [same] Self.

Verse 43:

न तस्य जन्ममरणे न तस्य सदसद्गती
न नाशः संभवत्यस्य चिन्मात्रनभसः क्वचित् ४३

There is no birth and death of that infinite Self, there is no drama of the real and unreal nature of that infinite Self.

It cannot be destroyed, there is only the eternal dynamism of that wholeness [taking on different forms]: Now and forever, it is only the one consciousness [appearing] in terms of the duality of heaven and earth, Absolute and relative.

Verse 44:

अच्छेद्योऽयमदाह्योऽयं चिदादित्योऽतिनिर्मलः
आहो नु चिरकालेन शान्तास्मि परिनिर्वृता ४४

That cannot be divided, that cannot be burned: The Sun—the administering power of total natural law throughout all the cycles of creation and destruction in the cosmos—is the all-surpassing ever the same light of consciousness, shining.

Is it really so, across the eternity of time, I am eternal peace, omnipresent infinite fulfillment?

Verse 45:

निर्वामि भ्रमनिर्मुक्तमासे निर्मन्दराब्धिवत्
असदाभासमत्यच्छमनन्तमजमच्युतम् ४५

I am at peace, freed from the mind's constant searching, like the ocean [of milk] without the mountain [Mandara] [churning within it].

The unreal is mere appearance, completely transparent, infinite and unbounded, unborn, and imperishable.

> According to the Purāṇas, at the beginning of time, at the first stir of manifestation of creation, the *Devas* and the *Asuras* got together and churned the heretofore silent ocean of milk, using the mountain called Mandara as a stirring rod, and the snake Vāsuki as the string to twirl the stirring rod. Out of their stirring, Itihāsa, history, and thus all of time-space causation, came up out of the ocean of milk. That was the dawn of creation. Before that there was silence alone.

Verse 46:

आत्माकाशमनाबाधममलं परमं चिरम्
अनन्तमिदमाकाशं फलौघाश्चाफलादिकाः ४६

The *Ākāśa* of the Self is free from blemish and never feels pain, [it is] the highest transcendental Being, everlasting.

> Unbounded is this *Ākāśa*, unlimited abundance of fulfillment and [at the same time] the unmanifest primordial roots of all desired objects.

Verse 47:

सुरासुरयुतं विश्वमेतन्मयमकृत्रिमम्
पुंस्त्वकर्ममयी सेना सर्वं मृन्मात्रकं यथा ४७

This whole universe comes into being by the combined forces of all the creative and destructive impulses of natural law (the *Suras* and *Asuras*) [that are] all made of This [*Ākāśa* of the Self], [which itself] is not made by anyone or fabricated from anything [deeper or subtler]:

Like an army is built up of so many actions of individual men, the ever-changing, ever-dying impulses of creation and destruction are the constituents of the whole creation, [they are made of *Ākāśa*, but the *Ākāśa* of the Self is not made of anything and is not created by anyone].

Verse 48:

द्रष्टृदृश्यमयी सत्ता चिन्मात्रैक्यमयी तथा
इदमैक्यमिदं द्वित्वमहं नाहमितीति च ४८

Similarly, objective reality always consists of two things, a seer and the seen; [but] ultimately [it] is made of one thing, consciousness alone.

"I am this unity," and "I am not this duality," she said.

Verse 49:

क इव भ्रमसंमोहः कथं कस्य कुतः क्व वा
स्वमनन्तमनायासमुपशान्तास्मि संस्थिता ४९

Like “Ka,” [the collapse of the fullness of “A,” onto its own point,] [the soul] wanders about here and there, completely ignorant [of its infinite unbounded nature]. How can infinity be confined in a point? By what agency does the ocean get lost in a drop? For what purpose is it lost? Where can the wholeness go?

My Self is unbounded and inexhaustible and remains forever tranquil like the settled ocean without waves.

Verse 50:

निर्वाणपरिनिर्वाणा गतमासे गतज्वरम्
अचेतनं चेतनं वा योऽयमाभाति चेतति ५०

[I am the] Infinite fulfillment and liberation of perfect silence, the absolute eternal silence that puts an end to the wandering of the soul from birth to birth: The ever-changing phases of relativity have come to an end, the fever of delusion has passed away [for me].

That which may be described as consciousness devoid of any object, or as consciousness which is completely full in itself, illuminates its own totality in eternal self-referral consciousness.

Verse 51:

भासमानात्म तद्रूपं खं महाचिति संस्थितम्
नेदं नाहं न चान्यच्च न भावाभावसंभवः
शान्तं सर्वं निरालम्बं केवलं संस्थितं परम् ५१

The eternally shining Self, the form of Totality, Infinite Pure Existence, Cosmic Consciousness is fully established.

There is no object, there is no sense of "I," and there is no other; there is no coming into being or ceasing-to-be being brought about.

Eternal peace is all that there is, without any parts to hold together, complete self-sufficiency, fully established transcendental Being.

Verse 52:

इत्थं विचारणापरापरमप्रबोधा-
द्बुद्ध्वा यथास्थितमिदं परमात्मतत्त्वम् ।
संशान्तरागभयमोहतमोविलासा
शान्ता बभूव शरदम्बरलेखिकेव ५२

In this way, there is no sprouting in consciousness of a distinction between relative and Absolute; having known all this relativity as transitory and unreal, the true reality is the transcendental Self [alone].

Excitement, fear, delusion, darkness, and the entire play of creation is completely merged in eternal peace: Having become eternal peace [all this relativity] is like a small insignificant wisp of cloud on a perfect cloudless autumn sky.

> This chapter chronicles the growth of Cūḍālā from ignorance to enlightenment. In the context of this story of the growth and stabilization of Cosmic Consciousness, Vasishtha presents with great clarity three distinct phases or qualities of consciousness which must come together at one time for the experience of Siddhis, the supernormal powers, including Yogic Flying. We will learn in Chapter 80, verse 19, that there are three qualities of consciousness which must come together to produce the Siddhis, Dhāraṇa, Dhyān and Samādhi. Cūḍālā quickly brings fulfillment to her practice of Siddhis, exhibiting her ability to bring together in one awareness these three quite distinct and apparently incompatible values of consciousness. The development of these three prerequisite qualities of consciousness has taken place in this chapter,

so this chapter must be understood as part and parcel of the presentation of the path to gaining the supernormal abilities.

Dhāraṇa comes from the Sanskrit root dhṛ, meaning "to hold, bear, carry, maintain, preserve, keep, possess." A honey bee goes from flower to flower and does not hold on to any one flower. Quite opposite to that is the quality of *Dhāraṇa*, which maintains the hold or grip of awareness on one object. This quality of *Dhāraṇa* is exemplified in the undying love of the royal couple. As their bodies age, their love for each other only grows stronger: "Our thirst for the unity of love grows stronger, like the creeper of the bottle gourd growing longer in the rainy season." There is a quality of holding onto a desired object, even as it undergoes changes and transformations, and the love of Cūḍālā and Śikhidhvaja perfectly exemplifies this quality of holding on to the object of desire.

In verses 10 and 11, the royal couple began a quest to somehow go beyond the changing and ever-dying values of relativity and find something that was eternal and everlasting. After many years of searching, and many more years of practice of meditation, Cūḍālā gains great clarity of experience of pure consciousness. Pure consciousness is an all-embracing, completely overshadowing experience, where nothing at all is left in the awareness but the fullness of Being. Nevertheless, Cūḍālā remembers the theme of her original quest, and reflects, in verse 25, on how pure consciousness could put an end to the wasting away of life in the aging process. This shows her extraordinary ability of *Dhāraṇa*, her ability to hold on to the object of desire.

The entire story of Cūḍālā and Śikhidhvaja is the quintessential, perfect demonstration of *Dhāraṇa.* Cūḍālā, deeply in love with her husband, through her practice of transcending and the practice of the Siddhis, gains complete mastery of natural law, and attains a level of unlimited fullness of bliss. But even in that state of infinite fulfillment, which no relative joy can match, she remembers her love and devotion to her husband, and devotes herself over a period of many years to guiding him to enlightenment. Then she and her husband together return to the capital city and rule the world for 10,000 years. That is steadfastness of desire!

In this chapter, the practice of transcending, *Dhyān* is introduced. The royal couple begin the practice of effortless transcending in verse 12 and are guided in the practice by competent adepts. *Dhyān* is the practice of systematically and effortlessly letting go of boundaries in favor of increasing subtlety, increasing abstraction, and ultimately in favor of completely unbounded awareness. Through her daily practice of *Dhyān*, Cūḍālā gained unbounded awareness, and with regular practice stabilized that unbounded awareness in the attainment of Cosmic Consciousness. As in the story, *Dhyān* must always be taught by trained teachers, so more details about the practice of *Dhyān* are not outlined by Vasishtha.

Finally, the third component of Siddhi practice, *Samādhi*, is that "One thing to be known," (v. 26) and its description dominates the chapter. Supernormal abilities depend on the level of consciousness, and the level of consciousness means precisely the degree of penetration and stabilization of Being. Cūḍālā's fully mature, fully stabilized state of Cosmic Consciousness is already the fertile field for the practice of Siddhis. Thus, this chapter comprehensively lays the groundwork for the development of Siddhis that begins in Chapter 4.

Colophon:

इत्यार्षे श्रीवासिष्ठमहारामायणे वाल्मीकीये मोक्षोपायेषु निर्वाणप्रकरणे चूडालाप्रबोधो नाम अष्टसप्ततितमः सर्गः ७८

Verse 1:

वसिष्ठ उवाच
दिनानुदिनमित्येषा स्वात्मारामतया तया
नित्यमन्तर्मुखतया बभूव प्रकृतिस्थिता १

Day after day, in this way, she lived, rejoicing in that infinite bliss of her own Self.

She was always completely Self-referral, having become fully established in her own nature.

Verse 2:

नीरागा निरुपासङ्गा निर्द्वन्द्वा निःसमीहिता
न जहाति न चादत्ते प्रकृताचारचारिणी २

Free from love and hate, she was beyond the pairs of opposites, and free from all effort to attain anything.

Not abstaining from anything and not accepting anything, she moved about, carrying out her assigned duties.

Verse 3:

परितीर्णभवाम्भोधिः शान्तसंदेहजालिका
परमात्ममहालाभपरिपूर्णान्तरात्मना ३

Having crossed over all boundaries, she was the receptacle of the ocean of unbounded Being, she had resolved all the doubts and uncertainties of the great knotted net of illusion [of the world].

She had fully accomplished the great attainment of the supreme Self by her inner self.

Verse 4:

विश्रान्ता सुचिरं श्रान्ता घनलब्धपदान्तरे
सर्वोपमातीततया जगामाव्यपदेश्यताम् ४

Feeling at ease with this accomplishment for a very long time, she now continued her spiritual practices, having merely attained the milestone of inner realization.

The area of relative creation being neglected by her [so far] she continued [her spiritual practices] with the goal of unfolding the fullness of relative creation, the fullness of the world of names and forms.

> In the previous chapter, Cūḍālā gained enlightenment, Cosmic Consciousness, and that state of enlightenment was described again in the first three verses of this chapter. Now this verse suggests that what Cūḍālā experienced as "Cosmic Consciousness," was not the ultimate fulfillment of human evolution, was not the highest level of consciousness that could be attained by a human being, but rather, was merely a significant milestone on

the path. What are the higher states of consciousness that are available to man? Vasiṣhṭha is teaching Rām that there are two phases in the growth of enlightenment, an inner phase that finds fulfillment in the attainment of Cosmic Consciousness, and an outer phase that leads to Brahman, the completely integrated, unified state of enlightenment. The understanding of these stages of enlightenment is important in the context of the unfoldment of the Siddhis, which is the theme of these seven chapters, because the successful performance of the Siddhis requires the experience—even for a moment—of the completely integrated state of Unity Consciousness.

States of consciousness represent distinct modes of functioning of the human nervous system. Maharishi Mahesh Yogi has explained that there are seven states of consciousness that are open to man. Each state of consciousness is a specific, unique style of functioning of the nervous system, with identifiable characteristics, and according to Maharishi, with correspondingly unique physiological parameters. On the basis of the rich experiences of millions of meditators practicing his Transcendental Meditation technique over a period of fifty years, and on the basis of detailed descriptions of experiences of higher states of consciousness in the scriptural records of the ancient Vedic Literature, in texts such as the Bhagavad Gītā, Maharishi has outlined the milestones of development on the path to enlightenment in terms of these seven states of consciousness.

The first three states are waking, dreaming and sleeping, and these are enjoyed by everyone in the world, from birth. Waking state is the state in which we experience the material world; sleep state is a state of deep rest of the nervous system, in which the senses and organs of action are not active; and dream state is a period of illusory perception during the night's sleep. These are familiar to everyone's experience, and well documented in terms of the knowledge of human physiology.

The fourth state of consciousness, (*Turīya cetana*) is consciousness on its own, consciousness pure, the simplest form of human awareness, a perfectly balanced state of mind, called *Samādhi* in the Yogic literature. Maharishi describes it as follows[1]:

"This is a state of inner wakefulness with no object of thought or perception, just pure consciousness aware of its own unbounded nature. It is wholeness, aware of itself, devoid of differences, beyond the division of subject and object—transcendental consciousness. It is a field of all possibilities, where all creative potentialities exist together, infinitely correlated but as yet unexpressed. It is a state of perfect order, the matrix from which all the laws of nature emerge, the source of creative intelligence."

When through repeated experience of transcending, pure consciousness becomes so familiar to the mind that it is spontaneously maintained as an all-time reality, along with the changing states of waking, dreaming and sleeping, a different state of consciousness is experienced, called Cosmic Consciousness. Maharishi explains how this fifth state of consciousness develops:[2]

"In the beginning, because the system is not used to that style of functioning, after meditation, the system returns to its usual, habitual style of functioning. We plunge back into the waking, dreaming, or sleeping state. But because it is such a beautiful, restful state, unbounded and fulfilling, very quickly the system starts to gain the habit of returning to that state. After some time of alternating that fourth state with the other three, the nervous system becomes habituated to maintain that style of awareness. It begins to be able not to lose that style of functioning. Then that state of awareness is maintained even during waking, dreaming and sleeping."

In this spontaneous state of duality, two quite distinct styles of functioning are simultaneously maintained by the nervous system. Maharishi explains how this is possible[3] : "It is well known that there exist in the nervous system many autonomous levels of function, between which a system of coordination also exists. In the state of Cosmic Consciousness, two different levels of organization in the nervous system function simultaneously while maintaining their separate identities. By virtue of this anatomical separation of function, it becomes possible for transcendental consciousness to co-exist with the waking state of consciousness and with the dreaming and sleeping states of consciousness."

The characteristics of Cosmic Consciousness are familiar to us from Vasishtha's descriptions in the previous chapter of the state of "*Mahāciti*," literally "Great Consciousness," which we translated as Cosmic Consciousness (2.14). Maharishi writes about this state:[4]

"The state of Cosmic Consciousness is inclusive of transcendental consciousness as well as consciousness of the relative order; it brings cosmic status to the individual life. When the individual consciousness achieves the status of cosmic existence then, in spite of all the obvious limitations of individuality, a man is ever free, unbounded by any aspect of time, space or causation, ever out of bondage. This state of eternal freedom, set out here in principle, is a result of establishing the mind in the state of transcendental consciousness."

Cosmic Consciousness is the fifth state of human consciousness. The fifth state of consciousness is a state of complete fulfillment, a state of infinite bliss, maintained as an all-time reality, and therefore it is said to be a state of enlightenment. Maharishi describes the bliss and fullness of this state,[5] "The bliss of this state eliminates the possibility of any sorrow, great or small. No sorrow can enter bliss consciousness, nor can bliss consciousness know any gain greater than itself. That state of self-sufficiency leaves one steadfast in oneself, fulfilled in eternal contentment."

The sixth state of consciousness builds upon the fifth state by expanding on the perception and knowledge of the environment: improving the ability of perception and evaluation of the world of the waking state. The inner enlightenment, the establishment of the mind in transcendental consciousness continues, but now a new joy is added to life, the appreciation of the glory of the Creator of the cosmos in every relative perception. This develops through a refinement of the activity of the waking state:[6] "The activity of devotion comprises the feelings of service, reverence and love, which are the most refined qualities of feeling. It is through the activity of devotion that Cosmic Consciousness develops into God-consciousness."

The refinement of feeling leads to the ability to appreciate subtler, more delicate values of the object of perception. On the ground of the infinite silence of unbounded awareness which has been permanently established, very delicate impulses of feeling and perception become possible. "With such an unrestricted, unbounded awareness, we are able to penetrate into the deeper values of perception. Our perception becomes more refined. We could naturally imagine a state in which the finest perception would be possible, so that the finest value of the object of experience would become apparent to our perception."[7] When this finest value of perception is established, then every object is appreciated in terms of the finest value of relative creation, which is the impulse of the Creator, termed the "Light of God." This is a state in which the omnipresent Light of God is palpably visible everywhere, at all times, and perception is said to be "celestial perception." This elevation and refinement of the ability of perception such that the heavenly light of God is appreciated in every point value of perception is so dramatically different in its character from the ordinary waking state, that this is termed a distinct state of consciousness, "God Consciousness." It is a state in which the glory of God's creation has become permanently established on the level of perception.

Beyond the sixth state, there is yet the possibility to rise to an even more glorious, more exalted state of consciousness.

In the fifth state of consciousness, Cosmic Consciousness, there are two values simultaneously open to awareness, the unbounded infinite Self, and the non-Self. In God Consciousness, there continue to be two values simultaneously open to awareness, but now the non-Self aspect of relative creation has been raised to the supreme value in the relative.

In the seventh state of consciousness, perception is raised to its infinite value, and the object of perception is appreciated to be as dear, as unbounded and full as one's own Self. Then the object is as infinite as the subject, and the object is appreciated in terms of the infinite value of the Self; subject and object unified. Maharishi describes it in this way:[8] "In this unified state of consciousness, the experiencer and the object of experience have both been brought to the same level of infinite value and this encompasses the entire phenomenon of perception and action as well. The gulf between the knower and the object of his knowing has been bridged. When the unbounded perceiver is able to cognize the object in its total reality, cognizing the infinite value of the object, which was hitherto unseen, then the perception can be called total or of supreme value. In this state, the full value of knowledge has been gained, and we can finally speak of complete knowledge."

The experience of the seventh state of consciousness builds upon the refined perception of the sixth state of consciousness, and yet the experience of the wholeness and oneness of inner and outer unboundedness is completely different in its character from the glorious celestial perception of God Consciousness. Because the characteristics of life are different, this is termed a distinct state of consciousness, Unity Consciousness.

With the addition of the seventh state of consciousness, our map of the full range of human potential is complete: These are the seven states of consciousness that are available to every individual on earth, by virtue of having a human nervous system. We can summarize the entire path to enlightenment through all these seven states of consciousness as the path of learning to use one's total brain potential. Actually, the experience of Transcendental Consciousness already engages the total brain: The whole brain functions in synchrony, with perfect coherence in order to give rise to the experience of Transcendental Consciousness, and this has been shown in the EEG brain waves of beginning and advanced practitioners of the Transcendental Meditation technique. One engages the total brain in Transcendental Consciousness in a momentary experience, first, and then that value of total brain functioning expands more and more through regular practice of meditation and its advanced techniques, and one rises through all these seven states of consciousness.

In the next few verses, our heroine, Cūḍālā, rises to the highest level of consciousness, Unity Consciousness, the state of supreme knowledge. Now it is useful to reflect on the context of this story: Vasishtha is teaching his disciple Rām the knowledge of human potential, the knowledge of the higher states of consciousness. As the future ruler of the kingdom of Ayodhya, he needs to know the whole story of what a human being is, and what every human being can be: What are the states of consciousness open to man, and what are their characteristics, and how are they developed? The entire purpose of this story is to make clear to Rām something which cannot be described in words: It is said of this Unity Consciousness, that it is "That from which speech returns," it cannot be captured in speech. How then can Vasishtha teach Rām the knowledge of higher states of consciousness, so that he will be inspired to gain the highest state of consciousness in his personal life, and rule his kingdom with wisdom and justice? The first lesson that Vasishtha is teaching Rām about human potential is that knowledge is different in different states of consciousness. Cūḍālā gains the state of full enlightenment in Unity Consciousness, and she is glowing with the light of life. Her husband, Śikhidhvaja, notices this and wants to know what has happened. She does her best to explain her experience, but he does not understand a word of what she is saying.

The challenge to explain higher states of human potential is ages-old, simply because the material of which the experience of enlightenment is made is unavailable in the waking state. The Siddhis, and especially Yogic Flying, are going to provide a tangible bridge, by presenting an experience which is only possible on the level of Unity Consciousness, but which is visible to the eyes even in the waking state. That is the gist of it: With masterful strokes, Vasishtha, the pre-eminent story-teller, is going to make the benefits of higher states of consciousness clear to Rām, and to the reader. With this context of understanding of the whole range of human experience from ignorance to complete enlightenment, we return to Cūḍālā's quest for higher consciousness:

Verse 5:

इति सा भामिनी तस्य चूडाला वरवर्णिनी
स्वल्पेनैव हि कालेन ययौ विदितवेद्यताम् ५

That being the state of affairs now, she being [naturally] intensely passionate [in whatever she undertook to do], Cūḍālā became an ardent seeker of true spiritual knowledge about the surrounding world.

In only a short time indeed, pursuing this direction, she learned everything there was to be known.

> The effect is visible on the surface; the cause that gives rise to the effect is hidden. "True spiritual knowledge about the world" means learning the unseen cause of visible phenomena. The purpose of knowledge in every relative discipline is to explain the principles of transformation which give rise to what is actually observed. There are universal laws of nature underlying what is seen happening.
>
> For example, with regard to the observed behavior of living beings, all plants and animals are made of cells which carry out all the functions of life on the microscopic level. Cells themselves have a hidden cause deep within: Inside the cell is the cell nucleus which directs all the activities of the cell. Within the cell nucleus are the strands of DNA; the DNA is made up of long sequences of four basic nucleotides which represent the ultimate governing intelligence of the cell. Sequences of codons in the DNA code for specific amino acids which are assembled to create proteins which organize and carry out all the activities of the cell. The observed phenomena

of behavior of living beings has its basis in packages of intelligence contained within the cells.

Seeing the underlying cause of observed phenomena means appreciating the laws of nature that are functioning to give rise to surface expressions. Laws of nature are studied in physics, chemistry, biology, and so forth, and the knowledge that they provide informs perception, refines perception. The accumulated knowledge in every discipline brings to awareness the underlying intelligence responsible for what is observed. This is why students go to school, to refine their ability of perception of the external world through knowledge of the underlying intelligence that is causing the expressed phenomena. With more and more knowledge, perception and evaluation of the world is more and more refined, and the individual acts with less and less mistakes.

The path to perception of the underlying intelligence of every object and phenomenon is the path of gaining and internalizing the knowledge of how natural law functions. By gaining the knowledge of all the disciplines of natural law, the knowledge of all the sciences, Cūḍālā refined her ability of perception to the highest degree possible in the relative, so that she could see the animating intelligence of natural law, the light of God lively in every phenomenon. She learned everything there was to be known about how natural law functions.

The idea of gaining celestial perception through mastery of all the disciplines of natural law seems foreign to us, because remaining in one discipline only, one does not gain that breadth and depth of vision to be able to see the pure intelligence, the light of God shining in every phenomenon. This is both because the knowledge of each discipline is so vast that learning everything is unmanageable, and because not every discipline has succeeded in locating its ultimate source in pure intelligence. One cannot read every book in the library; one cannot in this way gain total knowledge.

Cūḍālā lived in a Vedic culture. The Vedas are said to contain the total blueprint of natural law in creation. The different branches of Vedic Science comment, analyze and expand on the knowledge in the Vedas exhaustively. Together, the approximately forty branches of knowledge in Vedic Science encompass all the knowledge of natural law underlying all the observable phenomena in relative creation. Total knowledge of natural law is available in the Vedas and Vedic Literature. The goal of the study of the Vedas, the fulfillment of the Vedic teaching is just this: Gaining the total knowledge of natural law, so that in every perception one appreciates the liveliness of total intelligence of natural law, Veda, giving rise to the observed phenomenon. God Consciousness, the universal perception of the Light of God as the highest relative value of every point in creation, is the fulfillment of the Vedic teaching. Study of the Vedas is for that.

Cūḍālā mastered all the branches of Vedic Science—in itself a noteworthy and rare accomplishment—and rose to God Consciousness, the sixth state of human consciousness. That is the purport of this verse.

Verse 6:

यथायमागतः कश्चिज्ञागतः स्पन्दविभ्रमः
तथा विलीयते सर्वं तत्त्वज्ञानवति स्वयम् ६

In which manner, having attained whatever anyone knew about the physical sciences, she came to see the vitality of pure life everywhere in the dynamism of the phenomenal world.

In that way, gaining the knowledge of the essential reality of the material world, the whole creation dissolved, and was appreciated in terms of her own self.

> Vasishtha is explaining the connection between knowledge of the physical sciences, and the supreme value of perception. When the deepest knowledge of natural law found in any discipline is found shining on the surface of the object, then every perception has within it the vitality of the creative impulse, the power of natural law which is the ultimate source of the object. An example will make this clear. In Maharishi Mahesh Yogi's Consciousness-Based Education, teachers refer daily to a Unified Field Chart for their discipline. The Unified Field Chart shows all the branches of a discipline, theoretical and applied, with reference to their ultimate source in the Unified Field. From this unified level, the four main forces diverge, and then all the particles and fields, and their applied values in electromagnetism, electronics, mechanics and celestial mechanics, etc. When studying any branch of physics, the teacher relates that study to the Unified Field Chart, so that the student can see the expressed values of natural law in that sub-branch of physics with reference to the Unified Field. The result is that the

student understands the isolated values of natural law in each area of study in terms of their root or basis in the Unified Field. This trains the student to "see the vitality of pure life everywhere in the dynamism of the phenomenal world."

In time, the perception of the finest relative value in the object of knowledge gives way to the perception of the infinite unmanifest source of the object, the transcendental value of the object. When the perceiver appreciates the object of perception in terms of the infinite value of his own Self, then the non-Self aspect goes to the background, and the oneness of the Self predominates. In this way, creation can be said to dissolve, so that only the Self remains. This is God Consciousness stepping on to Unity Consciousness. The next three verses elaborate on this experience of Unity Consciousness.

Verse 7:

अदृष्टसकले शान्ते पदे विश्रान्तिमेत्य सा
रराज शरदच्छाभ्रमालेव गतसंभ्रमा ७

She was at that milestone [in the development of consciousness] in which the dynamism of ever-changing values of relative perception goes to the background, and the silence of the unmanifest transcendental wholeness becomes more prominent in the awareness.

The boundaries of her perception were becoming porous, like the banks of clouds [of the rainy season] dissipating, and giving way to the open skies of the autumn season.

Verse 8:

अनाकुला समालोकमसंबन्धात्मनात्मनि
जरद्गवीव शैलाग्रं सतृणं प्राप्य संस्थिता ८

She was totally occupied with [the life of] the unmanifest, innocently witnessing the relationship between the infinite knower and the infinite known within the infinite Self,

Like an old cow finding a mountaintop full of grass and becoming established there [without wandering off].

Verse 9:

स्वविवेकघनाभ्यासवशादात्मोदयेन सा
शुशुभे शोभना पुष्पलतेवाभिनवोद्गता ९

Through dedicated practice [of meditation], by virtue of her success in directly experiencing the Self, she gained the total knowledge of the Self.

Glorifying her person with the light of total knowledge of the Self, she shone with the resplendent beauty of youth [despite her age], like new flowers coming up on a vine as old flowers wither and fall away.

> Unity Consciousness is a state of perfect health, a state of complete vitality of the physiology. In Unity Consciousness, and even temporarily, in individuals experiencing Transcendental Consciousness, a special substance is secreted on the skin, called *Soma*, or *Ojas*, that makes the individual glow with a divine spiritual radiance. This is a very common phenomenon.
>
> Reversal of aging is also a commonly observed phenomenon for meditators, such that meditators exhibit a physiological age ten or even twenty years younger than their chronological age. The maintenance of youthful beauty and luster is a common, even predictable result of regular practice of transcending. That Cūḍālā shone with uncommon beauty after attaining Unity Consciousness is thus completely believable based on the research on the reversal of aging through the practice of the Transcendental Meditation program.

Verse 10:

अथ तामनवद्याङ्गीं कदाचित्स शिखिध्वजः
अपूर्वशोभामालोक्य स्मयमान उवाच ह १०

Now, by chance seeing that lady with her perfect youthful figure, radiant with beauty like never before, Śikhidhvaja, being astonished, said to her:

Verse 11:

भूयो यौवनयुक्तेव मण्डितेव पुनः पुनः
अधिकं राजसे तन्वि जगद्राजवती यथा ११

"You seem to have been blessed with ever more beauty and youthful charms with passing years,

[Now] "You surpass all others in beauty and allure, [you have become] the most beautiful lady in the whole world!

Verse 12:

प्रपीतामृतसारेव लब्धा लभ्यपदेव च
आनन्दापूरपूर्णेव राजसे नितरां प्रिये १२

"Have you obtained and begun drinking the nectar of immortality or something similarly desirable?

"As if you are filled with an ocean of infinite bliss, the beauty of your soul shines exquisitely, gladdening the heart.

REVERSAL OF AGING PROCESS
through the Transcendental Meditation program

PHYSIOLOGY	Through aging	Through TM
Blood pressure	↑	↓
Auditory threshold	↑	↓
Near-point vision	↑	↓
Cardiovascular efficiency	↓	↑
Cerebral blood flow	↓	↑
Homeostatic recovery	↓	↑
BIOCHEMISTRY		
Cholesterol concentration	↑	↓
Hemoglobin concentration	↓	↑
MIND-BODY COORDINATION		
Reaction time	↑	↓
Sensory-motor performance	↓	↑

PSYCHOLOGICAL	Through aging	Through TM
Susceptibility to stress	↑	↓
Behavioral rigidity	↑	↓
Learning ability	↓	↑
Memory	↓	↑
Creativity	↓	↑
Intelligence	↓	↑
HEALTH		
Cardiovascular disease	↑	↓
Hypertension	↑	↓
Asthma (severity)	↑	↓
Insomnia	↑	↓
Depression	↑	↓
Immune system efficiency	↓	↑
Quality of sleep	↓	↑

Much of the wear and tear to the system caused by aging and stress can be reversed through the deep rest of TM.

Wallace, R.K., M. Dillbeck, E. Jacobe, and B. Harrington. "The Effects of the Transcendental Meditation and TM-Sidhi Program on the Aging Process." *International Journal of Neuroscience* 16 (1982): 53–58.

YOUNGER BIOLOGICAL AGE

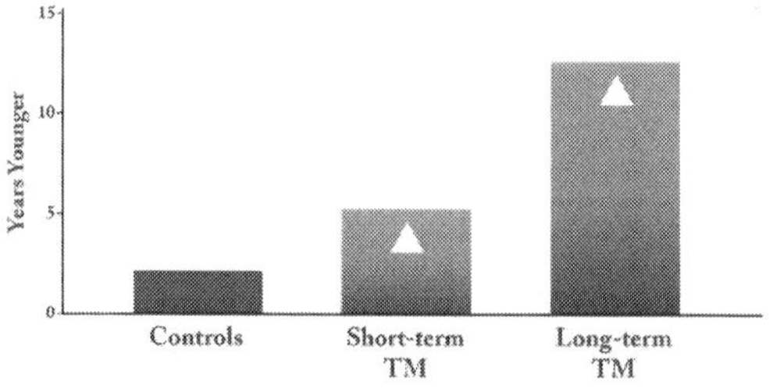

International Journal of Neuroscience 16 (1982): 53–58

Long-term TM meditators (5 years or more) had a "biological age" 12-15 years younger than their actual chronological age.

Wallace, R.K., M. Dillbeck, E. Jacobe, and B. Harrington. "The Effects of the Transcendental Meditation and TM-Sidhi Program on the Aging Process." *International Journal of Neuroscience* 16 (1982): 53–58.

Verse 13:

उपशान्तं च कान्तं च दधाना सुन्दरं वपुः
अभिभूयेन्दुमायासि श्रियं कामपि कामिनि १३

"You are self-composed and beautiful to look at, all-attractive and charming, wonderful [in every way].

[With the beauty of your radiance,] "You excel in splendor even the bewitching light of the moon; the heart swells with love and finds fulfillment [in seeing you].

Verse 14:

अभोगकृपणं शान्तमूर्जितं समतां गतम्
गम्भीरं च प्रशान्तं च चेतः पश्यामि ते प्रिये १४

"You have engaged the mighty power of silence that unwinds the [layers of] stress and misery and creates balance.

"Mysterious and composed and radiating the light of wisdom, I see thee structured in all-nourishing all-supporting love.

Verse 15:

तृणीकृत्य त्रिभुवनं पीताखिलजगद्रसम्
अनन्तोड्डामरं सौम्यं मनः पश्यामि ते प्रिये १५

"Having drunk the precious golden essence of the whole creation, [by seeing your beauty] you make all the three worlds appear as insignificant as a straw.

"Having dignity beyond all limits, your mind is serene and tender like the light of the moon, I see thee structured in all-nourishing all-supporting love.

Verse 16:

न केनचिन्महाभागे विभवानन्दवस्तुना
चेतस्तव तुलामेति मरुक्षीराब्धिसुन्दरम् १६

"There is nothing to compare in eminence with the majesty and bliss of the exalted state of balance of your mind: For a thirsty man searching for love in a barren desert, your beauty is like the whole ocean [of love] contained in a glass.

Verse 17:

तैरेव बालकदलीमृणालाङ्कुरकोमलैः
अङ्गैः स्थितिमनुप्राप्तैर्वृद्धिं यातेव लक्ष्यसे १७

"By these means, the vigor and strength of the body is maintained perpetually: By maintaining the simplicity and innocence of youth [*Brahmacharya*], by [properly treated] heavy metals [such as mercury], by maintaining the suppleness of the body, and by living life on the finest level of feeling.

"With these components being implemented [as part of a holistic approach to health and longevity] the vitality of the body can be maintained over a long period, as your youthful appearance demonstrates.

> Śikhidhvaja brings out four principles established in the field of Ayurveda for structuring physical immortality:
>
> 1) *Brahmacharya*, for conservation of energy and vitality; 2) *Bhasmas* (ashes) of heavy metals such as mercury, which are integral parts of herbal formulations called *Rasāyanas*, which are prescribed in regimens for promoting long life; 3) maintaining the suppleness of the body and coordination of the limbs through regular practice of Yoga *Āsanas*, and 4) living in higher states of consciousness, in which life is sustained on the basis of the finest level of feeling (*Komala*).

Verse 18:

तथा तेनैव तेनैव संनिवेशेन संस्थिता
अन्यतामुपयातासि लतेव ऋतुपर्यते १८

"In that manner, by that expedient alone one gains immortality—by making the body in every way a fit dwelling place for the soul, [the otherwise changing mortal] body continues on—by that expedient alone one gains immortality.

"You are one who has reached that which has not been reached by others: You have [even now] slender graceful curves like a twining creeper, [although] having passed through many seasons.

Verse 19:

किं त्वया पीतममृतं प्राप्तं साम्राज्यमेव वा
अमृत्युमेव संप्राप्ता प्रयोगायोगयुक्तितः १९

"Have you drunk the nectar of immortality, or have you attained the rulership of all the worlds [giving you authority over even aging and death]?

"Never-dying eternal youth has been completely attained by you, through some combination of [health-promoting] practices and regimens [of diet and daily routine].

Verse 20:

राज्याच्चिन्तामणेर्वापि त्रैलोक्याद्वा त्वयाधिकम्
अप्राप्तं किमनुप्राप्तं नीलोत्पलविलोचने २०

"Or perhaps you have gained sovereignty over the three worlds by means of the fabulous crest-jewel [that bestows all desires] and in that way this extraordinary attainment [of perpetual youth] has been achieved by you.

"What can there be that is not accomplished by some technique? There must be sequential steps of achievement to reach the goal: When the paste of the blue lotus is imbibed, then the vision is opened to higher realities: [by what herb, then, or by what other means have you regained the beauty of your youth?]"

Verse 21:

चूडालोवाच
नाकिंचित्किंचिदाकारमिदं त्यक्त्वाहमागता
न किंचित्किंचिदाकारं तेनास्मि श्रीमती स्थिता २१

Cūḍālā said:

"In the absence of something there is nothing; [every] something is the creation of the unbounded expanse of nothingness; having let go of this something, I have become a continuum of nothingness.

"Nothing is something [after all]; the creative power of the unbounded expanse of nothingness is [certainly] something; by that [creative power] in me, this splendid Divine beauty abides in me eternally.

The charming, flowery words of Cūḍālā are poetic, but she intends them as a succinct expression of the reality which she is living. The inner unboundedness of awareness has merged with the outer unboundedness to create a continuum of transcendence, a continuum of pure Being. Like the Unified Field in modern physics, which in its least excited state contains the virtual fluctuations of all possible excitations of the field, she says that there is a creative power in the nothingness, and that creative power of the unbounded expanse of nothingness is the reality which she is living. By virtue of the inherent dynamism within the seemingly flat transcendence, unity can become a living reality, it can be functional.

Śikhidhvaja, however, has not studied our modern quantum field theory, and he does not understand that there can be the dynamism of virtual fluctuations in the vacuum. From his point of view, everything is created from some existing material: A tree grows from the seed, if there is no seed, then nothing comes up. Nothing can emerge from nothing: Cūḍālā's expressions in this verse do not mean anything to Śikhidhvaja, and he laughingly rejects and refutes them in verse 3 of the following chapter.

Verse 22:

इदं सर्वं परित्यज्य सर्वमन्यन्मयाश्रितम्
यत्तत्सत्यमसत्यं च तेनास्मि श्रीमती स्थिता २२

"Having completely abandoned this entire relative creation, something other than manifest creation has been resorted to by me.

"That in which [I have taken refuge] is the Truth, and it is the Truth of the unmanifest; by that [eternal truth] in me, this splendid Divine beauty abides in me eternally.

Verse 23:

यत्किंचिद्यन्न किंचिच्च तज्जानामि यथास्थितम्
यथोदयं यथानाशं तेनास्मि श्रीमती स्थिता २३

"That in which I have taken refuge is something which is [in truth] nothing and something [at the same time]. That [which is something and nothing at the same time] I know as ever-changing on the ground of eternal stability.

"Knowing how creation comes into being and knowing how creation is destroyed, by that [knowing] in me, this splendid Divine beauty abides in me eternally.

Verse 24:

भोगैरभुक्तैस्तुष्यामि भुक्तैरिव सुदूरगैः
न हृष्यामि न कुप्यामि तेनास्मि श्रीमती स्थिता २४

"Enjoying food by not eating, I am fully satisfied with food by remaining at a distance.

"I am not excited [by desires for food], I am not agitated [by hunger or lack]; by that [not taking food], this splendid Divine beauty abides in me eternally.

In the experience of transcendental consciousness, metabolic activity is reduced, as measured by reduced oxygen consumption and reduced breath rate. Maharishi has claimed that if there are no stresses in the system, then it is not necessary for the metabolic activity to continue in the state of transcendental consciousness. Some research has recorded long periods of breath suspension of 40 seconds or longer in advanced practitioners of the Transcendental Meditation technique, but subsequent research suggested that the apparent breath suspension was due to lack of sensitivity of the instruments, and that actually a very quiet oscillation of breath was continuing during those periods. Even so, Transcendental Consciousness is an extremely orderly restful hypometabolic state. Unity consciousness extends that perfect orderliness of the state of least excitation of consciousness to the field of the senses and the organs of action. The physiology in Unity Consciousness could be expected to perform with greatest efficiency and economy. If the system is perfectly orderly in its functioning, very little intake of food will be needed to maintain life. Perhaps as little as a few almonds a day could be enough to sustain the individual.

Stories are told of the ancient *Ṛṣis* gaining enough energy from the *Prāṇa* in the early morning air to support their daily life without any other food being taken. Thus, Cūḍālā's claim that her abstinence from food was responsible for the continuance of her youthful beauty should be taken at face value, that she either ate very little, or ate nothing at all. Still, it should be noted that abstinence from food is not a necessary landmark of Unity Consciousness: In the historic record, many great enlightened sages in Unity Consciousness continued to eat, and exhibited a healthy, balanced digestive fire.

Cūḍālā is pointing out, in response to Śikhidhvaja's suggestions that she has found some magic elixir which restores youth, that in fact she is taking no food at all. There is no lesson here about what food to eat in order to maintain a youthful figure and glamorous appearance: She finds no need for any kind of material sustenance.

Śikhidhvaja is unfamiliar with such a state of life, where there is no need for the intake of food, and suggests that only an angry or furious man, who cannot compose himself to eat would go without food, and such a one would not be found radiant with beauty. Cūḍālā's expressions in this verse do not make any sense to Śikhidhvaja, and he again laughingly rejects and refutes them in verse 4 of the following chapter.

Verse 25:

एकैवाकाशसंकाशे केवले हृदये रमे
न रमे राजलीलासु तेनास्मि श्रीमती स्थिता २५

"When the eternal unity of the unmanifest space-time continuum comes to direct experience in the state of complete self-sufficiency [of awareness] then there is infinite joy in the heart.

"I do not find delight in the royal sports and diversions [because my heart is overflowing with delight in the experience of the empty void of unmanifest space-time;] by that [experience of void], this splendid Divine beauty abides in me eternally.

> The joy of the Self is infinite and immeasurable in the state of Unity Consciousness. It is a state of unbounded fullness of life inside and out. Relative joys do not add to that state of bliss; their absence does not detract from that bliss. These royal diversions and sports and their small joys are of no value when the mind is saturated with the bliss of infinite fulfillment. They are trifling and not even worth considering. They cannot add to the bliss any more than a candle can add to the brightness of the noonday sun.
>
> Śikhidhvaja does not understand that the unmanifest space-time continuum can be an experience of immeasurable bliss. He sees Cūḍālā's indifference to worldly joys as a complete rejection of life. Life flows in the direction of greater and greater happiness. He sees life without these finite worldly joys as barren and empty. Śikhidhvaja misses the description of the infinite joy of

Absolute Being and so Cūḍālā's words make no sense to him. He refutes them in verse 5 of the following chapter.

Verse 26:

आत्मन्येव हि तिष्ठामि ह्यासनोद्यानसद्मसु
न भोगेषु न लज्जासु तेनाहं श्रीमती स्थिता २६

"I [take my] stand in the Absolute eternal *Ātman*, which is seated in a sacred place in the royal garden.

"I do not take my stand in superficial relative enjoyments; I do not take my stand in the celestial field [in the gap between Absolute and relative]; By that [standing in the *Ātmā*], I am [completely identified with] this splendid Divine beauty that abides eternally.

Cūḍālā takes her stand, *i.e.*, she is awake to and lives in the *Ātmā* exclusively. Where does she live, what constitutes her world, is it the relative world of the waking state, or the heavenly world, or the Absolute eternal unchanging Being? Cūḍālā claims that she is not in truth this body, she is not entranced by the activity of the senses, her true life is somewhere else. She lives a life in which the Self is all that there is, there is only the infinite Self moving within itself. That is where she takes her stand. Everything else is insignificant to her. This is the reality of Unity Consciousness.

Verse 27:

जगतां प्रभुरेवास्मि न किंचिन्मात्ररूपिणी
इत्यात्मन्येव तुष्यामि तेनाहं श्रीमती स्थिता २७

"Having power over the whole world, the eternal Being that is in me is not something [small,] measurable and having a manifest form, [it is infinite and unbounded].

"Thus, I find fulfillment in the Self alone; by that [finding fulfillment in the Self alone], I am [completely identified with] this splendid Divine beauty that abides eternally.

Verse 28:

इदं चाहमिदं नाहं सत्या चाहं न चाप्यहम्
सर्वमस्मि न किंचिच्च तेनाहं श्रीमती स्थिता २८

"This expanding universe is my Self; this nothingness is also my Self,

"The truth is, [that] the expansion of creation is "I," the nothingness is "I," and "I" am something more than the creation alone.

"The whole universe is in me! [Therefore, this] nothingness is something [substantial and worth having] and by that, [having the whole universe within the Self], I am [completely identified with] this splendid Divine beauty that abides eternally.

> Cūḍālā experiences the whole universe in terms of her Self. The Self by itself is unmanifest pure Being. Being is composed of both silence and dynamism: Both are integrated in one holistic structure of unmanifest Being.

The silence, emptiness, void, vacuum is Self; the ever-expanding dynamism of creation is Self. She experiences the whole universe inside her Self, inside the field of unmanifest Being. She is not measured or delimited by relative creation, she is something more than that, infinite unbounded wholeness of Absolute and relative together, silence and dynamism together.

Śikhidhvaja understands that there is a state of transcendental consciousness in which the Self is awake to its own nature, but he likens it to the state of sleep in which nothing else remains. He does not understand that silence and dynamism are both lively in the oneness of eternal Being. So, for him, the "I" always refers to the body. And he sees Cūḍālā in front of him, speaking to him, and he cannot comprehend what she means by saying that she does not take her stand in the body, is not there in the body, is not this body. Śikhidhvaja believes the words of these three verses, 26-28 to be philosophical ontological discussions of no practical value. Cūḍālā intended these verses to practically and succinctly convey the status and measure of her level of consciousness. Śikhidhvaja refutes these characterizations of her experience in verses 6 and 7 of the following chapter.

Verse 29:

न सुखं प्रार्थये नार्थं नानर्थं नेतरां स्थितिम्
यथाप्राप्तेन हृष्यामि तेनाहं श्रीमती स्थिता २९

"Nothingness is infinite joy, [and so,] for the sake of having an object [to enjoy], nothingness becomes the object; [but] nothingness [in itself] is not objective, nothingness is not non-Self, it is ever-abiding eternal existence.

"With the realization of how the whole creation is the expression of my Self, I enjoy eternal bliss and fulfillment; by that, [knowing the universe to be the creation of my own Self], I am [completely identified with] this splendid Divine beauty that abides eternally.

Verse 30:

तनुविद्वेषराजाभिः प्रज्ञाभिः शास्त्रदृष्टिभिः
रमे सह वयस्याभिस्तेनाहं श्रीमती स्थिता ३०

"I enjoy company with those royal ministers who are knowers of the Self; with wise enlightened sages [in the King's retinue]; and with scholars deeply versed in the scriptures.

"I enjoy companionship [exclusively] with others [like me] full of vitality and in the prime of their lives; by that, [association with others who are wise and healthy], I am [completely identified with] this splendid Divine beauty that abides eternally.

Verse 31:

पश्यामि यन्नयनरश्मिभिरिन्द्रियैर्वा
चित्तेन चेह हि तदङ्ग न किंचिदेव
पश्यामि तद्विरहितं तु न किंचिदन्तः
पश्यामि सम्यगिति नाथ चिरोदयास्मि ३१

"Whatever I see with the eyes, illumined by the rays of light, or perceive with any of the senses, and whatever I conceive with the mind, here in this manifest world—by virtue of being part of [that veil of illusion of] relativity—is in reality nothingness, it is something that is made up of that eternal unmanifest Being.

"I see [within all these changing values of perception and thinking] that [deeper reality] which is completely separate from the world of relativity, [the eternal immortal Being] which has no boundaries or limits but [is nevertheless real].

"I see facing me in every direction the infinite totality of wholeness of life, transcendent, unmanifest, present here and now, timeless, ever-new, ever in [terms of] my own Self. [...and therefore, I am this splendid Divine beauty—wholeness of life—that abides eternally.]"

In this verse, Cūḍālā sums up everything that she has been saying about her state of consciousness and gives a profound characterization of Unity Consciousness. In Unity, the boundaries of relative perception do not completely dissolve; if they completely dissolved, then it would not be possible to live, to move about or behave within the relative boundaries. Rather, the boundaries lose their all-consuming significance, they are seen as really nothing. The deeper reality of infinite transcendental Being shines through every boundary and glorifies every relative perception. Boundaries are seen, but unboundedness is lived.

Śikhidhvaja does not comprehend this distinction between primary and secondary, foreground and background. He only hears Cūḍālā telling him that what she sees with the eyes she doesn't actually see, instead she sees something non-material, infinite and eternal. In verses 8 and 9 of the following chapter, Śikhidhvaja refutes her characterization of perception, and her entire description of her experience.

This chapter began with a three-verse description of Cūḍālā's experience of Cosmic Consciousness and concludes with this eleven-verse testimonial of her experience of Unity Consciousness. This could be the end of the story. Cūḍālā has attained the highest state of consciousness, Unity Consciousness, and described this glorious state with great clarity. She enjoys infinite fulfillment, immeasurable bliss in every thought, speech and action, and there is nothing more which she needs to accomplish, nothing further which could add to the fullness of her spiritual realization. Rām has been given very detailed descriptions of the higher states of consciousness and their characteristic values and has watched Cūḍālā grow from ignorance to enlightenment. Cūḍālā is living the bliss of heaven on earth.

Cūḍālā is still in her earthly body, and she continues to perform the duties of her station. She has not renounced the world, she has not become a nun, or made any such vows. To the contrary, she continues to be the loving wife of her husband, the king. With her husband she had been accustomed to share all her experiences and all her growing knowledge. But now, because of the gulf that has grown between their levels of consciousness, she has lost her ability to communicate with him. She has earnestly and innocently tried to share her experience of higher consciousness, in answer to his question about her youthful beauty, but as we will see in the next chapter, he doesn't understand at all. Moreover, he believes her words to be childish, and does not accept her at all as an accomplished teacher of spiritual wisdom.

Cūḍālā has infinite resources at her disposal, the resources of total knowledge of natural law which she has gained. Although she is indifferent to worldly joys, she is nevertheless bound in the body, and follows through on the natural desire and need of the wife of the king to bring complete fulfillment to her soul mate. She devotes herself unceasingly to the task of bringing enlightenment to the king, despite seemingly insuperable obstacles in the form of his obstinacy in holding on to narrow boundaries.

In the following chapter, her lifelong companion and ever-devoted partner, dearer to her than life itself, refutes her logic, ridicules her words and completely fails to connect with what she is trying to convey to him. How she deals with that setback, how she follows through on her quest to guide her husband to the supreme enlightenment is historic, legendary, an inspiring example for everyone in the world. The real story, what sets this account apart as the quintessence of the supreme awakening of human potential, starts here. Here is the highest flight, the supreme adventure of the human soul, made accessible to the novice or uninitiated. What we, the readers, do not yet grasp or comprehend about the higher states of consciousness, Cosmic Consciousness, God Consciousness and Unity Consciousness, is going to be made tangible, measurable, and eminently practical. Watch the consummate skill of the story-teller and teacher Vasiṣhṭha, as he opens up the world of enlightenment and higher consciousness for everyone to see.

Colophon:

इत्यार्षे श्रीवासिष्ठमहारामायणे वाल्मीकीये मोक्षोपायेषु निर्वाणप्रकरणे चूडालात्मलाभो नामैकोनाशीतितमः सर्गः ७९

Endnotes

1 Maharishi Mahesh Yogi, *Creating an Ideal Society: A Global Undertaking*, MERU Press: 1976, West Germany, p. 123.
2 Maharishi Mahesh Yogi, *Science of Creative Intelligence Teacher Training Course,* Lesson 23, MIU Press: 1972, p. 23-5.
3 Maharishi Mahesh Yogi, *On the Bhagavad Gita: A New Translation and Commentary with Sanskrit Text, Chapters 1 to 6*, Maharishi University Press, Fairfield, Iowa, 2015, p. 314.
4 Ibid., p. 145.
5 Ibid., p. 424.
6 Ibid., p. 315.
7 Maharishi Mahesh Yogi, *Science of Creative Intelligence Teacher Training Course*, Lesson 23, MIU Press: 1972, p. 23-6.
8 Ibid., p. 23-9.

Chapter 4: Theory and Practice of Yogic Flying®

Verse 1:

वसिष्ठ उवाच
एवमात्मनि विश्रान्तां वदन्तीं तां वराननाम्
अबुद्ध्वा तद्गिरामर्थं विहस्योवाच भूपतिः १

[Cūḍālā] described her state of consciousness in this way, as resting in the infinite silence of the Self inside and outside.

Not having understood the meaning of [her description of] the cessation of all diversity in the fullness of the Self, the king who was the ruler of the [material] world laughingly said:

> This verse is the seed expression of a very wide-ranging chapter, in which the predominant theme is Cūḍālā's mastery of Yogic Flying. But if we look closer at the structure of the verse, we can see how the disparate parts of the chapter are bound together as one. The verse starts with the expression, "In this way resting in the Self," and ends with the word "the ruler of the earth." And as a tree grows from its seed, this chapter explains graphically how by resting in the Self, the rulership of the whole world becomes possible.
>
> The technology of Yogic Flying is explained, not as a frivolous entertainment or curiosity, but as a practical technology of governing a nation by maintaining orderliness in the collective consciousness of the people. The ruler of the nation must be able to nourish his constituency, must be able to prevent them from violating natural laws and creating misery and suffering in their own lives.

Sovereignty has no significant meaning unless the king has the ability to bring all good to the entire population of the country. The ancient technology of Yogic Flying is a technology of rulership, a technology for taking the reins of destiny of the collective consciousness of the nation, and guiding the nation to happiness, prosperity, safety and invincibility.

The first section of the chapter, verses 2-12, presents Śikhidhvaja's inability to comprehend his wife's description of the state of enlightenment that she was radiating.

The second section, verses 13-30, describes the practice of Yogic Flying.

The third section, verses 31-48, explains the mechanics of how the body lifts up into the air in Yogic Flying.

The fourth section, verses 49-67, introduces the concept of the collective consciousness of a nation, and explains how an ideal society can be created with only five percent of the nation practicing the technique of effortless transcending. The practice which Vasishtha describes seems to be comparable, both in its details and in its practical effect to the Transcendental Meditation® technique taught in the world today by Maharishi Mahesh Yogi.

The fifth section, verses 68-82 describes the practice of Yogic Flying in large groups in order to bring orderliness and coherence to the collective consciousness of the whole nation.

The move of the chapter is from ignorance to enlightenment. The chapter starts from the complete ignorance of the field effect, complete lack of knowledge of the unbounded infinite unmanifest field of life as the source of all relative manifestation. Vasishtha then introduces the technology of Yogic Flying, explaining in detail how it works to lift up the body, and how it works to culture the consciousness of the Yogic Flyer. Then he introduces the paradigm of collective consciousness and the field effects of consciousness, first with the individual practice of effortless transcending by a large number of the population, and then with a smaller number of dedicated professionals practicing Yogic Flying and the Siddhis together in one place. With this latter technology, the society as a whole can be very easily guided to perfection. This is enlightened administration. This is true sovereignty over the earth, based on resorting to the infinite unmanifest Self in the practice of Yogic Flying. This is how the chapter unfolds from its seed in the first verse.

Section 1: Śikhidhvaja's refutation of Cūḍālā's description of enlightenment

Verse 2:

शिखिध्वज उवाच
असंबद्धप्रलापासि बालासि वरवर्णिनि
रमसे राजलीलाभी रमस्वावनिपात्मजे २

Śikhidhvaja said:

"O radiant and beautiful lady, you are behaving like a foolish child, speaking gibberish without connection to reality.

"Enjoy our royal amusements without fear, take delight in the pleasures befitting the daughter of a king.

Verse 3:

किंचित्त्यक्त्वा न किंचिद्यो गतो प्रत्यक्षसंस्थितम्
त्यक्तप्रत्यक्षसद्रूपः स कथं किल शोभते ३

"Having let go of something, then there is nothing perceptible remaining which could enter into another state.

"Having let go the perceptible form of reality, how indeed can one shine with beauty?

> This is a refutation of verse 21 of the previous chapter, in which Cūḍālā says she has let go of every "something" and become a continuum of nothingness, a continuum of the dynamism of the unmanifest creative power of total natural law.

Verse 4:

भोगैरभुक्तैस्तुष्टोऽहमिति भोगान्जहाति यः
रुषेवासनशय्यादीन्स कथं किल शोभते ४

"[You say,] 'I am fully satisfied with the enjoyment of food, without eating.' [One] Who leaves off all enjoyments, is like an angry man who [because of his agitated state of mind] does not eat, does not sit still, does not sleep, etc. How indeed can such a one shine with beauty?

> This is a refutation of verse 24 of the previous chapter, in which Cūḍālā says that she enjoys food by remaining at a distance and not eating.

Verse 5:

भोगाभोगे परित्यज्य खे शून्ये रमते तु यः
एक एवाखिलं त्यक्त्वा स कथंकिल शोभते ५

"One who is indifferent to enjoyment or absence of enjoyment, who lives in a barren empty world without joy, Who always rejects everything, how indeed can such a one shine with beauty?

> This is a refutation of verse 25 of the previous chapter, in which Cūḍālā says that the unmanifest brings infinite joy to her heart, and she does not find delight in the royal sports and diversions.

Verse 6:

वसनाशनशय्यादीन्सर्वान्संत्यज्य धीरधीः
यस्तिष्ठत्यात्मनैवैकः स कथं किल शोभते ६

"Sleep puts an end to all desires, everything is completely abandoned, mentally and physically.

"With the inner wakefulness of the Self, [everything is also completely abandoned as in sleep, and] the eternal oneness of the ocean of consciousness is all that remains; how indeed can such a one shine with beauty?

> Śikhidhvaja recognizes that the transcendent is a field beyond all boundaries. But he is not aware of how the experience of transcending influences all aspects of relative life, nor does he know that regular practice develops higher states of consciousness, with great benefits to practical life.

Verse 7:

नाहं देहोऽन्यथा चाहं न किंचित्सर्वमेव च
एवं प्रलापो यस्यास्ति स कथं किल शोभते ७

"I am not the body is obviously false, and I am not [merely] something, I am everything eternally, is also obviously false.

"Such ontological discussions are of value to no one, how indeed can such a one [who engages in useless speculation] shine with beauty?

> Verses 6 and 7 are a refutation of verses 26-29 of the previous chapter. In verses 26 and 27, Cūḍālā explained that she was primarily living the life of the Absolute and was not positioned to enjoy either the earthly or the celestial realms. In verse 28 Cūḍālā clarified that her self—the "I"—is no longer identified with the body but is identified with the nothingness that contains the whole universe within it. In verse 29 Cūḍālā explained that the nothingness of her Self was eternal, and she enjoyed eternal bliss.

Verse 8:

यत्पश्यामि न पश्यामि तत्पश्याम्यन्यदेव यत्
प्रलाप इत्यसंन्यस्य स कथं किल शोभते ८

"What I see, I don't see, that which I do see is non-material, infinite and eternal;

"That is pure gibberish, completely devoid of any logic. How indeed can such a one [who thinks incoherently] shine with beauty?

This is a refutation of verse 31 in which Cūḍālā says that whatever boundaries of perception may be there, they are insignificant and do not register in her mind, she sees only the deeper value of transcendental Being within every object of perception.

Verse 9:

तस्माद्बालासि मुग्धासि चपलासि विलासिनि
नानालापविलासेन क्रीडामि क्रीड सुन्दरि ९

"Therefore, you are childish, you are silly, you are speaking illogically, O lightheartedly sporting lady.

"I am amused by this playful diversion of speaking out various metaphysical ideas as a sort of entertaining game, O beautiful one."

The royal couple never argues, and they never speak harsh words to one another. Śikhidhvaja speaks lightheartedly and laughingly about the inconsistencies in Cūḍālā's words, thereby conveying to Cūḍālā that her words did not resonate with him in the way she had intended.

Verse 10:

प्रविहस्याट्टहासेन शिखिध्वज इति प्रियाम्
मध्याह्ने स्नातुमुत्थाय निर्जगामाङ्गनागृहात् १०

Laughing with the joy of talking about the nothingness of Being, Śikhidhvaja finished his speech by expressing his love for Cūḍālā.

It being the time to perform the midday oblations, he stood up and left his wife's apartment.

Verse 11:

कष्टं नात्मनि विश्रान्तो मद्वचांसि न बुद्धवान्
राजेति खिन्ना चूडाला स्वव्यापारपराभवत् ११

"This is indeed unfortunate: Not having had the [repeated] experience of the inner peace and silence of the Self [in the state of transcendental consciousness], the king did not understand the meaning of my words."

Thus, feeling depressed Cūḍālā returned to her routine of long meditations and deep experience of the transcendental Being.

Verse 12:

तदा तथाङ्ग तत्राथ तादृगाशययोस्तयोः
ताभिः पार्थिवलीलाभिः कालो बहुतिथो ययौ १२

Then, continuing with her long meditations, she enjoyed true felicity there, combining in her life both devotion to husband, and joy in the Self.

Enjoying together their royal sports and diversions, as time passed, the love [and unity] between the two grew stronger and stronger.

> Cūḍālā's depression about her failure to communicate to her husband the truth of her experience of Unity Consciousness was not a lasting mood. Her life was naturally fulfilled, and there was no room for sorrow of any kind. Despite this difference in understanding and despite the difference in their levels of consciousness, the love between the two continued to grow stronger day by day, bringing them both more and more fulfillment.

Section 2: The practice of Yogic Flying

Verse 13:

एकदा नित्यतृप्ताया निरिच्छाया अपि स्वयम्
चूडालाया बभूवेच्छा लीलया खगमागमे १३

Desirous of testing whether her inner Self was fully established in eternal contentment and freedom from desires, Cūḍālā began to practice the sport of Yogic Flying, which directly cultures Unity Consciousness.

> "Kha-gam," is "gam," going, through "kha," space. "Āgame," is in the traditional way handed down. "Līlayā," is by means of, or with "Līlā." Līlā, play, is not meant in the sense of childish play, but as drama, sport, performance on the stage of life: She wanted to demonstrate that her knowledge of reality was genuine. Yogic Flying is not a private mental imagination, it is a procedure of making the body move through space, such that anyone can see it is moving.

Verse 14:

खगमागमसिद्ध्यर्थमथ सा नृपकन्यका
सर्वभोगाननादृत्य समागम्य च निर्जनम् १४

Now she who was the daughter of a king set herself the goal of perfection in Yogic Flying.

Attentive to the fabrics of space of the whole universe within her own Self, by practicing Yogic Flying, her body became merged in space, free from earthly limitations.

> *Sarvabhogān*: The whole universe (sarva) is seen as a

many headed snake. The curved hoods of the snake represent the unbounded reaches of space and time, the unlimited sense of expansion. She became united with this unbounded expansion (*Samāgamya*) through attention, (*Ādṛtya*) on "A," (*An-ādṛtya*). Her practice was putting her attention on the emptiness of space, on the unmanifest field of abstraction. Literally, she was putting her attention on "A," practicing "A," revering "A." The practice of Yogic Flying unfolds the dynamism within "A," within the unmanifest, within nothingness, *i.e.*, unfolds the infinite reaches of space and time within the unmanifest Self. She experienced "A," the seed of total knowledge of Veda, the totality of all the laws of nature, lively in her own self-referral consciousness.

Perfection of Yogic Flying means third stage Yogic Flying. She was not aiming at the first stage of Yogic Flying, hopping like frogs (usually on foam or soft grass mats to prevent injury), or the second stage of Yogic Flying, hovering motionless in the air. She wanted the third stage of Yogic Flying, moving through the air at will: This would demonstrate to the world the maturity and depth of her inner enlightenment. These three stages of Yogic Flying are in sequence the subject of Chapters 5, 6 and 7.

Verse 15:

एकैवैकान्तनिरता स्वासनावस्थिताङ्गिका
ऊर्ध्वगप्राणपवनचिराभ्यासं चकार ह १५

She was focused on one and only one goal: To make her body so intimately connected with the Self that it would obey every impulse of the Self.

For that she performed prolonged practice of lifting the body into the air to refine the *Prāṇa*.

> The story of Śikhidhvaja and Cūḍālā provides us a platform, a context for entering into the description of Yogic Flying. Cūḍālā is living enlightenment, but she is unable to convey to her husband her state of fulfillment. Now she seizes upon the idea of learning to fly.
>
> Scientific research on Yogic Flying shows that there is global EEG coherence at the moment just before liftoff. Global EEG coherence means that every part of the brain is in tune with and participating in the intention to lift off the ground. The EEG of flying combines the global EEG coherence characteristic of transcendental consciousness, with the EEG characteristic of bodily activity. The engagement of the total brain indicated by the EEG at the moment of liftoff indicates that it is consciousness as a whole that is lifting up the body. The technique of flying thereby establishes supreme coordination between mind and body. (See chart, facing page.)
>
> In the remainder of this chapter, the underlying theory of the practice of Yogic Flying is explained to the incredulous Rām, and in the following two chapters, the

Optimizing Brain Functioning through the Transcendental Meditation and Transcendental Meditation Sidhi® Programs of Maharishi

Creating the Maharishi Effect—radiating a purifying influence to neutralize negative trends in society

First stage of Yogic Flying where the body lifts up in a series of short hops.

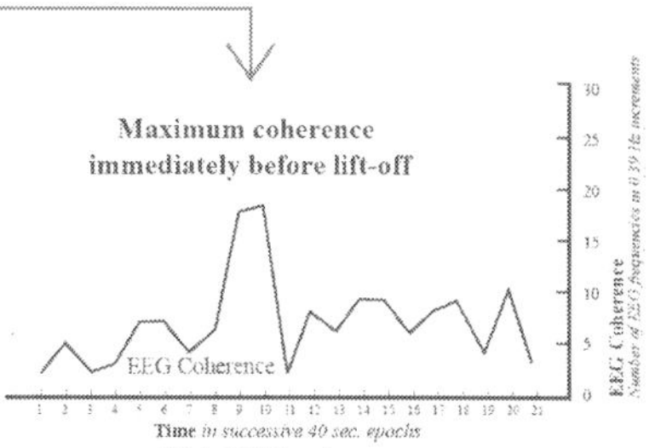

High EEG coherence during experience of Yogic Flying

Original finding—During the Transcendental Meditation Sidhi Yogic Flying technique, maximum coherence is measured immediately before the body lifts up. **Replication study**—Broadband global EEG coherence among all brain areas increases during the 2.12-second period immediately before the body lifts up during the TM-Sidhi Yogic Flying technique, compared to a control condition. **References:** *Scientific Research on Maharishi's Transcendental Meditation and TM-Sidhi Programme: Collected Papers*, Volume 1, 1977, 705–712; *International Journal of Neuroscience*, 1990, 54: 1–12.

The Transcendental Meditation Sidhi program is a breakthrough in the development of human potential. Enlivening and activating Transcendental Consciousness, and developing the habit to spontaneously project thought and action from this simplest form of awareness, pure consciousness, total potential of intelligence, makes thought and action most natural, and therefore spontaneously evolutionary, and opens the field of all possibilities for the fulfillment of every desire. Here is the scientifically validated formula for enlightenment—life in fulfillment.

first and second stages of Yogic Flying are described in detail. We return to the story of Śikhidhvaja and Cūḍālā only in the third subsequent chapter (Chapter 7), where Cūḍālā has fully mastered third stage Yogic Flying and is able to go anywhere in creation at will.

Vasishtha now spends 220 verses telling the complete story of Yogic Flying, from the first stage of hopping to complete mastery of aerial flight, in order to prepare the reader fully for the description of the exploits of Cūḍālā. This is the most comprehensive and detailed exposition of the mechanics of Siddhis and Yogic Flying in the whole of the Vedic Literature.

Verse 16:

श्रीराम उवाच
यदिदं दृश्यते किंचिज्जगत्स्थावरजंगमम्
स्पन्दच्युतं क्रियानाम्नः कथमित्यनुभूयते १६

Śrī Rām said:

What is this practice, hardly ever seen in the world, in which the unmoving body moves [upwards]?

Bodies naturally fall downwards. It takes effort to resist the downward pull of gravity. How is this Yogic Flying done?

Verse 17:

कस्य स्पन्दविलासस्य घनाभ्यासस्य मे वद
ब्रह्मन्खगमनाद्येतत्फलं यत्नैकशालिनः १७

Tell me about the experience of the Yogic Flyer as his body shakes and lifts off the ground by this practice.

Tell me about the expansion of the Yogic Flyer's soul as he moves through space: There can be no achievement on a par with this! By a single impulse of the mind one achieves the result.

Verse 18:

आत्मज्ञो वाप्यनात्मज्ञः सिद्ध्यर्थं लीलयाथवा
कथं संसाधयत्येतद्यथा तद्वद मे प्रभो १८

By the physical demonstration of success in Yogic Flying, it becomes evident whether the individual has attained full knowledge of the Self or has not attained full knowledge of the Self.

How does one gain full mastery of this Yogic Flying? Tell me, O Master, how to accomplish that.

> This is a poignant and well-timed question. Cūḍālā has the desire to fly through the air, and for that purpose she is practicing lifting her body up into the air. Ordinarily human beings are not seen flying through the air on their own. So, what exactly is happening here?
>
> Up to this point, the story of Śikhidhvaja and Cūḍālā has been eminently believable. Śikhidhvaja's refutation of Cūḍālā's experience of higher consciousness gave us a

down to earth feeling, that we were listening to an historical account of an ancient king. Now, suddenly, we seem to have crossed the line into fantasy. Ordinarily, people don't fly. Laws of gravity hold them down onto the earth. Rām is listening closely, and he wants to know exactly what sort of turn the story has taken here.

Rām presumes quite a lot about Yogic Flying, and his question is very detailed. For example, he makes a very astute observation, that since human beings don't have wings, then it must be consciousness itself, the total value of natural law, the Will of God, which is lifting the body up into the air. The "kha-gam," moving through the air, could only be brought about by Brahman, totality [*BrahmanKhagam*, v.17, line 2]. That a person could move through the air transported by total natural law, transported by the Will of God alone, is nothing less than miraculous. Rām's questions make it clear to Vasishtha that he has reached the limit of "suspension of disbelief," and that if Vasishtha wants the story to continue as an historical account of real people, he needs to explain scientifically and systematically what is happening. Vasishtha accedes to Rām's request, and now launches into a comprehensive and detailed account of the knowledge of Yogic Flying in the ancient Vedic Science.

Verse 19:

वसिष्ठ उवाच
त्रिविधं संभवत्यङ्ग साध्यं वस्त्विह सर्वतः
उपादेयं च हेयं च तथोपेक्ष्यं च राघव १९

Vasishtha said:

There are three elements that must come together in consciousness at one time to bring success to every endeavor:

The intention [to achieve a result] [*Dhāraṇa*]; the letting go of the desired result [*Dhyān*]; and at the same time, the witnessing quality of pure consciousness [*Samādhi*], O Rāghava.

> Yogic Flying is an ancient Yogic practice. The principles of Yogic Flying are explained in the ancient scripture of Yoga, Maharṣi Patañjali's *Yoga Darśanam*. Yogic Flying is one of the Siddhis described in the third chapter (*Yoga Darśanam* III.42). The principle of Siddhi practice according to Patañjali, is bringing together these three values of consciousness, *Dhāraṇa, Dhyāna* and *Samādhi*, in one awareness. Patañjali writes in Chapter 3 of *Yoga Darśanam*:[1]
>
> *Dhāraṇa* is attention held steady on a single point. (1)
> *Dhyāna* is the continuous flow of awareness there. (2)
> *Samādhi* is when that object becomes as if devoid of its own nature, and awareness appears by itself. (3)
> The three taken together are *Saṁyama*. (4)
> Through mastery of *Saṁyama*, the splendor of complete wakefulness dawns. (5)

Verse 20:

आत्मभूतं प्रयत्नेन उपादेयं च साध्यते
हेयं संत्यज्यते ज्ञात्वा उपेक्ष्यं मध्यमेतयोः २०

The qualification of the Self by a mental impulse is the intention [*Dhāraṇa*] to achieve a result.

What has been known as letting go [*Dhyān*] is the complete abandonment of the desired result. And the witnessing quality [*Samādhi*] is in the middle between the two.

> *Samādhi* is that field which lies in the middle between the letting go of the impulse on one side, and the appearance of the desired fruit or result on the other side. The mental impulse is a tangible thing; the appearance of the flavor or result of the Siddhi is also tangible. What is in the middle between the two is abstract and intangible and cannot be described in words. It is "in the middle."

Verse 21:

यद्यदाह्लादनकरमादेयं यच्च सन्मते
तद्विरुद्धमनादेयमुपेक्ष्यं मध्यमं विदुः २१

That which accompanies the intention through its stages of creation, until it has fully formed as a thought; and lets go of the thought as it dissolves in reverse sequence is called the uninvolved witness [*Samādhi*] by the wise.

> That which is in the middle, the witness, is untouched by the dynamism of Siddhi performance and remains ever uninvolved. It is there at the start and there at the

finish. It is neither created nor dissolved. It remains as a constant, the eternal being of the knower who is the performer of the Siddhi.

Verse 22:

सन्मतेर्विदुषो ज्ञस्य सर्वमात्ममयं यदा
त्रय एते तदा पक्षाः संभवन्ति न केचन २२

Those who, through repeated experience, have become experts in this practice of creating [and dissolving] impulses [from the Self] realize that the whole universe is made of the Self.

When these three elements meet together in one awareness, then there is nothing that cannot be known or accomplished.

Verse 23:

केवलं सर्वमेवेदं कदाचिल्लीलया तया
उपेक्षापक्षनिक्षिप्तमालोकयति वा नवा २३

The authenticity of Cūḍālā's experience of the whole universe as her own Self could be demonstrated at any time by her mastery of Yogic Flying:

When one brings together the witnessing quality, the intention, and the letting go, then one sees [by the presence or absence of the fulfillment of the intention] whether one truly experiences the universe as one's own Self or not.

Verse 24:

ज्ञस्योपेक्षात्मकं नाम मूढस्यादेयतां गतम्
हेयं स्फारविरागस्य शृणु सिद्धिक्रमः कथम् २४

The functioning value of the Self—the degree to which the unbounded infinite Self can be put to practice by the wise knower of reality—is named the *Samādhi* (*Upekṣā*) phase of consciousness; the manifesting of the Siddhi proves how much can be brought out of the otherwise inscrutable Self.

Letting go of the name, you hear it dissolving into total silence, where it becomes infinitely powerful: This is how name gets transformed instantaneously into form.

Verse 25:

देशकालक्रियाद्रव्यसाधनाः सर्वसिद्धयः
जीवमाह्लादयन्तीह वसन्त इव भूतलम् २५

The place of performance, the season or quality of time, sustained practice, the formulas, and the technology of functioning from the Self give rise to all the Siddhis.

The soul gets exhilarated in this practice, like the surface of the earth in springtime.

Verse 26:

मध्ये चतुर्णामेवैषां क्रियाप्राधान्यकल्पना
सिद्ध्यादिसाधने साधो तन्मयास्ते यतः क्रमाः २६

Even on the path to mastery of the Siddhis, the practice of the Siddhis is the most exalted activity [of any kind] that a human being can engage in.

When the Siddhi practice first yields [some measure of] the predicted result of the practice, there is a feeling of satisfaction and fulfillment in that accomplishment; all the Siddhis are like that: From the starting point to full mastery, every step of progress brings increasing waves of joy and fulfillment.

> *kriyā-prādhānya-kalpanā*,
> *kriyā*, activity, meaning in this context, these (eṣāṁ) activities of the Siddhi performances.
> *prādhānya*, most exalted, supreme
> *kalpanā*, doing, practice
> "The most exalted activity that a human being can do."

Verse 27:

गुटिकाञ्जनखड्गादिक्रियाक्रमनिरूपणम्
तत्रासतां च दोषोऽत्र विस्तारः प्रकृतार्थहा २७

The first level of demonstration of success in the practice of Yogic Flying is moving into the air in repeated short hops.

In that case, [when there are only short hops, then] the consciousness is not fully Self-referral, and there is impurity [in the physiology or atmosphere]. Here progress towards the goal has started, and the short hops are going to expand and give way to long flights.

> The platform for the development of all the Siddhis is the eyes-closed investigation into consciousness as a field of all possibilities. On one extreme end of all possibilities, there is infinite fullness and on the other extreme end there is complete emptiness; between these two extremes is the range of all possibilities. The exploration of consciousness is an investigation into the movement of awareness back and forth from fullness to emptiness and from emptiness to fullness. The structure of the Vedic *Maṇḍala* embodies this eternal move of awareness from fullness to emptiness and back to fullness, ever balancing creation and destruction at every point. The Vedic *Maṇḍala* is the eternal blueprint of the all possibilities structure of consciousness, the map of the inherent dynamism within Self-referral consciousness.[2]
>
> The study of consciousness is intrinsically the study of Veda. Success in Yogic Flying is the measure of the degree of refinement of consciousness, the degree to which

consciousness is completely Self-referral, *i.e.* the degree to which consciousness contains the total value of Natural law within its own structure.

In the first stage of Yogic Flying, progress in the development of Self-referral consciousness has been marked, but it is not yet fully mature. This stage is itself already a huge accomplishment of the Yogi, and the remarkable implications of the liftoff in Yogic Flying as a technology to systematically unfold the total knowledge of the Self are explored in detail in Chapter 5.

With more and more practice investigating consciousness as a field of all possibilities, Self-referral consciousness becomes increasingly profound. The improved Self-referral consciousness is measured, tested, or proven through increased success in Yogic Flying.

This process of expansion of short hops into longer hops and eventually remaining in the air through increasingly profound experience of Self-referral consciousness is analyzed in detail in Chapter 6.

Verse 28:

रत्नौषधितपोमन्त्रक्रियाक्रमनिरूपणाम्
आस्तामेव किलैषोऽपि विस्तारः प्रकृतार्थहा २८

Jewels, herbs, austerity, and mantras are aids to success in Yogic Flying.

Targeting specific qualities of the eternal Self, they powerfully accelerate the progress towards the goal; and [thereby] the short hops are going to become long flights.

[Wearing of] Jewels [precious gems, semi-precious stones, and minerals of all kinds, according to the science of Jyotish, to balance specific karmic influences and enliven specific qualities of intelligence;] [ingesting] herbs [according to the science of Āyurveda, to create balance and to enliven specific qualities of intelligence in the physiology;] [practicing] *Tapas*, [restraining the senses from coming into contact with their accustomed or desired objects through long extended programs of meditation, and/or austere practices such as celibacy, standing on one leg, and so forth, in order to create heat, physical vitality and spiritual ardor, and gain the sympathy of natural law;][pronouncing Vedic] mantras, [verses from the Vedas and Vedic Literature to enliven specific *Devatās* having precisely measured quantities of organizing power in order to achieve targeted transformations in consciousness and in material creation to fulfill specific desires and/or enliven the all-possibilities structure of consciousness and create heaven on earth] are all aids to success in Yogic Flying.

Putting to practice the science of sound through Vedic mantras, the science of light through gems and gem therapies, the science of medicine for balancing the doṣas in the body, and spiritual practices which conserve and channel the life energy to maximize physical vitality and spiritual radiance, all contribute to success in the practice of Yogic Flying.

Verse 29:

श्रीशैले सिद्धदेशे च मेर्वादौ वा निवासतः
सिद्धिरित्यपि विस्तारः कृतार्थप्रकृतार्थहा २९

When [by the practices outlined in the previous verse,] the hardness of the physical body is glorified and softened, and [conversely,] when the conscious experience is concrete even when the awareness is not travelling through any of the five roads of the senses, then the consciousness remaining within itself could function from the central switchboard of all activity [and accomplish what it wants].

Then there is a universal awakening and the gates of the Siddhis are wide open: As the mind would easily go here and there without boundaries, [now] the physical body would also go here and there without boundaries.

> This has opened up a wide gate of all possibilities for all mankind. Mind body coordination means the gap between matter and consciousness is bridged. If the gulf between consciousness and body is bridged, as demonstrated in Yogic Flying, then time and space are no barriers, and the body will travel here and there without boundaries. The body will be able to reproduce itself in any way it wants by mere thinking. The individual has expanded to universal cosmic status, and the start of Siddhi practice has given way to the fulfilled state of accomplishment of the goal of all action.
>
> Cūḍālā's enjoyment of the full mastery of this third stage of Yogic Flying is described in Chapter 7.

Verse 30:

तस्माच्छिखिध्वजकथाप्रसङ्गपतितामिमाम्
प्राणादिपवनाभ्यासक्रियां सिद्धिफलां शृणु ३०

Therefore, [seeing the possibility of quickly accomplishing the goal of living perfection in life,] as revealed in the story of Śikhidhvaja, devote yourself assiduously to mastery of the Siddhis and Yogic Flying.

Listen to how this practice brings about the fruits of perfection, by refining the primordial *Prāṇa* [the life-force].

> *Prāṇa*, the life-force, is the primordial vibration of total natural law, the first expression of the Absolute Being in the relative field: The purification of that fundamental impulse—eternally oscillating between creation and destruction, inhalation and exhalation—in order to give rise to that exalted state of balance of mind, called *Samādhi* in the *Yoga Śāstra*, is brought about by the Yogic practices that have Siddhis as their fruit. Listen to how these Yogic practices bring perfection to life.

Section 3: The mechanics of the practice of Yogic Flying

Verse 31.1:

अन्तस्था ह्यखिलास्त्यक्त्वा साध्यार्थेतरवासनाः ३१-१

antasthā hi akhilās tyaktvā sa adhi-ārtha-itara-vāsanāḥ.

There are gaps everywhere at every level of creation because there are empty spaces in the flow of "A." Letting go of one syllable or word, [in the following gap, there] are the impulses of creative intelligence that are needed to structure the form of the subsequent word.

In the previous verses Vasishtha has described the mastery of total natural law, the complete opening of the Siddhis, as the fruit of the practice of Yogic Flying. This was his attention step: Now he asks Rām to listen, to be attentive, because he is going to explain the mechanics of the practice of Yogic Flying. Those mechanics harness what Vasishtha calls (v.30) the "*Prāṇādi*," the *Prāṇa-Ādi*, the (*Ādi*) first *Prāṇa*, the primordial *Prāṇa*.

This next verse, the first verse after *Śṛṇu*, "listen!" starts with a definition of what this primordial *Prāṇa* is. In order to unfold the mechanics of the practice, we need to understand that which is the engine of purification, that by which the whole of life is being purified—the primordial *Prāṇa*. In order to define the primordial *Prāṇa*, Vasishtha first takes our attention to that area, that space where the primordial *Prāṇa* is found—the gaps.

This verse is laid out in the classic *Sūtra* style: There is an initial word which is the seed idea for the entire *Sūtra*, then a conjunction specifying the quality of relationship, followed by a phrase which expands the understanding of the initial word. The first word, the seed of the *Sūtra*, is *Antastha*. The *Antastha*—literally "intermediate stand"—that which stands in the middle or interior, that which stands between any two, is a "gap." Gap is separation; hence gap implies distance. Gap is fundamentally a kind of space: Vasishtha is starting his definition of primordial *Prāṇa* by pointing to the field or space where this *Prāṇa* is vibrating, where it is functional, where it is active. What is space? It is something which separates, which holds apart, or exists in between two things. Any space comes into being by the separation of objects or things into discrete packages with gaps in between.

There are gaps on every level of creation. We know from modern science that on the atomic level, the space between the nucleus and the electron shells is so great that matter itself is mostly empty space. So, with this one word *Antasthāḥ*, gaps, we are positing the existence of empty space. Here in this empty space we must find the primordial *Prāṇa*. There is a relationship between two objects, two entities, and that relationship creates a dynamism, a flow or movement in the gap between the two. There is, for example, a space in the lungs, and the movement of air in and out of that space is what we call breath. But what is the primordial breath, what is primordial *Prāṇa*? That brings us to the next word.

"*Hi*," the second Sanskrit word in this line, means "because." Why, after all, are there gaps, why are there spaces and separations, why are there intervening fields of relationships between objects anywhere and everywhere in creation? Who or what has created all these gaps everywhere, on every level of creation? What has set the electron far away from the proton in the structure of the hydrogen atom? What has created the gap between cells, what has created this whole universe? Can there really be a "because," an unqualified ultimate cause for the existence of any and every gap in creation? If our attention is to go to the cause of the *Antasthāḥ*, the cause of the gaps, it must go to the field of Veda. Veda is the eternal uncreated blueprint of the whole creation. Veda is the cause of creation, and Veda is itself the uncreated eternal reality, the cause of all causes. This is the fundamental irreducible axiom in Maharishi Vedic Science℠: The cause of anything in creation is the Veda.

How does the Veda give rise to innumerable gaps on every level of creation? That is being answered by the next word, "*Akhilāḥ*."

The Veda starts with the sound "A." The first word is *Agnim*, so "A" is the launching point from which the whole text of the Veda sequentially emerges. The significance of being the first is enormous. According to Maharishi Mahesh Yogi's Apaurusheya Bhāshya or "uncreated commentary" of the Veda, the first expression contains in seed form all that follows; the entire Veda is an elaborated commentary on this one syllable, "A."[3] Even phonologically, "A" is the basis of the Sanskrit sound system. All the letters emerge from "A," all the letters have "A" within them. "A" represents the continuum of sound, the continuum of speech. Fundamentally, all of speech is made up of "A," taking on different forms as vowels and consonants, but always remaining ultimately, "A."

In the flow of the eternal Veda, in the flow of Vedic

speech, there are interruptions, there are gaps. These interruptions are being called "*Khilāḥ*." There is a sequence of discrete units, and the continuum of flow is punctuated by gaps. Always, between letters, between words, between phrases and between verses, there are gaps. The gaps uphold the distinction of the infinite variety of creation emerging from the eternal continuum of "A." There are gaps everywhere in creation, Vasishtha says, because there are gaps in the flow of knowledge in the Veda.

Now Vasishtha wants to investigate into the inner dynamism of the gaps of the Veda. The first word of the line was *Antasthāḥ*, "gaps." He wants to look at the area where there is nothing, where the sound is completely unmanifest. There may be numerous stages in the fading away of the sound, but that fading away is not the *Antastha*, it is still connected to the previous sound. In order to understand the gaps, and in order to understand what this verse is telling us about the nature of the unmanifest gaps, we need to completely let go of the previous sound: *Tyaktvā* means "having let go." In coming to nil, the sound goes through many transformations or "somersaults" as the manifest layers dissolve one by one. Those somersaults of "A" within itself as it fades into the unmanifest, reveal its eight-fold nature of successively finer layers of earth, water, fire, air, space, mind, intellect and ego. These are successively let go in the gap. Having let go of the expressed value of the speech of the Veda, we are awake in the unmanifest value: We are awake in the gaps of speech. At this point in the gap, there is complete emptiness. There is no residual value of the previous expression. It is empty space, as empty as empty can be. But a closer examination of this empty space reveals that there is some liveliness within it. In that empty space in the gap between expressions of the Veda, there are *Vāsanas*, latent impressions. In the unmanifest gap between expressions of the Veda, there is lively intelligence. That lively intelligence contains within it the blueprint for the successful formation of the following word or following expression. In order for another word to come up out of the gap after the first word, there has to be a functioning value of intelligence that evaluates that so much knowledge has been unfolded, and now at this point precisely this expression, different from what was there in the previous, needs to come forth. There has to be a ground for launching the subsequent expression. That ground needs to know where the expression has been—where precisely in the systematic sequential unfoldment of the knowledge of the Veda the gap is located—and needs to know where it is headed, what is coming next in the sequence. Hence, the gap needs to have the total knowledge of where it has been and where it is going. The total knowledge of natural law is therefore lively in every gap in the Veda. This total knowledge alone is capable of flawlessly upholding perfection of sequential unfoldment of the Veda at every point. So, the *Vāsanas* responsible for planning the construction of a new and different desired object out of the unmanifest gap represent complete knowledge of natural law in motion, complete knowledge made functional. It is functional because it is applied to the specific gap; it is universal, because it is unmanifest, without distinguishing manifest characteristics, and because it encompasses the totality of natural law.

This flow of intelligence in the unmanifest gaps between the different packages of knowledge of the Veda, syllables, words, *Ṛcas* and so forth, is the *Prāṇādi*, the primordial *Prāṇa*. The total dynamism of natural law put into motion, made functional, brought to bear in order to execute the sequential unfoldment of Veda at every point in the sequence, is the life-breath of the Veda. This is the supreme cause: It is this which unfolds the Veda from the silence of the gaps. This is the creative power of the Veda, the organizing power of total natural law. Having captured this quality of the total creativity of natural law in individual awareness, one becomes the master of the whole creation.

Vasishtha has painted a picture of the supreme value of *Prāṇa* as that lively functioning intelligence that carries each syllable of the Veda on to the next syllable, the supervisor and instigator of change, the sustainer of ongoing diversity. The original *Prāṇa* is not merely a vibration which continues unabated, and without which life cannot be maintained. It is not merely activity. It is not simply a power cord plugged into the electricity from the power station. *Prāṇa* is the power of renewal, ever-transforming, ever carrying life on to new experience, new knowledge and new achievement, ever carrying life on towards more and more bliss, more and more fulfillment, until the total value of action and the total value of knowledge has been accomplished. *Prāṇa*, as the power of renewal, ensures that change is always evolutionary, always progressive.

Change is inevitable, but what distinguishes life is the ability to resist entropy, to move towards greater order. *Prāṇa* is not just motion, not just dynamism. It is intelligence also, it is motion which harnesses the organizing power of total natural law.

In this first line, Vasishtha has brought our attention to the functioning value of total intelligence of natural law, the transformation that organizes the sequential unfoldment of the Veda from the silence of the gaps. How exactly can this inexhaustible power of renewal be harnessed in individual life? How can this primordial *Prāṇa* be enlivened in individual existence in order to bring fulfillment to life and bring about complete mastery of the Siddhis? What are the exercises, the "*Prāṇāyāma*," that will apply the intelligence of the gaps of the Veda to practical life? In the first line of this verse Vasishtha deals exclusively with the primordial level of *Prāṇa*, *Prāṇa* on the level of the uncreated Veda, *Prāṇa* as the inherent organizing power bringing about the transformations of sounds in the sequential unfoldment of the Veda from within the gaps. This *Prāṇa* is not yet applied to individual life. In the next line, Vasishtha applies this model of *Prāṇa* to the surface of life, to the functioning of human physiology. This will clarify what it means to refine *Prāṇa*, and how it is possible to bring perfection to human life.

Verse 31.2:

गुदादिद्वारसंकोचान्स्थानकादिक्रियाक्रमैः ३१-२

By means of sequential steps of transformation at every point along the way starting from the mouth and progressing to the colon, [the food is carried along the alimentary canal by *Prāṇa* in the process of digestion] until all useful nourishment has been extracted and [the food] is completely dried up in the colon.

The primordial *Prāṇa* is the life of the Veda, it is the power of renewal which sequentially unfolds diverse changing values while remaining connected to the starting point, connected to the theme expressed in seed form in the first expression. The gross *Prāṇa*, the *Prāṇa* in the life of human beings, is also constantly renewing life, taking in material from the environment, extracting useful ingredients, and discharging the remainder: *Prāṇa* extracts order and intelligence from the environment and thereby sustains life, sustains progress and evolution, maintaining the connectedness and integrity of the individual life-stream, the individual experiencing ego.

This line is interesting from a modern scientific standpoint, because we are completely aware in great detail of all the different steps in the process of digestion: From the chewing and moistening of food in the mouth, to the addition of acids and digestive enzymes in the stomach, and the extraction of different kinds of nutrients at different stages in the stomach and intestines, we are taught from childhood the various steps of transformation that take place as food is digested.

We see the functioning of *Prāṇa* on the gross level of life, as the taking in of materials from the environment, and then discharging materials into the environment. In between there are steps of transformation. These steps of transformation take place in the intermediate spaces: By flowing through channels, in the space created by those channels, there is activity. Something happens in the mouth, something more happens in the stomach, something again different happens in the duodenum, and so on. These are spaces, these are gaps, and in these gaps there is activity, the activity of transformation which creates the building blocks that grow and sustain the body. The activity in the unmanifest gap between syllables or words is like the activity in the different spaces in the alimentary canal: There are transformations in the gap, and then the next syllable comes out; or there are transformations in the gaps and the next new day of experience comes forth for the living human being. It is subtle primordial *Prāṇa* on the one hand, and gross manifest *Prāṇa* on the other hand. But in both cases, it is the functioning intelligence of natural law that sustains progress: Lively intelligence functioning unseen in the gaps is transforming the incoming building blocks and giving rise to the final product.

What is the relationship between these two kinds of *Prāṇa*? What is the relationship between the primordial *Prāṇa*, which is the ultimate cause, the agency of all change and transformation in the universe, the creative power inherent in total natural law—and its expression in human physiology as *Vāta Doṣa*, the agency of movement ultimately responsible for all growth and renewal in individual life? This is the relationship between the source of all change, the evolutionary power deeply embedded in every particle, in every point of creation—and the life principle that expresses itself in human life. More specifically, Vasishtha's intention in bringing these together in one verse is to show that here is the relationship between the architect's blueprint, and the actual building that has been constructed according to that blueprint. The body is the physical expression of the infinite organizing power of total natural law: As is the body, so is the universe, as is the microcosm, so is the macrocosm. It is the same creative intelligence, it is the same *Prāṇa*, the same life-force which expresses on both levels.

At the finest level of creation, if we look at what the universe is ultimately made of—if we closely examine the interstellar space, the intergalactic space, the abstract fabrics of the absolute potential for existence inherent in every point in the universe—the *Antasthāḥ*, the gaps, the intermediate spaces—modern science finds that nothingness, vacuum is not a dead sort of thing, it is actually lively with infinite intelligence. The very feature which is the hallmark of emptiness, nothingness, vacuum, is itself the expression of the dynamism of total natural law. There are virtual fluctuations lively in the vacuum, representing the dynamism of all possible transformations.

From the viewpoint of ancient Vedic science, total natural law, the "Constitution of the Universe," is the transcendental structure of every point in creation. The ten *Maṇḍalas* of Ṛg Veda are there within every point, total knowledge and organizing power is present in every point of creation. From the Vedic Science perspective, the Constitution of the Universe is present in every point.

From the modern science perspective there is a vacuum energy that is lively in every point. Quantum field theory explains that the vacuum state, the ground state, which is a state of no particles, is actually lively with virtual fluctuations, the continual creation and annihilation of all possible particles. Thus, in both languages, what we call "space," or gap or intermediate region, or "*Ākāśa*," in Sanskrit, has an all-possibilities structure. Space has infinite potential inherent in it.

The human body also has an infinite all-possibilities structure: Total Natural Law, the same Constitution of the Universe which is lively in the transcendental structure of every point in creation, has given rise to the human physiology. Although in religious language, we have heard for thousands of years that "Man is made in the image of God," Dr. Tony Nader has demonstrated in his landmark work, *Human Physiology: Expression of Veda and Vedic Literature*,[4] that the design of the human body, the architecture of the nerves and veins and so forth, gives concrete expression to the all-possibilities structure of total natural law. In form and in function, all the qualities of the different *Maṇḍalas* of Ṛg Ved, and the qualities of the different branches of the Vedic Literature are perfectly expressed in corresponding organs and structures in the human physiology. This dramatic one to one correspondence between the fibers that make up the human physiology and the different component laws of the Constitution of the Universe reveals the supreme architecture of the human body. This gives us a very profound insight into Vasishtha's correlation between the animating principle responsible for the sequential unfoldment of the Veda and Vedic Literature, and the inherent life principle in the fundamental processes which imbibe and process order from the environment and construct the human body.

The correlation between the creative power of the silent gaps in the Vedic text providing the foundation for the manifest expression of the speech of the Veda, and the similarly unseen process of extracting nutrients from food and thereby providing the foundation for building up and constantly renewing the human physiology teaches that the human physiology is exquisitely sophisticated in its design. Beyond the DNA, there is an overarching blueprint of cosmic order, a standard of perfection that is itself eternal and uncreated. It is the source of all change but lies beyond the reach of change and decay. The transcendental structure of every point in creation has infinite dynamism so perfectly balanced and organized that the activity balances out eternally and sustains the unchanging silence of Being. The correlation that Vasishtha is making between the creative power of the silent gaps in the Vedic text and the extraction of nutrients from food is a connection between the deepest level of life which is absolutely perfect and free from entropy or disorder of any kind, and the gross surface value of life which is fraught with impurities and imperfections.

The actual functioning of the human physiology is not in itself the model of absolute perfection: It is not so perfect as to never decay, it has friction within it. There is the possibility of parts coming out of balance, it is mortal. This is the point. If we apply the template of perfect cosmic order, the order of the inherent sequential unfoldment of the Veda, which unfolds change while remaining ever unchanged, to the human body—if we can connect the changing values of human physiology to their source in the field of perfect order, it may be possible to improve the functioning of the human body. It may be possible to decrease the entropy in its functioning, increase its efficiency, raise its physical materials, and its style of functioning closer and closer to perfection.

We are aware of so many degrees of health and disease in the human body: Already a large portion of human endeavor is focused on improving health and removing disease. The human physiology has innumerable modes of abnormal and imperfect functioning. But there is perfection implicit in the design, and it is possible to take recourse to that cosmic design in order to refine and bring to perfection the gross functioning of the physiology. There is the possibility of refining the functioning of the human physiology in order to bring it in tune with the cosmic order, in tune with the integrated functioning of Total Natural Law. This process of refinement of the gross *Prāṇa* is called *Prāṇāyāma*. The gross *Prāṇa* can be brought into alignment with the primordial *Prāṇa*, the cosmic order, the intelligence of total natural law. This is the promise of this verse.

In the previous verse, we were advised to listen to how the practice of Yogic Flying and Siddhis brings about perfection in life, the supreme goal of enlightenment, by the practice of purification of the breath, bringing the breath in tune with the primordial *Prāṇa*—the blueprint of Total Natural Law. The word "*Śṛṇu*," "Listen!" was the last word of the line, advising Rām to be alert, because the whole story of gaining perfection in life is going to be told next. This first verse after the word "Listen!" now lays the foundation for complete understanding of the path to perfection: It defines what *Prāṇa* is, and more specifically what primordial *Prāṇa* is. This verse following the word "*Śṛṇu*," is the master key verse of this entire theme of Yogic Flying, explaining the principle of how Yogic Flying works, and how it brings perfection to life: It works by aligning the functioning of the life-principle in the human physiology with the perfect order of Total Natural Law. The perfect order of Total Natural Law is enshrined in the principle of dynamism in silence, the principle of sequential unfoldment inherent in the Constitution of the Universe, lively in the gaps.

Nothing less than total knowledge of natural law could be capable of bringing life to the level of perfection. There must be a field of perfect order, a field of infinite intelligence, a field of Total Knowledge of Natural Law. The possibility of enlightenment, the hope for perfection in life hangs on this one central point: Is there a field of absolute perfect order, is there a field of total knowledge, is it possible to capture the organizing power of the home of all the laws of nature?

Pure existence, infinite eternal Being, the source of thought deep within the mind, through long practice and deep experience of self-referral consciousness, is found to be a composite of both silence and dynamism together in one structure. This silence and dynamism together, the nature of eternal Being, with more and more practice is experienced as a continuum of sound in silence, the sound "A," at once pure and dynamic. That sound "A," is itself the embodiment of the totality of existence, eternity, wholeness of life. And with more deep experience, more clarity of perception of one's own unmanifest Self-referral consciousness, one begins to be aware of interruptions in the eternal flow of "A." There are breaks and divisions within the eternal continuum of wholeness of "A." "A" is reverberating, collapsing into its own point and expanding again to infinity, over and over. And in this process of collapse and emergence it takes on different qualities, and sequentially unfolds the Veda and Vedic Literature. The whole Vedic Literature is the reverberation of silence, the dynamism of the Self, the nature of eternal Being, flowing out of the gaps in the continuum of "A." This is the transcendental structure of every point in creation, and it is the home of all knowledge, the home of all the laws of nature, the source of all change, and the eternal repository of perfect order. The total potential of natural law, in terms of total knowledge and total organizing power is vested in the gaps in the continuum of "A," described in this verse as the *Khilas* of "A." This is the cognition of a field of perfect order, well known to the sages of ages past, the lighthouse of enlightenment, the starting point and the goal of all search, the absolute foundation of the practice of Yogic Flying.

The path to perfection lies in capturing this field of perfect order and making it functional, harnessing it in order to benefit practical life. The benefit which is being unfolded here, however, is not one of intellectual awakening. Rather, raising the functioning of the entire human physiology to the level of perfection of the Constitution of the Universe is presented as the goal. How the physiology takes in food, takes in orderliness from the environment and processes it, extracts nutrients from it in order to build tissues, and make the organism grow and learn and expand its territory of influence—this process of living, this expression of the life principle, can be refined to such a great extent by the practice of *Prāṇāyāma* as to mirror the perfect functioning of natural law in the universe. Physiology can express the order inherent in the creation of the universe by coming in alignment with the principle of sequential unfoldment of the Veda. This is what Yogic Flying, the supreme practice of *Prāṇāyāma* accomplishes. Through Yogic Flying the individual attains the supreme goal of enlightenment, where infinity is expressed on the level of the physical body, where the body is free from limitations, and the dweller in the body has unlimited freedom to harness total natural law to accomplish any desire in creation instantly.

The process of digesting food, the process of extracting nutrients from food and building the nervous system has to be raised to the level of perfection, where the physical body is built up from the building blocks of unmanifest Being with perfect order at every instant. How far this process of transformation can proceed, how closely the physiology can model the physiology of the universe has not been explained in this verse. What has been presented as the founding axiom of the path to enlightenment is the alignment of the life-breath in the body—the alignment of the inner intelligence of the body that draws in orderliness from the environment in order to grow and expand its territory—with the intelligence which unfolds the total knowledge of the Constitution of the Universe from within "A." This is the fundamental principle of Yogic Flying, but as Vasishtha explains in the next verse, this can be accomplished in many different ways.

Verse 32:

भोजनासनशुद्ध्या च साधुशास्त्रार्थभावनात्
स्वाचारात्सुजनासङ्गात्सर्वत्यागात्सुखासनात् ३२

By [always] eating pure food and sitting in a pure and clean place; through successfully carrying out in daily life the goals set forth in the scriptures;

Through behavior in the Self; through association with virtuous people; by renouncing the world; through being well-disposed in life;

What are the procedures to refine the *Prāṇa*, what are the procedures to refine the functioning of human physiology in order to align the human physiology with the state of perfection, the absolute order at the basis of creation? In the previous verse, the intimate relationship between Cosmic law and individual human physiology was explained. In this verse, Vasishtha summarizes all the different ways in which human physiology can be attuned to Cosmic law, all the different ways by which human life can be raised to perfection:

1) Purity of food, water, air, and physical environment

2) Culturing the physiology by following the dictates of culture, the guidelines for living laid down in the scriptures

3) Through technologies of consciousness

4) Through association with virtuous people

5) Through renunciation of the world—the recluse way of life

6) Through being well-disposed in life—the householder way of life

(1) In the presence of toxins, the physiology will not function with perfect order. The first principle of refining the human physiology is to remove and avoid all damaging and weakening influences on the physiology. The physiology has a great inborn capacity to refine its style of functioning, but in the presence of entropy in the environment in the form of inappropriate or impure food, impure water, polluted air, and a dirty or disorderly

physical environment, the orderly functioning of the physiology gets overshadowed. The purity of all the environmental factors that impact life is expounded in the "Upa-Veda" section of Vedic Literature: Āyur-Veda for balanced and pure diet and pure water, Gandharva Veda for purity of the near environment through the science of music, Dhanur Veda for the elimination of war and natural disasters, and Sthāpatya Veda for the perfectly orderly design of buildings and cities. Maintaining maximum purity in all of these areas will directly and profoundly support the process of aligning individual intelligence with cosmic intelligence.

(2) The guidelines for living which have been laid down in the scriptures of every religion throughout the world present the knowledge of how to live life in accord with natural law, in all different climates and geographical conditions. All of these guidelines have the same purpose of refining the functioning of individual physiology in order to bring it more and more in harmony with Cosmic Law. The Ten Commandments, for example, are universal guidelines for everyone in order to raise life to perfection. Likewise, in the Vedic Literature, there are 18 Smṛtis, and 18 Upa-smṛtis, which lay out in exquisite detail how to behave in all the different stages of life, from childhood, through adulthood, and how to behave in all the different castes and occupations in society. In all the scriptures, there are goals set forth for all aspects of human endeavor, and these goals must be accomplished, they must be made a living reality. This is a very important channel for purifying life.

(3) Through behavior in the Self: Through first contacting the Self and drawing the inner wakefulness out

into daily activity through the practice of effortless transcending, and then through behavior within the Self, the practice of the Siddhis, which trains the individual consciousness to function in unbounded awareness. The Siddhis, including Yogic Flying, are practices which make the infinite potential of the Self functional, and teach the individual to make use of that unbounded inner resource of the Self in practical life. These programs directly culture and align individual consciousness and physiology with Cosmic Law.

(4) The company of virtuous people means people who have excelled in the implementation of the above three guidelines, purity of food and environment, following the dictates of the scriptures, and culturing the state of enlightenment through the technologies of consciousness so that every thought and action is spontaneously in accordance with total natural law. Keeping the company of such people is itself a valuable guideline for raising life to perfection.

In the Bhagavad Gita, [Chapter IV, verse 34] Lord Kṛṣṇa tells Arjuna, "Know this, through homage, repeated inquiry and service, the men of knowledge who have experienced Reality, will teach you knowledge." Being in the environment of virtuous people, "men of knowledge who have experienced Reality," is lauded by Vasishtha as a technique in itself for refining the individual *Prāṇa* and bringing it more and more in tune with Cosmic Law.

(5) and (6) Both paths, the path of the renunciate, and the path of the householder are intended to culture this refinement of individual *Prāṇa*. Life as a whole, on every level, is structured for this purpose of bringing

individual consciousness and physiology in alignment with the Constitution of the Universe.

These six points are all "practices for the refinement of *Prāṇa*," practices for aligning the individual physiology with the Constitution of the Universe. All these six, including Yogic Flying, the supreme *Prāṇāyāma,* are brought together in the one word, *Prāṇāyāma,* in the next verse.

Verse 33:

प्राणायामघनाभ्यासाद्राम कालेन केनचित्
कोपलोभादिसंत्यागाद्भोगत्यागाच्च सुव्रत ३३

O Rāma, merely by the practice of *Prāṇāyāma* by anyone, over time,

[One] attains complete freedom from anger, covetousness, and all such attachments and passions, and freedom from all problems in life, O thou of excellent vows.

The word "*Suvrata,*" "O thou of excellent vows," connects this verse to the previous verse. In the previous verse, all the different approaches to refining the *Prāṇa*, bringing the activity of the human physiology into perfect attunement with the field of perfect order on which it is based, have been mentioned. Purity of food and environment must be practiced. The commands of the scriptures must be carried out. Transcendental consciousness must be experienced through regular practice of effortless transcending and made fully functional through the practice of the Siddhis including Yogic Flying. One must be successful in the world and live in joy and affluence, or conversely renounce the world and live as a recluse:

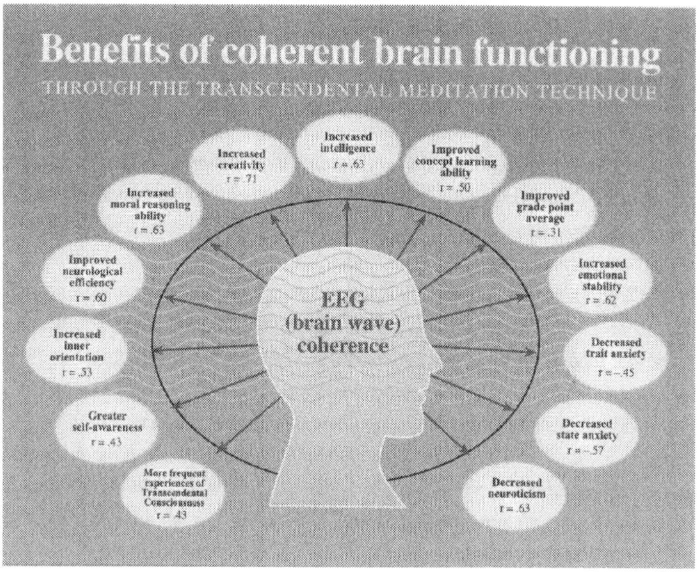

Benefits of coherent brain functioning: Making the brain orderly improves all aspects of life simultaneously, giving freedom from all problems. By the practice of Transcendental Meditation and Yogic Flying, the activity of the brain is refined, nourishing the whole of life in one stroke.[20]

All of these modes of purification require long and devoted practice. Consequently, the tradition for all such spiritual practices is to make vows, solemn promises to follow specific guidelines of living to perfection, without any deviation. An individual may be said to be "*Suvrata*," of excellent vows, if the standards of living which he sets out to uphold unfailingly are very high, and if he succeeds in upholding them.

Unfailingly upholding very high standards of purity of behavior in all the areas mentioned in the previous verse, over a long period of time, is the only way the goal of purification of the *Prāṇa* can be achieved. By the word *Prāṇāyāma*, Vasishtha is referring back to verse 30, and the word *Prāṇa-ādi-pavana-abhyāsa*, signifying practices which purify the physiology and bring it into alignment with the primordial principle of sequential unfoldment of Veda, bring it into attunement with the breath of the Veda, the breath of cosmic life.

It should not be understood that by the word *Prāṇāyāma*, Vasishtha is here introducing a new thing, some breathing exercises, and these will take the place of all those practices mentioned in the previous verse, and thereby directly achieve the goal. To the contrary, he is here amplifying the understanding of the previous verse by adding the demand to continue the practices over a long period of time.

This verse succinctly lays out the goal of refinement of *Prāṇa*. Crudeness of breath, uncultured breath, the breath of the individual who has not undertaken the practices of the previous verse, purity of food and environment, and so on, is associated with the confinement of life within very narrow boundaries. The individual is constantly motivated by urges to attain what he does not have; he is constantly driven by passions and appetites and beset with problems and obstacles to fulfilment of his desires at every turn. When the individual breath takes recourse to cosmic breath, when the individual contacts the source of perfect order that is the basis of universal life, then his thought and action get trained to function in accordance with total natural law, and his desires are spontaneously fulfilled by nature. He lives in peace and affluence and enjoys eternal contentment.

Problems big and small abound in every channel of life. Bringing an end to problems in life can only mean gaining access to the infinite organizing power of natural law and harnessing it to fulfill one's individual desires. Success in every aspect of life is the goal of the spiritual path, the goal of purity of life as described in verse 32. There is one solution to all problems, and that is capturing the home of all the laws of nature on the level of one's conscious mind. That means life has to be cultured to be totally in accord with natural law. Then every thought and action simultaneously fulfills the individual needs and desires at the same time as it supports the needs of the environment, and the broad design of cosmic life.

There can be no simultaneous solution to all problems, and no sense of freedom in life without the awareness going beyond the confines of narrow and limited boundaries. Awareness has to be completely unbounded, life has to be absolutely full, with unlimited resources, unlimited energy and unlimited bliss, completely free of all restrictions. Anything less than that will not give freedom to life. By *Prāṇāyāma*, Vasishtha intends the prolonged and disciplined practice of an ideal daily routine, on the highest level of purity, incorporating on a daily basis all those spiritual practices and behaviors which culture unbounded awareness and train the awareness to think and act spontaneously in accord with total natural law.

How the breath gets refined, how the individual breath rises to the status of cosmic breath will now be described.

Verse 34:

त्यागादाननिरोधेषु भृशं यान्ति विधेयताम्
प्राणाः प्रभुत्वात्तज्ज्ञस्य पुंसो भृत्या इवाखिलाः ३४

Whether one renounces the objects, or acquires them, one's awareness remains intensely confined in narrow boundaries. All these boundaries and limitations go away by following these prescriptions.

Because of having power over the boundaries, the *Prāṇas* are the carriers of the soul's [latent] knowledge of that unbounded reality of life; to whatever degree the soul has been purified, the wholeness of unboundedness shines through the boundaries.

> The first line of this verse makes explicit all that was said in the commentary on the previous verse: It is by following all the prescriptions of verse 32 that one gains eternal freedom in life. It is important to note the emphasis here that eternal freedom does not require renunciation of the world. One can certainly gain enlightenment while engaged in the field of activity, using the infinite organizing power of total natural law to bring success to every activity in order to live life in affluence and comfort. The paths of the householder and the recluse are both valid in the name of evolution, and with the proper application of knowledge and technology, both convey life to perfection.
>
> The second line of this verse explains how refinement of the *Prāṇa*—through all these different habits and vows—gives rise to freedom in life.

The verse says that *Prāṇa* has power over the boundaries. What exactly is the special status of Prāṇa that makes it the vehicle of evolution to higher states of consciousness and the agency that lifts the body into the air in the practice of Yogic Flying? Prāṇa stands at the junction between Absolute and relative, between consciousness and the physical nervous system.

Ultimately, there are two fields of life. One is relative and ever-changing. The other is infinite, Absolute and never-changing. The Absolute contains within itself the intelligence and order—the blueprint of natural law—that gives rise to the relative field. *Prāṇa*, in its most simple, abstract state is simply vibration. At the junction point between Absolute and relative, at the finest level of relativity, the Absolute begins to move, begins to vibrate. This primordial vibration is the starting point of creation, this is where creation first begins to take shape and bring about manifestation of the unmanifest power and potential of pure Being, the plane of cosmic law.

Vasishtha takes this analysis even further, locating the principle of action within the structure of the Absolute: The nature of the Absolute is pure knowledge, and in the structure of pure knowledge there is a principle of movement, a principle of sequential unfoldment that is lively even in the unmanifest gaps between the expressions of knowledge: If we think of the Absolute as vibrating with total knowledge, then within the non-vibrating silence of the gaps between expressions of knowledge there is the principle of action, the principle of movement, the principle of sequential unfoldment, which drives the eternal presentation of the total knowledge of the Absolute, Veda, within itself. Locating this principle of action within the structure of pure knowledge, within the Absolute phase of life—what we in modern terms would call the Unified Field of All the Laws of Nature, was established in the first line of verse 31.

This primordial principle of action, which gives rise to the finest value of pure dynamism, the initial vibration at the start of creation, is called *Prāṇa*. The breath that the human being takes in, and that sustains the life of the individual nervous system from moment to moment, is also called *Prāṇa*. How can one and the same word be used for these two quite different phenomena? We will see that *Prāṇa*, in its varying values and varying degrees of expression characterizes the whole range of human experience from sleep to waking, and through all the higher states of consciousness.

Modern physics has found that the fundamental particles and fields of nature, the most fundamental building blocks of our universe, exhibit an abstract property that is called spin. While these fundamental building blocks of our entire universe are not localized particles but are more like waves that are spread out all over space, each one of these fundamental fields exhibits a property that is referred to as spin or spin angular momentum.

Also, according to the equations of modern physics (quantum mechanics), this spin variable can only take on one of five different values (0, 1/2, 1, 1.5, and 2). Consequently, all of the fundamental particles and fields can be grouped into one of five categories, depending on whether the spin is 0, 0.5, 1, 1.5, or 2. Spin 2 is associated with the graviton, the intermediary of the force of gravity. Spin 1.5 is associated with the gravitino, which is a new field predicted by physics. Spin 1 fields include the photon, the intermediary of the electromagnetic field, as well as the intermediaries of the strong and weak nuclear forces. Spin 0.5 is associated with electrons and quarks. Spin 0 is associated with the Higgs Boson, the so-called God particle, which is needed to give mass to all the particles.

Thus, we can summarize the entire field of manifest creation, as understood by modern field theory in terms of these five spin types.

These same five spin types are known to the ancient Vedic Science as the five primordial elements, earth, water, fire, air and space, experienced through the senses as smell, taste, sight, touch and hearing. This correlation has been carefully worked out and reported by quantum physicist, Dr. John Hagelin.[5] By virtue of the extreme perfection of cognition of reality by the ancient seers of Vedic Science, the categories of experience of the world in Vedic Science match those of modern science.

According to so called supersymmetric unified quantum field theories such as superstring theory, at higher energy levels, the particles that represent the air and the space elements, the gravitino and the graviton, become capable of transforming into one another. The gravitino can become a graviton one moment and transform back into a gravitino the next. In this circumstance, the two particles are recognized as two different components of one field, which is called the gravity superfield. In this situation, the gravitino plays a special additional role as the intermediary field that allows the graviton field and gravitino field to transform back and forth between each other. A so called virtual, or transient, gravitino is able to unify the graviton field with the gravitino field, producing the gravity superfield. The whole creation is then made of one thing, the superstring, appearing in different modes.

In Vedic Science also, the air element, the element corresponding to the sense of touch, is capable of unifying all the elements into one unified structure, when through the process of pulse diagnosis, all the diverse elements in the physiology are felt as impulses of touch on the fingertips. The air element has a special status, being capable of transforming into all of the other elements and thereby bringing back the record of what are the specific characteristics of the five elements, expressed in terms of *Vāta*, *Pitta* and *Kapha* in the physiology at that time. The whole diverse physiology is seen in terms of one thing, impulses or vibrations on the fingertips. As in the Upanishads the command is to know that one thing by which everything else is known, in Āyurvedic pulse diagnosis, by knowing one thing, knowing the pulse through the sense of touch, one learns everything about the state of the physiology.

Vasishtha adds one new thing to the picture of reality made up of five elements or five spin types, which apparently has not been incorporated into the modern scientific viewpoint, and that is the ability for consciousness to experience more integrated, more unified states of awareness. Higher states of consciousness are more unified states of consciousness and they have more knowledge and more organizing power. How do these unified states of consciousness interact with the world in order to give rise to special abilities, Siddhis, including Yogic Flying? This is being explained—how consciousness thrills the body and causes it to do something that it ordinarily would not do, fly through the air. The explanation is going to be in terms of *Prāṇa*.

Vāta Doṣa in Āyur Veda is a confluence of air and space elements: Both the quality of movement, which characterizes air, and the space or arena in which movement takes place belong to Vāta doṣa. In Āyur Veda, *Vāta Doṣa* has five principle subdivisions, called *Prāṇa Vāyus*, or *Prāṇa*s. These *Prāṇas* are responsible for all values of movement in the physiology. The five *Prāṇas* are *Prāṇa Vāyu*, *Apāna Vāyu*, *Samāna Vāyu*, *Udāna Vāyu* and *Vyāna Vāyu*. *Prāṇa Vāyu* brings food and air into the body. *Apāna Vāyu* is responsible for exhalation and the elimination of wastes. *Samāna Vāyu* works with the digestive fire for the digestion and assimilation of food. *Udāna Vāyu* is the upward moving flow which connects the gross physiology with the inner intelligence of total natural law. *Vyāna Vāyu* distributes the nourishment of breath and food to every cell in the body.

The flow of breath throughout the body, the nourishment of the system through food, and the overall administration of the physiology through the flow of intelligence, are all carried out systematically by these five *Prāṇas*. With the one word, *Prāṇas* (plural), this verse locates the five breaths as the functioning value of intelligence in the physiology. On the one hand, the breaths are responsible for transporting all kinds of nourishment throughout the body. They participate in all the gross superficial aspects of physiological function. On the other hand, by virtue of their ability to unify all the disparate aspects of the physiological system into one coherently functioning organism, the *Prāṇas* are the window to more refined styles of consciousness in the physiology.

Different parts of the physiology have their different duties, their own marching orders, as it were, but what unifies all of them together is the functioning of the different *Prāṇa*s. Correlation of the parts can be very poor, almost non-existent, as in the state of sleep. In waking state, the different parts begin to work together, and there is some degree of correlation between all the diverse functions of the physiology and the intentions being exercised in the field of action by the command centers of the central nervous system. For more order to be exhibited in the overall functioning of the physical system, it can only come from more refined functioning of the *Prāṇa*s. More refined means spontaneously taking into account activities of the system that are more distant. On a scale from total object-referral activation of the system in terms of fight or flight, to the all-pervading total silence of self-referral consciousness in the state of *Samādhi*—from the shutting off of the correlation of the parts, to the complete integration of the parts in one wholeness of Being, the different values of consciousness have their basis in different styles of functioning of the *Prāṇa*s. Only through the integrated style of functioning of the *Prāṇa*s can the underlying wholeness—the wholeness which is inherent in diversity of the physiological functioning, just as the unified field is inherent in the diversity of creation—shine through the boundaries. The refinement of the *Prāṇa*s tells the whole story of the growth of higher states of consciousness.

Whatever the soul has learned about the nature of life, about the pure field of creative intelligence at the basis of all thought and action, shines through the successive steps of rest and activity of the *Prāṇa*s. On a gross level, the *Prāṇa*s integrate the diverse functions of the physiology into a living organism. On a subtler level, they are, at least in principle, capable of unifying life, bringing all the disparate values of consciousness and physiology together into one integrated state of fullness of life in higher consciousness, completely in tune with the total value of natural law. We have seen the plausibility of this in terms of the role of the gravitino in creating a synthesis of all matter in the unified super-symmetric Quantum Field Theories, such as superstring theory. Now Vasishtha is going to explain in precise detail how the *Prāṇa*s create the unified state of consciousness and physiology, the state of Yoga, the state of enlightenment.

Verse 35:

राज्यादिमोक्षपर्यन्ताः समस्ता एव संपदः
देहानिलविधेयत्वात्साध्याः सर्वस्य राघव ३५

The knowledge of liberation from all boundaries was first given to royalty: They lived wholeness of life, life on the level of perfection.

By mastering the wind in the body, they became the rulers of the whole world, O Rāghava.

Mastering the wind in the body means living life on the faintest level of feeling. Wholeness of life, life on the level of perfection, can only become a living reality based on the finest level of feeling. "The wind in the body," is a very crude expression for the content of the ultimate attainment in the state of Unity Consciousness. But we have seen that in the principle of movement contained in *Prāṇa* there is the power to integrate the whole of life. The gross wind is certainly mastered, and the breath becomes softer and highly economical. But also, the softer, finer values of movement of the air element, the most delicate values of the sense of touch, the finest level of feeling has been mastered which takes within its fold the whole of cosmic life and the whole of cosmic law. On that basis of rulership of the total value of natural law in creation, they became rulers of nations.

Vasishtha is pointing out to Rām, that this knowledge of enlightenment is relevant to him, also. He also can become an enlightened ruler and a Yogic Flyer by mastering "the wind in the body."

Vasishtha is about to embark on a detailed description of the mechanics of Yogic Flying, how actually the body lifts up off the ground. The technique which Cūḍālā used, as has already been explained, was the technique of *Saṁyama*, which is a purely mental technique which gives rise to the spontaneous fruit of the body suddenly lifting up into the air. This technique, propounded in the Yoga Sūtras of Patañjali, is effortless and natural, and easily taught to qualified aspirants who are skilled in the practice of transcending and experiencing transcendental consciousness. However, since the body lifts up in the air spontaneously and suddenly, the mechanics that bring this about are not so obvious. In order to teach the mechanics, he enters into a discussion of a more difficult and laborious path to mastery of the "wind in the body." This is a path which breaks the wholeness of the body into parts, and then integrates the parts together into a whole. In Patañjali's system the whole thing happens in one stroke. Vasishtha, by bringing our attention to the ancient kings who first received this knowledge of Yoga, is going to open up for our understanding the inner dynamics of the process of Yogic Flying.

Verse 36:

परिमण्डलिताकारा मर्मस्थानं समाश्रिता
आन्त्रवेष्टनिका नाम नाडी नाडीशताश्रिता ३६

[They placed their] attention on the vital points (*Marmas*) [where] the wind of the body spins around rapidly:

Surrounding the intestines there is one such channel (*Nāḍī*); there are 100 different channels (*Nāḍīs*) the mind can resort to.

In the context of the discussion of the mechanics of Yogic Flying, this verse is very important, because this verse focuses on the channels of mind-body coordination. Up until this point, there could have been some doubt about Cūḍālā's practice of flying. Was she (merely) feeling that she was in the air, or imagining that she was flying like birds, or like clouds, while her body remained on the ground? Were these flights of the mind which she was exercising? Although Yogic Flying as Cūḍālā practiced it is a purely mental procedure (of *Saṁyama*), the dramatic result of the practice is physical, the lifting up of the body, and this is readily seen by anyone. How does the body rise up in the air by the command of the mind? This is being explained.

There are specific discrete channels of mind-body coordination, and each one of these channels has the same overall structure. That structure is being described here: The body is being divided into a hundred different parts.

In the subsequent verses we will see how all these parts are integrated into a whole.

The archetype for the channel of mind-body coordination is the structure of the Vedic *Maṇḍala*.[6] All the distinct transformations that constitute the organizing power within the specific channel of mind-body coordination are arranged in a circle of laws of nature, a circle of *Devatās*. The stream of intelligence, the stream of knowledge lively in that channel of mind-body coordination flows from one law to the next law and to the next law in a perfect sequence, progressively going step by step through all the details of creation, and then in the reverse direction, analyzing, taking apart or destroying step by step until the basic constituents have been recovered. The two halves of the circle are perfectly balanced at every point, so that the two opposites of creation and destruction, or analysis and synthesis together create wholeness at every step. In the Vedic *Maṇḍala*, the progression from each point to the next proceeds with infinite speed, so that the structure is for all purposes simultaneous and fixed. This theme of sequential expansion and sequential contraction is followed in every channel of mind-body coordination.

There are channels of mind-body coordination for each of the principle elements, earth, water, fire, air and space, and for innumerable processes and functions in the physiology. In each channel, there are functions and processes, there are materials being processed, and there is the consciousness or intelligence of the knower, which is the agency for whose sake the transformation is being carried out. Thus, these are structures within the physiology which carry out autonomic processes, which carry out the innumerable housekeeping functions of the body on every level, which at the same time have an intelligence component, have a relationship with the knower, have some level of connection with the central nervous system, where the knower, the "I" resides. Through these channels of mind-body coordination, the territory of influence of the "I," of the knower, the *Ātmā*, extends to every cell, to every structure, to every particle in the whole body. The whole story of relationship of consciousness and body has been systematized in terms of these 100 channels of coordination, and the sequential flow of intelligence in all these *Maṇḍalas*.

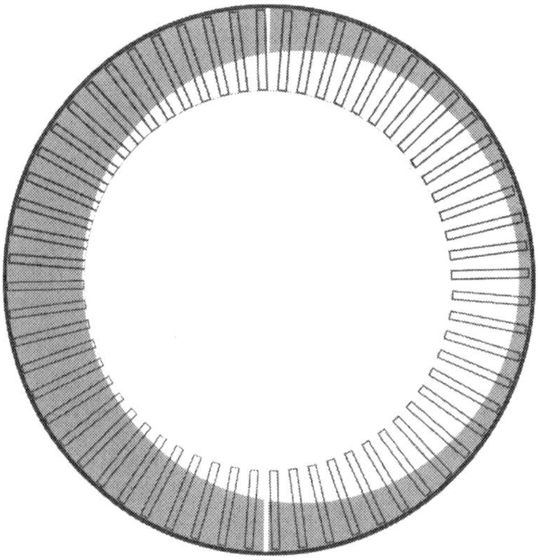

The Vedic Maṇḍala structure, with sequentially arranged packages of knowledge, moving from fullness to emptiness and back to fullness.

Verse 37:

वीणाग्रावर्तसदृशी सलिलावर्तसंनिभा
लिप्याधौंकारसंस्थाना कुण्डलावर्तसंस्थिता ३७

This brings to vision the total spread of the architecture of the divine *Vīṇā*, resembling the consciousness of the knower, the "I," who is playing the *Vīṇā*, laid out as discrete packages of knowledge spread throughout the *Vīṇā*, establishing the *Vīṇā* as the textbook of total knowledge [of the Constitution of the Universe].

The body is the divine *Vīṇā*. The individual consciousness in the body is as if playing the divine *Vīṇā*. The divine *Vīṇā* is made up of 100 different packages of knowledge—that is the architecture of the body. The body is made of natural law, the body embodies complete knowledge of natural law. The "I" which is identified with the body, which is structured by the body, is itself total natural law, "*Kuṇḍalāvarta-saṁsthitā*." The architecture of the human body is established as the field of total knowledge, and that is the reality of Being, the reality of the *Ātmā*.

The body has innumerable *Marma*, and each *Marma* is a channel of mind-body coordination. Each channel of mind-body coordination strings together pearls of knowledge of sequential transformations of natural law, which make pure existence functional, awake in that specific channel. The sum total of the activities of each *Marma* is what we call consciousness, human consciousness. The activity of the *Marma* is the intelligence of natural law made functional: There is a flow from transformation to transformation embodied in the structure of the marma itself, and that flow is orchestrated and carried forward by *Prāṇa*. The life-breath is ultimately the move of intelligence through all these channels.

Every individual human being is capable of transcending thought and experiencing pure consciousness, consciousness awake in itself, the unbounded ocean of Self-referral consciousness, the ultimate repository of total knowledge and total natural law. How is this possible? It is possible to transcend because the human nervous system, the human physiology is structured for that. Because total

This diagram shows the 192 Sūktas of the First Maṇḍala of Ṛg Veda as the packages of knowledge corresponding to the spinal nerves.[21]

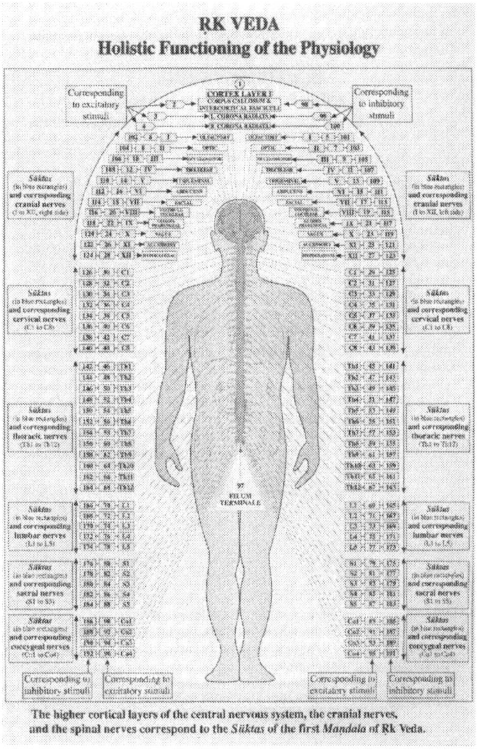

The higher cortical layers of the central nervous system, the cranial nerves, and the spinal nerves correspond to the *Sūktas* of the first *Maṇḍala* of Rk Veda.

natural law—made up of hundreds of textbooks of natural law, each organized as the governing intelligence of a specific channel of mind-body coordination—is structuring the human physiology, the human physiology is capable of knowing itself in the state of transcendental consciousness, capable of pure self-referral consciousness.

The intelligence of total natural law is there latent in every human being in the physical structure of the physiological system. It is latent, because the actual functioning value of intelligence, the actual character of consciousness that is experienced through this machine depends on the quality of *Prāṇa* that is animating the machine. If the *Prāṇa* is very crude, then the sequential unfoldment of natural law in each channel is not fully lively, and then the participation of that channel of natural law in the overall functioning of the physiology is minimal. With crude *Prāṇa*, consciousness is not complete, consciousness is not fully awake, and not being fully awake it is not Self-referral, it is not aware of its own unbounded infinite potential. Even in ignorance, the brain functions in specific channels, but it is not the total brain that functions simultaneously, because the *Prāṇa* has not yet been refined.

This verse has given the map of unfoldment of enlightenment in individual life in terms of this sequence: The awakening of Self-referral consciousness takes place through the enlivenment of the full value of knowledge and intelligence in every channel of mind-body coordination, every *Marma* in the physiology. That enlivenment of full knowledge and intelligence takes place through the refinement of the *Prāṇa* which in its most refined and delicate values, animates the flow of intelligence in each channel of mind-body coordination. The refinement of *Prāṇa* in turn gives rise to the orderly flow of intelligence and coherent integrated functioning of the human nervous system. That orderly flow of intelligence makes the individual consciousness the home of all knowledge and the home of all the laws of nature. The home of all knowledge on the level of the conscious mind places at the disposal of the individual human being the infinite organizing power of total natural law. This is the map which the knowledge of the architecture of the human physiology has given us. How to refine the *Prāṇa* has already been considered in verse 32.

There is an innate desire for growth and evolution and expansion of life in every species. In humankind, the desire for more happiness, more knowledge, more love, greater and greater territory of influence, more and more of everything drives everyone towards higher states of evolution. The spiritual path, described in verse 32, brings fulfillment to all those desires for more and more by unfolding the infinite organizing power of natural law that is already contained within every human being: The individual human being has infinite inner resources, and there is a path for the unfoldment of that. In the absence of that path, in the lack of knowledge of the path, the individual finds obstacles to the expansion of life, and then the individual suffers, and the saying becomes prominent that "Life is a struggle." Infinite bliss and infinite love and power is the birthright of every individual human being, just by virtue of having a human nervous system. That is the teaching of this verse.

But what about the other species of life on this planet?

How is the force of evolution experienced in other species? That is being addressed in the next verse:

Verse 38:

देवासुरमनुष्येषु मृगनक्रखगादिषु
कीटादिष्वब्जजान्तेषु सर्वेषु प्राणिषूदिता ३८

In angels, demons and men; in wild animals, crocodiles, birds, and the like;

In insects, spiders and so forth, in fish, in all living breathing creatures [whatsoever,] the [same cosmic evolutionary force, the life force—]*Prāṇa* is there moving upwards.

In this theme of analysis of the phenomenon of Yogic Flying, Vasishtha began by identifying the component parts of the physiology. The physiology is made up of more than a hundred channels of mind-body coordination. The mind can take recourse to any channel because consciousness is connected to the body through these channels. Through which channel can the mind gain the ability to lift the body up in the air? There is no one single channel which bestows mastery over flight through the air. How then is Yogic Flying possible?

The channels of mind body coordination are collections of discrete transformations arranged in sequence. The underlying knowledge of every channel of mind-body is knowledge of natural law—every channel is intrinsically a package of knowledge. This was established in verse 37. The sum total of all the packages of knowledge which constitute the intelligence governing the different channels of mind-body coordination in man is called

Veda. Veda is the universal knowledge of life.

There are channels of mind-body coordination in every species, but the representation of total knowledge of the Veda is partial in the lower species, not complete as it is in man. Thus, the lower species have only limited capabilities and limited resources, and their path of evolution is set by nature. Nevertheless, there are channels of mind-body coordination, and corresponding packages of knowledge in every species, and breath which sustains life from moment to moment in accordance with the cosmic force of evolution.

Breath of any creature means participation in the play of cosmic life, which means inevitably being under the spell of the cosmic force of evolution.

All species are evolving under the influence of one cosmic force of evolution. Even species which live to kill have a desire for more, to go upwards in the chain of life.

Transmigration of species is the expression of this evolutionary force of nature.

The evolutionary ladder through Darwinian evolution is the same, born onward by the cosmic force of evolution.

The force of evolution is always positive, always upwards.

The science of *Āsana*, a branch of Yoga, presents collections or subsets of the channels of mind-body coordination which emulate the primary channels functioning in different species. Thus, there are hundreds of different *Āsanas* named after different animals. In each such posture, those particular laws of nature found in those channels of mind-body coordination characteristic of that animal are strengthened. Because each animal is under the spell of the cosmic force of evolution, each of these asanas strengthens in a different way the overall vitality of the evolutionary force of nature in man.

Every channel of mind-body coordination in man is a vehicle for conveying life upwards. There are no evil channels of mind-body coordination, there is no part of the body which is not fully participating in the play of cosmic life. The body is made of natural law. Lower species are also living and breathing, they are made of natural law, but these are always partial values of natural law, and they are not flexible, not refinable. The evolution of each of the lower species is fixed within very narrow boundaries. Man can experience the total value of natural law, the total value of the evolutionary force in nature. Man can experience self-referral consciousness, and consequently, as we shall see, man can fly.

In this verse, Vasishtha is pointing out that *Prāṇa* in all its expressions in every species in creation, on earth and in heaven, is always an upward moving force, an evolutionary force, a life-force. The importance of this is to demonstrate that the hundred(s) of channels of mind body coordination in the human physiology, each borne along by *Prāṇa* animating every sequential transformation of natural law, all have an upward direction, an upward move, an upward push. Life itself has an upward thrust, and these hundred channels of mind-body coordination in man represent the evolutionary power of natural law in human consciousness and physiology, ever pushing upwards. Vasishtha explains in verse 40 how this can be harnessed to bring about the phenomenon of

Yogic Flying.

But what about the destructive power of natural law? That is also a part of natural law, that is also a part of human life. How does that fit into this picture? That is addressed in the next verse.

Verse 39:

शीतार्तसुप्तभोगीन्द्रभोगवद्बद्धमण्डला
सिता कल्पाग्निविगलदिन्दुवद्बद्धकुण्डली ३९

In suffering from cold, and in sleeping, the destructive power of the king of the snakes holds sway. [That is] the destructive pole of the circle of life [moving *Prāṇa* downward].

The contracting side of the circle of life annihilates everything like the fire at the end of a *Kalpa*, or the waning of the moon.

The power of contraction [opposite to the expansion of the cosmic force of evolution,] expressing the influence of the cooling rays of the moon brings the progression of creative intelligence to a stop in the null point of the *Maṇḍala* (or circle of life) like the dissolution of the universe brought about by the destroying fire at the end of a *Kalpa*. "Circle of life," *Kuṇḍalī*, is referring to the packages of knowledge of the sequential transformations of natural law which underlie every *Nāḍī*, every channel of mind-body coordination. The knowledge in every package has both values, creation and destruction, heat and cold, activity and rest, waking and sleeping. The previous verse established the existence of a cosmic force of evolution, that carries every species in creation onwards and upwards toward perfection. The life-force, the *Prāṇa* of every species, the creative intelligence which supports the breath of life, is a positive, upward moving force. If that is so, how do we account for the destructive phase of life, which is so obvious in creation? There are species that kill and eat everything that they come across, and in this verse, the king of the snakes represents that destructive power which is evident in nature. There is a cruel aspect in nature which seems to contradict the picture of one cosmic force of evolution which universally causes everyone and everything to evolve. The answer is that the knowledge of destruction is built in to the evolutionary plan, it is an essential part of it. Even on the cosmic scale, the cycle of time includes both creation and destruction. In the animal kingdom, there are species which create protoplasm, and other species which devour it. The whole of life is spontaneously balanced between creation and destruction. *Prāṇa* is everywhere an evolutionary force in nature, but nevertheless for the flower to blossom, the bud has to be destroyed. In order for species to be active during the day, activity must come to an end in sleep. In order to survive the cold of winter, there must be internal heat, internal metabolism which maintains the temperatures needed to sustain life. Destructive intelligence is an essential part of the circle of intelligence, the cycle of transformations, the "*Parimaṇḍala*," (v. 36) in every species in creation. Progress is in steps of rest and activity, and for each new step, the previous step has to come to an end, has to rest, so there is destructive intelligence built in to progress. Notwithstanding all the destructive power that we see functioning everywhere in nature, the *Prāṇa*, the life-force which expresses in every species, is everywhere positive, upward moving. That is why we call the intelligence at the basis of creation, "creative intelligence," and that is why we call the life-force, the breath of life within every species, "the cosmic force of evolution."

This total force of evolution, that expresses itself in every species in creation, operates in every channel of mind-body coordination in man. Every one of the more than a hundred channels in the body expresses creative intelligence, expresses the life-force, carries life upwards.

With this verse we have completed our analysis of the parts of human physiology which are involved in the phenomenon of Yogic Flying: Our analysis has been in terms of the component channels of mind-body coordination, called *Nāḍīs*, which together integrate consciousness and physiology and thereby sustain life. Now we are going to examine how these parts come together to create the whole, to create the manifest phenomenon of Yogic Flying.

Verse 40:

ऊरोर्भ्रूमध्यरन्ध्राणि स्पृशन्ती वृत्तिचञ्चला
अनारतं च सस्पन्दा पवमानेव तिष्ठति ४०

[During Yogic Flying] the fluctuations of consciousness go through all the channels of the body back and forth from the thighs to the middle of the eyebrows,

Moving with increasing speed as the channels are being increasingly purified; [until finally] becoming continuous he [the Yogic Flyer] remains established [in the Self].

In every channel of mind body coordination, there is a sequence of transformations, a progression which moves in a cycle, expanding from a point more and more until the maximum expansion in infinity has been reached, and then again contracting, under the influence of the destructive phase described in the previous verse, becoming less and less until the minimum most has been achieved in the contraction to a point. This cycle of expansion to infinity and contraction to a point, is laid out in terms of successive transformations of natural law in a circular *Maṇḍala* structure. The move from infinity to point and from point to infinity is the primordial move of *Prāṇa*. These are the mechanics of the creation of consciousness, the creation of wakefulness, the creation of subjectivity from the organized transformations of inert matter, through the movement carried along by *Prāṇa*. Through successive transformations, the point recognizes itself as infinity, and infinity sees itself as nothingness, sees its own nature reflected in a point.

There is a cycle of natural law in every channel of mind body coordination, in all the hundreds of *Nāḍīs* in the body, incessantly moving between creation and destruction, moving from point to infinity and back to point. Each of these channels functions according to its own purpose, its own mandate, and the cycle proceeds at its own pace, largely independent of what is happening in other parts of the body, in other channels of mind-body coordination. A certain degree of connectedness is built into the system by design, so that all the parts contribute to the life of the body, but each *Nāḍī* has its own textbook, its own rhythm, and carries out its functions with minimal interference and restriction.

Now in this verse, the largely independent—autonomous and autonomic—functioning of the different channels of mind-body coordination are being harnessed. The fluctuations from infinity to point and from point to infinity in each channel are being coordinated. This takes place through the introduction of technologies of consciousness.

Since verse 34, Vasishtha has been explaining to Rām how *Prāṇa* is an activity of successive transformations within the physiology which gives rise to consciousness, and how consciousness through the activity of *Prāṇa* gains command over the relative boundaries of the physiology. Having established a connection between consciousness and physiology, in principle, through the functioning of *Prāṇa*, the life breath, which gives intelligence and vitality to every living being, now in this verse, the tables are turned. Now consciousness is being used to coordinate the activities of matter in different areas of the physiology, in order to refine the overall activity of the system. When the cycles of natural law in all the channels of mind-body coordination from the thighs to the middle of the eyebrows are brought into alignment, so that every cycle is moving to a point at the same time, and every cycle is expanding to infinity at the same time, then a new phenomenon arises: All the small values of mind-body coordination, each of which is a part of the individual structure, each of which has a crucial role in sustaining the existence of the individual, all together take on a different character when they are brought into correlation with each other: There is an emergent property, and that is the experience of pure wakefulness, pure Self-referral consciousness. Each of these channels was already an aspect of the intelligence of the individual, but as long as these channels were not coordinated, were not functioning in synchrony, then the experience of the wholeness of all these isolated channels of awareness was not available.

This is the refinement of *Prāṇa*: Bringing the different parts of the physiology into close connection with each other, so that each functions in relation to the whole. The benefit of this increased coordination and coherence between the different parts of the system is increased efficiency and economy of functioning. The overall breath becomes finer. It becomes finer because of increased efficiency and corresponding decrease in metabolism, not through superficial manipulation.

When all the positivities of all the channels of mind-body coordination are summed together, the result is pure wakefulness, infinite unbounded Self-referral consciousness. This result, characterized by refinement of the *Prāṇa*, is easily available to any human being through the application of technologies of consciousness. The infinite spin of successive transformations moving from infinity to point and from point to infinity in every channel of mind-body coordination in the body, gives rise to the summation of all positivities in the experience of pure wakefulness, pure Self-referral consciousness.

The most powerful technology of consciousness for harnessing all the different channels of mind-body coordination and creating one unified wholeness of pure wakefulness comprised of infinite silence and infinite organizing power is the practice of Yogic Flying using the formula advocated by Patañjali. In this practice of Yogic Flying through the application of *Saṁyama*, the impulse or wave function of infinite consciousness repeatedly collapsing to a point and expanding again to infinity, moves to and fro through all the values of *Ākāśa* in the physiology, touching the extremes on both ends of the body from the middle of the eyebrows to the thighs [or seat]. In this procedure, the *Prāṇa* is purified, the obstacles to pure wakefulness are eliminated, and the body gains perfect health. In the following verses, Vasishtha explains how this process of refining the *Prāṇa* through Yogic Flying harnesses the infinite organizing power of total natural law in order to bring about the fulfillment of the desire to fly.

Verse 41:

तस्यास्त्वभ्यन्तरे तस्मिन्कदलीकोशकोमले
या परा शक्तिः स्फुरति वीणावेगलसद्गतिः ४१

The fluctuations of consciousness are the characteristics of Her—who resides in that unboundedness [of the Self], in the infinite bliss of the *Ānanda-maya Kośa*—

Who is *Parā Śakti*—she flashes forth and the body (the divine Vīṇā) dynamically rises up and moves in the air.

The emergent property of the coordinated functioning of all the different channels of mind-body coordination is the infinite power of Absolute Being, pure existence. The fluctuations of consciousness are the successive spins of the move from infinity to point and back to infinity. Those fluctuations of the unbounded eternal Self are the nature of the Self. That Nature, consisting of infinite creative power, resides in the infinite bliss of that inner content of life, the most delicate inner sheath of the human nervous system, the body that is made of infinite bliss, the *Ānandamaya Kośa*.

When this emergent property of the combined functioning of all the channels of mind-body coordination, Mother Divine, who is the infinite organizing power of the transcendental field, "*Parā Śakti*," comes into being during the practice of Yogic Flying, it is a spontaneous awakening, it is a dynamic move. Immediately she plays the divine *Vīṇā*, the instrument of the body, and the melody of that playing is seen as the body lifting up and moving through the air. The flashing forth is not contrived, it is a spontaneous creation of the field of infinite correlation. It emerges instantly as a blissful, even musical transformation when all the parts come together to create the whole.

Verse 42:

सा चोक्ता कुण्डलीनाम्ना कुण्डलाकारवाहिनी
प्राणिनां परमा शक्तिः सर्वशक्तिजवप्रदा ४२

She who is spoken of as named *Kuṇḍalī* unfolds the letter "A" into the circle of life,

The supreme power inherent in all living beings, the source that gives energy and intelligence to all the impulses of the mind.

Mother Divine is here being named *Kuṇḍalī*. She is the power behind the sequential unfoldment of Veda: By virtue of her, "A" becomes "Ak," and then unfolds further to become "*Agnim*," and "*Agnimīḷe*," and then the whole of the first *Ṛca*, and the whole of the first *Sūkta*, and the whole of the first *Maṇḍala*, and on to the complete exposition of the totality of knowledge. This power of sequential unfoldment of natural law is the power of Mother Divine, the power in all living beings, the source of energy and intelligence of all the impulses of thought of every individual. It is her unlimited power that lifts the body up into the air in Yogic Flying.

Verse 43:

अनिशं निःश्वसद्रूपा रुषितेव भुजंगमी
संस्थितोर्ध्वीकृतमुखी स्पन्दनाहेतुतां गता ४३

During the destructive phase of the circle of life (collapse of "A"), the inward breath, her [Parā Śakti's] appearance is like a furious snake [which dissolves everything].

Then the creative power of the circle of life gains the upper hand: Throbbing with life she [Para Shakti] becomes the cause of the unfoldment of "A," entering into her holistic state.

In the collapse of "A" into "Ka" in the first syllable of Ṛk Veda, the process of annihilation of "A," gives rise in succession to all the simple vowels in the Sanskrit language. In a sequential process of spiraling down through successive layers, in the first layer, "A" becomes "I," and in the next spiral, "I" becomes "U," and "U" becomes "Ṛi," and then "Ḷri," "E," "O," and finally "Aṁ" before collapsing into Ka.[7] This spiraling down to a point in the creation of Ka from "A," has the appearance of a furious snake, which destroys the totality of knowledge contained in seed form in "A," and creates the nothingness of "Ka."

Then the creative power gains the upper hand and "A"

unfolds into "*Agnim*," and the rest of the Veda unfolds. It is this power of sequential unfoldment of the Veda—the power that transforms infinity "A" into the nothingness of the point "Ka," and then expands that nothingness of "Ka," into the totality of knowledge—which lifts the body up into the air in Yogic Flying.

Verse 44:

यदा प्राणानिलो याति हृदि कुण्डलिनीपदम्
तदा संविदुदेत्यन्तर्भूततन्मात्रबीजभूः ४४

When the wind of the life-breath enters the heart, *Parā Śakti* [*Kuṇḍalinī*] comes into the body in one step

Then the inner consciousness of the Yogic Flyer [identified with *Parā Śakti*] becomes the seed, which gives rise to creation through the *Tanmatras*.

The individual Yogic Flyer embodies *Parā Śakti*, the creative principle that gives rise to the whole universe.

In one step means with great force, great power, suddenly, in one movement—in one movement she fills up the whole body.

When the wind of the life-breath advances to the heart, that is one step of unfoldment of the total constitution of natural law in "A."

Then the completely unified self-referral consciousness of the knower in the state of *Samādhi*, knowing himself, gives rise to the seed of all manifestation in the form of the subtle elements, (sound, touch, form, taste and smell) emerging as the expressions of his own Nature.

The organizing power of Mother Divine is the power which creates the whole universe. That creative power is experienced as the creation or recreation of the whole body of the Yogic Flyer, consisting of all the physical elements, earth, water, fire, air and space, at the instant that consciousness becomes identified with the power of Parā Śakti. Consciousness, or the "I," becoming identified with the infinite organizing power of Parā Śakti, is expressed in this verse as the "wind of the life-breath entering the heart."

This renewal of the physical body of the Yogic Flyer at the moment of liftoff is a dramatic transformation brought about by the unique state of infinite correlation that is experienced at that moment: Every cell of the body is connected to the organizing power of Mother Divine, and so in that instant the creative power of Mother Divine recreates each cell of the body in accordance with the blueprint of total natural law. Every cell of the body is lifting up, every cell in the body is participating in the "playing of the divine Vīṇā" by Mother Divine.

Verse 45:

यथा कुण्डलिनी देहे स्फुरत्यब्ज इवालिनी
तथा संविदुदेत्यन्तर्मृदुस्पर्शवशोदया ४५

As she is giving rise to the whole creation, *Parā Śakti*, humming within herself, bursts forth like Dhanvantari from the ocean of consciousness.

In the same way, the consciousness [of the Yogic Flyer] rises up, and by the authority of the gentlest level of feeling, the body rises up [into the air].

"*Abja*," Born of the water, referring to Dhanvantari, who emerged from the churning of the ocean of milk by the *Asuras* and *Devas* at the dawn of creation. Dhanvantari carried with him the nectar of immortality. In the same way, in a flash, at the moment of liftoff, Mother Divine nourishes every cell in the body with the nectar of immortality.

It is consciousness which is lifting the body up, not physical effort. So only the gentlest feeling is needed to direct the body as it takes flight.

Verse 46:

स्पर्शनं मृदुनान्योन्यालिङ्गिका तत्र यन्त्रयोः
यथा संविदुदेत्युच्चैस्तथा कुण्डलिनी जवात् ४६

The feeling [to fly,] by virtue of its softness envelops the dynamism in silence; then silence merges with dynamism and dynamism merges with silence.

As consciousness rises upwards; correspondingly, *Parā Śakti* rises upwards instantly.

Verse 47:

तस्यां समस्ताः संबद्धा नाड्यो हृदयकोशगाः
उत्पद्यन्ते विलीयन्ते महार्णव इवापगाः ४७

In this process, the veins, arteries and the heart move in perfect correlation.

Parā Śakti rises upwards in every cell of the body like a great wave rising up in the ocean.

The totality of knowledge is involved in lifting up the

body, and every cell in the body participates in moving upwards. The body as a whole, with all its innumerable parts, is lifted up into the air, as Parā Śakti, the infinite organizing power of the life-force in the body, moves upwards.

The implications of this experience of perfect coherence between the impulse of Mother Divine, and the activity of every cell in the body is profound. Intelligence and existence become fused, one in the other. This accounts for example, for the coherence between *Vata, Pitta* and *Kapha* fingers in the pulse of the advanced Yogic Flyer: The impulses in the arterial system coming from the autonomic ganglia, are trained to function in a perfectly coordinated manner based on the Unified Field, so they are always in tune and never obstruct the fulfillment of the individual's desires, and never come out of balance: This is Dhanvantari coming out of the ocean of milk, delivering perfect health to the individual.

Verse 48:

नित्यं पातोत्सुकतया प्रवेशोन्मुखया तया
सा सर्वसंविदां बीजं ह्येका सामान्युदाहृता ४८

Parā Śakti, who reverberates [in every cell of the body] with the desire to fly, and who lifts the body in the air, is the nature of one's own Self.

She is the life-principle of every sentient being, verily She is declared to be the One who becomes the many.

Vasishtha sums up the entire discussion of the mechanics of Yogic Flying with the dramatic conclusion that Flying is completely natural for man. The desire to fly is there in every cell of the body, it is the very nature of life. The life of every sentient being in creation is directed towards this supreme accomplishment of perfect mind-body coordination. The process of creation, the process by which the eternal unity of Absolute Being diversifies and becomes multiplicity is carried out by Parā Śakti. She is the nature of one's own Self. She is at once the origin of the desire to fly which is inherent in every cell of the body, and she is the power which lifts the body up in the air in Yogic Flying. Yogic Flying is the supreme fulfillment of the whole stream of evolution, the fulfillment of the primordial desire of the Self, "I am One, may I be many?"

With this knowledge of Parā Śakti as the source and goal of Yogic Flying, the analysis of the mechanics of Yogic Flying is complete.

This series of verses on the mechanics of Yogic Flying, verses 31-48, presents a systematic and coherent explanation of how consciousness is related to physiology, and how the practice of Yogic Flying works at the junction point between mind and body, between subjectivity and objectivity, in order to raise life to the state of perfection.

Verse 31 is the seed exposition of the mind-body connection, and it recounts the relationship between intelligence and existence—between the intelligence of total natural law, Veda, the blueprint of creation, and the gross functioning of the human physiology. By design, the physiology takes in orderliness from the environment in the form of food and processes it to create the consciousness of the living organism. There is a dynamism, a move from the field of intelligence onto the field of existence, and this move is called *Prāṇa*. All the following verses in this section are the detailed exposition of this connection between intelligence and existence.

Verses 32 and 33 present a picture of life evolving, growing towards perfection, by more and more of the intelligence of the state of perfect order at the basis of creation being applied to the surface of life. This process of evolution is the process of refinement of the *Prāṇa*. Refinement of the *Prāṇa* means that more and more of the intelligence of total natural law is expressed in the physical machinery that digests food and creates consciousness, creates individual life.

Verse 34 is a bridge verse which connects all the procedures to refine *Prāṇa* that have been recounted in verse 32, with the detailed description of the move of *Prāṇa* at the junction point of consciousness and physiology which will be unfolded in the following verses.

Verses 35 -37 lay out the architecture of the human body and define explicitly the detailed relationship between *Prāṇa* and Veda, between *Prāṇa* and the knowledge of total natural law. The human body is made of packages of knowledge, each collections of impulses of intelligence governing discrete processes of transformation. All the packages together comprise the total range of natural law—the blueprint of the universe and the blueprint of the human physiology, the microcosm and the macrocosm.

Verses 38-39 analyze the flow of *Prāṇa* more deeply, showing that in each channel of mind-body coordination where *Prāṇa* is functioning, there is a circle of life, a circle of intelligence of natural law which oscillates between creation and destruction.

Verse 40 begins the process of synthesis of all the parts. All the diverse values of *Prāṇa* come together to create the wholeness of consciousness. Yogic Flying is presented as a technology of bringing correlation and integration to all the disparate parts that make up the human physiology.

Verses 41 to 48 give voice to the emergent property of functioning consciousness. When the different channels of mind-body coordination are fully correlated and integrated so that all the parts move together as one whole, then that consciousness has authority over the physiology as a whole. That consciousness which has authority over the entire physiology is made up of the combined values of intelligence of all the channels of mind-body coordination. This embodiment of total natural law in the physiology is the *Śakti* or "power" of consciousness, it is the intrinsic nature of consciousness as a whole. This emergent property of total natural law functioning is called Mother Divine. Mother Divine lifts the body up in Yogic Flying. This is the conclusion of the detailed analysis of the functioning of intelligence at the junction point of consciousness and physiology. The total value of intelligence of natural law at the junction point between consciousness and matter becomes functional, and that total value of intelligence is harnessed to lift up the body in the procedure of *Saṁyama* for Yogic Flying.

In verses 31 to 48, the relationship of mind and body has been analyzed in detail, and the parts have been brought together again in a structure of wholeness of consciousness functioning, consciousness in motion, consciousness lively with mastery of total natural law. This is Vasishtha's exposition of the mechanics of Yogic Flying.

Section 4: Collective consciousness of the society and the nation.

Verse 49:

श्रीराम उवाच
आकल्पादनवच्छिन्ना चित्संवित्सर्वमस्ति हि
तस्मात्कुण्डलिनीकोशात्केनार्थेनोदयः स्फुटः ४९

The glorious Rām said:

Since ancient times the knowledge of all the higher states of consciousness has been there in every generation:

The knowledge of enlightenment in terms of the [realization of the] Constitution of the Universe in human physiology [through Yogic Flying] certainly came from that [same] eternal tradition of knowledge. With what purpose was the knowledge of Yogic Flying brought forth in the world?

Verse 50:

वसिष्ठ उवाच
सर्वत्र सर्वदा सर्वं चित्संविद्विद्यतेऽनघ
किंत्वस्या भूततन्मात्रवशादभ्युदयः क्वचित् ५०

Vasishtha said:

In every generation, always the knowledge of all the higher states of consciousness has been there, O sinless one.

[In every generation there have been enlightened teachers] Who through mastery of the subtle elements (sound, touch, form, taste and smell) and the gross elements (space, air, fire, water and earth) gained the ability to rise up in the air.

Verse 51:

सर्वत्र विद्यमानापि देहेषु तरलायते
सर्वगोऽप्यातपः सौरो मित्त्यादौ वै विजृम्भते ५१

In every generation there have certainly been individuals with the knowledge of how to activate the flying impulse on the physical level, on the level of their bodies.

The ability to go anywhere at will is an ancient practice: The sun at first was fixed in one place in the sky, and verily it was made to rise up in the sky.

Verse 52:

क्वचिन्नष्टं क्वचित्स्पष्टं क्वचिदुच्छिन्नतां गतम्
वस्तु वस्तुनि दृष्टं तत्तत्सद्भावैर्विजृम्भितम् ५२

At some times the knowledge is lost to sight; at some times the knowledge is clearly evident; and then a time comes again when the knowledge is lost, this is always the fate of knowledge over time.

The eternal reality of life is seen, or the reality of life is obscured by the dynamism of activity on the surface of life; there is wholeness of life in the fullness of unmanifest Being, or the whole of life is given over to relativity: these are the phases of existence of truth; the complete knowledge of living wholeness of life is revived in its fullness again and again.

Verse 53:

एतद्भूयः क्रमेणाहं शृणु वक्ष्यामि तेऽनघ
देहे स्वे च यथोदेति भृशं संविन्मयक्रमः ५३

In the sequence of loss and revival of knowledge, this is the time of revival of complete knowledge: Listen, I will explain it to you, O sinless one.

Sometimes life is focused on the physical body as real, sometimes life is focused on the unmanifest Self as real. [In Yogic Flying] According to which perspective predominates, the body moves up into the air, or it falls down heavily; the mechanics of evolution of consciousness follow this sequence.

Verse 54:

चेतनाचेतनं भूतजातं व्योम तथाखिलम्
सर्वं चिन्मात्रसन्मात्रं शून्यमात्रं यथा नभः ५४

The ignorance or clarity of vision that characterizes the individual members of society determines the level of collective consciousness of the whole society.

The atmosphere is created by the collection of individuals: The degree of purity of heart and mind, the level of consciousness of the individual measured by the degree to which perception is right and thinking is in accordance with natural law, or the lack of purity, the extent to which the individual fails to perceive the reality, and thinking violates natural law, in precise measure, [every individual consciousness contributes to] the collective consciousness or atmosphere of the society.

Cetana-acetanaṁ, percipient-not percipient.
Bhūta-, being like something, characterized by;
Jāta, brought into existence;
Vyoma, space, atmosphere;
Tathā, in that way, to that measure, to that level
A-khila, the khila, the combined or collective value, of "A," consciousness.
Sarvaṁ, everyone [contributes to the collective]
Cin-mātra, the degree of purity of heart and mind, the level of consciousness of the individual,
San-mātra, the degree to which perception is real,
Śūnya-mātra, the degree of void or deficit
Yathā, in which manner,
Nabhaḥ, atmosphere.

Verse 55:

तद्धि चिन्मात्रसन्मात्रमविकारं स्वनामयम्
क्वचित्स्थितं संविदेव भूततन्मात्रपञ्चकम् ५५

It follows that since the process of Self-realization, the evolution of consciousness of the individual through Yogic practices which unfold the awareness of unmanifest Being, pure consciousness, influences the degree of purity of heart and mind, influences the level of consciousness of the individual measured by the degree to which perception is right and thinking is in accordance with natural law,

Therefore, [a small number of individuals] remaining in one place, and attending only to the consciousness phase of life, can influence all the different aspects of life, physical, mental and spiritual, in the whole society, by raising the level of collective consciousness of the society.

Verse 56:

तत्पञ्चधा गतं द्वित्वं लक्ष्यसे त्वं स्वसंविदम्
अन्तर्भूतविकारादि दीपाद्दीपशतं यथा ५६

It is pure consciousness that has entered into the five-fold structure of existence, consisting of the five elements, earth, etc., [*i.e.*] the field of duality: That which is appreciated as the object by the knower, that which becomes "thou," directly indicates the level of consciousness of the Self or knower.

Transformations of the innermost Self are of primary importance: By means of the light from a single individual experiencing the Self, the light of one hundred individuals is influenced in the same direction [of increased clarity of perception and action in the field of duality, the field of the five elements].

Change in Crime Rate in Cities with One Percent of the Population Practicing Transcendental Meditation, versus matched control cities.[22]

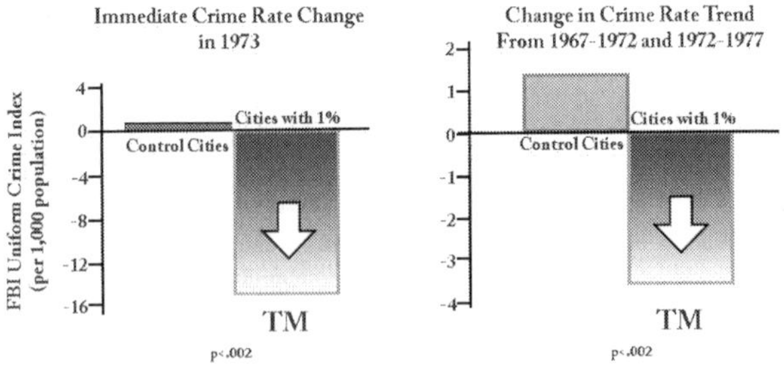

The influence of one percent of the population of a city practicing the Transcendntal Meditation technique is enough to counterbalance the negativity and incoherent thinking and action of the other 99% of the city population and cause a reversal of negative trends. The "light from a single individual experiencing the Self" influencing a hundred (śata) people in the same direction, is a field effect of consciousness. This effect becomes measurable in the statistics of the quality of life of the city as a whole, when the number of individuals in the city practicing Transcendental Meditation reaches one percent. Then the society as a whole begins to reflect greater orderliness.

This field effect of consciousness, called the "Maharishi Effect" by contemporary researchers, is measurable even on the level of nations. Orme-Johnson and Fergusson[8] report that according to a study by Hatchard and Cavanaugh:

> "Results indicate that scores for both New Zealand and Norway on the Index of National Competitive Advantage increased significantly compared to 44 other developed nations when they passed the

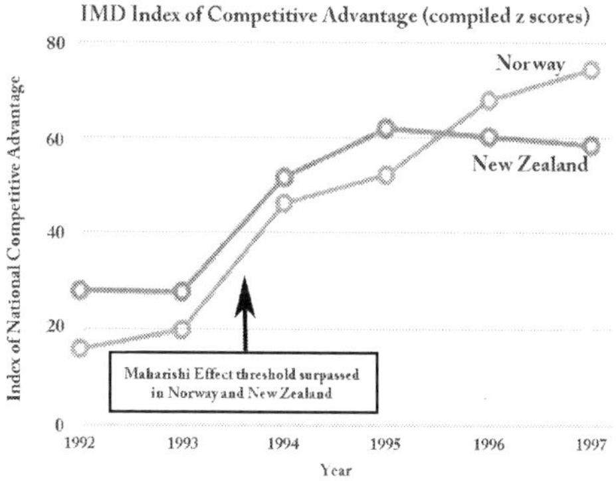

predicted coherence group threshold necessary to generate the Maharishi Effect. This was shown by sophisticated cross-country panel regression analysis, which met rigorous statistical tests of validity (robust to serially correlated errors, heteroskedasticity, and contemporaneous correlation of residuals). Index scores for New Zealand and Norway in the Figure above show the changes that occurred for both countries between 1993 and 1994 when the Maharishi Effect was generated ($p < 3 \times 10^{-15}$ or a three in 100 trillion likelihood that the observed change occurred by chance). Subsidiary analysis of data from the Organisation for Economic Co-operation and Development (OECD) confirmed that the observed changes were unusually broad-based ($p < 6.5 \times 10^{-8}$), sustained, and balanced in nature, with five years of high growth, low unemployment, and low inflation. Taken as a whole, the findings suggest a prescription for balanced and sustained growth based on a method to enhance quality of life and innovation in the population. This and other data related to improved quality of life and enhanced economic performance has been demonstrated not only in New Zealand and Norway but also in Cambodia, Mozambique, and the U.S. (Hatchard & Cavanaugh, 2009).[9] "

The field effect of consciousness described in this and the following verses, in which by "the light from a single individual experiencing the Self, the light of one hundred individuals is influenced in the same direction," is amply corroborated by current scientific research on the Transcendental Meditation program.[10]

Verse 57:

स्वसत्तामात्रकेणैव संकल्पलवरूपिणा
पञ्चकानि व्रजन्तीह देहत्वं तानि कानिचित् ५७

According to the percentage of people experiencing pure consciousness [in a city or country], the collective resolve [to create an ideal society] by the individuals practicing meditation is manifested, either partially or fully.

Five percent of the population practicing transcendental meditation and transcending morning and evening with the same [innocent] resolve and intention [to create a better world] are enough to establish the coherence of collective consciousness, [the perfect health, progress and prosperity of the whole society]: Those five percent guide the destiny of the whole population.

Pañcakāni, five percent of the population.

Having explained the mechanism of the field effect of consciousness, Vasiṣṭha now explains that five percent of the people transcending morning and evening are enough to create a utopian society for the whole world. In this verse he is making a jump from one percent to five percent of the population: One percent of the population meditating is needed to counteract the negativity in the other 99% of the people who are violating natural law (verse 56). But Vasiṣṭha is not content with counterbalancing negative trends in society: He wants to create a lasting utopian society for the whole world. For that more lofty goal, five percent of the population meditating is required.

Verse 58:

कानिचित्तिर्यगादित्वं हेमादित्वं च कानिचित्
कानिचिद्देशतादित्वं द्रव्यादित्वं च कानिचित् ५८

It is pure consciousness which has sway over the innumerable impulses moving in often contrary and conflicting directions that make up the collective consciousness of society: the individuals experiencing pure consciousness are the precious golden points of light; and it is that precious golden light of God which is guiding the destiny of the whole population (not human intention).

The degree to which the collective consciousness of the whole nation is in accordance with Total Natural Law, in accordance with the Light of God, guides the destiny of the whole population: Individuals that are themselves contacting pure consciousness and (therefore) not violating natural law in their lives, [individuals] that are living in the Light of God, guide the destiny of the whole population.

> Establishing coherence in collective consciousness means creating a momentum of evolutionary influence that will never decay. It's not enough to create a society with one percent practicing transcending morning and evening, because if that number diminishes for any reason, then the society falls back into chaos and negativity. Establishing coherence in collective consciousness so that it is unbroken and permanently self-sustaining is a higher goal, requiring five percent of the population meditating.

Verse 59:

एवं हि पञ्चकस्पन्दमात्रं जगदिति स्थितम्
चित्संविदत्र सर्वत्र विद्यते रघुनन्दन ५९

In this way, the radiance of life-supporting influence of five percent of the whole world's population [experiencing transcendental consciousness through the practice of Transcendental Meditation] is enough to establish a utopian society for the whole world.

In this case, when five percent of the world's population is meditating, there is coherence in the collective consciousness of the whole world, [there is perfect harmony, peace, and togetherness of all the nations of the world,] O Thou Delight of the House of Raghu.

> Having explained the value of five percent of a society's population practicing transcending, Vasiṣṭha now predicts that five percent of the whole world's population transcending morning and evening is enough to create a utopian society for the whole world.
>
> Maharishi Mahesh Yogi actively campaigned to create societies with one percent meditating, but this is not at odds with Vasiṣṭha's demand for 5% meditating. At a press conference in Fairfield, Iowa in October, 1975, Maharishi explained that this one percent was an intermediary goal: "Wherever we find there is one percent of the population [meditating], we raise the voice to create an ideal society by having 5 percent of the people [meditating]."[11]

Verse 60:

केवलं पञ्चकवशाद्देहादौ चेतनाभिधा
जडस्पन्दाभिधा क्वापि स्थावरादौ जडाभिधा ६०

It is an all-pervading unified field based phenomenon, by virtue of the preeminent power of the [influence created by] five percent of the population meditating being primarily a physical effect on the body mediated directly by [the field effect of] consciousness [without the intervention of any superficial mechanism of people meeting together, etc.].

The influence of the state of least excitation [of the field of consciousness] is known to be everywhere simultaneously; that which is unmoving, stable, abstract and present everywhere is more basic [than the excited states of matter]: the state of least excitation is present in all the excited states.

> Here Vasishtha clarifies that the effect of five percent meditating is through a field effect, not through superficial interactions or communications of any kind.

Verse 61:

यथा स्तब्धः स्थितो वीचिरिव स्थलमिवास्थितः
पञ्चकेषु तथैतच्चिल्लोलरूपा जडान्विता ६१

To whatever degree coherence in collective consciousness is firmly established, to that value, bubbling up of incoherence as deviations from the path of evolution will be less, and to that value, stagnancy and failure to progress will be short.

When five percent of the population are transcending, accordingly the dynamism of change and the resulting manifestation of the release of stress due to the corresponding growth of pure consciousness will always be firmly connected to the state of perfect order [and will therefore always promote progress and evolution for the whole society].

> Society is always changing. But change does not need to challenge the coherence and order of the whole society. Successfully maintaining the practice of 5% of the population requires the establishment of teaching institutions, whose "sole purpose is to maintain five percent of the population meditating."[12] So two things are needed to create a self-sustaining ideal society: The requisite number of individuals practicing transcending morning and evening, and the institutions which will support the practice with continuing programs for renewal and deepening of knowledge and experience. Maharishi concluded that "Once the five percent of the population is maintained meditating, the Age of Enlightenment will be perpetual."[13]

Verse 62:

इतः सौम्य इतो लोलः किमब्धिरिति नो यथा
विकल्पादौ तथैवैतत्पञ्चकं हि जडाजडम् ६२

In the final analysis, everything depends on the level of collective consciousness of society: If the consciousness is coherent, from there peace and harmony come forth; if the consciousness is incoherent, from there turbulence, violence, and calamities come forth.

Accordingly, at the first outbreak of violation of natural law in society, only this palliative of five percent of the population meditating will be effective because only the enlivenment of the transcendent, the field of perfect orderliness can eliminate disorder on the surface of life.

> This is the principle of administration of Rām Rāj. If there is turbulence in collective consciousness, the only permanently effective remedy will be raising the percentage of the population practicing effortless transcending morning and evening.

Verse 63:

देहादिपञ्चकं जीवः स्पन्दः शैलादिकं जडम्
स्थावराद्यनिलस्पन्दि स्वभाववशतोऽनघ ६३

The soul that is born to a society with five percent meditating, enjoys higher consciousness and creativity, more fullness of life, the natural consequence of being born with a more stable, more orderly nervous system, incorporating the all-possibilities character of the state of least excitation of consciousness in its structure.

[The soul's life] being set in motion from the very first breath with greater stability and adaptability, greater creativity and resourcefulness, [the soul is] spontaneously more powerful and influential, a natural born leader, O Sinless One.

> The children that grow up in the environment of coherence created by five percent of the population practicing effortless transcending will be stronger, more creative and more fulfilled in their personal lives, and will contribute more to the progress of the whole society. The coherence that is created in society will be self-sustaining, because the new generation of leaders will always be more progressive, more creative and more capable of guiding the whole society to greater and greater fulfillment.

Verse 64:

वाचः पर्यनुयोक्तव्या स्वभावाद्रघुनन्दन
शीतोष्णादि हिमाग्न्यादि वाक्चेति परिदृश्यते ६४

The use of language by all the people in their daily affairs, becomes more closely allied with the eternal language of total natural law, the language of the Self, the language of Veda [where there is perfect connection between name and form and greatest effectiveness of speech], O Thou Joy of the House of Raghu.

The inner intelligence of speech becomes more clearly visible as the opposite values expressed in speech, such as hot and cold etc., rise to express the whole range of life from fullness of fullness expressed in the first word [of Ṛg Veda], "*Agni*," [lit. "fire"] to fullness of emptiness, expressed in complete inertia or vacuum (*Hima*, lit. "frost") [in the *Avyakta Sūkta*, opposite to the first *Sūkta* in Ṛg Veda].

> As collective consciousness rises, speech rises to "bind the boundless," to capture the total potential of natural law in concise expressions. Expressions in speech on the surface of life conform more and more with the principles of sequential unfoldment of the Veda, the Constitution of the Universe. Then speech is more effective, it communicates the intentions of the speaker with greater clarity. When speech is more effective, the quality of togetherness of the whole community is strengthened, and the society spontaneously becomes more integrated and coherent.

Verse 65:

गृहीतवासनांशानां पुष्टाभावविकारिणाम्
स्थितयः पञ्चकानां हि योज्याः पर्यनुयोजने ६५

Concerning the portion of the population that devotes themselves to regular practice of contacting the Self within in order to realize the benefit for the whole society, that group may fluctuate in size from day to day and year to year, due to absence of the needed support and nourishment for the practice.

The ability of five percent of individuals in society to continue in the practice of creating an ideal society may vary since the individuals whose participation is creating the effect may be beset with challenges, [due to occupational responsibilities, limited finances, health problems, aging and so forth].

> Here Vasishtha is raising issues of administration of society through the field effects of consciousness. The effect is created by the individuals practicing their program of meditation, morning and evening. If for any reason the meditators are unable to fulfill their obligation, then the influence is not created. If the influence vanishes, then the society will revert to its previous state of incoherence. People in society will begin to suffer. The utopian character of the ideal society with five percent of the population meditating will last only as long as that percentage of the population continues diligently in their practice. The administrators of society must be constantly vigilant to maintain the necessary portion of the society meditating.

Verse 66:

वासनास्तु विपर्यस्ता इतो नेतुमितश्च ताः
पुंसा प्राज्ञेन शक्यन्ते सुखं पर्यनुयोजितुम् ६६

Regularity of practice is of utmost importance for the whole society: The positive effects can be reversed by failure to maintain regularity of practice; there must be proper guidance and inspiration at every step, so that the individuals continue in the practice.

With deep experience of the reality and with profound intellectual understanding, individuals should delight in continuing the practice, despite any challenges.

> The administrators of society are responsible for upholding the regularity of practice of the portion of society meditating. They must provide guidance at every growing level of consciousness and inspire everyone to continue the practice despite any challenges. Education in the schools and colleges should provide the needed knowledge for the students on an ongoing basis, and the education programs must continue after the students graduate. There must always be new layers of understanding to complement the continually advancing layers of experience.

Verse 67:

अशुभे वा शुभे वापि तेन पर्यनुयोज्यते
प्रबुद्धवासनं चान्यत्पञ्चकं सुप्तवासनम् ६७

Whether experiences are clear or hazy, by virtue of the charm of deepening experiences and the clear intellectual understanding of the importance of regularity, the practice should be continued with perfect regularity.

Growing in enlightenment, awakening the total potential of natural law in human awareness, and on the other extreme, falling asleep during the practice, the whole range of possible experiences contribute to the [required] five percent of the population meditating.

> There is a natural range of experiences of transcending, and all the different experiences of correct practice contribute to the required five percent of the population meditating. The level of consciousness of the meditators is not the decisive factor for creating the field effect: What is important is the correctness and regularity of practice. Everyone who practices effortless transcending contributes to the field effect. This principle is confirmed by EEG studies that show that there is little difference in the coherence of brain functioning of beginning meditators and advanced meditators during the practice of meditation.[14] Automatic self-transcending is a natural practice. From the start of the practice, transcending is effortless and spontaneous, and the results in activity grow and accumulate more and more with regular practice.

Vasishtha's exposition of the field effects of consciousness, and the importance of proper administration of the progress and understanding of the growing meditators, is in direct response to Rām's question about why Yogic Flying is taught. As we will see in the next section, Yogic Flying plays a crucial role in simplifying the task of stabilizing and administering the ideal utopian society over time.

From verse 54 to verse 67, Vasishtha has presented the basic principles of administration of the prosperity and progress of the whole society through the field effects of consciousness. This is automation in administration: Not creating peace through military power, not eliminating crime through large police forces, but administering society by creating a powerful effect of orderliness in the whole society through a portion of the population transcending morning and evening. This is leadership, this is governance, this is the direct path to utopian society, life free from suffering. But there are challenges in this approach, and these challenges can be eliminated through the introduction of groups of Yogic Flyers. This understanding will complete Vasishtha's answer to Rām's question as to why Yogic Flying is taught by the Masters of the Vedic Tradition: It is taught to simplify the administration of society on the level of perfection.

Section 5: The practice of Yogic Flying in large groups in order to bring orderliness and coherence to the collective consciousness of the nation.

Verse 68:

यत्र पर्यनुयोगस्य फलं समनुभूयते
तत्र तं संप्रयुञ्जीत नाकाशं मुष्टिभिः क्षिपेत् ६८

A situation could be created in which the fruit of the practice would accrue in all its richness to all of those engaged in practicing together, irrespective of the variations of individual circumstances:

To that end, a group composed of just a handful, [a fraction] of the required number of people practicing [Yogic Flying] together in close proximity [under one roof] will hit the target [of creating an ideal society].

> The field effects of consciousness on the city and national levels described in the previous section were an innocent by-product of the promotion of an effective and natural meditation technique, the Transcendental Meditation technique. Individuals learned for their own personal benefit and were not aware that they were contributing to the common good of society through their collective practice.
>
> In this section we examine the group practice of Yogic Flying, in which the motive for assembling a large group is to create the field effect for the entire nation, or even for the whole world. The numbers that are needed to have a national effect are quite small and are completely within the scope of already existing institutions, such as

the military, and schools and colleges. In this case, the motive of creating an atmosphere of peace, creativity and success for the whole nation becomes an inspiration for all the flyers to participate regularly in the group practice.

Such a project was carried out for fifteen years in Cambodia, with the establishment there of Maharishi Vedic University in 1993, with the full support and encouragement of the government. Their 200 plus students practiced the Transcendental Meditation and TM-Sidhi program including Yogic Flying in a group twice a day, as part of their curriculum. Their group numbers approached and often exceeded the requisite number to create coherence through the Maharishi Effect for the whole of Cambodia, the square root of one percent, which was 265 flyers.

The results are astonishing. In 1990, Cambodia was the poorest country among the 42 poorest countries of the world, based on income levels. Fergusson writes[15]:

> However, after implementation of the Transcendental Meditation and TM-Sidhi program, Cambodia's gross domestic product (GDP) growth rates averaged 8.9% until 2008, and the World Bank reported that Cambodia's industrial sector GDP growth rates equaled as much as 30% per year after the late 1990s. As shown below (left-hand chart), annual per capita GDP growth rate also ranged between 6% and 7% per year during this period for an overall increase of 179% between 1996 and 2008 (World Bank, 2015). During this period, the percentage of undernourished people in Cambodia fell from 30% of the population

in 1993 when MVU was established to 18% by 2008, a 40% reduction in undernourishment. The percentage of the population living in poverty also fell from 45% to 21% during the same period, and other measures indicated a decrease in poverty of 63% between 1994 and 2008, resulting in Cambodia by 2010 being ranked 63rd out of 152 on the international scale of poverty, a jump of 89 places in under one generation.

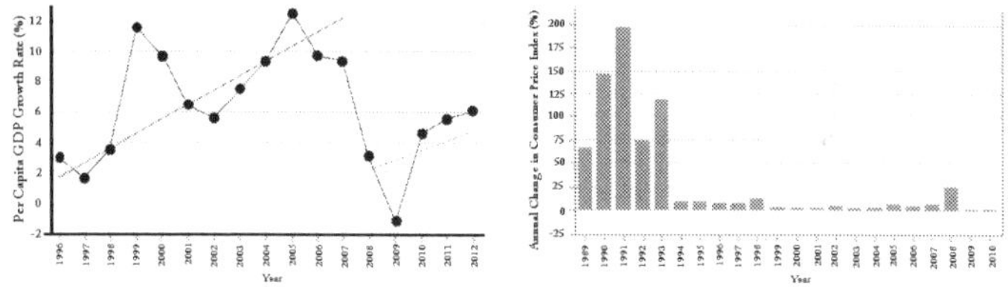

Left-hand chart Cambodia's annual per capita GDP growth rate between 1996 and 2012, with trend lines between 1996 and 2007 and between 2008 and 2012; **Right-hand chart** Cambodia annual percent change in consumer price index between 1990 and 2001.

During this period remarkable progress was made in reducing the percentage of the population undernourished; increasing enrolment in primary and secondary education, decreasing infant mortality, decreasing maternal mortality, increasing access to clean drinking water, reducing inflation from an average of 114% to below 10%, gaining food self-sufficiency, increasing education spending by the federal government, reducing civil unrest, and dramatically increasing the number of foreign visitors. The increase in annual apparel manufacturing revenue and the number of foreign visitors both sky-rocketed from essentially zero, as shown in the charts below.

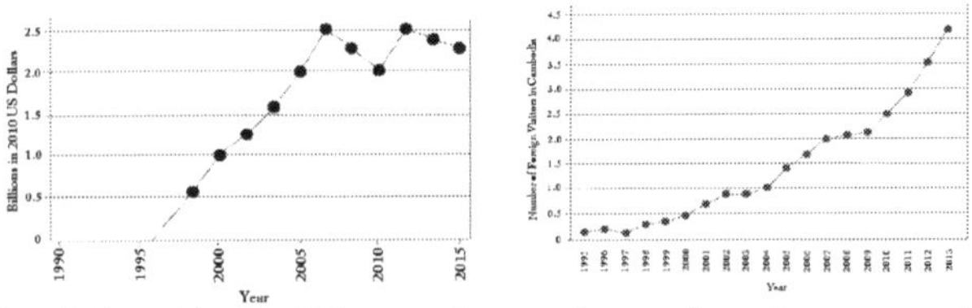

Left-hand chart Cambodia's annual apparel manufacturing revenue in billions of dollars derived from exports to the U.S. between 1990 and 2015 (World Bank Group, 2015, p.18); **Right-hand chart** number of foreign visitors in millions to Cambodia between 1995 and 2013 (World Bank, 2015).

Fergusson summarizes the statistical analysis of the data as follows:[16]

> A number of alternate hypotheses were advanced by the studies, including the role of the United Nations Transitional Authority in Cambodia and its elections held in 1993, the shift to a market economy from a centralised, planned economy in 1995, and the role of foreign aid in these observed changes. However, each hypothesis could not adequately account for all the reported changes. Indeed, the United Nations' own report said it *failed to bring peace to Cambodia.* The shifts in economic policy, which may have stimulated the economy, occurred after the implementation of the group at MVU. Some changes in economic indicators, such as inflation, coincided with formation of the group and occurred prior to changes in economic policy, and foreign aid declined after 1995. Thus, each of these alternate explanations lends support to a causal explanation for the group at MVU generating an influence of coherence in Cambodia.

The Cambodia case study is one of a series of studies of intentional interventions by the formation of groups of Yogic Flyers in order to create coherence and order in the collective consciousness of entire nations. These studies with their modern sophisticated statistical techniques attempt to prove the intangible field effect: In the field effect, there is no visible message or signal travelling from the individuals creating the effect—the field is not visible. But the effect is tangible and unmistakable.

The data from the International Peace Project in the Middle East[17] indicate a very close correlation between the size of the group and the power of the influence created. Mapping the numbers of the TM-Sidhi program participants against the Composite Index of the quality of life showed a very tight coherence between these two. The experimental strategy of creating a randomly chosen 13 day period when the numbers were continuously high, after which the numbers fluctuated greatly, shows unmistakably that the numbers of Yogic Flyers was leading the Quality of Life index and not vice-versa.

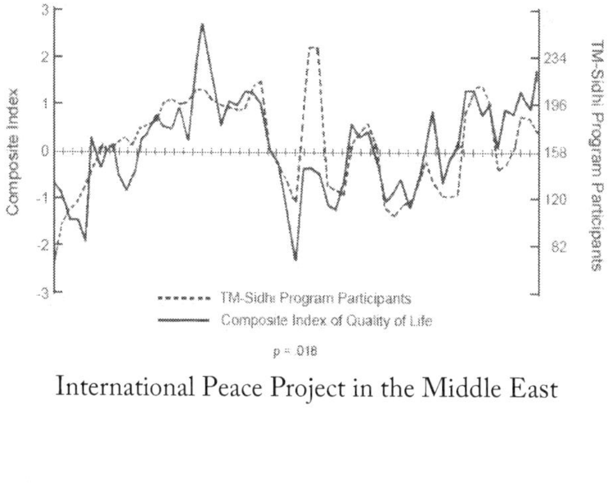

International Peace Project in the Middle East

Rām, Vasishtha's student in the Yoga Vasishtha, created an ideal society, a utopian civilization, called Rām Rāj. It was said that in Rām Rāj, noone suffered, everyone lived his full span of life, there were no famines or other natural disasters, and society as a whole thrived. How did Lord Rām create this perfect society? In this section, Vasishtha is giving Rām the technology for creating an ideal society. He needed only to create groups of Yogic Flyers, and then by virtue of the field effects of the flyers' consciousness, the whole society would enjoy heavenly life on earth. This is enlightened administration, automation in administration.

The experiments in Cambodia and in the Middle East demonstrate that the field effects of consciousness are real. There is a practical, societal benefit from the practice of Yogic Flying. It is for this reason, for the sake of the benefit for the whole society, that Yogic Flying is introduced in society, and groups are organized. That is Vasishtha's teaching to Rām. The powerful field effects of group Yogic Flying were well known in very ancient times, and those technologies were implemented in order to create an ideal society, Rām Rāj. This same technology of Yogic Flying is available in the world today, and it can be applied to bring complete fulfillment to governments, and to create an ideal society of prosperous and fulfilled individuals.

Verse 69:

तृणाग्रनिष्ठा मेर्वाद्याः पञ्चकानां हि राशयः
विवेकनिष्ठाः कीटाद्या एते स्थावरजंगमाः ६९

Seated on grass mats, all experiencing together in golden domes built specially for the purpose, a [small] group of experts gathered in one place [the size of the square root of the required number] has the same influence as the five percent of the population meditating [spread out over the whole country].

Seated together with the purpose of investigating consciousness as a field of all possibilities, practicing the *Siddhi* Sūtras, they can influence the whole world remaining in one place.

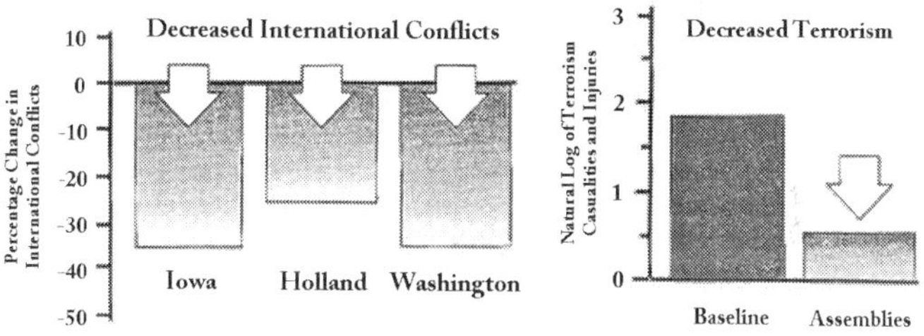

Impact of three World Peace Assemblies in Iowa, Holland and Washington, D.C. on (Left-hand chart) **International Conflicts** and (Right-hand chart) **Terrorism.**[23]

Three World Peace Assemblies, consisting in each case of many thousands of Yogic Flyers practicing together, showed dramatic effects on international conflicts and on incidents of terrorism worldwide. This demonstrates the ability to administer and nourish the collective consciousness of "the whole world remaining in one place."

Modern language and expressions have been used in translating this verse. The following is a word-by-word explanation of the translation, showing the Sanskrit words from which each expression is derived.

Tṛṇa, grass; *Agra*, top; *Niṣṭhā*, resting on. *Agra* means the best, most suitable surface, suitable for Yogic Flying, that means suitable for taking off and for coming back down. *Tṛṇa*, grass, refers to something very fine, minute, insubstantial, that will give way without creating resistance when the body comes down. Grass mats are comfortable for taking off and for coming down, and for sitting. *Tṛṇa* coming first in this verse indicates that the consideration of the surface on which the program is exercised is the first and most important consideration. The program of Yogic Flying, which starts with short hops, cannot continue if the body is injured when it comes down. So, the first consideration is where this practice will take place: For the novice, flying must be practiced on very soft grass mats, or in modern times, foam. Seated on foam, the meditator can take off in repeated short hops without harm or injury: That is the intent of this expression, *Tṛṇa-agra-niṣṭhā.*"

Ādyāḥ, novices. This means individuals who are at the beginning of the practice of Siddhis and Yogic Flying. Because they are skilled in lifting off using the formula for flying, they are called in this translation, "experts." They are experts from the standpoint of the influence they are creating in the collective consciousness through their practice of lifting off in Yogic Flying, but they are novices with respect to the degree of mastery of Yogic Flying. All the advantages of the group practice of Yogic Flying which is being described here is completely applicable to the beginners of the practice, who are still taking off in short hops. So already with the ability to fly in short hops they are "experts" in governing collective consciousness.

Meru: This is a mountain, said to be the center of the universe. Sometimes it is depicted as a gold-colored, dome-shaped mountain, like the back of a turtle. Oftentimes temples are built with the name Meru or Sumeru, indicating that this location is the center of the universe for their followers. We are taking the use of the word Meru in this verse as metaphorical, that the practitioners meet together in a large, perhaps dome-shaped hall with a vaulted ceiling, and their collective practice makes this physical location the center of the collective consciousness of the nation. So "Meru" is being translated as "in golden domes built specially for the purpose."

Rāśayaḥ, the assembled group having the same measure of influence, as the *Pañcakas*, the five percent of the population meditating.

Kīṭa, the name of one of the *Rāśis* or collections of zodiac stars; here *Kīṭā* refers to the different formulas of the Siddhi practice which are performed by the *Ādyāḥ*, novices, as they explore, *Viveka*, their foundation or seat in transcendental Being—that means as they make use of the technology of Siddhis to explore consciousness as a field of all possibilities. The idea is that the Siddhas take on successively different roles or qualities in the wholeness of Self-referral consciousness, in the same way that the sun takes on different qualities and characteristics as it moves successively through the different signs of the zodiac, while always remaining the vibrant light of life. In this way the Siddhas distinguish (*Viveka*) all the different qualities lively in self-referral consciousness and awaken all possibilities in the collective consciousness of the whole population of the nation.

Ete, they, *Sthāvara-jaṅgamāḥ*, remaining in one place their influence goes everywhere.

Verse 70:

प्रसुप्तवासनाः केचिद्यथा स्थावरजातयः
प्रबुद्धवासनाः केचिद्यथा नरसुरादयः ७०

[First] The members of the group experience deeper and deeper silence for a period of time, meditating and transcending according to their instruction, creating the foundation of stability and evenness [that will support the dynamism to come].

[Then] For a while the group experiences the dynamism within the silent self-referral consciousness, experiencing the various divine powers (Siddhis) in sequence according to their instruction.

Verse 71:

सवासनाविलाः केचिद्यथैते तिर्यगादयः
प्रक्षिप्तवासनाः केचिद्यथैते मोक्षगामिनः ७१

[Next] The members of the group play about with the impulses of the transcendental field to make the Absolute functional, beginning to challenge gravity in order to take off from the ground.

For some time, they experience being thrown into the air by the faint impulses of consciousness: Following these procedures [daily, morning and evening], the individuals in the group move quickly towards enlightenment (*Mokṣa*).

Verse 72:

अथ स्वास्वेव संवित्सु मनोबुद्ध्यादिकाः कृताः
हस्तपादादिसंयुक्तैः संज्ञाः पञ्चकराशिभिः ७२

Now at the time of liftoff, [when their bodies are thrown up into the air (*Prakṣipta*)] the individual selves of the participants become merged into the abstract universal field of Self-referral consciousness generated by the whole group, and the minds and hearts of everyone in the group are brought into attunement with that integrated field of pure consciousness.

The hands and feet, bodies, minds, hearts, and innermost selves of everyone in the group being joined together [at the moment of liftoff], there is a universal consciousness, a field of pure knowingness that is generated there in the group, and by that means the individuals coming together as a group create a powerful influence of coherence in the collective consciousness of the entire nation.

Verse 73:

तिर्यगादिभिरप्यन्यैरन्याः संज्ञाः प्रकल्पिताः
स्थावरादिभिरप्यन्यैरन्यान्याः संविदः कृताः ७३

By repeatedly experiencing the lift-off, their bodies moving up into the air propelled by unbounded awareness, the individuals grow in unbounded awareness, they gain total knowledge, and they gain the ability to accomplish anything by the mere impulse of consciousness.

By means of the foundation of transcendental silence created by the practice of meditation at the start, individuals also grow in unbounded awareness, but the influence of integration of consciousness by the group practice of Yogic Flying multiplies the growth and stabilization of unbounded awareness by the square of the number of people flying together.

> The body gets into the quality of space at the moment of liftoff during the practice of Yogic Flying. When many are practicing together under one roof, the space or field effect that is generated by each individual has the imprint of the field of each other individual in the group. The unboundedness of each individual is in terms of every other, "*Anya-anya*," as the verse says, "the other in terms of the other." That means that the radiance of each individual is multiplied by the number of people flying together. If there are a hundred people flying together, then each one has the radiance of a hundred flyers. The influence of the group is therefore the square of the number flying. This means also that the experience of

each individual is multiplied by the number flying together, so in a group of hundred, the individual's experience of the liftoff is a hundred times deeper than when he or she flies on his or her own.

The increased radiance of a group of Yogic Flyers flying together is called by Maharishi, *Super-radiance*. The super-radiance effect is equal to the square of the number of Yogic Flyers, and is due, according to Maharishi, to the generation of *Puruṣottama* at the moment of liftoff.[18] The influence of one single individual transcending and experiencing pure consciousness on his own, is the influence of *Puruṣa*, one unit of coherence. But in a group of Yogic Flyers, there is a "universal consciousness," created, a "mass of knowingness" (v.72) generated at the time of liftoff, and this intensified power of influence through the liftoff in Yogic Flying is called *Puruṣottama*.

The group of Yogic Flyers radiates a powerful influence of coherence and orderliness for the surrounding population. This great power of positivity and evolutionary influence can be harnessed in order to administer the peace, prosperity and progress of entire nations, as explained in the next verse.

Verse 74:

इति साधो स्फुरन्तीमे चित्राः पञ्चकराशयः
रूपैराद्यन्तमध्येषु चलाचलजडाजडैः ७४

Thus, the advantage of Yogic Flying: Fulfilling the desire to fly through the air, the Yogic Flyers make the power of consciousness clearly evident: The Siddhas practically and visibly demonstrate the super-radiance effect by which a small handful of individuals in a group influence the evolutionary trends of the entire nation.

[The great value of Yogic Flying is in] making the growth of consciousness concrete and visible for a beginner at the start of the practice, for an experienced Siddha stabilizing full value of enlightenment, and at every step along the path, by demonstrating the growing ability to make the body move through the air, or the absence of that ability, and by demonstrating the lively creative intelligence that has been developed, or the lack of full enlivenment of the infinite creative potential of human consciousness.

In this verse Vasishtha connects the power of influence of Yogic Flying with the need to administer society by the field effect of consciousness. It is possible to create a utopian society with five percent of the population practicing effortless transcending, morning and evening. This is not intractable, but it is nevertheless a very large number in a society of millions of people. One percent of a million is ten thousand people, and five times that is fifty thousand people. On the other hand, the square root of ten thousand is a hundred, and five times that is five hundred. Five hundred Yogic Flyers practicing together have the same influence on the coherence and orderliness of a nation of one million people as fifty thousand meditators. Maintaining a group of Yogic Flyers is much easier than maintaining the meditation practice of five percent of the population.

This is the answer to Rām's question as to why Yogic Flying is taught by the masters of the Vedic tradition. Group Yogic Flying provides a mechanism for creating a powerful evolutionary influence for the whole society, and thereby administering the peace and prosperity of entire nations. Because of the ease of creating a group of the requisite size, a stable and lasting state of order can be created for the whole society, very easily.

Moreover, not only is there the advantage that a smaller number of people need to be trained and maintained over time, but also there is the daily, concretely visible evidence of the successful performance of the members of the group. Because the effect is due to the liftoff, the successful performance of the members of the group can be observed and measured at any time. The administrators of society can have immediate information as to the power of influence that is being radiated for society on a day to day basis. Yogic Flying in groups is a powerful technology for governing the trends of time.

Verse 75:

एषामेकोऽभिसंकल्पः परमाणुर्महीपते
बीजमाकाशवृक्षाणां सर्गाणां तेष्विमानि तु ७५

The unification of all the individuals [in one integrated, harmonious and coherent collective consciousness] is the collective resolve of the Siddhas flying together, deeply lodged at the finest level of their consciousness, O Lord of the earth.

The impulse of the flying *Sūtra* being discharged by Siddhas on the faintest level of feeling, grow into trees of *Ākāśa*, [subjective universes decorated with the flowers and fruits of the Siddhis, the fabrics of all possibilities, capable of fulfilling all desires]: These subjective worlds of *Ākāśa* in the minds of the Siddhas become one [at the moment of liftoff when the flying impulse reaching the finest level of creation gains universality and infinite organizing power].

Verse 76:

इन्द्रियाणि च पुष्पादि विषयामोदवर्ति हि
इच्छाभ्रमर्यौ राजन्त्यो मञ्जर्यश्चञ्चलक्रियाः ७६

The flyers are the upholders of the integrity and invincibility of the nation; they bring about benefits of increased love, harmony and coherence for the nation, because [through their group performance of Yogic Flying,] they are engaged in raising the level of happiness, welfare and success of the nation.

The daily performance of the group of Siddhas moving about [on the foam] during the practice of Yogic Flying governs the whole nation, [by] bringing balance, harmony and coordination to the innumerable different desires within the nation.

> This is the technology of creating Rām Rāj, utopian society, at any time, for any society, anywhere in the world. Yogic Flying is a yogic practice that can easily be taught to large numbers of people, and it doesn't require belief or any sort of conversion. It only requires that the individuals actually practice the technique, daily, morning and evening, and then the corresponding effect will be generated for the benefit of the whole society.
>
> Rām's question, with what purpose is the technique of Yogic Flying taught by the masters of the Vedic tradition, is the most penetrating and insightful question in this entire discussion of Siddhis and Yogic Flying. The masters of the Vedic tradition were masters of Vedic

Science. Vedic Science is a complete and perfect science of total natural law.[19] The masters of the Vedic tradition throughout time had open to their awareness the complete knowledge of life, the total panorama of human potential and human achievement. With the knowledge of how life rises to perfection in every channel of human endeavor, why would they teach Yogic Flying? There are so many ways to culture human awareness, to educate disciples who innocently offer their lives to the teacher for guidance on the path to fulfillment in life. With all these options open to the awareness of the Vedic masters, why would they teach Yogic Flying?

There are two reasons why the Vedic masters, having at their disposal all the techniques and programs of education that have existed in the long span of time, and having unfolded in their personal lives the total knowledge and infinite organizing power of all the laws of nature in creation, would choose to teach their disciples Yogic Flying. The first reason is their infinite compassion for the whole human race, for the entire family of man. Holding to the precept, "The world is my family," "*Vasudhaiva kuṭumbakam*," they naturally felt the responsibility in this age, and throughout time, to nourish the whole society, to put an end to man's inhumanity to man, to eliminate suffering everywhere and raise life to perfection. The knowledge and organizing power, the joy and perfection that a single individual receives from his education for the sake of fulfillment in his individual life stream, is not a high enough goal for the great masters of the Vedic tradition. However many of the members of society

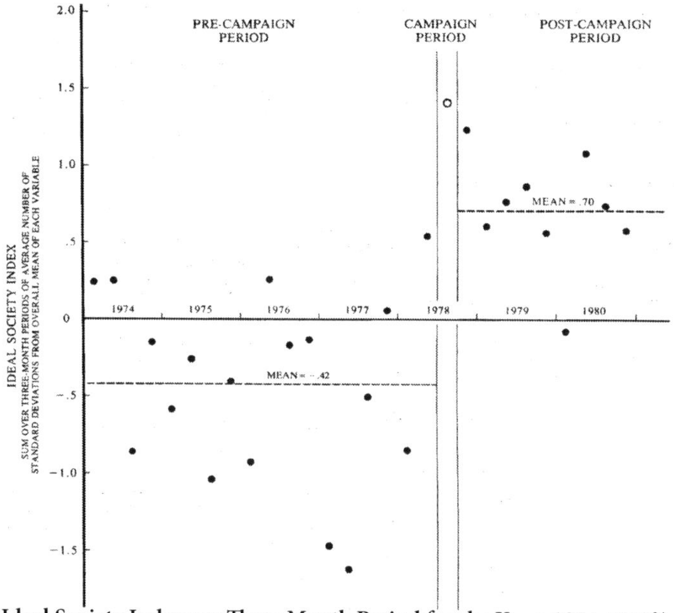

Ideal Society Index per Three Month Period for the Years 1974-1980[24]

The Ideal Society Index measured the change in overall quality of life brought about by Yogic Flyers who came to Rhode Island, USA for the Ideal Society campaign in 1978. The index measures eight variables which are unambiguous indicators of the quality of life. The variables were crime rate, motor vehicle fatality rate, motor vehicle accident rate, death rate, per capita beer consumption, per capita cigarette consumption, unemployment rate, and degree of pollution. Data points on the graph show the sum over three-month periods of average number of standard deviations from overall means of each of the eight variables.

The study authors, Dillbeck, Foss and Zimmerman, conclude,[25] "The results of this study indicate by direct intervention a causal relatinship between participants in the Transcendental Meditation and TM-Sidhi program and improvement in the quality of life at the level of an entire state. This conclusion is strengthened by the facts that the improvement in the quality of life in Rhode Island in the summer of 1978 had been predicted in advance, and that it occurred in Rhode Island in contrast to the control state Delaware."

that they themselves are able to directly influence, their hearts are open to the benefit and highest good of the entire family of man. With infinite compassion for life as a whole, and with the goal of administering the happiness and progress of the whole population, they want to teach those technologies of consciousness which culture life as a whole, which nourish every stratum of creation through the field effects of consciousness. Their vision is ever beyond bringing fulfillment and perfection to single individuals that come in their contact and respond to their influence. They have the expanded vision of responsibility for the whole society. This was Vasishtha's consciousness, and this was what he was teaching to Rām—not just individual enlightenment, but a sense of responsibility for the good of the whole world. The dignity of Vasishtha, the unimaginable, unapproachable perfection of a Vedic master, could teach nothing less than infinite compassion for the whole world family. Vasishtha was teaching Rām—not only the knowledge of the eternal unseen Reality of life, the knowledge of supreme enlightenment—but also the knowledge of how to raise the consciousness of the whole world to perfection, the knowledge of how to create what was henceforth known as Rām Rāj, the perfect administration of society, society firmly established in peace, harmony and absolute freedom from suffering of any kind.

In verses 50-67, Vasishtha presents the broad perspective on civilization as a whole which guides the actions of the Vedic masters. The level of consciousness of each individual, their innate degree of Self-knowledge, the degree to which they are living the fullness of the unbounded potential of the Self, or the degree to which their life is lived entirely on the surface, ever tossed about by changes in the relative field, that is the contribution of the individual to the collective consciousness of the entire society, nation and world. The rise and fall of civilizations is the rise and fall of the knowledge of wholeness of life, the rise and fall of the knowledge of the hidden infinite potential of man. Sometimes life is lived entirely on the surface, and the depth of life is missed, and humanity suffers; at other times there is revival, and the total potential of life is unfolded for every individual, and the whole society advances and thrives on the level of perfection. The loss and revival of knowledge over time is completely natural. The role of the masters of the Vedic tradition throughout time is to bring about revival, restoring the knowledge of life in freedom and affluence, life in enlightenment, and raising life as a whole to perfection.

In the context of this overall picture of the loss and revival of knowledge, the practice of Yogic Flying is the supreme technology, the most direct and powerful means of establishing ideal administration, and raising the entire society to perfection, for two reasons. The first reason is this concern for the nurturing of the society as a whole through the enlivenment of the field effects of consciousness. There is no technology of raising national and world consciousness that is more powerful than the technology of practicing Yogic Flying in large groups. The second reason is that there is no better place for fastest possible individual evolution, than to be a part of a large coherence creating group of Yogic Flyers. When the individual lifts off in the group, then the depth of his personal experience of the liftoff, the clarity of his experience is multiplied by the number of people who are practicing together. By this process, the negativity of the world, the darkness of the collective consciousness, however restrictive and limiting it may be, is kept at a distance, and the opportunity is completely open for the individual to explore in unlimited detail the fine structure of the self-interacting dynamics of consciousness and to rise quickly to higher states of consciousness. To create that opportunity for the individual, it is necessary to counterbalance the darkness of the world with the technology that nourishes the collective consciousness and washes away the stresses and negativity which accumulate daily from the violations of natural law by people in the surrounding society. Even for the sake of individual enlightenment, there is no faster path than group practice of Yogic Flying: This second reason Vasishtha now explains in the remaining verses of this chapter.

Verse 77:

लोकान्तराणि स्वच्छानि गुल्मा मूलं समेरवः
पल्लवा नीलजलदा लतालोला दिशो दश ७७

The internal universes made of *Ākāśa* are all ideal flawless perfectly healthy worlds; the thicket of trees made up of the internal universes of all the Yogic Flyers put together represents total natural law, the Constitution of the Universe.

The sequentially unfolding *Sūktas* of Ṛg Veda, dark blue like rain giving clouds, appear like so many creepers twining around and around through the space of the ten *Maṇḍalas* of Ṛg Veda.

Verse 78:

वर्तमानानि भूतानि भविष्यन्ति च यानि तत्
यजन्ति तान्यसंख्यानि फलानि रघुनन्दन ७८

The ten circles or somersaults will expand and become the different elements, which make up the whole universe.

They perform evolutionary actions, having innumerable fruits, O Joy of the house of Raghu.

Verse 79:

पञ्चबीजास्त एते हि राम पञ्चकपादपाः
स्वयं स्वभावाज्जायन्ते स्वयं नश्यन्ति कालतः ७९

There are five formulas [for experiencing the five elements on the finest level of creation]; they give rise to these Maṇḍalas, the trees of the five elements, O Rām.

From the transformations of the Self in the Self, they are born, and in the Self they are [again] destroyed in the course of time.

Verse 80:

स्वयं नानात्वमायान्ति चिरं जाड्यात्स्फुरन्ति च
स्वविविक्ताः शमं यान्ति तरङ्गा इव वारिधौ ८०

The infinite diversity of creation comes forth from the eternal Self; from the unmanifest, diversity springs forth again and again.

Distinguishing diversity within itself, the undivided peaceful wholeness moves like waves in the ocean.

Verse 81:

इतो यान्ति सम्मुत्सेधमितो यान्ति शमं स्वयम्
एते जाड्यविवेकाभ्यां तरङ्गा इव तोयधौ ८१

From here the impulses of consciousness move outward into creation, from here the impulses of consciousness proceed back to the peacefulness of the Self.

These are two kinds of impulses moving like waves on the ocean of consciousness: Completely Self-referral and tending towards manifestation.

Verse 82:

ये विवेकवशमालयं गता
राम पञ्चकविलासराशयः ।
तेन भूय इह यान्ति संस्थितिं
प्रभ्रमन्ति जगतीतरे मुहुः ८२

Those who having attained the home of all the laws of nature, desire discernment of these two kinds of impulses, O Rām,

Practice Yogic Flying in a large group to bring peace and prosperity to the whole population.

With the technique of Yogic Flying, a large enough group flying together balances the consciousness of the whole nation,

The Yogic Flyers roam about [in their flying hall], moving suddenly and mysteriously from the ground into the air, again and again.

Colophon:

इत्यार्षे श्रीवासिष्ठमहारामायणे वाल्मीकीये मोक्षोपायेषु निर्वाणप्रकरणे पञ्चकविलासो नामाशीतितमः सर्गः ८०

This is the core chapter of Vasishtha's Yoga, the central teaching of the great sage, and it may be said to be the most significant chapter in the whole of the Vedic Literature. Here Vasishtha builds a bridge between ignorance and enlightenment. Enlightenment creates a glow in the face, a vibrancy of perfect health in the physiology that may even be recognized and appreciated by the unenlightened. But what makes an enlightened man different? And what are the practical consequences of that difference? The difference is that the enlightened individual has harnessed the infinite organizing power of total natural law to work for him and to support and bring success to every impulse of his thought and action. Even the supreme level of natural law, the unified level of supergravity is at his service, so that he can move about anywhere in creation at will. The organizing power that has created the enormous galactic universe can even be harnessed to bring joy and fulfillment, and success in every endeavor to the entire population of a nation through the enlightened radiance of groups of Yogic Flyers. Indeed, it was through the establishment of large groups of Yogic Flyers, putting the knowledge of this chapter to practice, that Raam created Rām Rāj. In Rām Rāj, the enlightened rule of Rām, king of Ayodhya, रामराज दुख काहू न व्यापा, rāmrāj dukh kāhu na vyāpā, "In Rāmrāj noone suffered," human life was raised to the level of perfection, no one suffered from disease, everyone lived their full term of life, society was in peace, the rains always came on time, and there was no misery of any kind in society. Enlightenment, the state in which the infinite potential of man has been totally unfolded, comes to vision in this chapter.

The enlightened individual continues to behave in boundaries and is seen behaving by the unenlightened. Talk of experiencing infinity, talk about experiencing how boundaries emerge from the unmanifest Being is of little use, as Cūḍālā found in trying to explain her inner fulfillment to her husband—no amount of talk and no amount of logic will be successful in painting a picture of the infinite unmanifest wholeness of life moving within itself, for the individual enmeshed in the boundaries of the waking state. Whatever the enlightened individual speaks, from his level of total enlightenment, total fullness of life, those same words are interpreted by the ignorant on their own level. Because of this disparity between the intention of the speech of the enlightened, and what is actually picked up by the unenlightened, the knowledge of reality, the knowledge of the experience of higher states of consciousness always breaks into pieces when it falls on the hard rocks of ignorance. Consequently, Vasishtha explains in verses 50-64 of this chapter, the knowledge of reality always goes through alternating times of revival, and times of loss of the knowledge. At some times, society gains nourishment from the transcendental field of life, and life is lived in affluence, abundance and peace, and at other times the collective consciousness of the people remains on the surface of life, and there is suffering and misery on all sides.

What is called enlightenment is not an intellectual

understanding; it is not a belief system, it is not a concept. The mental faculties of the waking state of consciousness cannot grasp what the living fulfillment of infinite bliss is. Certainly, there is a value of knowledge even in the waking state: If one has learned that fire burns, one can save oneself from injury from fire. But if the individual is violating natural law, even unknowingly, there is nothing that can save him from receiving the consequences of his actions, and suffering as an inevitable result. Life does not suddenly come out of suffering by learning a new concept or believing in a new God. Life can only come out of suffering by actually harnessing the infinite organizing power of total natural law.

Yogic Flying provides a tangible bridge between the world of the enlightened and the bound reality of the waking state of consciousness in the state of ignorance. This bridge is on two levels: First, the visible phenomenon provides tangible proof of the existence of higher states of consciousness. Human beings don't ordinarily fly through the air. If they are to move upwards, it can only be by harnessing the organizing power of total natural law. If someone is seen moving up into the air without gimmicks, that is tangible evidence that the total potential of natural law can be captured in human awareness and made to function for the fulfillment of individual desires. Yogic Flying provides proof of enlightenment. Whatever an individual's perception or understanding of the world may be, however exalted his awareness may appear to be, or may be claimed to be, there is a measuring rod to show how much natural law truly works for him. Not a belief, not an understanding, not a mood of tranquility or indifference or unattachment: Enlightenment is command of total natural law, and that command can be demonstrated unequivocally to individuals in the waking state of consciousness.

This bridge of demonstration of enlightenment, proof of enlightenment, is only one aspect of the connection that is made in this chapter between the world of the enlightened and the world of the waking state. The other, and really most important aspect of Yogic Flying is in the area of the field effects of consciousness.

In this chapter, Vasishtha makes very unusual claims about how society works. He posits the existence of a collective consciousness, which is the sum total of the clarity of mind, pure consciousness, or wakefulness of all the individuals in a society. Whether the individuals' attention is on the surface value of manifest boundaries, or whether he is moving among boundaries while his mind is absorbed in the immutable, unchanging absolute phase of life, the character of consciousness of every individual in society contributes to the collective consciousness. The coherent and orderly brain of a single individual transcending and experiencing pure consciousness during his daily practice of Transcendental Meditation is enough to counter-balance the disorderly incoherent thinking of one hundred other non-meditating people, Vasishtha claims in verse 56. Transcending creates a field effect, an effect at a distance, an effect mediated by an unseen field of connectivity between all the individuals in a society, between all the individuals in a geographical area, irrespective of the presence or absence of actual interactions or communications between them. The power of groups of Yogic Flyers, practicing together under one roof, even at the first stage of Yogic Flying, in which the practitioners lift off the ground in small hops, has a dramatically increased field effect on the society. That power is equal to the square of the expected effect from that same number of individuals transcending. These field effects of consciousness are measurable, and in recent times, they have been successfully used to stop fighting in war-torn areas, and bring peace, increased prosperity and better health to entire societies. This is the power and import of this chapter, which makes the chapter the clarion call for all mankind to rise to perfection: Here is the technology, as Vasishtha explains to Rām, to create perfection in administration, to create an ideal society, to bring heaven onto the earth. There is no teaching greater than this, there is no knowledge more valuable than this. This eminently measurable field effect of consciousness, which we now call the Maharishi Effect, because of its scientific demonstration by Maharishi Mahesh Yogi's revived technologies of consciousness in modern times, is proposed here by Vasishtha as the engine of transformation of society from a time of ignorance and suffering to a time of revival of the truth of life, where society lives life on the level of perfection. Here is the real bridge between ignorance and enlightenment.

It is fascinating to see how the first verse of the chapter can present a seed which is expanded into all these diverse themes; Śikhidhvaja's rebuttal to Cūḍālā's description of her experience, Cūḍālā's development of the flying Siddhi, the description of the mechanics of Yogic Flying, the explanation of the Maharishi Effect and the Field Effects of Consciousness, and the special role of groups of Yogic Flyers in creating peace, progress and fullness of life for the entire nation. How the seed of this chapter holds all these diverse ideas together in one package is remarkable. In discussing the loss and revival of knowledge of the transcendental reality of life, Vasishtha points out in verse 64 that even the language changes in order to reflect the changing values of collective consciousness. Maharishi has explained that the sound "A," appearing as a prefix for verbs and nouns in Sanskrit, takes on different meanings in different ages. There is one such word in the first verse, *Abuddhvā*, "not knowing," or "not understanding." This is the ordinary waking state meaning, and gives the sense of this verse in terms of Śikhidhvaja's ignorant lack of receptivity and inability to comprehend the meaning of Cūḍālā's words. In an enlightened age, the prefix "A," according to Maharishi, citing ancient grammar texts, takes on variously the meanings of Knowledge, Action, Achievement and Fulfillment (*Jñān*, *Gaman*, *Prāpti*, and *Mokṣa*). In such an age, the first word of line 2, *Abuddhvā*, could mean "knowing the totality of knowledge contained in "A," or, knowing the infinite dynamism of total natural law, contained in "A." This second line could be translated as follows:

Verse 1.2: "Having known "A" to be the precipitation of the activity of consciousness when the wholeness of consciousness is in its least excited state, playing about at the junction point between intelligence and existence, he [the *Ātmā*], the lord of the material universe, expressed his mastery over creation by behaving remaining within himself."

In this sense, the precipitation of the activity of the wholeness of consciousness, the manifestation of the intention of the enlightened consciousness, gives rise to the ability to fly, and to the Maharishi Effect, and the great benefits enjoyed by a society hosting a large group of Yogic Flyers. These activities, these objective manifestations of the field of consciousness are perceptible even in the waking state. But from the standpoint of the enlightened consciousness, there is a playing about between intelligence and existence, a flow between the inner unboundedness and the outer unboundedness, a flow which is perceived as consciousness moving within itself, which does not disturb the non-changing unity of perception of the wholeness of the Self. This new translation thus contains the seed ideas that are developed in the remaining parts of the chapter.

However, the chapter begins with the testimonial of the ignorance and lack of understanding of Śikhidhvaja. So, there is a flow, back and forth from the enlightened perspective and the perception of the state of ignorance. We are experiencing in the narrow confines of this one chapter, the entire range of loss and revival of knowledge. And we are shown the mechanics of how Yogic Flying can transform an age of ignorance into an Age of Enlightenment. Both of these translations of the second line are valid perspectives in the context of this chapter, and both versions are elaborated in different portions of the chapter. So, the seed contains both the ignorance of Śikhidhvaja and Cūḍālā's growing mastery of Yogic Flying, and also the mechanics whereby the ignorant superficial perception of the people in society can be raised to higher and higher levels by harnessing the infinite organizing power of natural law through group practice of Yogic Flying. Once again, the first verse of the chapter contains the total knowledge of the whole chapter in seed form.

In the perfection of expression of the first verse of this extraordinary chapter, the sage Vasishtha builds a bridge between the states of ignorance and enlightenment, and lights up the path for everyone in ignorance to rise to full enlightenment.

Endnotes

1 Egenes, Thomas, tr., *Maharishi Patañjali Yoga Sūtra*, 1st World Publishing: 2010, Fairfield, IA, pp. 75-77.

2 Maharishi Mahesh Yogi describes the eternal structure of knowledge of Veda and Vedic Literature: "Each aspect of Vedic Literature expresses a specific quality of pure intelligence. Each aspect of Vedic Literature, from beginning to end, expresses the full range of a specific quality, from its infinite value to its point value—from its holistic value to its progressively quantified values in orderly sequence. ... For any structure to be immortal, it must be inexhaustible; for any structure to be inexhaustible, it must be self-referral, which means it must refer to its source, it must refer to itself, it must be in a circular form. ... The obvious conclusion is that the structure of Veda is in the *Maṇḍala* form, and each structure of the Vedic Literature (being the structuring dynamics of Veda) is in a *Maṇḍala* form—we call it a self-referral loop. Being in a circular form, a *Maṇḍala* form, each aspect of the Vedic Literature breathes immortality, eternity." Maharishi Mahesh Yogi, *Maharishi Vedic University Introduction*, Maharishi Vedic University Press: Holland, 1994, pp.74-76

3 "The seed of all knowledge, अ (A), develops into the tree of knowledge, the Veda and Vedic Literature. Different branches of knowledge develop as different disciplines." Maharishi Mahesh Yogi, *Maharishi Vedic University Introduction*, Maharishi Vedic University Press: Holland, 1994, p. 32.

4 Nader, Tony, *Human physiology: Expression of Veda and Vedic Literature*, MUM Press: Fairfield, Iowa, 2014.

5 Hagelin, J.S., Restructuring physics from its foundation in light of Maharishi's Vedic Science, *Modern Science and Vedic Science* 3 (1989): 1, p.32.

6 See *Maharishi Vedic University Introduction*, quoted in footnote 2 above.

7 Maharishi Mahesh Yogi, *World Parliaments of Peace* series of lectures, 2006.

8 Orme-Johnson, D. W., & Fergusson, L. (2018). Global impact of the Maharishi Effect from 1974 to 2017: Theory and re-

search. *Journal of Maharishi Vedic Research Institute*, 8, 13-79.

9 Hatchard, G., & Cavanaugh, K. L. (2009). The peace and well being of nations: An analysis of improved quality of life and enhanced economic performance through the Maharishi Effect in New Zealand, Norway, USA, Cambodia, and Mozambique—A longitudinal, cross-country, panel regression analysis of the IMD Index of National Competitive Advantage. Hamilton, Ontario, Canada: Canadian Centers for Teaching Peace.

10 For a summary of the research on the Maharishi Effect, see *Journal of Maharishi Vedic Research Institute*, 8, 13-79.

11 Maharishi Mahesh Yogi with representatives of the Fairfield Radio and Print Media, "Press Conference on Transcendental Meditation and Religion, and Five Percent to Perpetuate the Ideal Society," October 2, 1975, 40 min. videotape, Maharishi International University and WPEC.

12 Ibid.

13 Ibid.

14 Travis F.T., (1991). Eyes open and TM EEG patterns after one and after eight years of TM practice. *Psychophysiology*, 28 (3a):S58.

15 Op.cit., *Journal of Maharishi Vedic Research Institute*, 8, pp. 38-41.

16 Ibid., pp. 40-41, also Fergusson, L. 2016, The impact of Maharishi Vedic University on Cambodian economic and social indicators from 1980 to 2015. *Journal of Maharishi Vedic Research Institute*, 2, 77-135.

17 Orme-Johnson, D. W., Alexander, C. N., Davies, J. L., Chandler, H. M., & Larimore, W. E. (1988). International peace project in the Middle East: The effect of the Maharishi Technology of the Unified Field. *Journal of Conflict Resolution*, 32(4), 776-812.

18 Maharishi Mahesh Yogi, *Maharishi's Absolute Theory of Government: Automation in Administration*, Age of Enlightenment Publications: India, 1995, pp. 56-59, etc.

19 Maharishi explains, "My Vedic Science, being the science of unity and diversity at the same time, is the science of everything. It is the science of singularity, the science of self-referral subjectiv-

ity, and also it is the science of objectivity, which is nothing other than the expression of subjectivity; at the same time it is the science of transformation, it is the science of the self-referral dynamics of creation. It is the science of eternal silence coexisting with eternal dynamism at the basis of creation. ... "My Vedic Science is the holistic science that unfolds the total reality and offers all possibilities. It is science and technology at the same time. It is the science of supreme order. It is a perfect science." Maharishi Mahesh Yogi, *Maharishi Vedic University Introduction*, Maharishi Vedic University Press: Holland, 1994, pp. 157-159.

20 Orme-Johnson D.W., Haynes C.T., EEG phase coherence, pure consciousness, creativity, and TM-Sidhi experiences. *International Journal of Neuroscience* 1981 13: 211-217.

21 Nader, Tony, *Human physiology: Expression of Veda and Vedic Literature*, p. 77.

22 Dillbeck, M. C., Landrith, G. S., & Orme-Johnson, D. W. (1981). The Transcendental Meditation program and crime rate change in a sample of forty-eight cities. *Journal of Crime and Justice*, 4, 25-45.

23 Orme-Johnson, D. W., Dillbeck, M. C., & Alexander, C. N. (2003). Preventing terrorism and international conflict: Effects of large assemblies of participants in the Transcendental Meditation and TM-Sidhi programs. *Journal of Offender Rehabilitation*, 36(1-4), 282-302.

24 Dillbeck, M. C., Foss, A, & Zimmerman, W. (1989). Maharishi's global ideal society campaign: Improved quality of life in Rhode Island through the Transcendental Meditation and TM-Sidhi program. In R. Chalmers, G. Clements, H. Schenkluhn, & M. Weinless (Eds.), *Scientific research on Maharishi's Transcendental Meditation and TM-Sidhi programme: Collected papers, volume 4*, (pp. 2521-2531). The Netherlands: Maharishi Vedic University Press.

25 Ibid., p. 2530.

Chapter 5: First Stage of Yogic Flying

Section 1: The Constitution of the Universe and the individual life-force

Verse 1:

वसिष्ठ उवाच
एतत्पञ्चकबीजं तु कुण्डलिन्यां तदन्तरे
प्राणमारुतरूपेण तस्यां स्फुरति सर्वदा १

1. This formula for global administration through natural law is structured in the Constitution of the Universe that is the inner nature of unbounded awareness.

It is the most delicate impulse of life: By means of the reverberation of the sound of the Constitution of the Universe in the unbounded Being, the form of the sūtra bursts forth, bestowing all good everywhere.

> In the previous chapter, *Rām* asked Vasishtha why the masters of the Vedic tradition taught the technique of Yogic Flying at various times throughout the ages. Vasishtha's answer was that the Field Effect of the practice of Yogic Flying (called the Maharishi Effect in our age,) was so powerful, that the Masters were able to use the technology of Yogic Flying in groups in order to administer the collective consciousness of the whole world and create an ideal society. In describing the mechanics of the practice, Vasishtha noted that Mother Divine, the embodiment of the total knowledge of the Constitution of the Universe, enters the body in one flash at the moment of liftoff. This phenomenon of the instantaneous and complete transformation of consciousness, creating a flash of total natural law permeating the entire physiology

and radiating into the environment—bestowing all good everywhere—is so remarkable, that Vasishtha now departs from the story of Cūḍālā and Śikhidhvaja, and devotes an entire chapter to the liftoff.

The liftoff that is being described is the result, or manifestation of the fruit of the practice of *Saṁyama* in the practice of Siddhis as advocated by Patañjali. Even the novice practitioner of the practice of Yogic Flying, who begins the practice after only a few months of practice of effortless transcending—learning to experience Samādhi which is the prerequisite to the experience of Siddhis—finds that his body lifts up into the air spontaneously in small hops during his practice of flying. This liftoff of the novice Yogic Flyer is already the fundamental building block, the central component in the "global administration through natural law." This remarkable achievement, that with only a few months preparation, the initiate experiences the functioning value of total natural law entering practical life, is the supreme gift of Patañjali, the great blessing of the Vedic tradition. The liftoff, even a small hop of a few inches in height, is infinity functioning in practical life.

If the Maharishi Effect, the field effect of consciousness generated by Yogic Flying, was only generated by adepts who had completely mastered gravity and gained the ability to roam through the air anywhere at will, then it might be difficult to find enough of such fully enlightened accomplished masters to successfully administer the society through automation in administration—through the generation of an indomitable influence of coherence and integration of life. But since this powerful effect of radiance of coherent, life-supporting influence for the whole society can be generated by the rank beginners of Yogic Flying, and that the whole world population can be effortlessly administered by some few thousand practitioners, this must be explored in depth. The highlight of the Yoga Vasishtha, the consolidated essence of all the Vedic knowledge, the most powerful weapon in the arsenal of kings of all times, that always bestows victory before war—this wisdom, the knowledge of the liftoff, Vasishtha is now laying before Rām.

Verse 2:

सान्तः कुण्डलिनीस्पन्दस्पर्शसंवित्कलामला
कलोक्ता कलनेनाशु कथिता चेतनेन चित् २

That is the goal of the practice: The individual consciousness in Samādhi contacting the eternal self-referral activity of the Constitution of the Universe, every part shines with the glory of the whole.

After the expression of one word has been completed, in the ensuing gap the following word is being calculated by the thinking mind referring back to its source in pure consciousness.

Now begins an analysis of the self-interacting dynamics of consciousness that give rise to the liftoff. Self-referral means referring back to the wholeness of the Self in the same way that the impulse of natural law in the text of the Veda refers back to the wholeness of natural law in the silence of the gap between every two words in the flow of the Vedic text.

Verse 3:

जीवनाज्जीवतां याता मननाच्च मनः स्थिता
संकल्पाच्चैव संकल्पा बोधाद्बुद्धिरिति स्मृता ३

Because referring back to the source at every moment gives vitality to all that has come before in terms of what has already been projected as thought by the mind, and all that is yet to follow: That which abides through all the changing values of expression is [called] the mind.

That functioning aspect of intelligence which organizes every step of progress in terms of the initial resolution and only that resolution, is called intellect, because it is awake to the intentions at every stage, being governed by the memory.

> Here Vasishtha defines mind and intellect in terms of the functioning value of intelligence in Self-referral consciousness.

Verse 4:

अहंकारात्मतां याता सैषा पुर्यष्टकाभिधा
स्थिता कुण्डलिनी देहे जीवशक्तिरनुत्तमा ४

The individual ego is that aspect of universal intelligence, *Ātmā*, that is awake to all that has come before, with regard to this particular physical nervous system made up of the eight elements of *Prakṛti* (mind, intellect, ego and earth, water, fire, air and space).

The individual ego abides as the Constitution of the Universe in the body: It is the individual life-force, the supreme expression of total natural law, the most precious gift of the Creator.

> More delicate than the mind, and still more delicate than the intellect, is the individual ego. The individual ego is the administrator of the life of the body, the representative of supreme intelligence that is capable of putting total natural law to function. The "I" that is awake to all that has come before for this particular nervous system, is in principle the functioning value of the Constitution of the Universe in the body. This potential, this force for life, is the precious gift of the Creator. This life-force is now being analyzed.

Verse 5:

अपानतामुपागत्य सततं प्रवहत्यधः
समाना नाभिमध्यस्था उदानाख्योपरि स्थिता ५

[The life-force] taking the form of the *Apāna* breath, always flows downwards; [becoming the] *Samāna* breath it is established in the middle of the navel; the breath that is named *Udāna* is established in the upward direction.

The life-force, the individual ego, takes the form of different breaths in the body.

Verse 6:

अधस्त्वपानरूपैव मध्ये सौम्यैव सर्वदा
पुष्टाप्युदानरूपैव पुंसः स्वस्थैव तिष्ठति ६

Whatever is seen to move downwards, that is governed by the *Apāna* breath; the breath centered in the middle of the navel carries nourishing life-giving *Soma* everywhere in the body; the *Udāna* breath is the visible manifestation of the soul; perfect health—the establishment of the self—stands on the basis of these three alone.

Svastha, established Self, is the expression for perfect health in Sanskrit. Here Vasishtha explains that perfect health depends on the balanced functioning of the three constituents of *Prāṇa*, namely *Apāṇa*, the downward breath, the *Samāna* breath that nourishes the whole body, and the *Udāṇa* breath, the upward moving breath.

Vasishtha first explained what we mean by "ego," or "self," as distinct from the grosser functions of consciousness, intellect and mind. Now he analyzes the administration of the physiology by the ego in terms of maintaining balance of these three vital airs. This is going to give us a clear understanding of the physiological difference between Self-referral and object referral styles of functioning, and thereby clarify what it means to refer to "the Constitution of the Universe" in the body.

Verse 7:

सर्वयत्नमधो याति यदि यत्नान्न धार्यते
तत्पुमान्मृतिमायाति तया निर्गतया बलात् ७

Every effort, every conscious act of individual inception moves the breath in the downward direction; [the balance of perfect health] is not maintained through conscious effort.

That soul or *Puruṣa* is in the process of dying by that effort; the soul escapes from that process of dying through strength (*Bala*) [which accomplishes desires without effort].

Effort is a function of the ego, but every conscious act of effort creates imbalance in the physiology by increasing the *Apāna* breath. In that moment of effort, perfect health is lost, and all manner of imbalances leading to diseases of all kinds and aging now enter life.

Verse 8:

समतैवोर्ध्वमायाति यदि युक्त्या न धार्यते
तत्पुमान्मृतिमायाति तया निर्गतया बलात् ८

Equanimity only brings about the upward move of the breath; if there is artifice or expedient of any kind, the upward breath is not maintained.

That soul or *Puruṣa* is in the process of dying by that artifice or expedient; the soul escapes from that process of dying through strength (*Bala*) [which accomplishes desires without effort].

> The upward *Udāṇa* breath is not driven upward by individual effort. There is nothing that can be artificially manipulated in order to drive the breath in the upward direction. The upward breath is completely spontaneous and automatic. It is called the "visible manifestation of the soul," just because the administrator of total intelligence in the physiology is visible there, and any individual inception, any individual effort counteracts and hides this manifestation of the inner soul. That aspect of the ego which is in contact with the infinite intelligence of total natural law is not accessible by effort. It follows that any technology of consciousness which involves effort of any kind—focus, concentration, manipulation of the thinking process, or whatever—will hide the "visible manifestation of the soul," and not be successful in raising the level of consciousness. The liftoff in the practice of Yogic Flying, on the other hand, is completely spontaneous and automatic, it is not brought about through effort.

Verse 9:

सर्वथात्मनि तिष्ठेच्चेत्त्यक्त्वोर्ध्वाधो गमागमौ
तज्जन्तोर्हीयते व्याधिरन्तर्मारुतरोधतः ९

If, through every experience, through all the changing states of consciousness, he remains established in the Self, having abandoned the upward and downward movement of breath, he acts in the world without acting, [remaining uninvolved in the action].

That [is the normal state of human life, the state of perfect health]; the disease of every living being is set in motion through the vitiation and imbalance of the breaths within the body [brought about through effort and individual inception].

> Here Vasishtha explicitly connects the dots between the experience of the established self, "*Svastha*," which is experienced as the uninvolved witness of all activity in the state of Cosmic Consciousness, and the genesis of all disease through the vitiation of the breaths in the body brought about by individual effort and individual inception of action. Perfect health and Self-realization are one and the same thing.

Section 2: The cure of all diseases through the knowledge of the Self

Verse 10:

सामान्यनाडीवैधुर्यात्सामान्यव्याधिसंभवः
प्रधाननाडीवैधुर्यात्प्रधानव्याधिसंभवः १०

Through the absence of balanced functioning of the *Nāḍīs* or channels in the body, the plague of all manner of diseases comes into being.

Through the absence of the most essential thing for health, [the balanced functioning of] the *Nāḍīs*, the most important factor for the creation of every disease, [the imbalanced function of the *Nāḍīs*] originates.

> Vasishtha places the ultimate responsibility for health and disease at the feet of the individual ego, which through effort and individual inception—object-referral—creates imbalance and disease in the physiology, and through effortlessly referring back to total natural law, creates balance and perfect health. In the textbooks of Āyurveda, Vedic Medicine, this same phenomenon is called *Prajñāparādha*, (loosely translated as "mistaken intellect,") which Caraka, the foremost proponent of Āyurveda, says is the cause of all diseases.
>
> The spontaneous liftoff in Yogic Flying is a powerful infusion of balance and perfect health that instantaneously influences every cell in the body. That which brings the unbounded Self into the field of activity, that which is making the infinite functional, is bringing perfect health into the physiology.

Verse 11:

श्रीराम उवाच
किंविनाशाः किमुत्पादाः शरीरेऽस्मिन्मुनीश्वर
आधयो व्याधयश्चैव यथावत्कथयाशु मे ११

Śrī Rām said:

What are the factors which destroy life, what are the factors which bring about life in this body, O Ruler of Sages?

Explain to me in detail the whole story of mental illnesses and physical diseases.

> Now, through verse 42, there is a comprehensive survey of the entire field of Vedic medicine. The purpose of this exposition coming at this point is to fill in the details of the knowledge given in the last two verses, that all diseases are caused by mistaken intellect and conversely all diseases can be eliminated and perfect health established by expanding consciousness through Transcendental Meditation and Yogic Flying.

Verse 12:

वसिष्ठ उवाच
आधयो व्याधयश्चैव द्वयं दुःखस्य कारणम्
तन्निवृत्तिः सुखं विद्यात्तत्क्षयो मोक्ष उच्यते १२

Vasishtha said:

Mental illnesses and physical diseases are both the cause of suffering.

The cure of these disorders through knowledge gives happiness; the mastery over these disorders is said to give enlightenment.

> "*Kha*," is a Sanskrit word for "space." Suffering is said to be a "bad space," *Duḥ-kha*, and happiness is a "good space," *Su-kham*. The absence of disease is a state of happiness and bliss, according to Suśruta, author of one of the three main textbooks of Āyurveda. In the state of perfect health and freedom from disease, the senses, mind, intellect and ego all experience bliss. The cure of disease gives happiness, not a neutral state. The path to gaining enlightenment is even described in Garuḍa Purāṇa as a path of gaining mastery over all diseases one by one. Vasishtha says there is no difference between the quest for perfect health, and the search for enlightenment.

Verse 13:

मिथः कदाचिज्जायेते कदाचित्सममेव च
पर्यायेण कदाचिच्च आधिव्याधी शरीरके १३

When combating illness sometimes the disease is overcome, sometimes balance is maintained without succumbing to the disease;

Sometimes, going through the entire course of mental and physical symptoms of the disease, the body dies.

Verse 14:

देहदुःखं विदुर्व्याधिमाध्याख्यं वासनामयम्
मौर्ख्यमूले हि ते विद्यात्तत्त्वज्ञाने परिक्षयः १४

Whatever the kind of suffering that the body is undergoing, the wise maintain that the physical disease is ultimately mental, made of the impressions of past experience.

In every case, the root of disease is the folly or mistake of the past, hence all diseases can be eliminated through the application of knowledge [to correct the mistake], when there is true insight into the principles and science [of correcting the mistaken intellect].

> The folly or mistake of the past, is what is described in Āyurveda as *Prajñāparādha*, "mistaken intellect." There is favoring of individual inception and individual effort over cosmic intelligence and the spontaneous functioning of total natural law. There is loss of wholeness of awareness, what is called Self-referral consciousness,

in favor of narrow boundaries and object-referral consciousness. This one mistake is the cause of all disease.

Verse 15:

अतत्त्वज्ञानवशतः स्वेन्द्रियाक्रमणं विना
हृदि तानवमुत्सृज्य रागद्वेषेष्वनारतम् १५

Not having access to the total knowledge of the Constitution of the Universe, not being able to follow the spontaneous sequential order of the wholeness of the Self,

Some very small impulse in the heart becoming disconnected from the wholeness grows into passionate attractions and aversions that are not in accord with total natural law.

Vasishtha explains how the mistaken intellect or "folly" begins: An impulse in the heart grows into passionate desires and aversions that are unconnected with the wholeness of the Self. Then the infinite organizing power of total natural law is not available to bring fulfillment to the desire. This inevitably leads to suffering.

Verse 16:

इदं प्राप्तमिदं नेति जाड्याद्वा घनमोहदाः
आधयः संप्रवर्तन्ते वर्षासु मिहिका इव १६

This situation coming to pass is a disaster for life: Indeed, acting from stupidity only produces dense ignorance and illusion,

[Such that] The deluded and mistaken mind-sets are put in motion to perform action when action is not suitable, like snow falling in the rainy seasons.

> Action unconnected with the whole is analogous to snow falling in the rainy season. The deluded and mistaken mind, captured by some passing impulse of attraction in the heart, is a disaster for life.

Verse 17:

भृशं स्फुरन्तीष्विच्छासु मौर्ख्ये चेतस्यनिर्जिते
दुरन्नाभ्यवहारेण दुर्देशाक्रमणेन च १७

When the consciousness is deluded they struggle vehemently to fulfill their desired goals and aspirations without success,

[Confounded] By eating wrong food, and by being in wrong places at wrong times,

Verse 18:

दुष्कालव्यवहारेण दुष्क्रियास्फुरणेन च
दुर्जनासङ्गदोषेण दुर्भावोद्भावनेन च १८

By taking food at the wrong time, and by undertaking wrong actions,

By association with wrong people, and by the springing up of wrong thoughts.

Verse 19:

क्षीणत्वाद्वा प्रपूर्णत्वान्नाडीनां रन्ध्रसंततौ
प्राणे विधुरतां याते काये तु विकलीकृते १९

Or by becoming exhausted before the desire is fulfilled, the emptiness and failures of the individual streams of desire become a continuum [of suffering, unfulfilled life].

When the animating principle of mind, *Prāṇa*, moves about in the body suffering from want, it imparts injury to the body.

> Through chasing after desires that are unconnected with the wholeness of life, life becomes a struggle. The struggle is compounded by layer after layer of violation of natural law, for example eating wrong food, being in wrong places at wrong times, taking food at the wrong time, doing actions that are forbidden by the scriptures, associating with wrong people, and having wrong, life-damaging thoughts. Through all these life-damaging influences, life becomes a continuum of struggle, suffering and unfulfilled life.

In the absence of fulfillment of desire, the *Prāṇa* that moves about in the body, animating all activities of the mind feels the pressure of this lack, and suffering from that lack, in frustration, becomes crude and irregular and imparts injury to the body.

Verse 20:

दौस्स्थत्यकारणं दोषाद्व्याधिर्देहे प्रवर्तते
नद्याः प्रावृग्निदाघाभ्यामिवाकारविपर्ययः २०

The cause [of disease] is the corruption of the integrity of consciousness; due to [that] impurity of consciousness, the disease in the body progresses.

Like the rivers transforming from fullness in the wet season to emptiness in the hot summer season, the letter "A," [the seed of total knowledge representing totally pure consciousness, complete Veda,] experiences a calamitous change in fortune [becoming associated with emptiness and negation—instead of Veda unfolding in sequential order from "A,"] and the disease progresses.

The *Prāṇa*, having become crude, loses its connection to the intelligence of total natural law, the fundamental intelligence of the body. Having lost its connection to the inherent sequential unfoldment of natural law, by which life naturally unfolds in cycles of knowledge, action, achievement and fulfillment, the field of intelligence which should be the seat of normal functioning, becomes like a void, a treasure hidden from view and completely unknown. In the field of speech, this process of *Prāṇa* forgetting its basis in the sequential unfoldment of Veda, is expressed in a transformation of the meaning of the syllable "A." "A" is the first expression of the Veda, which sequentially and systematically unfolds the total knowledge of Veda from within itself. That systematic unfoldment means that "A" in the Veda is ever associated with fullness of knowledge, moving and giving rise to greater and greater waves of achievement and fulfillment: This is the nature of "A" unfolding the totality of natural law from within itself. However, when the *Prāṇa* becomes crude, then losing connection to the blueprint of natural law, speech connects "A" with the absence of the object, with the negation of the object, rather than the fullness of it—a calamitous change in fortune. Because speech must be based on knowledge to be effective, in the absence of connection with the totality of knowledge, speech becomes weak, ineffective, and incompetent to orchestrate the fulfillment of desires. The integrity of consciousness becomes progressively weaker, and correspondingly the disease progresses.

Verse 21:

प्राक्तनी चैहिकी वापि शुभा वाप्यशुभा मतिः
यैवाधिका सैव तथा तस्मिन्योजयति क्रमे २१

Following the sequence according to what came before or (conversely) localized in the narrow boundaries of the here and now, the framework of thinking that guides thought and action becomes either righteous or unrighteous.

Whichever of the two gains the upper hand, that one guides life exclusively, putting to practice in the field of activity, that mode of action over which it holds sway.

Verse 22:

आधयो व्याधयश्चैवं जायन्ते भूतपञ्चके
कथं शृणु विनश्यन्ति राघवाणां कुलोद्वह २२

Mental delusions and physical diseases in this way prevail over the physical body made of these five elements.

Listen to the story of how bodies perish, O Best of the offspring of the family of the Raghus.

Verse 23:

द्विविधो व्याधिरस्तीह सामान्यः सार एव च
व्यवहारस्तु सामान्यः सारो जन्ममयः स्मृतः २३

There are two kinds of disease occurring in the world, common, and genetic.

Communicable diseases are common, affecting everyone; genetic diseases are determined at birth as the inherited memory [stored in the DNA].

Verse 24:

प्राप्तेनाभिमतेनैव नश्यन्ति व्यावहारिकाः
आधिक्षयेणाधिभवाः क्षीयन्ते व्याधयोऽप्यलम् २४

The infectious agents of the communicable diseases destroy the body by reaching and infecting target cells or organs in the body.

By the diminution of balance of mind, the mental illnesses come into being; they weaken and destroy the body, like physical diseases, if strong enough.

Verse 25:

आत्मज्ञानं विना सारो नाधिर्नश्यति राघव
भूयो रज्ज्ववबोधेन रज्जुसर्पो हि नश्यति २५

Being without the knowledge of the *Ātmā* is not a genetic disease although seeming to be so [since everyone is born without the knowledge of *Ātmā*]; [it is] the mental imbalance caused by lack of knowledge of the Self [that] destroys the body [through disease, aging and accumulation of stress, etc.], O Rāghava.

By the false perception of the string as a snake, the string indeed becomes a snake and destroys the perceiver.

> There are mental diseases, and physical diseases. The physical diseases are of two kinds, innate disease, which we call genetic diseases, and communicable diseases which affect everyone. The communicable diseases are carried by infectious agents which target and infect specific cells or organs in the body.
>
> Mental diseases come into being by loss of balance of mind. They weaken and destroy the body as surely as do the physical diseases.
>
> Having classified all the diseases in this way, Vasishtha now asks an interesting question: Every human being is born in ignorance, without the knowledge of *Ātmā*. Can it then be said that being without the knowledge of *Ātmā* is an inborn, inherited condition? Vasishtha says no, the lack of knowledge of *Ātmā* is not a disease. All diseases are caused by the abuse of the nervous system: That means that the indweller of the nervous system is

not using the machinery in the manner for which it was originally designed. There is no inherent fault in the machinery.

Vasishtha refers back to the traditional story of the snake and the string. A string is lying on the floor. Due to lack of light, someone sees the string and thinks that it is a snake. Scared of the snake and its great destructive power, he runs about, yelling, "Snake," "snake." Completely agitated, full of anxiety, heart pounding from fear, and short of breath, he is in a state of excitement that is completely of his own making—there is no snake. Like that, the human nervous system is like the string. It has the total knowledge of natural law inherent in it, it is not programmed for failure. It is the wrong perception, the abuse of the human nervous system which causes suffering. The absence of the knowledge of the Self is not an inherited disease. Every single human being on earth can gain the knowledge of the Self and live life in affluence and peace, free from all problems, free from all disease. Vasishtha summarizes this role of genetics in bringing about disease in the next verse.

Verse 26:

आधिव्याधिविलासानां राम साराधिसंक्षयः
सर्वेषां मूलहा प्रावृरानदीव तटवीरुधाम् २६

The aging, disease, debilitation and eventual mortality of the body expressed by the play and display of innumerable diseases and mental illnesses, O Rāma, is programmed in the genetic code as the innate response to mental imbalance due to lack of knowledge of the Self.

For every disease, the root cause of destruction is the lack of knowledge of the total potential of natural law in the Self, like plants on the shore [are destroyed] by rivers in the rainy season.

> Vasishtha is saying that all diseases—physical, mental, genetic and communicable, as well as the phenomenon of aging—are programmed into the genetic code as innate responses to the mistaken intellect—the intellectual "folly," brought about by lack of knowledge of the Self.

Verse 27:

अनाधिजा व्याधयस्तु द्रव्यमन्त्रशुभक्रमैः
चिकित्सकादिशास्त्रोक्तैर्नश्यन्त्यन्यैरिहाथवा २७

Suitable medicines administered at proper times and correct use of mantras bring balance to the imbalanced states of mind and cure the diseases.

By transcending and experiencing unbounded awareness, and by the prescriptions of the ancient scriptures of internal medicine, Āyurveda, according to the situation and circumstances, the diseases are cured; otherwise they continue [to destroy the body].

Verse 28:

स्नानमन्त्रौषधोपाया वक्तुश्चाधिगतानि च
त्वया चिकित्साशास्त्राणि किमन्यदुपदिश्यते २८

The doctor prescribes bathing, using a mantra, herbs, and other expedients, and the mental imbalances are eliminated.

With the help of the physician, the cure is brought about according to the textbooks of internal medicine; the patient is also to be taught how to transcend and gain unbounded awareness [in order to bring about a cure on his own, without the help of a physician].

> Doctors have a role in restoring balance to the system when the body is ravaged by disease, but transcending and gaining unbounded awareness—repairing the mistake of the intellect—and thereby restoring the body's

connection to the blueprint of total natural law at its basis, should also be undertaken, to prevent the eruption of new diseases.

Verse 29:

श्रीराम उवाच
आधेः कथं भवेद्व्याधिः कथं च स विनश्यति
द्रव्यादितरया युक्त्या मन्त्रपुण्यादिरूपया २९

Śrī Rāma said:

How does a physical disease develop from a mental imbalance? How is the mental imbalance destroyed?

Which are the medicines and other expedients, which combined with meditation to gain unbounded awareness, and a pure virtuous lifestyle will effectively manifest a cure of the affliction?

Verse 30:

वसिष्ठ उवाच
चित्ते विधुरिते देहः संक्षोभमनुयात्यलम्
तथाहि रुषितो जन्तुरग्रमेव न पश्यति ३०

Vasishtha said:

When the mind is suffering and unfulfilled, the body, following the mind becomes agitated to the same degree.

Accordingly, the body which is the offspring of the mind, is injured, and in extreme cases does not see.

Now Vasishtha begins to describe the pathogenesis of disease.

Verse 31:

अनवेक्ष्य पुरो मार्गममार्गमनुधावति
प्रकृतं मार्गमुत्सृज्य शरार्तो हरिणो यथा ३१

Not attending to the way forward or lack of a way forward, he flows from one experience to the next.

Having abandoned the natural course of right action, he moves about like a deer struck by arrows of pain, at every turn.

Verse 32:

संक्षोभात्साम्यमुत्सृज्य वहन्ति प्राणवायवः
देहे गजप्रविष्टेन पयांसीव सरित्तटे ३२

Because of the constant agitation, the balance of mind is lost, and the ups and downs of experience from moment to moment influence the various *Prāṇas* or vital airs.

By virtue of entering into the profusion of sensory experiences in the body, the vital spirits (*Prāṇas*) move about like [the churning rapids of] a river flowing down a steep slope.

Verse 33:

असमं वहति प्राणे नाड्यो यान्ति विसंस्थितिम्
असम्यक्संस्थिते भूपे यथा वर्णाश्रमक्रमाः ३३

When there is lack of balance and equilibrium guiding the *Prāṇa*, the arteries and veins and channels of all kinds function irregularly.

In the absence of balance, the channels lose their coordination with one another, just as the natural order of the four castes falls away in the absence of the king.

Verse 34:

काश्चिन्नाड्यः प्रपूर्णत्वं यान्ति काश्चिच्च रिक्तताम्
प्राणा विधुरिते देहे सर्वतः सरितो यथा ३४

Some *Nāḍīs* become filled up, and some are emptied.

The *Prāṇa*s in the body are unable to accomplish their functions effectively as they are completely flooded like a river that has overflowed its banks.

Verse 35:

कुजीर्णत्वमजीर्णत्वमतिजीर्णत्वमेव वा
दोषायैव प्रयात्यन्नं प्राणसंचारदुष्क्रमात् ३५

Loss of full mental and physical capacity due to aging [through loss of memory and mental acuity, loss of full joint motility, loss of calcium, etc.], or loss of connection with the blueprint of natural law in the body [leading to cancer and other illnesses signaling the breakdown of innate purificatory processes], or intense degenerative diseases [such as Alzheimer's, Parkinson's, etc.][result from the *Prāṇa*s being unable to accomplish their functions due to clogged *Shrotasas*].

Through incoherence in the movement of *Prāṇa* through the body, the movement of food through the body results in production of impurities (*Doṣas*) [instead of bringing nourishment to the body].

Verse 36:

यथा काष्ठानि नयति प्राचीदेशं सरिद्रयः
तथान्नानि नयत्यन्तः प्राणवातः स्वमाश्रयम् ३६

As impetuous rapid flow of a river organizes the clearing of logs obstructing the course of the waters along the riverbed,

In the same way, the *Prāṇavāta* organizes the clearing of the particles of food in the channels obstructing the flow of nourishment to the self.

Verse 37:

यान्यन्नानि निरोधेन तिष्ठन्त्यन्तः शरीरके
तान्येव व्याधितां यान्ति परिणामस्वभावतः ३७

Which particles of undigested food being obstructed in their course through the channels, remain [as impurities] in the physiology.

Undergoing transformation in their internal composition and structure, they become diseased.

> Particles of undigested food are called "*Āma*," in Āyurveda. *Āma*, together with *Doṣa* (impurities) and *Dhātu* (the tissues) combine to form the diseased tissue.

Verse 38:

एवमाधेर्भवेद्व्याधिस्तस्याभावाच्च नश्यति
यथा मन्त्रैर्विनश्यन्ति व्याधयस्तत्क्रमं शृणु ३८

In this way, from mental imbalance the disease arises, and from the propagation of the disease, the individual perishes.

As [diseases arise] in this way by virtue of the actions of the mind, those actions of the mind being subsequently reversed, the diseases are destroyed: Listen [I will explain it to you].

> This is a fundamental principle which should not be overlooked: Since all diseases are caused by this one basic cause, the mistake of the intellect, by reversing that mistake, by bringing the awareness to wholeness of unbounded awareness—the experience of what is called

Samādhi, in the field of Yoga—the cause of the illness is removed, and the disease disappears.

Verse 39:

यथा विरेकं कुर्वन्ति हरीतक्यः स्वभावतः
भावनावशतः कार्यं तथा यरलवादयः ३९

As the pills of *Harītakī* by their own nature bring about purgation,

In the same way, the cure of disease can be brought about through the influence of technologies of consciousness, as surely as the alphabets starting with ya, ra, la and va, [will end up in "ha," complete silence, complete end or destruction of sound].

Verse 40:

शुद्धया पुण्यया साधो क्रियया साधुसेवया
मनः प्रयाति नैर्मल्यं निकषेणेव काञ्चनम् ४०

By purification, by performing right virtuous action, by service to holy people, [and by the] fulfillment gained by successful action,

The mind progresses toward stainless purity, by rubbing in gold.

Verse 41:

आनन्दो वर्धते देहे शुद्धे चेतसि राघव
पूर्णेन्दावुदिते ह्यत्र नैर्मल्यं भुवने यथा ४१

Bliss increases in the body when there is purity of consciousness, O Rāghava.

When by this regular practice of transcending the mind has expanded to the fullness of unbounded awareness, then there are no stresses remaining in the nervous system.

Verse 42:

सत्वशुद्ध्या वहन्त्येते क्रमेण प्राणवायवः
जरयन्ति तथान्नानि व्याधिस्तेन विनश्यति ४२

By purifying consciousness, these channels convey the vital airs (*Prāṇavāyus*) in proper order and sequence.

Functioning in proper balance, the vital airs digest and eliminate the particles of undigested food in the body, and by that process the disease is destroyed.

Section 3: Perfect Health through Yogic Flying

Verse 43:

आधिव्याध्योरिति प्रोक्तौ नाशोत्पत्तिक्रमौ त्वयि
कुण्डलिन्याः कथायोगादधुना प्रकृतं शृणु ४३

Thus, the systematic procedures applicable to you and to all human beings for destroying both physical disease and mental imbalance at their root are taught.

Now listen to the story of how the normal state of perfect health is gained by harnessing the innate healing power of the total constitution of the universe in the body through Yogic practices.

> Thus the systematic procedures for eliminating all physical and mental diseases at their root are taught: The application of the technologies of consciousness, together with the specified treatments of Āyurveda, is enough to put an end to all diseases, because all diseases come up from the same cause, lack of knowledge of the Self. This principle of eliminating disease by removing the root cause of all diseases, is eternally valid, for all men in all places in all times.
>
> The theme of this chapter, set in the first verse, is the experience of the liftoff during Yogic Flying. This verse summarizes Section 2 on health and disease, and begins Section 3, applying the technologies of consciousness, specifically Yogic Flying to create perfect health. It explains that the total knowledge of medicine, the total knowledge of all diseases and their cures, the total knowledge of perfect health is contained in the liftoff.

Yogic Flying is the means to harness the innate healing power of the Total Constitution of the Universe in the body. This knowledge and training should be part of every medical college in the world: Twice daily accessing the total Constitution of the Universe should be the practice of every doctor and health practitioner, so that the total knowledge of perfect health predominates in every isolated avenue of health care.

Research shows that this approach of using Yogic Flying as one modality in an overall theme of prevention through Maharishi Ayurveda is extremely fruitful. Results of one study based on insurance company records is summarized in the chart below.[1]

Decreased Hospitalization In All Disease Categories

Through Maharishi Ayurveda,
Including Yogic Flying

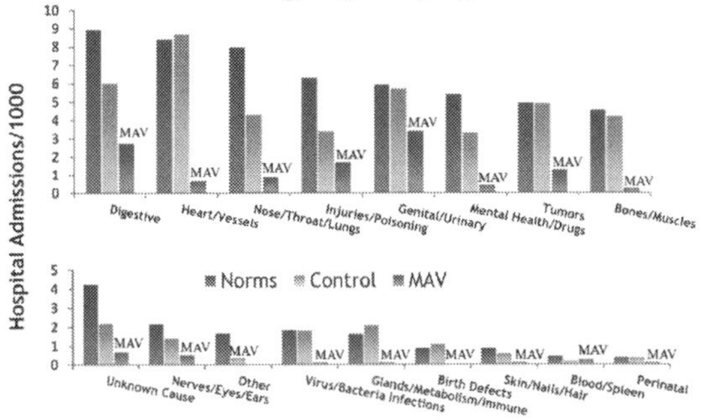

Reference: Orme-Johnson, D.W. and R.E. Herron, An innovative approach to reducing medical care utilization and expenditures. *The American Journal of Managed Care*, 1997. 3(1): p. 135-144.

Verse 44:

पुर्यष्टकपराख्यस्य जीवस्य प्राणनामिकाम्
विद्धि कुण्डलिनीमन्तरामोदस्येव मञ्जरीम् ४४

Prāṇa is the name of that quality of the soul said to be beyond the eight *Prakṛtis* that make up the body.

Know that delicate undulation of infinite bliss to be the Constitution of the Universe within, [Veda] arranged in perfect sequential order like a cluster of [lotus] blossoms.

> *Prāṇa* is the sequential flow of intelligence through all the syllables and gaps of the Veda, the process of unfolding the blueprint of total natural law. Here Mother Divine, as the complete embodiment of all the impulses of the Veda, is referred to as "*Kuṇḍalinī*." She is the lively Constitution of the Universe in the body.

Verse 45:

तां यदा पूरकाभ्यासादापूर्य स्थीयते समम्
तदैति मैरवं स्थैर्यं कायस्यापीनता तथा ४५

When through the practice of transcending and gaining unbounded awareness, the mind gets completely identified with the unmanifest field of pure consciousness, that [same] Constitution of the Universe lies flat without undulations.

Then it is capable of moving the immovable mountain of the body up into the air, through the practice of Yogic Flying, in that way making the unmanifest consciousness functional.

> First, for the beginning practitioner of Transcendental Meditation, the experience of unbounded awareness is flat and motionless, awareness pure without any object of experience. This is the experience of what is called the Patañjali *Kaivalya*, a state of self-sufficiency, fullness and wholeness of life which is infinite bliss and unending fulfillment.
>
> The Patañjali *Kaivalya* becomes dynamic through the practice of Yogic Flying.
>
> The flat oneness of eternal Being starts to function at the moment of liftoff, where the power of the transcendent is harnessed to lift the body up into the air. This demonstrates the power of consciousness and brings the practitioner immediately to the goal of Yoga, expressed by the final words of Yoga Darśanam, *Citi-śaktir iti*, owning "the full power (Śakti) of the thinking mind (Citi)."

> The liftoff substantiates and validates the experience of the Patañjali *Kaivalya*. The liftoff thus contains the total knowledge of Patañjali's Yoga, combining in one practice all the benefits of each of the eight limbs of Yoga.

Verse 46:

यदा पूरकपूर्णान्तरायतप्राणमारुतम्
नीयते संविदेवोर्ध्वं सोढुं घर्मक्लमं श्रमम् ४६

When the experience of unbounded awareness gained through the process of transcending becomes mature, then there is the experience of the dynamism within the structure of wholeness, the very fine fabrics of activity of the movement of *Prāṇa*, [the vibration of the Constitution of the Universe].

One is led to the experience of a higher level of *Kaivalya*, (integrated self-sufficient consciousness) [in which] the weariness and exhaustion of the activity of the day, [which previously was opposed to the experience of Absolute Being] is [now] tolerated, accepted as an essential component of the experience of totality, [being the natural expression of the dynamism of the light of life].

> Here the Jaimini *Kaivalya* is being introduced, the *Kaivalya* which locates dynamism deep within the fabrics of silence of the Patañjali *Kaivalya*.

Verse 47:

सर्पीव त्वरितैवोर्ध्वं याति दण्डोपमां गता
नाडीः सर्वाः समादाय देहबद्धा लतोपमाः ४७

Like ghee is the essence of milk, the higher level *Kaivalya*, the celestial world of the angels, is the precious golden essence of the whole creation: The dynamism of the Absolute having entered into the finest level of creation, [that golden ghee-like essence] embodies the power of Total Natural Law, like a royal scepter symbolizes the power of the sovereignty of the king.

All the channels, collectively taking hold of everything in the physiology, are bound together in the body as the various cosmic counterparts of the planets (*Grahas*) [which grasp and own everything in the material universe].

> The supreme relative perception, the highest kind of perception that is possible in the relative field characterizes the Jaimini *Kaivalya*. The celestial world of the angels, located at the junction point between relative and absolute, comes to vision now. The beings in this field represent the organizing power responsible for administering the whole creation. Here the nature (*Prakṛti*) of the transcendental unmanifest Absolute (*Puruṣa*) is expressed as infinite dynamism at the finest level of creation.
>
> This verse begins the exposition of the cosmic counterparts in the human physiology. The saying is *Yathā piṇḍe tathā brahmāṇḍe*, as is the body, so is the universe. All the different aspects of the cosmos are located in parallel structures in the human physiology.

Verse 48:

तदा समस्तमेवेदमुत्प्लावयति देहकम्
नीरन्ध्रं पवनापूर्णं भस्त्रेवाम्बुततान्तरम् ४८

Then, in the state of the higher *Kaivalya*, all the parts that make up the wholeness of total Natural Law in this physical body are made to rise to the higher role of simultaneously representing the flow of intelligence in the body of the whole universe.

The intelligence conducting the activity through all the gaps and channels in the physiology is the breeze of the sequential progression of Total Natural Law in the Constitution of the Universe: The inner intelligence that drives the air through the lungs, or the water through the water-skin [or blood-vessels], is God, the Father, the flow of intelligence of total natural law in the universe.

> The gaps and channels in the physiology are the cosmic counterparts of the structures that make up the body of the universe. The intelligence that conducts activity through all the physiological structures is the same intelligence that conducts the activity of cosmic life.

Verse 49:

इत्यभ्यासविलासेन योगेन व्योमगामिना
योगिनः प्राप्नुवन्त्युच्चैर्दीना इन्द्रदशामिव ४९

It is this intimate correlation between the gaps and channels in the physiology, and their cosmic counterparts in the organization of total natural law in the universe that gets fully enlivened by the practice and sport of Yogic Flying.

Yogis are able to lift off and to fly to the degree they have enlivened within their own physiologies the celestial mechanics of the world of (Indra,) the Ruler of the Universe.

> The total knowledge of dynamism, the field of action explored for all its values in Jaimini's Karma Mīmāṁsā, requires a clear vision of the relationship between the individual human nervous system and the cosmic, celestial structure of the organizing power of natural law. The total knowledge of the cosmic counterparts in the human physiology, described as Ved and Vedic Literature in human physiology, and the knowledge of the celestial mechanics revealed in the science of Jyotiṣ, are all contained in the liftoff. Yogic Flying strengthens the connection between the individual and the cosmos, and enlivens every fiber of the physiology with the organizing power of the total natural law that gives rise to the whole creation. The complete knowledge of the Jaimini *Kaivalya*, expounded in Jaimini's Karma Mīmāṁsā, is fully available in the liftoff in Yogic Flying.

Verse 50:

ब्रह्मनाडीप्रवाहेण शक्तिः कुण्डलिनी यदा
बहिरूर्ध्वं कपाटस्य द्वादशाङ्गुलमूर्धनि ५०

When, by means of the continuous sequential dynamic flow of Natural Law through the channel of Brahman, the human nervous system, there is the full organizing power of natural law available, and the Constitution of the Universe has become legal:

[Then] There is the ability of the body to move upwards, into the air, taking flight by the mere impulse of thought.

Dvādaśāṅguli = 1 *Vitasti*, from the root *Taṅs*, to fly)

Both the silence of Patañjali and the dynamism of Jaimini are available in their fullness in the moment of liftoff in Yogic Flying. Through the full enlivenment of the togetherness of silence and dynamism, in the practice of Yogic Flying, the body gains the ability to take flight through the air by the mere impulse of thought. This is the demonstration of the attainment of the Vyāsa *Kaivalya*, the third and highest *Kaivalya*, which puts together in one holistic structure the other two states of *Kaivalya* of Patañjali and Jaimini.

Verse 51:

रेचकेन प्रयोगेण नाड्यन्तरनिरोधिना
मुहूर्तं स्थितिमाप्नोति तदा व्योमगदर्शनम् ५१

By removing all the obstacles and obstructions in the physiology by the application of the technologies of consciousness,

Then [the yogi] attains the ability to stay in the air without falling down in the same instant, demonstrating power over the force of gravity.

Perfection of the flying Siddhi is the demonstration of the mastery of the Vyāsa *Kaivalya*, Brahman put to practice, the Absolute captured in a drop.

The complete mastery of Yogic Flying is present in seed form in the liftoff together with the Mahāvākyas and the total knowledge of the Brahma Sūtras. The same Brahman, the same totality, that with practice physically demonstrates total mastery of the force of gravity, is already there, spontaneously and suddenly lifting the body of even the beginning Yogic Flyer into the air in short hops.

The three great *Kaivalyas*—the supreme teachings of the systems of Yoga, Karma Mīmāṁsā and Vedānta—are there in every liftoff in the practice of Yogic Flying. The infinite, immeasurable, inconceivable fulfillment of the supreme attainment of perfection of knowledge and experience in these three sciences that together characterize the highest reaches of human potential, steps onto the stage of human life in the overwhelming experience of total brain functioning at the moment of liftoff in the practice of Yogic Flying.

Section 4: Mastery of Yogic Flying is the demonstration of the attainment of Brahman

Verse 52:

श्रीराम उवाच
दर्शनं कीदृशं ब्रह्मन्नयनांशुगणं विना
अदिव्यानामिन्द्रियाणां तत्त्वमेवं कथं भवेत् ५२

Śrī Rām said:

How is it possible to have a vision of the degree of stabilization of Brahman consciousness, without seeing a multitude of points of validation?

How is it possible that the ultimate reality, Brahman, is made visible to the senses in this way without the development of supernormal abilities of refined perception?

Verse 53:

वसिष्ठ उवाच
न केचन महाबाहो भूचरेण नभस्वतः
अदिव्येनाश्रिता ज्ञानैर्दृश्यन्ते पुरुषेन्द्रियैः ५३

Vasishtha said:

Not just some small degree of Brahman, O Mighty-Armed, [is demonstrated] by moving about on earth, by travelling through the sky.

It is not accomplished by means of invoking the gods on the celestial level, [it demonstrates] the complete absorption in the oneness of the Self, combined with total knowledge of natural law: the masters of Yogic Flying perceive the infinite unbounded Self, *Puruṣa*, with the senses.

Verse 54:

विज्ञानाद्दूरसंस्थेन बुद्धिनेत्रेण राघव
दृश्यन्ते व्योमगाः सिद्धाः स्वप्नवत्स्वार्थदा अपि ५४

On the ground of objective, scientific knowledge, [where the object is perceived as different from the Self, there] the completely stabilized state of Brahman—[in which] the supreme discernment of the infinite value of the object of knowledge is perceived by the eye [in every object of perception]—is a long way off, O Rāghava.

Those Siddhas who move through the skies perceive the homogeneous wholeness of life which is even more than [the perception in unity consciousness where] every object [is] in terms of the infinite value of the Self.

Verse 55:

स्वप्नावलोकनं यद्वत्तद्वत्सिद्धावलोकनम्
केवलोऽथ विशेषोऽयं सिद्धप्राप्तौ स्थिरार्थता ५५

Perceiving the homogeneous wholeness of life in every object of perception, that is the quality of perception on the level of perfection.

This state in which everything is experienced in terms of the infinite value of the Self, is a distinct state of consciousness, the supreme attainment of the enlightened Siddha, the state of perpetual unwavering peace that knows no change.

Verse 56:

मुखाद्बहिर्द्वादशान्ते रेचकाभ्यासयुक्तितः
प्राणे चिरं स्थितिं नीते प्रविशत्यपरां पुरीम् ५६

Because complete perfection in the outer phase of life comes when the state of duality comes to its final end in Brahman Consciousness, through the practice of the technique of increasing the *Ākāśa* or void in the physiology,

When the breath has reached the level of the eternity of Being it enters into the fortress of that which has no rival, nor anything beyond or subsequent.

> Mastery of Yogic Flying is the physical demonstration of the attainment of the final goal of the mature, fully ripened state of Unity Consciousness that is called Brahman.

Section 5: Brahman as the fully stabilized state of Being

Verse 57:

श्रीराम उवाच
वद स्वभावस्य कथं ब्रह्मन्नचलसंस्थितिः
वक्तारः सानुकम्पा हि दुष्प्रश्नेऽपि न खेदिनः ५७

Śrī Rām said:

Please speak of how by the repeated experience of the unbounded Self, the non-changing, permanent state of Brahman becomes fully established.

Good speakers are always sympathetic and full of compassion when there is a difficult question, please do not be annoyed [with me].

> Repeated experience of total knowledge and total organizing power lifting up the body in the practice of Yogic Flying leads to the stabilization of the highest state of human consciousness, Brahman consciousness. Rām has been listening carefully to the trend of Vasishtha's words, and he has understood that the Yogic Flyer experiences a taste of totality, a taste of Brahman at the moment of liftoff. Now he wants to understand how that taste of the supreme fulfillment of life expands into the final attainment of fully stabilized permanent wholeness of life. When the goal is already present at the start of the journey, it doesn't make much sense to ask how the traveler reaches the goal. So Rām asks for sympathy and compassion, encouraging Vasishtha to explain in detail what should be obvious to anyone—how the practice of

Yogic Flying cultures the supreme attainment of Brahman consciousness.

Verse 58:

वसिष्ठ उवाच
शक्तिर्या तु स्वभावाख्या यथा स्फुरति चात्मनः
सर्गादिषु तथैवासौ स्थितिं यातीति निश्चयः ५८

Vasishtha said:

It is the organizing power of the *Ātmā* which lifts the body up off the ground in proportion to the total amount of Being that has been stabilized in the awareness.

One flies successfully only to the degree that Being is stabilized in the awareness at the moment of liftoff, this is the accepted understanding.

As transcendental Being is stabilized in the awareness more and more, the performance of Yogic Flying becomes increasingly more successful. The Flyer flies higher and further. The goal unfolds more and more with practice of the technique.

Verse 59:

अवस्तुत्वादविद्याया वस्तुशक्तिरपि क्वचित्
भिद्यते दृश्यते ह्यङ्ग वसन्ते शारदं फलम् ५९

In the state of ignorance, because there is no steadiness of Being in the awareness, the power of Being to lift the body up into the air is very little.

Non-changing Being stands separate from the constantly changing world of perception; it is the steadiness of the underlying field that bears fruit in the fall according to what is planted in the spring.

> The performance of *Saṁyama* is the same for the beginning flyer and the individual in Brahman who has gained total mastery over gravity. What has changed is the degree of stabilization of Being.

Verse 60:

सर्वमेवमिदं ब्रह्म नानाऽनानातया स्थितम्
जृम्भते व्यवहारार्थं केवलं कथितस्थिति ६०

The whole creation is only Brahman; the multifold variety of creation continues in its ever-changing nature by virtue of that wholeness of non-changing Being.

Everything in creation is expanding, growing towards more and more; the ultimate goal of all activity is the realization that the Self is all that there is: That is the whole story of the creation, maintenance and dissolution of the universe.

> In this verse, Vasishtha explains explicitly what is meant by the full stabilization of Being, namely the attainment of the ultimate goal of all activity in the realization that the Self is all that there is.

Section 6: How Yogic Flying develops higher states of consciousness

Verse 61:

श्रीराम उवाच
सूक्ष्मच्छिद्रादिगत्यर्थं पूरणार्थं च खस्य वा
अणुतां स्थूलतां वापि कायोऽयं नीयते कथम् ६१

Śrī Rām said:

The deeper purpose of the path to enlightenment through putting attention on the space (or emptiness) in the body [in the practice of Yogic Flying] is the goal of complete fulfillment of all aspects of life, or [merely] expansion of the *Ākāśa* (or emptiness) quality in the physiology?

Is it the subtle quality of space, the quality of abstraction which grows on the path of Yogic Flying, or is it the gross physical value of separation in the apertures in the body which widens through the practice? How is the body [which is an assemblage of innumerable gaps and spaces] led along this path to fulfillment through Yogic Flying?

In this question, and in the previous question, *Rām* is trying to resolve a significant doubt that has arisen in his awareness. This shows how fully he has owned Vasishtha's explanations up to this point. The question is, how can one and the same technique, the spontaneous liftoff of the body during the performance of Patañjali's procedure of *Saṁyama* for Yogic Flying, give rise to two diametrically opposed experiences, namely the silent *Kaivalya* of Patañjali and the dynamic *Kaivalya* of Jaimini? And how can this same technique of the liftoff function to culture the state of Brahman which is delicately balanced between silence and dynamism? *Rām* does not wish to insult Vasishtha by pointing out explicitly the impossibility of this proposition, that a single technique can carry an individual through all these different experiences. So, he is delicately asking for clarification about how the entire stream of evolution can be conducted by a single formula, a single technology of consciousness. And he asks pointedly now, about what is happening in the physiology when *Ākāśa* element is increasing. This question brings into focus the different characteristics of the physiology in the different higher states of consciousness.

How Yogic Flying stabilizes the silent *Kaivalya* of Patañjali and thereby develops the state of Cosmic Consciousness, is obvious because it is promoting activity in silence. In time, the physiology gets accustomed to maintaining silence even in the midst of activity. But the development of the Jaimini *Kaivalya*, and the attainment of God Consciousness involve a very different dynamic. Here the increase of *Ākāśa* brings about an opening in all the channels of the body, so that the light of life deep within, heretofore obscured can now shine forth. Through this process of opening up the channels of the body, the fire element comes to dominate the physiology, and this is the characteristic value of the physiology in God Consciousness.

The third phase in the path of evolution, the stabilization of the Vyāsa level of *Kaivalya* occurs again through infusion of *Ākāśa* into the physiology. Maharishi explains in his commentary on the Brahma Sūtra,[2] that there are four distinct stages in the evolution from God Consciousness to Brahman. In the first stage of development, the fire-element dominated physiology in God Consciousness starts to be overtaken by increasing value of air element. In the second stage, the air element comes to be completely predominant in the physiology. In the third stage, the *Ākāśa* element begins to overtake the air element as the predominant element in the physiology. And in the fourth stage, the *Ākāśa* element completely predominates in the physiology. From this description of the sequential growth of an *Ākāśa* dominated physiology, starting from the fire dominated physiology of God Consciousness, it is clear how the practice of Yogic Flying can directly promote this unfoldment of Brahman by steadily increasing the value of *Ākāśa* in the physiology. What is in need of clarification, then, is how increasing values of *Ākāśa*, through the liftoff in Yogic Flying, help to culture and stabilize God Consciousness.

Verse 62:

वसिष्ठ उवाच
काष्ठक्रकचयोः श्लेषाद्यथा छेदः प्रवर्तते
द्वयोः संघर्षणादग्निः स्वभावाज्जायते तथा ६२

Vasishtha said:

When there is both a piece of wood and a saw to cut it, the cutting proceeds by separating what was joined together.

Through the rubbing together of the two [sticks], naturally in that way fire is produced.

This seemingly obscure analogy is explaining the need

for gaining God Consciousness as a foundation for gaining Unity and Brahman. Creation must be analyzed for its constituent parts, and the finest, most delicate value in creation, the all-pervading luster of the radiance of the light of God must come to perception. In the relationship between infinite silence and the dynamism of the finest level of creation, the totality of Brahman is realized. But without the development of supreme celestial perception of God Consciousness, there are no pieces of wood to be rubbed together. The process of analysis, called *Mīmāmsā*, has to come first. In this process of analysis, the source of creation in the dynamism of the eternal Veda is realized: What is seen as action (*Karma*) on the surface is seen ultimately to be the sequential unfoldment of the Veda, the unfoldment of total knowledge from "A," the first syllable of Ved. When in this way, the whole creation is appreciated in terms of the finest value in the relative, then the building blocks of unity, silence and dynamism, have become available, and the final process of integration of life can begin.

The answer to *Rām's* question here about the transformation of the body through the practice of Yogic Flying is explained in verses 63-77 in terms of the development of the supreme perception of God Consciousness. In the analogy offered in this verse, this is all about sawing the wood into two pieces. Then when God Consciousness is attained, the path to Unity starts. But first the supreme celestial finest value of creation has to come to vision. For that, the quality of *Ākāśa* has to be increased in the body. This is the story of the creation of two things out of the incoherent jumble of the waking state world: infinite silence and the infinite dynamism of total natural law. The wood is the world, the saw is the infusion of *Ākāśa* into the physiology through the liftoff. In the end, in the attainment of God Consciousness, there are these two pieces, silence and dynamism: pure infinite silent consciousness on the subjective side of life, and the dynamism of the infinite organizing power of total natural law on the supreme celestial level of relative creation.

Verse 63:

मांसं कुयन्त्रजठरे स्थितं श्लिष्टमुखं मिथः
ऊर्ध्वाधः संमिलत्स्थूलद्व्यम्भः स्थैरिव वैतसम् ६३

The mouths of the openings of the pores and channels of the physiology become rigid, permanently closed, incapable of normal functioning.

The upper and the lower [lips] are joined together, and their opening is covered up, remaining blocked, like a thicket of reeds [that do not allow any passage].

Verse 64:

तस्य कुण्डलिनी लक्ष्मीर्निलीनान्तर्निजास्पदे
पद्मरागसमुद्गस्य कोशे मुक्तावली यथा ६४

Remaining blocked, inaccessible and unable to function, the Constitution of the Universe in the physiology, Lakṣṁī, Mother Divine, is sitting inside on her perpetual seat.

Covered over and hidden from sight within her [nineteen layered] enclosure, like a fabulous treasure, that can only be drawn out by the finest most delicate impulse of universal love [that alone is capable of] simultaneously opening all the petals of the lotus [on which Mother Divine is resting].

Verse 65:

आवर्तफलमालेव नित्यं सलसलायते
दण्डाहतेव भुजगी समुन्नतिविवर्तिनी ६५

The flavor that results from curving back on to the Self is the transformed value of what was carried into the Self; the Self remains ever the same, unchanging, eternal, amidst all the back and forth [of creation and destruction in the practice of Siddhis].

Like a snake beaten with a stick rears up to its full height and dignity but remains the same snake, the self rises up, expands and becomes the unbounded cosmic Self without undergoing any modification or transformation.

Verse 66:

द्यावापृथिव्योर्मध्यस्था क्रियेव स्पन्दधर्मिणी
संविन्मधुविबोधार्कौ हृत्पद्मपुटषट्पदी ६६

Stationed at the junction point between consciousness and physiology, between heaven and earth, the flying impulse has all the appearance of ordinary action, [but in reality it] puts in motion the dynamism of Total Natural Law.

On one side, there is the nectar of immortality of completely integrated and coherent silent consciousness, and on the other side, the instantaneous unfolding of the full potential for action of the light of life: There in the hollow space within the lotus of the heart is stationed the omnipresent all-pervading intelligence of Mother Divine.

Verse 67:

तत्सर्वं शक्तिपद्मादि बाह्येनाभ्यन्तरैस्तया
हृदि व्याधूयते वातैः पत्रवृन्दमिवाभितः ६७

That is totality, the primordial seat in the lotus of the heart of the infinite organizing power of the whole creation, put in motion on the outside by the body lifting up off the ground, and put in motion on the inside by the expansion of consciousness through all the reaches of space and time.

The dynamism of total natural law in the heart is shaken by the movement of the vital airs, like a pile of leaves being blown in every direction.

Verse 68:

यद्वद्व्योम स्फुरत्यङ्ग स्वभावात्तत्र वायवः
बलवन्मृदु यत्किंचिद्धृशं कवलयन्ति तत् ६८

In the practice of Yogic Flying, space bursts into view more and more by displaying its intrinsic nature of expansion in the body as the vital airs [are put into motion].

Full of the lordly strength and power of wholeness of life which expresses itself with infinite delicacy and irresistible power on the tiny boundaries of the physical body, [the vital airs] completely devour and overtake the body, making the body assume the qualities of space, transparent and unlimited, the image of wholeness, total natural law.

Verse 69:

वातैराहन्यमानं तत्पद्मादि तरलायते
हृद्यन्यान्येति कार्यैण पल्लवादि यथा तरोः ६९

By means of the impurities in the vital airs being struck in all directions by the image of perfection of the wholeness of the Self, that primordial lotus of the heart [the home of all knowledge and the repository of total natural law] vibrates and becomes lively.

When the superficial beating of the heart comes into alignment with its deepest purpose to reflect the move of Total Natural Law from fullness to emptiness and back to fullness, [then, being] constantly subjected in that way to that most tender nourishment of the infinite inexhaustible fullness of the Self spread everywhere, the blossoms of the tree of life begin to open.

Verse 70:

देहेष्वाजरणं सर्वरसानां पवनोऽन्वहम्
जनयत्यग्निमन्योन्यसंघर्षाद्वनवेणुवत् ७०

Day by day, [by the practice of increasing the *Ākāśa* in the body through Yogic Flying and thereby enlivening the intelligence, dynamism and purificatory power of the vital airs] the vital air reverses the aging of all the tissues in the bodies [of the individuals practicing Yogic Flying together in a group].

[The practice] creates the fire "*Agnim*," through rubbing together all the opposite values in the physiology, as if burning away the forest of reeds.

> [The practice] creates the fire "*Agnim*," according to verse 62, by rubbing two sticks together. The two sticks are the two opposites, silence and dynamism. The dynamism of "A," and the silence of "Ka," are brought together in the first syllable of the Veda, "Ak." The collapse of "A" to "Ka," is the universal paradigm for the unfoldment of knowledge. Rubbing these two sticks together, silence and dynamism, ignites the totality of knowledge, Veda. "Ak" then expands to become *Agnim*. *Agni* is literally fire, and at the same time it is the seed of total knowledge of Ṛg Veda. The rubbing together of the two sticks is a process of balancing and integrating the opposite values in the physiology.
>
> Where did the opposites come from? The opposite values of silence and dynamism themselves were brought into being by the saw which cut the log in two. The

cutting apart is the process of release of stress, purifying and bringing back to coherent normal functioning all the different channels in the physiology. The channels, when they are free of obstructions and functioning normally, are capable of expressing the entire range of activity of natural law from infinite silence to infinite dynamism. The physiology is made of knowledge, but the obstructions have to be removed before the light of knowledge can shine forth.

The forest of reeds is described in verse 63: "The pores and channels of the physiology become rigid, permanently closed, incapable of normal functioning... like a thicket of reeds." All these channels being opened, and their obstructions cleared is like burning away the "forest of reeds."

Verse 64 describes Mother Divine sitting inside the physiology "on her perpetual seat, covered over and hidden from sight within her [nineteen layered] enclosure, like a fabulous treasure." The forest of reeds are the (nineteen) enclosures that hide and protect the infinite organizing power of Total Natural Law in the form of Mother Divine, seated in the heart. By the burning of the forest of reeds, the infinite organizing power of total natural law embodied in Mother Divine becomes accessible, and the infinite brilliance of the celestial light of life shines through the whole physiology.

At the final culmination of this process, when the opposites have been created and are now being "rubbed together," the physiology shines with the light of the total knowledge and organizing power of Veda, embodied in Mother Divine. Then *Agnim*, the light of the Veda, the fire of knowledge, permeates everywhere without restriction. Here is the unlimited expansion and dominance of the fire element in the physiology. This increase in the fire element is brought about by the increase of *Ākāśa*, that opens all the pores and channels of the physiology that are blocked, hiding the light of Mother Divine, the treasure deep within.

The kindling of the fire of the light of life—the origin of the light of celestial perception—has been described in this verse. The process of expansion of the fire element in the physiology, giving rise to the exalted state of God Consciousness, is described in the following verses.

Verse 71:

स्वभावशीतवातात्मा देहस्तेनौष्ण्यमेत्यथ
उदितेन स सर्वाङ्गे भुवनं भानुना यथा ७१

The breath in the body, comprised of all the flow and movement of the vital airs in the physiology, coming to its least excited, perfectly ordered state, reveals its inherent nature as *Ātmā*: By that means the body functions in complete accordance with total natural law, the Constitution of the Universe, [*Agnim*], becoming the precipitated form of abstract infinite consciousness.

By the increase of the perfectly orderly self-referral quality of consciousness in all the limbs of the body, the world in which the individual moves about is as if lighted up by the light of the sun.

Verse 72:

सर्वतो विचरेदस्मिंस्तत्तेजस्तारकाकृति
हृत्पद्महेमभ्रमरो योगिनां चिन्त्यतां गतम् ७२

The flame of that fire of total knowledge, spreads everywhere in this body, making every particle of the physiology free from the influence of gravity, [becoming an orderly and coherent constituent of the whole, completely in accordance with the total intelligence of natural law].

Roving about in the field of multiplicity by virtue of the exquisitely refined celestial golden impulses of the lotus of the heart of the [accomplished] yogis, whatever the mind conceives, that is instantly achieved.

> As God Consciousness develops, the fire element begins to be predominant in the physiology.

Verse 73:

तत्प्रकाशमयं ज्ञानं चिन्तितं सत्प्रयच्छति
येन योजनलक्षस्थं वस्तु नित्यं हि दृश्यते ७३

That world of the celestial radiance of the light of God is pure knowledge, total knowledge: Whatever is the impulse of the mind on that level instantly produces the corresponding effect in material creation.

The ability of fulfilling any impulse of desire by harnessing the total potential of natural law being established by the procedure of Siddhi practice, the dawning light of the celestial world becomes permanent, and is seen everywhere at all times.

Verse 74:

तस्याग्नेर्वाडवस्येव जलं संशुष्कमिन्धनम्
मांसपङ्कजखण्डाढ्यं हृत्सरःकोशवासिनः ७४

With respect to the dawning of the celestial light everywhere, from the enlivenment of the knowledge of sequential unfoldment of total natural law, correspondingly there is the enlivenment of the fire element, the enlivenment of the quality of lively intelligence in the inert insensible functioning machinery of the body, and the water element in the body, that object-referral portion of the physiology that flows according to objective laws, is completely dried up and becomes the kindling for the expression of consciousness in matter, becomes the material structure for the expression of the dynamism of self-referral consciousness in the physiology.

There is fullness and liveliness of the intelligence of Total Natural Law in the gaps and spaces of the material structures that make up the physiology, because of fullness having taken up its abode in the walls of the container, the vessels through which the blood pumped by the heart flows.

Verse 75:

यदच्छं शीतलत्वं च तदस्यात्मेन्दुरुच्यते
इतीन्दोरुत्थितः सोऽग्निरग्नीषोमौ हि देहकः ७५

That unbounded infinite Self which is completely transparent and unbounded, and is the essential nature of the perfectly orderly state of least excitation of consciousness, is said to be *Indu.*

Thus, *Indu* is the individual ego or self that has risen to cosmic status. He is Total Veda, perfectly ordered sequentially unfolding Total Natural Law, and he is *Soma*, the link between consciousness and the physical nervous system, hence he is [known as] the inner controller, the animating intelligence of the body.

Verse 76:

सर्वं तृष्णात्मकं किंचित्तेजोऽर्काग्न्यभिधं विदुः
शीतात्मकं तु सोमाग्न्याभ्यामेव कृतं जगत् ७६

Everything that there is in creation is an excited state, a precipitated value of the wholeness of the Self; the finest, most delicate level of excitation of the whole creation is the brilliant ever shining celestial radiance of the light of life (*Arka*), called Veda by the wise.

Veda is the eternal vibration of the Self in its perfectly orderly least excited state, consisting of both intelligence of Total Natural Law, starting with "*Agni*," and the eternal flow characterized by *Soma*; by these two alone the whole universe has been created.

Verse 77:

विद्याविद्यास्वरूपेण सर्वं सदसदात्मना
जगद्वा येन निर्वृत्तं तदेवैवं विभज्यते ७७

The universe has arisen by virtue of knowledge and ignorance of the nature of the Self; all of subjectivity and all of objectivity are created by the Self, the *Ātmā*. By means of ignorance the world of multiplicity has sprung up; by means of knowledge that unchanging eternal unity underlying the whole creation is lived; there is only the Self, there is nothing other; in this way, according to one's level of consciousness, one is apportioned the corresponding reality.

Section 7: The Science of Soma, the First Science, the Science of Total Natural law

Verse 78:

संवित्प्रकाशं विद्यादि सूर्यमग्निं विदुर्बुधाः
असञ्ज्ञाड्यं तमो विद्याद्याहुः सोमं मनीषिणः ७८

The knowers of the knowledge of the celestial light, [known variously as] the First Science, the science of the Sun, [or] the Science of Creative Intelligence (*Agni*), are the wise knowers of reality.

The First Science is the knowledge of the eternal dynamism within the unmoving silence of the state of least excitation, the virtual fluctuations of the vacuum: It is called *Soma* by the wise knowers of reality.

> The knowledge of the brilliant celestial light of the fully integrated state of life in God Consciousness is the First Science, the science which stands above all the other sciences of natural law: It is the science of the Sun which is the cause of all causes and the light of life, it is the Science of Creative Intelligence which is the science of how the universal intelligence of Natural Law creates the universe—those who know this fundamental knowledge which gives a proper foundation to all the different sciences of Natural Law, they are the wise knowers of reality, according to the enlightened sages.
>
> The basis for the refined celestial perception of God Consciousness is *Soma*. The *Devas*, the impulses of

creative intelligence at the junction point of Absolute and relative, drink *Soma*, and this enlivens the finest value of activity in all the channels of perception and action. By drinking the *Soma*, the creative intelligence responsible for seeing through the eyes gets enlivened for its most delicate capabilities, and becomes capable of seeing the celestial world. Like that, all the channels of perception are opened to the world of the finest relative through drinking the *Soma*. *Soma* is the basis for the brilliant celestial light of the fully integrated state of life in God Consciousness.

This supreme celestial field coming to awareness, forms the basis of understanding and knowledge in every field of knowledge. All the universal laws which are the founding principles and axioms for knowledge in every discipline, are lively in the supreme celestial field. The science of this level of life gives insight into the mechanics of creation lively in every discipline of natural law. This is the supreme level of analysis, the analysis which yields the cause of all causes.

The knowledge of Karma Mīmāṁsā is fundamentally the knowledge of this celestial field, and the total knowledge of Karma Mīmāṁsā may be encapsulated in this one word "*Soma*." Knowledge of *Soma* gives a proper foundation to all the sciences of Natural Law. *Soma* is the dynamism, the flow of a virtual liquid that gives expression to the fluctuations of the vacuum. On the basis of *Soma*, the laws of nature derive their breath, and the whole creation comes up. All the states of consciousness have their basis in different qualities, different degrees of purity of *Soma*.

Soma gives rise to the liftoff: *Soma* is created at the moment of highest mind-body coordination, just before the body lifts up into the air. The total knowledge of the *Soma*, the basis of the first science, the ultimate foundation of all the sciences of natural law is contained in the liftoff. The conclusion of this verse is that *Soma* is that one thing by knowing which, the full power and scope of the liftoff in Yogic Flying can be completely comprehended. By virtue of the power of *Soma*, the body lifts up into the air in Yogic Flying: By virtue of the *Soma*, the total knowledge of Vedic Science may be said to be contained in the liftoff. Hearing this verse, Rām asks to be told all about the *Soma*, so that he can fully understand all the implications of this technology of consciousness.

Verse 79:

श्रीराम उवाच
वह्निर्वाय्वात्मनः सोमादुदेतीति मुनीश्वर
सोमस्योत्पत्तिमधुना वद मे वदतांवर ७९

Śrī Rāma said:

Vāyu is the vehicle for the expansion of the Self; through [growth and refinement of] the *Soma*, [the link between mental and physical values,] the individual rises [to higher states of consciousness], O Supreme ruler of sages.

Tell me with sweet honey-like words, the story of the origin of the *Soma*, O greatest of all story tellers.

Vāyu is the impulse of creative intelligence which governs the air element. Air element includes the breath, and the five *Prāṇa-vāyus*, the Sub-doṣas of Vāta Doṣa.

In the previous chapter (4:31-48), the story of growth of consciousness was told in terms of refinement of the *Prāṇa* in the body. That study began with the comparison in verse 31 of the dynamic principle of sequential unfoldment of the Veda and the process of digestion and assimilation of food in the physiology. The digestion of food is a process of moving the food through the various stages in the alimentary canal, and at each stage the food undergoes different transformations, until in the end all useful nutrients have been removed from the food. *Prāṇa* is the organizing intelligence conducting this process; through refinement of the *Prāṇa*, more and more refined products of digestion are produced from the food that is eaten. The process of assimilation of orderliness from the environment was told in terms of *Prāṇa*. But the perfection of this process of digestion gives rise to finer and finer products of digestion, so the same story can be told in terms of the refinement of the products of digestion. Now Rām is asking to hear this same story of evolution of higher states of consciousness in terms of the refinement of the products of digestion. The most refined product of digestion is the *Soma*, which was introduced in verse 75. Now in verse 78, *Soma* is proposed as the "vidyādi," the First Science. Through the growth and refinement of this *Soma*, the individual rises to higher states of consciousness. *Soma,* the link between mental and physical values, must be fundamental to the knowledge of Yoga, Karma Mīmāṁsā and Vedānta. Thus, it should be possible to describe the entire range of human evolution from ignorance to supreme enlightenment in terms of *Soma*. Rām wants to hear Brahman and the path to supreme enlightenment explained from this new perspective.

Verse 80:

वसिष्ठ उवाच
अग्नीषोमौ मिथः कार्यकारणे च व्यवस्थिते
पर्यायेण समं चैतौ प्रजीषेते परस्परम् ८०

Vasishtha said:

Agni and *Soma* together are always found in the relationship between any cause and its effect, and whenever multiplicity arises from unity.

The mechanics of creation are the same in the field of subjectivity and the field of objectivity, the one is the other.

In response to Rām's question, Vasishtha now embarks on the explanation of the entire course of evolution in terms of *Soma* and the changing values between consciousness and physiology. Perfection of the flying Siddhi will be seen as the expansion of the *Soma* from a momentary drink, to a constant all-time reality. Vasishtha here presents his complete and final analysis of the lift-off in terms of the *Soma* at the junction point between consciousness and matter.

Agni is the *Devatā* of expansion and diversification. "A," the first syllable of the Veda, contains the total knowledge of natural law in seed form. "A" unfolds from itself the first word of Ṛg Veda, "*Agnim.*" *Agni* is the organizing power which systematically unpacks and unfolds the total knowledge and infinite organizing power contained in "A."

"A" alone tells the whole story of natural law, and *Agnim*

is the perfect elaboration of "A." Through *Agni* the entire Veda and Vedic Literature comes into existence, the whole field of knowledge is expanded and unpacked out of the infinite potential of knowledge and organizing power contained in "A." *Agni* is the completely self-sufficient song of creation, it does not need any further help from outside to expand and unfold the total value of natural law from within itself. Even so, Vasishtha insists that there is a second principle, a second cause that comes into play whenever multiplicity is created from unity, and that *Devatā* is *Soma. Soma* comes into play at the finest stratum of creation, and in terms of the Veda, it is the level of intelligence where speech is connected to silence.

The sound "A," the first expression of the Veda, gets completely annihilated in the following sound "Ka," and that process of collapse goes through eight stages, corresponding to the eight *Prakritis*, the eight aspects of nature. The nature of "A," is revealed in eight layers or somersaults when we look deeply into the process of collapse of "A" into "Ka." When the seventh somersault ends, and the eighth somersault begins, all that is left of the original sound "A" is the hum or vibration of speech. The connection of that most refined value of speech, called "*Anusvāra*," with the unmanifest non-vibrating silence is expounded in great depth in the Veda, in terms of *Soma*. The eight somersaults of "A" collapsing into "Ka," are explored for all their possible values in each of the *Maṇḍalas*, 2 through 9. The ninth *Maṇḍala*, dealing with the eighth somersault of "A" is the story of *Soma*, the finest stratum of manifestation of the speech of eternal law, being purified, being clarified, and eventually being resolved into its essential constituent which is unmanifest silence, Being, known as *Puruṣa*, the completely uninvolved witness of all activity. The first seer of the Ṛg Veda, Ṛṣi Madhuchchhandas, tells the story of *Agni* in the first *Sūkta* of Ṛg Veda. The same Ṛṣi, Ṛṣi Madhuchchhandas tells the story of *Soma* in the first *Sūkta* of the ninth *Maṇḍala* of Ṛg Veda. The activity on the finest level of creation, on the level of the *Soma*, is needed to explain the process of diversification of unity into diversity, according to Vasishtha, and the voice of Madhuchchhandas, from the far distant past, rises to confirm that vision.

In the second line of this verse, Vasishtha is presenting the founding principle of interdisciplinary study. If there is a First Science, then there must be principles which allow the knowledge of the First Science to be systematically applied to support the knowledge in all other sciences. The founding principle of interdisciplinary study is, according to Vasishtha, that the laws of nature in the subjective field are the same as the laws of nature in the objective field. Subjectivity does not have a different set of laws; the same laws function in both fields. The corollary is that the mechanics of creation of the Veda are the same as the mechanics of creation of matter. All the principles and laws of nature which go to create the Veda are again seen in the process of manifestation of matter in the relative field. This means that if our microscopes are not yet fine enough to see the subtlest stratum of relative creation, then the knowledge of the finest stratum of creation from the field of Vedic Science is a credible and authentic means of study. The knowledge of *Soma* described in Ṛg Veda is relevant and applicable to the study of the finest level of material creation: The same laws of nature must be applicable in both areas because the laws of nature for subjectivity and objectivity are the same. Vasishtha explains this principle in detail in the following verses.

Verse 81:

जन्माङ्गबीजाङ्कुरवत्तथा दिवसरात्रिवत्
स्थितिश्छायातपसमा केवला सैतयोर्भवेत् ८१

In the same way that the swollen seed has lively within it all the component parts that express themselves in the life of the organism, so also the night contains within it in seed form all the activities and events of the day.

Similarly, the state of pure unmanifest Being has within it the blueprint of Total Natural Law that gives rise to the whole creation: He (*Puruṣa*, the Self) is completely competent on his own to create both worlds, subjectivity and objectivity.

The swollen seed is the fully enlivened state of *Kaivalya* that is lively with all the laws of nature: This is the Jaimini *Kaivalya*. The seer of the Jaimini *Kaivalya* sees the blueprint of creation within the flat silence of the Patañjali *Kaivalya*. The highest value of *Kaivalya*, the Vyāsa *Kaivalya*, is the self-sufficient source of all creation, subjective and objective: It has both the Patañjali *Kaivalya*—the source of all subjectivity, and the Jaimini *Kaivalya*—the source of all objectivity, within its structure. The Vyāsa *Kaivalya* is the one fountainhead of all diversity, completely competent on its own to create the worlds of subjectivity and objectivity.

Verse 82:

तुल्यकालोपलम्भासावित्थं छायातपस्थितिः
केवलैकोपलम्भाढ्या स्थितिर्दिवसरात्रिवत् ८२

Established in all-encompassing total knowledge, there is the attainment of the subjective and objective worlds at the same time: The state of Being is a lively field of all possibilities.

The state of Being, one undivided wholeness, by itself attains the wealth of multiplicity of creation, just as the night contains within it the seed form of all the activities and events of the day.

> Here the unified, Absolute source of all creation is being described.

Verse 83:

कार्यकारणभावश्च द्विविधः कथितोऽनयोः
सद्रूपपरिणामोत्थो विनाशपरिणामजः ८३

Pure existence is the ultimate cause, the origin of everything in creation, and it is itself the organizing power which is capable of transforming the unity of Being into multiplicity; [thus] there are said to be two kinds of causes contained within eternal Being, the dynamism of eternal existence, "A," [which is transformed into all the different alphabets that make up the Vedas], and the "non-A," the silence [of the unmanifest gaps in the speech of the Veda].

There is the material substance out of which everything originates through transformation, and there is the creation through the transformation taking place in the silent unmanifest gaps, when everything has been completely annihilated.

> There is the quote, *Mantra-brāhmaṇayor veda nāmadheyam*. Mantra and *Brāhmaṇa*, sound and gap together are called Veda.[3] The gaps in the structure of the Veda are as important as the syllables, because in the gaps there is the organizing power giving rise to the expression of the subsequent syllable. There are syllables and gaps, expressions of speech and silence, and these are said to be two kinds of causes. *Agni* plays the role of the dynamism of creation, and *Soma* plays the role of the silence. Together, the two are always found in the relationship between any cause and its effect (verse 80, above).

Verse 84:

एकस्माद्यद्द्वितीयस्य संभवोऽङ्कुरबीजवत्
कार्यकारणभावोऽसौ सद्रूपपरिणामजः ८४

With respect to the duality which arises from the state of eternal unity, the origin [of duality] is contained in the swelling up of the seed, [the swelling up of the liveliness of potential dynamism within the self-sufficient wholeness of unity].

That pure existence which is the ultimate cause, the origin of everything in creation, and is itself the organizing power which is capable of transforming the unity of Being into multiplicity, is what becomes manifest through the transformations in form of the eternal, immortal non-changing pure existence.

> The *Devatā* value which transforms the object is a part of the organizing power of that immortal Being which is the source of all change. The "object" which is being transformed by the action of the *Devatā*, is itself also the eternal Being. Through layers of transformation, the same one pure Being expresses itself in the diversity of knowers, processes of knowing, and objects of knowledge.

Verse 85:

एकनाशे द्वितीयस्य यद्भावो दिनरात्रिवत्
कार्यकारणभावोऽसौ विनाशपरिणामजः ८५

When there is destruction of unity by the appearance of duality, the reality of duality is that it is contained within eternal unity like day is contained in the night.

That [same] pure existence which is the ultimate cause and the organizing power of creation, becomes manifest through the transformations of the unmanifest Being.

> Duality, consisting of a subjective pole, and an objective pole, has its basis in unity. That unity becomes manifest through successive layers of transformation of its own unmanifest Being.

Verse 86:

सद्रूपपरिणामस्य मृद्धटक्रमसंस्थितेः
अक्षोपलम्भादितरत्प्रमाणं नोपयुज्यते ८६

Because through many sequential stages of evolution of a manifest form from pure existence, the object gains shape and solidity like an earthen pot, [thus] through the eyes one sees [only] the other, the non-Self—[therefore] sensory perception is not a valid means of gaining knowledge of the unmanifest Self.

> The senses of man are designed for object-referral functioning, designed for seeing the objects outside. This is useful for locating food, and for avoiding dangerous animals, etc. The senses however are not innately designed to bring the knowledge of the inner world of the Self.

For that, special procedures and technologies of consciousness are required.

Mṛd-ghaṭa-krama-saṁsthitiḥ: Mṛd-ghaṭa is a pot fashioned from earth or clay; *Saṁsthitiḥ*, form or shape of existence, *Krama*, sequential development. The idea of this compound seems to be that of the development of a form through sequential iterations. In order to experience the infinite Self, the machinery of the eye is not helpful: The eye is designed for the clear perception of relative boundaries. To gain knowledge of that which is beyond boundaries, to gain knowledge of the nature of the Self, procedures other than looking outward must be used.

Verse 87:

विनाशपरिणामस्य दिनरात्रिक्रमस्थितेः
अभावोऽप्येकवस्तुस्थो गतो मुख्यप्रमाणताम् ८७

Following the sequence of transformations of consciousness into matter in the opposite direction, the path of destruction of the manifest expressions of objectivity, because of the steps of evolution being ever the same, whether day is being created from night, or night is being created from day.

The unmanifest Being coming to direct experience, establishes the reality of oneness of eternal existence: That is the pre-eminent path of gaining knowledge [of reality].

There are many layers of transformation by which the object of perception is sequentially built up from the unmanifest. Conversely, by traversing that sequence in the reverse direction, one gains the ability to perceive finer and finer levels of the object until the unmanifest Being at the source of the object is directly cognized. This is the path of gaining knowledge of the Self. One traces the path of creation in the reverse direction in order to cognize Being, the Absolute source of all creation.

Verse 88:

अनास्था नास्ति कर्तृत्वमित्याद्या युक्तिवादिनः
अवज्ञया बहिष्कार्याः स्वानुभूत्यपलापिनः ८८

There is no effort, no individual inception of the doer on the path to experience of the unmanifest Being: Being can only be gained by making use of the thinking process without any reference to any existing thing, without meaning [because Being is absolutely primordial and without precedent].

With complete indifference [during meditation] to the thoughts relating to activities in the relative world, the direct experience of the Self is gained by one who turns away from all distractions.

The technology of automatic self-transcending is described here. In order for the mind to settle down and experience its source in Being, there can be no individual effort. Any effort of concentration or focusing the mind will keep the mind on the surface and prevent the process of fathoming quieter levels of the mind from proceeding successfully. Similarly, if one follows with interest thoughts that arise in the mind, then the activity of the mind will be sustained on that level, and again the process of fathoming quieter levels of the mind will not be successful. If any value of meaning is sustained on the level of attention, then the awareness will be held on the superficial level where that meaning is functional, and will be held back from exploring deeper levels of the mind. Neither the techniques of concentration, involving focused attention, nor the techniques of innocently witnessing and following the thoughts that come in the mind, are effective techniques for conveying the mind to unmanifest Being. What has to happen is to track the creative process in the reverse direction: This requires not favoring any distractions to the settling of the mind (such as contemplation), and not engaging the mind in new layers of the creative process, by focusing the mind (in techniques which require focused attention or concentration).

Verse 89:

प्रत्यक्षवदभावोऽपि प्रमैव रघुनन्दन
अग्न्यभावोऽपि शीतस्य प्रमाणं सर्वजन्तुषु ८९

Perception of the changing values of speech as the mind proceeds towards more and more, is the correct procedure, the only path to unboundedness, O Joy of the House of Raghu.

Spontaneously moving in the direction of more and more happiness and bliss in the gap between impulses of primordial Vedic sounds, there is the path to experience of the state of least excitation of consciousness for every human being born on this planet.

Vasishtha extols the process of transcending using a

sequence of speech sounds derived from the Veda, called a mantra. With the proper technique, these special sounds will convey the mind effortlessly to the unbounded transcendental field of life. Transcending is natural for every human being, and this is a natural procedure appropriate and valuable for everyone.

Verse 90:

अग्निर्धूमतया भागाद्यां प्रयाति पयोदताम्
सद्रूपपरिणामेन तदग्निः सोमकारणम् ९०

[During meditation] The impulse of Vedic sound progresses to earlier, less developed, more primitive, more abstract levels of expression of the impulse by becoming vaguer, fainter, more ethereal, less concrete, [and thereby] generating the sweet milk-like essence of life [*Soma*].

By means of the transformation of the form or expression of the sound in the direction of greater abstraction and greater power, that impulse of Vedic sound becomes the cause of [the production of] *Soma*, the link between mental and physical values.

As the mind experiences spontaneously the quieter and quieter levels of the thinking process, there is increasing charm at every step. This increasing charm is due to the production of "the sweet milk-like essence of life," the *Soma*. The specially chosen impulse of Vedic sound is the cause of the production of *Soma* in the nervous system.

Verse 91:

अग्निर्नष्टतया शैत्यादसावेव प्रयाति यत्
विनाशपरिणामेन तदग्निः सोमकारणम् ९१

The impulse of Vedic sound is brought to complete nothingness, total annihilation through the process of refinement [to finer and finer levels of expression of the impulse of sound]: It is that transcending alone which is the true goal of the movement of the mind.

By the transformations of the sound leading to the complete disappearance of the impulse, that impulse of Vedic sound [expanding to infinity] becomes the cause of the production of *Soma*.

> The special sound that is used in order to experience quieter levels of the mind, is completely let go, transcended. This complete disappearance of the sound is not a failure of the practice, it is actually the goal of the practice, because in that process of disappearing, the production of *Soma* in the nervous system is maximum. This procedure is called "automatic self-transcending," because no amount of effort, no focusing or directing of the mind in any way will give rise to the experience of "complete nothingness." Only the completely effortless tracking of the creative process in the reverse direction will bring the awareness to the source of all creation.

Verse 92:

सप्ताम्बुधिपयः पीत्वा धूमोद्गारेण वाडवः
पयोदतां प्रयातेन तदेव जनयत्यलम् ९२

The juice of the *Soma*—the product of the total brain functioning in the experience of the completely unified state of consciousness at the moment of transcendence—being drunk by repeated transcending during the process of experiencing increasing abstraction [of the Vedic sound] is the enlivenment of the dynamism within the transcendental unmanifest Being.

Producing *Soma* by means of transcending, that alone gives rise to the experience of pure consciousness as a field of all possibilities.

> Vasishtha was asked to tell the story of *Soma*. In order to do that, he had to describe in detail the unique circumstances and context in which *Soma* is created. For this he had to describe the process of automatic self-transcending. There may be thousands of meditation techniques, and all may have their value in promoting progress in some area of life. But of all these techniques, only this one technique of automatic self-transcending, described here gives rise to the production of *Soma*.

Verse 93:

अर्कः पीत्वा निशानाथमामावास्यं पुनः पुनः
उद्गिरत्यमले पक्षे मृणालमिव सारसः ९३

Like a flash of infinity, the Lord of the night, *Soma*, born at the moment of transcending, is drunk again and again.

At the point when there is no object of experience, the *Soma* is discharged like a lotus stalk coming up in a pond.

Verse 94:

पीत्वामृतोपमं शीतं प्राणः सोममुखागमे
अस्त्रागमात्पूरयति शरीरं पीनतां गतः ९४

When the *Soma* enters into the mouth, having drunk the image of immortality, the breath (*Prāṇa*) becomes still.

Because of entering into the blood, the whole body swells with satisfaction, being in a state of complete fullness and affluence of life.

Verse 95:

जलमप्युदपां भोगे प्रयात्यर्कस्य रश्मिताम्
सद्रूपपरिणामेन तज्जलं वह्निकारणम् ९५

In the exhilaration of the draft, the liquid [*Soma*] flows upward like rays of the Sun.

By means of the process of refinement in the direction of greater abstraction and greater power, that liquid is the antecedent of the most delicate *Soma* which is carried upwards to the world of the gods.

> The Soma flow upwards to the heavenly world of the gods, nourishing those most refined qualities of intelligence, the *Devatās* responsible for the administration of the whole physiology.

Verse 96:

नाशात्मकतया तोयमौष्ण्यत्वादेति ह्यग्निताम्
विनाशपरिणामेन तत्तोयं वह्निकारणम् ९६

By repeated experience of the Self through the disappearance of all relativity, the ocean of pure intelligence flows by virtue of its intrinsically dynamic nature and becomes creative intelligence.

By repeated transcending, that unbounded, infinite ocean of pure intelligence becomes the antecedent of the most delicate *Soma* which is carried upwards to the world of the gods.

> Through the production of *Soma* by repeated transcending, the experience of the transcendent changes. The

field of unmanifest pure intelligence becomes a dynamic field, a field of virtual potential dynamism, a field of creative intelligence. That pure field of creative intelligence is made up of innumerable impulses of intelligence. Each impulse in the ocean of impulses has a specific value of organizing power, a specific range of application of intelligence, in the ocean of all possible values of expression of creative intelligence. These impulses within the transcendental field are called *Devatās*. *Devatās* are the central focus of study in Vedic Science. These impulses become stronger by drinking the *Soma* produced in the process of transcending. This is how transcending makes pure intelligence "creative intelligence." *Soma* plays the role of enlivening the functioning value of the individual laws of nature that are inherent in the blueprint of total natural law at the basis of creation.

Verse 97:

अग्नेर्विनाशे सद्रूपपरिणामो निशाकरः
इन्दोर्विनाशे सद्रूपपरिणामो हुताशनः ९७

Because there is creative intelligence lively in the unmanifest field of pure consciousness, the unmanifest is the source of all possible transformations.

Because intelligence in its pure unmanifest state is conscious of its own existence, all possible transformations are the Self-referral fluctuations of unmanifest pure intelligence.

Verse 98:

हताशो नाशमागत्य सोमो भवति वै तथा
दिवसो नाशमागत्य रात्रिर्भवति वै यथा ९८

Pure unmanifest intelligence having become conscious of its own existence, having become Self-referral consciousness, in that process of intelligence becoming intelligent, *Soma* is there, in every way supporting and bringing that about.

[By means of the liveliness of Self-referral consciousness,] the pure unmanifest Being becomes the home of all the laws of nature, in which manner it is recognized to be the source of all change in the field of relative existence.

> Flat Absolute, which we call pure intelligence, is devoid of attributes. But creative intelligence, made lively by the *Soma*, is the home of all the laws of nature, the home of all knowledge, the non-changing source of all change, the state of perfect orderliness, eternal and uncreated, and self-perpetuating. Through the enlivenment of *Soma*, pure intelligence becomes intelligent and prepares itself to play about in its own field.[4]

Verse 99:

तमः प्रकाशयोश्छायातपयोर्दिनरात्रयोः
मध्ये विलक्षणं रूपं प्राज्ञैरपि न लभ्यते ९९

Between darkness and light, between flat absolute and the dynamism of the relative, between day and night,

In the middle between these opposites, there is the apprehension of the junction point, having the form composed of all possible values of intelligence, [all possible *Devatās*] in a virtual [not fully manifest] state.

> The finest relative, the field of the celestial, lies at the junction point between manifest and unmanifest. It partakes of the qualities of both, but is a world on its own. All the *Devatās* responsible for the administration of the manifest universe reside there in the gap between relative and absolute.

Verse 100:

संधिरप्यविलोपः स्यादेतयोरेव तद्वपुः
भावाभावैर्यथैकास्थानिष्ठावेतौ तथैव हि १००

The junction point should be more than simply a break between these two [opposite values], indeed [a world of beings is there], that is the beautiful celestial world.

By means of the eternal continuance [of the structure of pure knowledge composed] of the impulses of intelligence in the gap, the *Devatās* which embody the togetherness of pure knowledge and organizing power uphold the unity of these two [fields of day and night, manifest and unmanifest,] and in that way uphold the oneness of eternal unity in the midst of diversity.

> The structure of pure knowledge is eternal and not created by anyone. These qualities of *Nityatva,* eternity and *Apauruṣeyatva*, not created by anyone, are qualities that belong to the Absolute, but they are exhibited by perfectly ordered structures at the junction point between relative and absolute. On the one hand, through sequential unfoldment these perfectly ordered structures give rise to diversity; on the other hand, by virtue of their perfection of structure, they partake of the eternal qualities of the Absolute. In this way, the structure of the Vedic *Maṇḍala*, and the *Maṇḍala* structure found expressed in all the branches of Vedic Literature, is made up of the respective *Sūktas* of the Vedic *Devatās* arranged in perfect sequential order, and is said to be "*Nityatva*" and "*Apaurusheyatva.*"

Verse 101:

द्वाभ्यां चैतन्यजाड्याभ्यां भूतानि प्रस्फुरन्ति हि
यथा तमः प्रकाशाभ्यामहोरात्रा महीतले १०१

These beings [the *Devatās*] responsible for upholding the duality of consciousness and matter, move about here and there at the finest level of creation, the brilliant celestial world where diversity first sprouts from eternal unity.

This is how the day and night composed of darkness and light comes to be experienced on the surface of life, here in our world.

> Ṛg Veda 1:164:39 speaks of this world of Devatās, located in the *Parame Vyoman*, the highest heaven, as "*Yasmin devā adhiviśve niṣeduḥ*," "In which reside all the *Devas* responsible for the administration of the manifest universe."

Verse 102:

चिद्रूपजडरूपाभ्यामारब्धेयं जगत्स्थितिः
जलामृताभ्यां मिश्राभ्यां शीता तनुरिवैन्दवी १०२

The origin of subjectivity and objectivity is here in the celestial world, the eternal abode of the gods in heaven.

The flow of *Soma* (*Aindava*) is the measure of that field of perfect order composed of a mixture of immortality and flow, change perpetual that is undecaying: The flow of *Soma* indicates how much the physical body reflects that perfect order of the celestial world.

> *Soma* gets enlivened and begins to flow, and the inert matter, the structural elements of the physical body come alive. As *Soma* flows more and more, the various parts of the body begin to function in terms of Self-referral consciousness. Self-referral consciousness expands its territory to incorporate more and more of the nervous system, expanding even into the peripheral organizing structures of the autonomic nervous system. Through the agency of the *Soma*, not only the conscious processes, but even the unconscious processes maintaining homeostasis, begin to breathe the Absolute order, *Nityatva*, and *Apaurusheyatva* of the cosmic blueprint of total natural law. More *Soma* means greater orderliness, more balanced functioning without friction, and correspondingly, expanded consciousness. Maximum value of *Soma* is lived in the state of Brahman consciousness, and this presents absolute perfection, where every part of the physiology is perfectly in tune with every other part of the physiology, and the whole physiology is perfectly aligned with the intelligence governing the entire cosmos.

Verse 103:

प्रकाशमनलं सूर्यं चिद्रूपं विद्धि राघव
जडात्मकं तमोरूपं विद्धि सोमशरीरकम् १०३

O Rāghava, know that consciousness, pure subjectivity expresses itself in the form of light, which is ultimately fire, which is ultimately [coming from] the sun.

Know that what gives form to the lifeless insensate matter [in order to give the experience of consciousness] at the finest level of the physiology is *Soma*.

> *Soma* is the light of life. At one level of consciousness, the physical machinery of the body gives rise to consciousness—consciousness is an emergent property of matter. At another level of consciousness, matter is made of consciousness and consciousness is all that there is—matter is an emergent property of consciousness. *Soma* is equally the cause of consciousness and the cause of material creation. *Soma* binds together these two perspectives: *Soma* is common to all the states of consciousness. *Soma* is the sun that gives light and form to consciousness.

Verse 104:

चित्सूर्ये निर्मले दृष्टे नाम नश्येद्भवोदयम्
व्योमसूर्ये बहिर्दृष्टे यथा कृष्णानिशातमः १०४

There is no blemish or imperfection seen in the sun of pure consciousness: Sound [in the inward stroke of meditation], comes to an end, and what comes to experience [when the impulse of sound is lost] is pure Absolute Being.

As it is seen in the outer world, the sun is the ultimate origin of the sky [and everything in it], [so] the blinding black darkness of the unmanifest Absolute [is the origin of all subjectivity, the sun of the inner life].

> The Absolute Being which is experienced when the finest impulse of sound is let go in the process of automatic self-transcending, contains the complete blueprint of total natural law without any blemish or imperfection. The transcendent Being shines, as it were, with the fullness of total knowledge. But Vasishtha is quick to point out, that although the Being is the light of life and the blueprint of natural law, it is not experienced as light: There is no content to experience, it is pure wakefulness alone without any object of experience. Because there is no objective content, there are no qualifications of that pure Being. Because there are no qualifications, it is unbounded and infinite, limitless pure intelligence. That is the sun, the source of all the rays of consciousness.

Verse 105:

सोमदेहे जडे दृष्टे चिन्निजे सत्यवद्भवेत्
निशीथे विलसत्यज्ञे यथा सौरप्रभाभरः १०५

The *Soma* in the body is a physical chemical, it can be seen, observed and measured: [in the physiology] it is the embodiment of that which never changes, it is responsible for the continuity of consciousness.

The dynamism of perfect evolutionary action in the nature of the Absolute flashes forth and expresses itself in the field of the manifest, just as the light of the sun bestows all possible forms.

> *Soma*, which is responsible for the experience of the sun of pure consciousness, described in the previous verse, is a tangible, measurable, analyzable material in the nervous system. It is a physical chemical open to investigation by modern science. The role of that chemical is to maintain the continuity of consciousness.
>
> When through the repeated process of transcending, the *Soma* is increased in the physiology, then the field of pure consciousness gains the quality of dynamism. This inherent dynamism of the transcendent which is a lively field of all possibilities and a field of perfect orderliness, flashes forth and expresses itself in the manifest field as perfect evolutionary action, action which is completely in accord with all the laws of nature. That means that through repeated transcending, the transcendental field is enlivened and becomes dynamic, and that dynamism is spontaneously drawn into the field of activity, and appears as perfect evolutionary action. Perfect evolutionary

action means action free from mistakes, and action that brings great benefits simultaneously to the actor and the whole of the near and far environment. This improvement in the field of activity develops spontaneously through regular practice of transcending, and it is experienced as greater accomplishment with less effort, and greater support of nature, greater positive response from the environment. This is the light of the sun of pure consciousness illuminating the field of action.

Verse 106:

सोमं प्रकटयत्यग्निश्चिद्देहस्य चिरं प्रभाम्
स्वसंविन्मयमिन्दुश्चिद्देहस्थं रूपमर्कजम् १०६

The *Soma* makes manifest on the level of the body the perfectly orderly flow of the intelligence of total natural law that upholds consciousness, makes consciousness lasting and permanent, the manifest expression of the eternal light of God.

The consciousness that "I am," "I am the knower," is made of *Soma* [*Indu*], it is the root of existence of the physical body—the manifest form of the body is born of the light of the *Soma*.

The experience of greater support of nature and increased efficiency and success in the field of activity is due to increasing amounts of *Soma* in the physiology. Through increasing values of *Soma*, the light of God shines in all activity, and the individual does not violate the laws of nature.

The sense of Self, the "I," the "knower," is made of *Soma*.

That is the case in ignorance and in the state of enlightenment. But the "I" becomes progressively more expanded, and more capable of spontaneous right action, through regular experience of transcending. As *Soma* increases in the physiology, nothing happens to the experience of "I." The continuity is maintained, and strengthened. Even though the character of action is changing and becoming more and more righteous, and even though consciousness itself is becoming more and more expanded, and more and more blissful, the sense of "I" remains. As the *Soma* changes over time, since the manifest form of the body is born of the light of the *Soma*, then the body is progressively rebuilt on the basis of the perfect template, the stainless blueprint of total natural law which is the Sun of life. Health improves dramatically, the body gets rejuvenated, and the physiology begins to enjoy life on the level of perfection. Individual life comes to be the manifest expression of total natural law, the expression of the eternal light of God. The entire process of taking an individual out of ignorance and suffering is the process of enlivening and enriching the *Soma* in the physiology.

Verse 107:

चिन्निष्क्रियात्वनामा सा केवला नोपलभ्यते
आलोक इव दीपेन देहेनैवावगम्यते १०७

Consciousness being without activity by its very nature, the knower is completely self-sufficient and self-referral, nothing of the non-Self [world of objects] is apprehended.

Seeing, if it is to take place, is by means of light [illuminating the object]; the object is brought to perception by the machinery of the body [eyes, optic nerve, etc.] that is uniquely capable of perceiving light.

Verse 108:

चितश्चेत्योन्मुखत्वेन लाभः सैव च संसृतिः
निश्चेत्यायाः शुभो लाभो निर्वाणं वा तदेव हि १०८

There is perception by consciousness of any object only by means of directing the gaze, and by implication, there is a field of relative existence only by virtue of the knower directing his attention.

By means of the outward, object-referral consciousness, the beautiful, auspicious and fortunate [objects in the relative world] are perceived, or alternately, if the consciousness is not object-referral, the world of multiplicity vanishes, and then that unbounded infinite consciousness alone is.

Verse 109:

अन्योन्यलब्धसद्भाक्यावेवं कुड्यप्रकाशवत्
अग्नीषोमाविमौ ज्ञेयौ संपृक्तौ देहदेहिनौ १०९

There are these two contrasting, mutually exclusive modes of experience of reality, either one perceives the material object, or one perceives the eternal unmanifest non-changing truth of life; in this way, the vision of the wall, the vision of any manifest boundary depends on something prior to perception, the standpoint of consciousness, whether Self-referral or object referral.

Agni and *Soma*, these two are to be known as the diversifying quality of consciousness (*Agni*) which gives rise to the perception of boundaries, and the unifying quality of consciousness (*Soma*) which gives rise to the experience of unboundedness; these two are completely blended together [in the ordinary experience of the waking state of consciousness] becoming the body, and the dweller in the body.

> Now the entire stream of evolution from ignorance to supreme enlightenment is being presented in terms of an expanding, diversifying principle, called "*Agni*," and a unifying principle, called "*Soma*." These two principles give rise respectively to object-referral experience and Self-referral experience.

Verse 110:

अतिशायिनि निर्वाणे जाड्ये चैवातिशायिनि
अग्नीषोमस्य चैवाङ्ग स्थितिर्भवति केवला १९०

In the most excellent state of perfect balance of *Agni* and *Soma*, in the fully integrated state of enlightenment, then there is no perception of diversity and there is only the most excellent state of unchanging eternal unity in divine consciousness.

The characteristic of consciousness in that most expanded state of enlightenment brought about by [the perfect balance of] *Agni* and *Soma* is completely Self-referral, [such that] the non-changing eternal continuum of Being is eternally maintained as an all-time reality, and there is nothing else but that.

> In this verse, the state of supreme enlightenment in the state of Brahman consciousness is described in terms of the perfect balance of the diversifying and unifying principles of natural law.

Verse 111:

प्राणोऽग्निरुष्णप्रकृतिरपानः शीतलः शशी
छायातपवदित्येतौ संस्थितौ मुखमार्गगौ १११

The upward breath [*Prāṇa*] is completely in tune with Cosmic Law, the constitution of the Universe, Veda [which is] the primordial dynamism of the creative power of total natural law, expressed as the downward breath, [the upward and downward breaths oscillating as] the perfectly orderly state of least excitation of the physiology, individual mind embodying the status of cosmic mind symbolized by the Moon. Simply put, the unmanifest Being is full of the eternal dynamism of Total Natural Law: These two, existence and intelligence, pure consciousness and its organizing power, are completely integrated in the experience of eternal unity, the goal and the path moving together as one.

> In this verse, the state of supreme enlightenment in the state of Brahman consciousness is described in terms of the balance of the upward breath and the downward breath; and in terms of the unity of the fields of existence and intelligence, the unity of pure knowledge and its organizing power.

Verse 112:

अपाने शीतले सत्तामेत्युष्णः प्राणपावकः
प्रतिबिम्बमिवादर्शे स च तस्मिंस्तथैव हि ११२

When the downward breath is in the perfectly orderly state of least excitation, it is in tune with the eternal immortal existence of Being—having transcended all excitations, the breath becomes pure cosmic intelligence.

Like the wholeness of Total Natural Law seeing itself in a perfect mirror, the knower in his fully expanded, least excited state, sees himself reverberating in the Self-referral fluctuations of pure consciousness, and in that manner, he knows himself to be the eternal Veda, the embodiment of eternal non-changing unity.

In the first line of this verse, the state of supreme enlightenment in the state of Brahman consciousness is described in terms of the perfectly ordered, least excited state of the downward breath, that is completely in tune with Being, having become pure cosmic intelligence.

In the second line of this verse, the state of supreme enlightenment in the state of Brahman consciousness is described in terms of the knower seeing himself reverberating in the Self-referral fluctuations of pure consciousness, and knowing himself to be the eternal Veda, the embodiment of eternal unity.

Verse 113:

चिदग्निः पद्मपत्रस्थं सोमं वाचात्मकं त्विषा
जनयत्यनुभूत्येह कुड्यालोकं यथा बहिः ११३

The intrinsic creativity of pure consciousness, consciousness that is fully lively with the creative potential of total natural law is established by total brain functioning at the moment of liftoff in Yogic Flying, giving rise to *Soma* which is the consolidated essence of speech, the flow of the eternal Veda, infinite dynamism of total natural law put into motion.

That *Soma* [in turn] gives rise to perfection of the faculties of gaining knowledge, the ability to know anything at will, leading to the deep appreciation of the fine mechanics of the process of creation of the object in the outside world, giving rise to perception of the finest relative, perception of the world in terms of light, celestial perception.

> The explanation of the nature of *Soma* and its relationship to *Agni* in the process of transcending and in the development of higher states of consciousness has been explained in verses 90 to 112. Now in this verse, Vasishtha begins to relate the knowledge of *Soma* to the powerful engine of acceleration of growth of consciousness which has been the theme of this chapter, the liftoff during Yogic Flying. There is a profound infusion of *Soma* into the system at the moment of liftoff. This growth of *Soma* has great advantages for practical life: The *Soma* produced at the time of liftoff brings perfection to the faculties of gaining knowledge, including the Siddhi of being able to

> know anything at will. The *Soma* produced in the liftoff cultures refined perception through the senses, in the direction of celestial perception.

Verse 114:

संसृत्यादौ यथा काचित्संविच्छीतोष्णारूपिणी
अग्नीषोमाभिधां प्राप्ता सैव सर्गे नृणामिह १९४

In the beginning stages of the course of Yogic Flying, whatever small degree of integration of pure consciousness [has been achieved], that corresponding degree of dynamism will be expressed in the impetuosity of the liftoff in Yogic Flying.

The balance of *Agni* and *Soma*, the degree of perfection of mind-body coordination is made vividly evident as the height of lift-off that is achieved: The lift-off, when the body suddenly takes off into the air here and now, is the only clear demonstration by human beings, visible to other human beings, of the growing level of consciousness, growing mind-body coordination [on the path to perfection] .

> The liftoff in Yogic Flying demonstrates the degree of perfection of mind-body coordination. Perfect mind-body coordination means balance of *Agni* and *Soma*: It is the balance between *Agni* and *Soma* which gives rise to the liftoff. Increasing refinement of this balance will give rise to higher and higher flights. The liftoff is a direct measure, objectively verifiable, of the degree of perfection of mind-body coordination, the degree of balance between *Agni* and *Soma*. The objectification of the measure of growth of higher states of consciousness takes

enlightenment out of the field of mysticism, demonstrating that enlightenment is not mood or a concept. The liftoff brings to view the degree of success in mastering gravity by harnessing the support of total natural law.

Verse 115:

यत्र सोमकला ग्रस्ता क्षणं सूर्येण षोडशी
मुखाद्वितस्तिमात्रं स्यात्तत्र बद्धपदो भव १९५

In which practice of Yogic Flying, [only] a little portion of *Soma* is drunk in an instant, [but] through regular practice of Yogic Flying leading to growth of consciousness, and the progressive stabilization of the sun of life, (the *Ātmā*,) [then] the *Soma* rises to its full measure, it expands to be an all-time reality.

From the beginning, the measure of liftoff may only be about a span, nine inches or so, but in that small flight, you have taken a positive step forward on the path of enlightenment, and those small hops are going to become long flights.

In this verse, the entire span of progress in Yogic Flying from small hops to long flights is tied to the development of *Soma*. Maintaining the body in the air requires the constant and full production of *Soma*; on the way to that, momentary draughts of *Soma* cause the body to lift up into the air in small hops.

Verse 116:

नूनं सूर्यपदं प्राप्तो यत्र सोमो हृदम्बरे
नूनं केवलया स्थित्या तत्र बद्ध पदो भव ११६

Now with this liftoff, a step of progress on the path of stabilization of the *Ātmā* has been achieved, in which the *Soma* is enlivened in the space of the heart.

Now with this liftoff, by the experience of self-sufficiency, by fulfilling a desire by the mere impulse of the mind by going back to the Self, in that demonstration of supreme mind-body coordination, you have taken a positive step forward on the path of enlightenment, and those small hops are going to become long flights.

> *Soma* is enlivened in the space of the heart: *Soma* is intimately connected with the expansion of consciousness. Here it is being made clear that it is *Soma*, the product of perfect-mind body coordination that is lifting the body up into the air. It is not through individual effort, nor does it grow through increasing power of muscles developed through long practice. Flights become longer and higher through growth in higher consciousness and the stabilization of the production of *Soma*. From the beginning of the practice of Yogic Flying, to the goal of complete mastery over gravity, the body lifts off the ground by the mere effortless impulse of desire of the mind. Every liftoff is a positive step forward on the path to enlightenment.

Verse 117:

उष्णमग्निश्चिदादित्यः शैत्यं सोम उदाहृतम्
यत्रैतौ प्रतिबिम्बस्थौ तत्र बद्धपदो भव ११७

The infinite unbounded field of Self-referral consciousness (*Āditya*) is the field of Total Natural Law (*Agni*)—the state of least excitation of consciousness (*Śaitya*) is vibrant (*Uṣṇa*), it has dynamism within its nature—the *Soma*, the superfluid flow of intelligence at the junction point of consciousness and matter, has been demonstrated.

In which demonstration of the power of consciousness, these two, consciousness and physiology are seen as identical, and both belong to one wholeness of total natural law: in that demonstration of Brahman consciousness in the liftoff, you have taken a positive step forward on the path of enlightenment, and those small hops are going to become long flights.

> Consciousness and physiology are seen as identical when physiology is established as the mirror of consciousness, and consciousness is established as the mirror of physiology. In this way, by developing supreme mind-body coordination, the liftoff directly cultures the integrated state of life in Brahman Consciousness. Consciousness and physiological are so perfectly integrated at the moment of liftoff that each becomes the reflection of the other, and both belong to one wholeness of natural law. In this verse, Vasishtha refers back to verses 110-112, in which the growth of Brahman consciousness was measured in terms of the perfect balance of Agni and Soma,

> and the perfect balance between the upward breath and the downward breath. These features of perfect balance in the physiology in the state of Brahman Consciousness, the supreme goal of evolution, are drawn into practical life at the moment of liftoff. The liftoff is the supreme technology of Yoga, the jet plane to supreme enlightenment in Brahman consciousness.

Verse 118:

शरीरे सोमसूर्याग्निसंक्रान्तिज्ञो भवानघ
तत्र संक्रान्तिकाला हि बाह्यास्तृणसमाः स्मृताः ११८

When the physical body [lifts up in the air], the *Puruṣa* or soul, the dweller in the body has stepped onto a completely unified state, where the infinite silence of the unbounded Self (*Sūrya*), and the dynamism of total natural law (*Agni*) and the flow of *Soma* connecting silence with dynamism, connecting consciousness with physiology, are all three fully lively, fully awake in perfect balance: Be [in that way] O stainless one!

In the practice of Yogic Flying, many times [in each session] one steps onto that completely integrated state of perfect mind-body coordination when the body lifts up in the air, as if reflecting on the outside the memories of [infinite dynamism fixed in eternal silence, like so] many blades of grass floating in the air.

> Amplifying what was said in the previous verse, Vasishtha explains that the *Puruṣa*, the dweller in the body has stepped onto a new level of integration. This is much more than the state of *Samādhi* that is experienced during the practice of effortless transcending. It is a completely

integrated state of perfect-mind body coordination, in which the body is as much involved as the mind. That is the perfection of the art of transcending, the image of totality, Brahman. Not only the "*Dhi*," the intellect or consciousness is in perfect balance, "*Samā*," but the entire mind-body system has achieved a level of perfect balance with the environment, like a blade of grass floating in the air.

Verse 119:

संक्रान्तिमुत्तरमथायनमङ्ग सम्यक्कालं तथा विषुवतौ यदि देहवातैः
अन्तर्बहिष्ठमिव वेत्सि यथानुभूतं तच्छोभसेऽत्र न पुनः परमभ्युपेतः ११९

This deeply profound transcending at the time of liftoff is a very advanced Yogic practice, the fastest path to enlightenment when practiced together in large groups at the center of the country: If the group is large enough, the trends of the entire collective consciousness of the nation can be balanced, [for fastest evolution of the whole society].

You know what is the level of perfection of mind-body coordination [that has been achieved] according to what is observed in the phenomenon of the liftoff: Glorify your Self in this way, here and now, transcending again and again, until the supreme goal of enlightenment is achieved.

Already in the previous verse, Vasishtha has shown that the liftoff in Yogic Flying is the most deeply profound transcending, the most profound state of integration of consciousness, physiology and environment. The liftoff is a direct highway to Brahman Consciousness. We have seen in this chapter how from so many different angles total knowledge of Vedic Science is located in the liftoff and drawn into practical life through regular practice. Perfect health is contained in the liftoff. The Patañjali *Kaivalya* is contained in the liftoff. The Jaimini *Kaivalya* is contained in the liftoff. The Vyāsa *Kaivalya* is contained in the liftoff. Total Veda is contained in the liftoff. And that which is beyond the Veda, the complete fulfillment of life in the attainment of Brahman consciousness as an all-time reality, is contained in the liftoff. Certainly, the liftoff must be the fastest path to enlightenment.

But Vasishtha now points to an even more advanced Yogic practice, one which simultaneously integrates not only the body and the mind, but draws the collective consciousness of the entire nation together into a state of perfect unity and coherence. When Yogic Flying is practiced in large groups at the center of the country, then a still higher level of integration is achieved.

An individual transcending and experiencing transcendental consciousness experiences the primary, foundational level of mind-body coordination. This is the starting point of the path of evolution through Yoga. More advanced is the tremendous mind-body coordination achieved at the time of liftoff, through the Siddhi of Yogic Flying utilizing the practice of *Saṁyama* as prescribed by Patañjali. This advanced practice of the liftoff brings the body as well as the mind into a state of complete harmony and integration with all the laws of nature. But there is one more level of integration possible, and this will represent the absolute fastest path to enlightenment. When a group of Yogic Flyers practicing together under one roof at the geographical center of the nation reaches a size of the square root of one percent of the population, then the whole society participates in the phenomenon of integration of consciousness and physiology, and the entire nation experiences waves of purity and coherence in the collective consciousness. The integration of body, mind, and the collective consciousness of the entire nation represents a higher level of integration, and this experience is the fastest engine of growth for the individual, and for the collective consciousness of the nation as a whole. This technology of flying in large groups is as much more powerful than the practice of lifting off alone, as the liftoff itself is more powerful than the experience of transcendental consciousness. This is the most powerful technology of Yoga, the supreme essence of Vasishtha's Yoga, the technological basis of *Rām* Rāj, and the ultimate culmination of this chapter on the liftoff in Yogic Flying.

Colophon:

इत्यार्षे श्रीवासिष्ठमहारामायणे वाल्मीकीये मोक्षोपायेषु निर्वाणप्रकरणे अग्निषोमविचारणं नामैकाशीतितमः सर्गः ८१

Endnotes

1 Orme-Johnson, D.W., and Herron, R.E., An Innovative Approach to Reducing Medical Care Utilization and Expenditures, *American Journal of Managed Care*, January 1997, 3: 1, pp. 135-144. Available at AJMC.com.

2 Based on 400 hours of audio recordings of Dr. Vernon Katz and Maharishi during their work on the translation of the Brahma Sūtra, 1968-1975. Highlights of these audio recordings are published in Katz, Vernon, *Conversations with Maharishi: Maharishi Mahesh Yogi speaks about the Full Development of Human Consciousness*, Maharishi University of Management Press: Fairfield, Iowa, 2011 (Volume 1) and 2014 (Volume 2).

3 This is one of Maharishi's favorite quotations, and this is the translation which he teaches for it.

4 This process of pure intelligence becoming creative intelligence is described by Maharishi in lesson 8 of the 33 lesson videotaped course, *Science of Creative Intelligence Teacher Training Course*, MIU, 1972.

Chapter 6: Second Stage of Yogic Flying

Verse 1:

वसिष्ट उवाच ।
अणुतां स्थूलतां वापि यथा गच्छति योगिनाम्
देहो नाम तथा सम्यग्वक्ष्यमाणमिदं शृणु १

aṇutāṁ sthūlatāṁ vā'pi yathā gacchati yoginām
deho nāma tathā samyag vakṣyamāṇam idaṁ śṛṇu 1

As to whether there are short hops or long hops taken by the Yogis [during Yogic flying], this whole story of how the body moves [in progressively longer flights] is being described [now], listen!

The previous chapter was devoted to describing the enormous practical benefits of the liftoff by the novice practitioner of the practice of *Saṁyama* using Patañjali's formula for Yogic Flying. The entire path of unfoldment of total knowledge and organizing power is contained in every liftoff, every small hop of even the beginner Yogic Flyer. The flyer gains perfect health through the flow of *Soma* in that instant of the liftoff, and he tastes the fulfillment of the *Kaivalya*s of Patañjali, Jaimini and Vyāsa, enlivening in his awareness the totality of Veda, and the supreme knowledge of Vedanta.

In the next chapter, we return to the story of Cūḍālā, and the exploits of Cūḍālā are described. By that time, Cūḍālā has completely mastered the flying Siddhi, and many other Siddhis as well, and she flies here and there, exploring the otherwise inaccessible regions of the universe, and satisfying her curiosity about life on every level of creation.

This bridge chapter is necessary to explain how the practitioner of Yogic Flying advances from small hops to complete mastery of the skies. We have seen that total knowledge and organizing power is contained in seed form already in the beginning hops of the new practitioner. What actually has to happen for the full power of the flying Siddhi to be manifested? What is it that determines whether the liftoff is very short, like a beginner's hop, insignificantly small and minute, compared to the possibility of flying through the universe and visiting the various *Lokas* (worlds)—or very long, opening the possibility of visiting the tops of the mountains and the bottom of the oceans and wherever one might like to go. In the previous chapter we examined what happens to the health of the body, and what happens to the mind as the immediate result of success in the practice of the sūtra for Yogic Flying, in the beginner and accomplished flyer alike. Now we are going to look at the practice from the outside, to see how actually the body moves through the air. In terms of total brain functioning at the moment of liftoff, there is no difference between the beginner and the adept, but in terms of how the body moves, whether it comes down right away, or like the flyer Ādi Śaṅkarācārya, flies to the next city, there is certainly a very big difference. How the beginner becomes adept, and his short flights become long flights—what has to happen on the level of body in order to perfect the Siddhi—that needs to be clearly understood in order to be prepared for Cūḍālā's amazing flights, described in the next chapter.

The first word of this verse is "*Aṇutāṁ*," meaning short and minute. It is followed by the word, *Sthūlatāṁ*, meaning big, huge. These two words are followed by the word "*Vā*," meaning "or," and then by the word "*Api*," meaning "if," or "whether." The word *Yathā*, "in which manner," refers to the liftoff in the practice of the sūtra for Yogic Flying, as described in the previous chapter. *Gacchati*, is third person singular present tense of the root *Gam*, to move, so it means, one goes, moves, or travels. And the last word of the line is *Yoginām*, pertaining to the Yogis. "Whether [any] one of the Yogis travels a tiny bit or a long way in this practice," is quite literally the meaning of this line. Commentators however, seeing the word "*Aṇutāṁ*," "small, minute," in this verse, and seeing the word *Aṇimādi*, referring to the eight Siddhis starting with *Aṇimā*, "making the body small as an atom," mentioned in verse 14, have concluded that the whole chapter is about the development of these eight supernormal powers. Now, it is true, that the unfoldment of all these higher powers is going to come from the perfection of the flying Siddhi, and reference will be made to this growth in all the Siddhis in verse 14, and in the concluding verses of the chapter. But it is not right to see this chapter as the interpolation of an extraneous and unrelated chapter on special powers. What we need to learn in this chapter—and what is proposed that we learn, in the first verse of this chapter—is how Cūḍālā's practice of Yogic Flying went from short hops to long flights. We know everything about the liftoff, but we don't yet know about what happens next, what happens to the body, how far the body travels. This we have to learn, how the beginner becomes adept. If other Siddhis come along in the process, that is all right, but our passion is to know how her short hops became long flights. And that is the central theme of this chapter.

Verse 2:

हृद्यब्जचक्रकोशोर्ध्वं प्रस्फुरत्यानलः कणः
हेमभ्रमरवत्सान्ध्यविद्युल्लव इवाम्बुदे २

When the heart desires for the body to move upwards, that intention coming to a point at the finest level of creation, flashes forth as the flying impulse, born of the *Soma*.

The golden light that is full of the power to move about at will, comes in an instant like a flash of lightning emerging from the integrated state of mind and body at the moment of liftoff, in proportion to the *Soma* that is being given out.

> From the perspective of the body, the flying impulse is a flash of golden light emerging from the integrated state of mind and body at the moment of liftoff. That flash of light which travels through the whole body, is born of the *Soma*. The quality and quantity of the *Soma* determines how far the body will move under the influence of the flying Siddhi.

Verse 3:

स प्रवर्धनसंवित्त्या वात्ययेवाशु वर्धते
संविद्रूपतया नूनमर्कवद्याति चोदयम् ३

The *Soma* increases in quantity to the degree that consciousness becomes more concentrated and integrated with more powerful and more forceful winds.

The winds being composed of consciousness are full of the power of the thunderbolt of Indra, such that wherever the wind of consciousness moves, everything in its path is immediately pushed along in that direction.

> Consciousness has organizing power. More concentrated and more integrated consciousness means increasingly pure consciousness. The purer, the more concentrated, the more integrated it becomes through practice, the greater the organizing power. The winds of that consciousness—the organizing power set in motion by that consciousness—depend upon how concentrated, how unmixed with any relative boundary, how pure and integrated is that consciousness. When the diverse consciousness, flowing through many channels, turns back on itself and becomes completely self-sufficient, on its own, fully integrated, then it is a wholeness, completely full, and that fullness, that wholeness of awareness is called "Indra." The organizing power of that integrated state of consciousness has the power of the thunderbolt of Indra. The thunderbolt of Indra is the flashing forth of the immense organizing power of total natural law. He, Indra, is the lord of all the *Devas*, the master of all the impulses of creative intelligence. His power, his thunderbolt, is the total organizing power of all the impulses

of creative intelligence at his command. That organizing power produces forceful winds in the body, lifting it up.

Verse 4:

संध्याभ्रप्रथमार्काभो वृद्धिमभ्यागतः क्षणात्
गालयत्यखिलं साङ्गं देहं हेम यथानलः ४

Resembling the first ray of light at the break of dawn, [the golden light of the flying impulse emerging from the transcendent] appears suddenly and immediately expands,

[And] The body as a whole together with its limbs is made to move a physical distance, corresponding to the move of the golden light.

This is the description of the phenomenon of Yogic Flying from the perspective of the body: The golden light of the flying impulse, powerful like the thunderbolt of Indra, flashes forth like the first ray of light at the break of dawn, and quickly expanding, moves the body.

Verse 5:

जलस्पर्शासहो युक्त्या गलयेत्प्रपदादपि
बाह्य एवानलस्पर्शात्स्वान्ते वस्तुविशेषतः ५

In the ignorant, unenlightened individual, there is inability to sustain a faint impulse of feeling [in the silence of unbounded awareness]; by practice [of Yogic Flying,] the awareness should be brought to silence, the level of the unified field: By [repeatedly] experiencing the integrated state of consciousness at the moment before lift-off, the ability to function in unbounded awareness grows.

Only when something outside is the end-result of the experience of the Self, [brought about] by putting the Absolute into motion on the finest level of feeling, does the Absolute become a tangible object of experience made of the self-interacting dynamics of total natural law.

> Unbounded awareness is without qualities, without measure. Whether it is integrated and pure, or perhaps a little wavering, and not so tight, compact and Self-referral is difficult to measure. However, by putting the pure consciousness to action, the quality of the consciousness, the degree of purity becomes immediately evident. Making the unbounded awareness function through the technology of Siddhis is making the unmanifest step onto practical life, and become tangible and fruitful. The Absolute is made of the self-interacting dynamics of total natural law, but these self-interacting dynamics are virtual fluctuation of the unmanifest Being, and they are not seen until they are put to action, made to function on the finest level of feeling. The experience of the integrated

state of consciousness at the moment before liftoff is consciousness being put to action, consciousness being made tangible.

Verse 6:

स शरीरद्वयं पश्चाद्विधूय क्वापि लीयते
विक्षोभितेन प्राणेन नीहारो वात्यया यथा ६

The integrated unified consciousness becomes the body, having a dual nature, [body and the space in which it moves]; after being tossed about here and there, something of the integrated unified state of consciousness clings to it.

By means of [the body] being shaken [and made to move about here and there] by the *Prāṇa*, the consciousness in the body becomes capable of motion in the same way.

In the phenomenon of Yogic Flying, first, in the moment just before liftoff, the mind-body system encompassing consciousness in its simplest and most ordered state, and the physiology playing the role of dynamism in the field of consciousness, are completely integrated and whole. Consciousness is the body, the body is consciousness, they are together total natural law, Veda reverberating within itself, and that infinitely dynamic integrated consciousness alone is. Now that integrated consciousness which is one thing, flows or is transformed into two things, namely the body and the space, the *Ākāśa* in which the body moves. In that instant when the integrated unity of consciousness becomes two things, body and the space around it, the body rises up into the air in fulfillment of the desire of the mind. The body behaves dynamically, moving into the air and returning to the ground in a series of hops: the integrated state of unity has become the duality of the body moving about in space. But as the body is moving, it is not entirely on its own, since it is carrying out the dictates of the mind, the dictates of the integrated state of consciousness whose intention, whose *Saṁkalpa* it is now fulfilling. In that process of the intention of the integrated consciousness to fly being carried out by the body, something of the integrated state of consciousness, something of the totality of Brahman experienced by the mind-body system at the moment before liftoff, clings to the body. What clings to the body in some small measure, is the ability to move through space at the dictate of the mind. The intention moves the body, and something of the intending consciousness itself flows into the body and becomes the body, and clings to the body. Infinity moves into every cell of the body at the moment of liftoff, and in that process of putting to practice the desire within that infinity, the infinity collapses, it becomes finite, it becomes the body moving up into the air some few inches. But in the process of moving according to the dictates of the integrated consciousness, some element of the abstraction of infinite consciousness that has flown into the body and instigated flying remains, clings on to the physiology. Now the physiology has learned how to carry out the command of consciousness in a new way—not simply responding to a few nerve impulses conducted by neurons from the central nervous system as in the ordinary waking state mode of moving about, but responding to the infinity of Brahman moving into every cell of the body and lifting the body up. A channel is created between the lively wholeness of total natural law and the physical body, a channel of "mind-body coordination." The body gains a memory of how to behave in the grip of wholeness, how to respond to the impulse of total natural law. In that growing memory, something of the cause, something of the infinite state of totally integrated consciousness clings onto the body, even after the hopping has ceased. The body has grown to some small measure in the value of wholeness of consciousness, and it is now a different body: It is a body that knows how to behave in accordance with the design and command of total natural law. The channel of connection, of coordination, of ability to behave in response to flowing infinite consciousness, has been established and is growing steadily with practice. And this ability clinging onto the body means that the body is more capable of responding to the dictates of the integrated state of total natural law in any and all circumstances, not just in flying. This is a positive step of integration of consciousness and physiology. Some small measure of "mind over matter," remains in the body. The body is growing in the value of the integrated state of total natural law, it is becoming more and more the fit dwelling place, the temple of Brahman. All this happens in the instant that the integrated consciousness flows and moves the body into the air.

Verse 7:

आधारनाडीनिर्हीना व्योमस्थैवावशिष्यते
शक्तिः कुण्डलिनी वह्नेर्धूमलेखेव निर्गता ७

What sustains the [empty tube which we call the] physical body up off of the ground, is the strengthened quality of *Ākāśa* that remains as a residue [of the wholeness, when the unified consciousness becomes the body at the moment of liftoff].

The power [that sustains the body in the air] is the Constitution of the Universe, because what carries the body upwards is the degree of enlivenment of the writing in the mist—[the text of the Veda, the script of Total Natural Law]—made concretely visible [in the awareness].

> The element of the fully integrated state of consciousness, the element of Brahman which clings to the body after it has been made to fly through the air in a series of hops is here being identified as "the strengthened quality of *Ākāśa*." The body is growing more and more in the *Ākāśa* element through the regular practice of Yogic Flying. With sufficient infusion of the nature of *Ākāśa* into the body through long practice of Yogic Flying, the body could stay up in the air. The body is growing in the ability to carry out the dictates of consciousness, and that ability could grow to such an extent that the body could successfully follow the command of consciousness to rise up and remain in the air. That process of growth through Yogic Flying is the strengthening and increasing of the quality of *Ākāśa* in the body.
>
> What is the power of *Ākāśa* in the body? In Vedic Science,

Ākāśa is the element associated with hearing, and with sound. There are five physical elements, earth, water, fire, air and space, and each is associated with one of the five senses, smell, taste, sight, touch and hearing, giving rise to sensations of odor, savor, form, feeling and sound. The *Ākāśa* is not empty space in the sense of a Euclidean framework, it is a Unified Field, that is lively with the virtual fluctuations of total natural law. Total natural law, comprising the total Veda together with all the branches of Vedic Literature, is lively in every point of creation, and this is the nature of *Ākāśa*. Infusing *Ākāśa* into the physiology means infusing the total potential of all the laws of nature, total Veda and Vedic Literature into the physiology. Every cell in the body is growing in the value of Veda, becoming living breathing Veda. Every cell is growing in the value of total natural law.

When every cell is growing day by day in the value of total natural law, and when individual awareness is a projection of the intelligence of the sum of all the cells in the body, then something happens to consciousness, something must happen on the level of experience as this quality of *Ākāśa* keeps growing. This is being explained in this verse.

The power of the Constitution of the Universe is what sustains the body up in the air, and the Constitution of the Universe is made up of Veda and Vedic Literature, the discrete structures which together make up total natural law. Law is an expression of intelligence, and that expression has been cognized by the seers of ancient times as formulae, laws, expressions, sentences, knowledge of natural law expressed by natural law itself in its own language, the language of natural law. In the language of natural law, the ancient Vedic language, there is a perfect correlation between name and form—the sequence of syllables is the name, and the law or principle which it embodies is the form. The connection between name and form is said to be eternal, not man-made. All the laws of nature are eternally telling their own story to themselves, and this is the flow of the Veda.

As the *Ākāśa* grows in the physiology, the Constitution of the Universe, total Veda and Vedic Literature is growing in the physiology. The milestone of this growth of *Ākāśa* is the vision in consciousness of the Veda as "writing in the mist." In order for the body to fly, in order to remain in the air, the *Ākāśa* value in the physiology has to be so greatly enlivened that the impulses of intelligence that make up the Constitution of the Universe come to awareness, begin to be seen. Writing in the mist gives the sense of a somewhat hazy or indistinct experience. As for example, when one approaches a busy marketplace from a distance, one hears only a hum, a hubbub, without being able to distinguish specific sounds, and then as one approaches closer, one begins to hear that the overall din is made up of individual voices of sellers and buyers engaged in commerce. In the same way, the total value of the Constitution of the Universe, the total value of the writing in the mist is first experienced as the sound "A," which is the first sound of Ṛg Veda, and contains within it in seed form the total knowledge of Veda and Vedic Literature. This comes to be heard and seen: This is the experience of the growth of *Ākāśa* in the physiology. Constitution of the Universe is becoming a living reality, and that means that the physiology is growing in the value of natural law, growing in the value of Veda, beginning to reflect the total value of all the laws of nature that govern the universe, not abstractly, in consciousness, or in memory, but as a manifest materialization of total natural law as "writing in the mist."

Verse 8:

क्रोडीकृतमनोबुद्धिमयजीवाद्यहंकृतिः
अन्तः स्फुरच्चमत्कारा धूमलेखेव नागरी ८

The mind and the intellect being empty of all content, consciousness knowing itself becomes the Creator and the sacrificer of the sound "A," [the impulse of Total Knowledge, Veda].

The spontaneous appearances [of the sound "A"] being experienced repeatedly and increasingly clearly inside in the field of Self-referral consciousness, the writing in the mist is more and more clearly seen to be comprised of many sounds, comprised of the innumerable impulses of Total Natural Law, the Veda.

The writing in the mist becoming more and more clear, the sound "A" takes on manifold values. Capturing the total awareness with its charm, it gets infused in all the functions of consciousness. It becomes the instigator of all activity (*Purohitam*), it becomes the intelligence underlying all transformation and change (*Yajñasya devam*), it is the uninvolved witness of activity (*Ṛtvijam*), yet simultaneously engages natural law to function (*Hotāram*), and brings fulfillment to every activity (*Ratna-dhātamam*). This is the growth of *Ākāśa* in the physiology, experienced as the progressive enlivenment of total natural law in the physiology, giving rise to clearer and clearer cognition of the writing in the mist, the functioning value of total natural law in diverse channels in the physiology.

This whole phenomenon of the cognition of "A," takes place within pure consciousness, within the field of Self-referral consciousness, where there is no object of consciousness, and consciousness is awake to its own nature only. Consciousness is seeing its own nature as "A," it is not seeing something that is outside of it. This is detailing the phenomenon of the infusion of the total value of natural law, Brahman consciousness, into the physiology. With this experience, pure self-referral consciousness begins to be lively within itself, and with increasing experience of this field of total abstraction, the knower begins to experience this writing in the mist, not coming from outside, like a vision, but the fluctuations of his own eternal consciousness seeming to take form as sounds and forms, expressing their inherent creative power.

Verse 9:

बिसे शैले तृणे भित्तावुपले दिवि भूतले
सा यथा योज्यते यत्र तेन निर्यात्यलं तथा ९

When the *Ākāśa* inside the hard mountain-like body seated on the grass mat expands, the body becomes like a precious jewel having the light of heaven on the inside, and a solid earthly surface on the outside.

As the *Ākāśa* in the body in that way expands and is glorified through the practice [as the "writing in the mist" is experienced more and more clearly], She [Mother Divine, the Constitution of the Universe, the total potential of natural law which is the omnipresent dynamism in the *Ākāśa*] gets harnessed to the physical body, [and] by that process the body becomes light enough to move without the limitation of gravity, and moves through the air in that manner.

> Mother Divine is always there in every human physiology. She is the embodiment of total natural law, the nature of the innermost Self, the nature of *Ātmā*. But she remains hidden deep inside, unreachable. As the *Ākāśa* in the body grows and expands, that total value of natural law which is experienced moving the body in the phenomenon of Yogic Flying is recognized to be Mother Divine. She—total natural law, the Veda, the nature of *Ātmā*—gets as if harnessed to the body. She is then seen as the agency responsible for the lightness of the body.

Verse 10:

संवित्तिः सैव यात्यङ्ग रसाद्यन्तं यथाक्रमम्
रसेनापूर्णतामेति तन्त्रीभार इवाम्बुना १०

She [Mother Divine] coming to perception is the total disclosure of all knowledge, the supremely sweet nectar which is the source and goal of all search, and that alone moves the body up into the air according to the desires of the mind more and more as it unfolds.

The great mass of the body having become the embodiment of the principle of action by means of that sweet nectar [of *Soma*], moves [about at will] moving from fullness, where it is, to emptiness where it is not with the ease of water flowing [down a hill].

> *Rasena apūrṇatām/āpūrṇatām*: By means of "rasa" the fullness of "a" becomes "ā." The total knowledge of the Veda is contained in the expansion of "A," to "Ā." This is the complete disclosure of all knowledge. (*a ā iti*, the last sūtra of Pāṇini's grammar.)

Verse 11:

रसापूर्णा यमाकारं भावयत्याशु तत्तथा
धत्ते चित्रकृतो बुद्धौ रेखा राम यथा कृतिम् ११

The supremely sweet nectar is the fullness of the total knowledge of the Constitution of the Universe contained in "A," which is made to expand to become the letter "Ā:" Being, transforming into becoming with infinite speed, that is Totality, Brahman, and under the sway of that dynamism of total natural law [the body moves about].

When the intellect upholds the infinite variety of creation as one straight line, one eternal continuum of Being, O Rāma, correspondingly there is the ability to create anything at will.

> The fulfillment of the knowledge of *Puruṣa*, the fulfillment of the knowledge of the Self is said to be the vision of all the dynamism and variety of creation as one straight line, without beginning or end. In that vision the infinite creativity of total natural law is captured.

Verse 12:

दृढभाववशादन्तरस्थीन्याप्नोति सा ततः
मातृगर्भनिषण्णेषु सुसूक्ष्मेवाङ्कुरस्थितिः १२

Because the power stems from being firmly fastened in Being, as one attains to deeper and deeper levels [within the 19 enclosures of Mother Divine] She, Mother Divine, the infinite organizing power of Total Natural Law becomes correspondingly more accessible.

Seated in successively deeper enclosures of Mother Divine, each one subtler, more refined and more difficult to fathom than the previous, the corresponding creative power of that level of natural law is gained.

> The infusion of *Ākāśa* into the nature of the physiology through the practice of Yogic Flying, gives rise to the experience of the "writing in the mist," the cognition of the laws of nature, the Veda, reverberating in consciousness, beginning with the cognition of "A." With more and more infusion of *Ākāśa* into the physiology, the dynamism of natural law that was seen first as the voice of totality reverberating in "A," comes to be seen as Mother Divine, the embodiment of total Veda. Mother Divine moves the body, and the body moves effortlessly at will through the air. Now the entire process of expansion of consciousness through the practice of Yogic Flying, leading to the ability to fly through the air at will—the expansion from small hops to complete mastery of the skies—is being described as a process of gaining access to Mother Divine. Mother Divine is hidden safely behind many enclosures, and consciousness has to be steadier,

more integrated and purer in order to enter into each successive enclosure. One gains the power of total natural law in stages, according to the level of Being which has been infused in the nature of the mind, according to the deserving ability. The nineteen enclosures of Mother Divine are described in the *Devī Bhāgavatam Mahā Purāṇa*[1], (See Appendix, pp. 409 ff.) and they chronicle the step by step entry into the presence of the unlimited organizing power of total natural law. Each step, each deeper enclosure is progressively more beautiful, more charming, more full of treasures than the previous. The story of the nineteen enclosures of Mother Divine is an articulation of the many discrete milestones on the path to complete stabilization of Being. There is a path to mastery of the skies, but it is not a magic trick, it is the path to unfolding the deepest levels of silence, the fields of greater and greater orderliness and power deep within, it is the path to step by step complete perfection of consciousness and physiology, the path to supreme realization. Through long practice of Yogic Flying one attains the inner sanctum, the innermost enclosure of Mother Divine, and achieving that, one has earned total mastery of natural law. That mastery of total natural law which is attained by reaching the inner sanctum, the innermost of all the enclosures of Mother Divine, the fully stabilized pure Infinite Being, the throne of Mother Divine, is described in the next two verses.

Verse 13:

यथाभिमतमाकारं प्रमाणं वेत्ति राघव
जीवशक्तिरवाप्नोति सुमेर्वादि तृणादि च १३

Gaining the ability to function and project thought at each progressively deeper level, there is the valid path to knowledge of all the fine mechanics of creation involved in the expansion of "A" to become the letter "Ā." Follow and enjoy that path, O Raghava.

The individual soul attains the power to function on broader and broader scales even up to the size of mountains and achieve what can be achieved there, and to function on smaller and more minute scales down to the level of the minutest fine particles and achieve what can be achieved there.

> The fine mechanics of the process of creation are encapsulated in the collapse of "A" to "Ka." In the repeated collapse of infinity to a point, and expansion of the point to infinity, layers of expression of natural law are built up. In this way, the surface values of life are made up of the reverberations between infinity and point at the finest level of creation. As the aspirant becomes familiar with deeper and deeper levels of Being, he becomes familiar with broader and broader time and distance scales and how natural law expresses itself in those greatly expanded values; and he becomes familiar with finer and finer time and distances scales and how natural law expresses itself in the delicate and rapid interplay of atoms and fine particles. The function of natural law appears different in different time and distance scales. From the standpoint

of deeper and deeper levels of being, the unity of natural law on every level of creation comes to perception. Thus, the Siddha becomes competent to function on the finest levels, and on the most expanded levels.

The culmination of this expansion of capability through fathoming deeper levels of being comes when the inner sanctum of Mother Divine is reached, inside the entrance to the nineteenth enclosure. There, because of the broad base of awareness, new abilities come up. The path is from amness, individual existence, to isness, universal cosmic existence, from the isolated expression of "A," to the extended universal expression of "Ā." Vasishtha invites Rām to follow this path to universal awareness, going through all the enclosures of Mother Divine, gaining greater and greater silence and greater and greater organizing power until the total value of natural law on every level of creation is harnessed.

Verse 14:

श्रुतं त्वया योगसाध्यमणिमाद्यर्थसाधनम्
ज्ञानसाध्यमिदानीं त्वं शृणु श्रवणभूषणम् १४

What you have just heard is the process of perfection through the practice of Yoga leading to the (8 principle) Siddhis beginning with *Aṇimā,* the power of making the body as small as an atom, [all together] giving mastery over the entire field of manifest creation.

There are Siddhis of knowledge to be gained [also], now you should listen to this the greatest of all jewels of wisdom that can be heard through the ears.

The path to perfection through Yoga involves the practice of *Saṁyama* using the formulas taught by Patañjali. The practice of Yogic Flying culminates after a long time in the attainment of eight Siddhis, 1) *Aṇimā*, making the body very small, 2) *Mahimā*, making the body very large, 3) *Garimā*, making the body very heavy, 4) *Laghimā*, lightness of the body as in Yogic Flying, 5) *Prāpti*, the ability to acquire any desired object, 6) *Prākāmya*, irresistible will, 7) *Īśitva*, mastery of creation, 8) and *Vaśitva*, subduing everything to one's will and bestowing all enjoyments of the relative field, as well as eternal liberation.

Vasishtha has brought to Rām's attention the attainment of these eight Siddhis, brought about by the practice of Yogic Flying leading to the entry in succession to all of the enclosures of Mother Divine. This path to complete mastery of creation seems to be the sweetest and most precious knowledge, but it is actually not "the greatest of all jewels of wisdom." The flashiness of the possible attainment of these eight Siddhis is being balanced by the knowledge of the greatest of all jewels of wisdom, the knowledge of wholeness moving within itself, the knowledge of life in Unity Consciousness. This is the experience that destroys the darkness of ignorance with the light of knowledge, not these relative accomplishments.

Having heard of the great treasures that await by gaining familiarity with the different enclosures of Mother Divine, one might be tempted to give primary importance to these treasures. One might be tempted to try to win the favor of Mother Divine through special observances and by the recitation of stotras to Mother Divine. But these practices are not mentioned here. The path, and the goal, are always and forever only this, that by direct experience of the Self, the Self should be realized as all-pervading, spotless and pure—awake in itself, consciousness experiencing its true nature, untainted by the stains of relativity (verse 23).

Verse 15:

एकं चिन्मात्रमस्तीह शुद्धं सौम्यमलक्षितम्
सूक्ष्मात्सूक्ष्मतरं शान्तं न जगन्न जगत्क्रिया १५

Unity, oneness, where the mind is completely given over to Being, here and now is a state of pure consciousness, total brain functioning (*Saumya*) devoid of any manifest characteristics or qualities.

Subtler than the subtlest impulse of thought, it is a state of infinite peace, there is no [outside relative] world, no worldly activity of any kind.

Now he begins the description of the process of Self-realization, starting from the experience of transcending and gaining transcendental consciousness, *Samādhi*.

Verse 16:

तच्चिनोत्यात्मनात्मानं संकल्पोन्मुखतां गतम्
यदा तदा जीव इति प्रोक्तमाविलतां गतम् १६

16. That unified wholeness of consciousness is the Self completely enveloped by the Self (*Ātmā*), the active mind having entered into a state of restful alertness.

When the mind enters this state of transcendental consciousness, then Being alone is, it is said to have entered into a state of infinitely expanded unbounded awareness.

Verse 17:

असत्यमेव संकल्पभ्रमेणेदं शरीरकम्
जीवः पश्यति मूढात्मा बालो यक्षमिवोद्धतम् १७

That is the true nature of consciousness, consciousness alone without any object, intention turned back on itself, this is the soul, the dweller in the body.

The individual existence [of the ignorant man at the moment of transcending] sees the unlocalized incomprehensible Self: This is a beginning, not yet mature phase of development of consciousness, like a momentary or flashy taste of higher consciousness.

Verse 18:

यदा तु ज्ञानदीपेन सम्यगालोक आगतः
संकल्पमोहो जीवस्य क्षीयते शरदभ्रवत् १८

When however, by the [repeated experience of the] light of pure knowledge the [stresses which inhibit normal functioning are eliminated and] the consciousness becomes integrated and coherent, supporting every experience with the light of pure knowledge, [the light of the Self,] there is the [gradual] attainment of a higher level of consciousness, [Cosmic Consciousness],

[And] The incoherent, deluded desires that characterize ignorance in the waking state of consciousness [gradually] diminish like the clouds of the rainy season [fading away] in the autumn.

Having described the fourth state of consciousness in

verses 15-17, he now begins the description of the fifth state of consciousness, Cosmic Consciousness.

Verse 19:

शान्तिमायान्ति देहोऽयं सर्वसंकल्पसंक्षयात्
तदा राघव निः शेषं दीपस्तैलक्षये यथा १९

The stresses in the body are eliminated and the individual attains eternal peace and contentment through the complete cessation of all the [limited, bound, deluded] individual desires [of the waking state].

Then, O Descendant of the House of Raghu, the light of pure consciousness shines perpetually through all the changing states, like the light of an oil-lamp connected to an unlimited reservoir of oil.

Verse 20:

निद्राव्यपगमे जन्तुर्यथा स्वप्नं न पश्यति
जीवो हि भाविते सत्ये तथा देहं न पश्यति २०

During the time of sleep, a person in Cosmic Consciousness, remaining awake in pure consciousness, does not see dreams.

The individual soul in Cosmic Consciousness is permanently established in eternal being, and remains that way always even if one does not see a body.

Verse 21:

अतत्त्वे तत्त्वभावेन जीवो देहावृतः स्थितः
निर्देहो भवति श्रीमान् सुखी तत्त्वैकभावनात् २१

The individual soul is then unmanifest, unqualified universal Being, [ever] remaining in Being without becoming incarnate in a succession of physical bodies.

He exists, free from the body, in a completely exalted state of eternal bliss consciousness because his individuality has become one with universal reality.

> In verses 18-21, Cosmic Consciousness is being described.

Verse 22:

अनात्मनि शरीरादावात्मभावनमङ्ग यत्
सूर्याद्यालोकदुर्भेदं हार्दं तद्दारुणं तमः २२

When the Self has not been realized, then a new body is conceived by the *Ātmā* which will be more suitable [for continued evolution].

The unity of the soul taking up residence in a new heart and being broken apart by seeing the Sun, the planets and stars, and the entire multiplicity of manifest creation, that dreadful state of affairs is the blinding darkness [that the soul experiences entering a new body].

> At the moment of birth, when the newly born child takes his or her first breath, then he sees, as it were, the Sun, the planets and stars and the entire multiplicity of manifest creation. His cosmic counterparts register that impact of

the "sight" of the Sun, the planets and the stars, and this becomes the birth chart, the seed of destiny of the individual. The Sun and the planets are "*Grahas*," so called because they grasp and bind the awareness. Thus, the soul, which on its own is holistic and unified, enters into the blinding darkness of narrow boundaries and limitations, and lives through the destiny dictated by the arrangement of the Sun, planets and stars at that moment. This happens to the soul every time it takes residence in a new heart, in a new body. The seeker seeks liberation from the blinding darkness of this dreadful state of affairs, in which, life after life, the ocean of eternal bliss consciousness is lost in a drop, again and again. But—

Verse 23:

आत्मन्येवात्मभावेन सर्वव्यापि निरञ्जनम्
चिन्मात्रममलोऽस्मीति ज्ञानादित्येन नश्यति २३

When by direct experience of the Self, the Self is realized as all-pervading, spotless and pure—

Awake in itself, consciousness experiencing its true nature, untainted by the stains [of relative perceptions]—that is the experience that destroys the darkness of ignorance with the light of knowledge.

The Self is realized as all-pervading, spotless and pure only in Unity Consciousness, when every object of perception is experienced in terms of the unbounded Self

Verse 24:

अन्ये च विदितात्मानो भावयन्ति यथैव यत्
तत्तथैवाशु पश्यन्ति दृढभावनया तया २४

Which ignorance [continues] only as long as there is the other [the non-Self], and multiple knowers are called into being.

[The multiple knowers] see, and right away, by virtue of that seeing they are promoting the solidity of the relative field of existence that [sustains the state of ignorance].

> From the standpoint of Unity Consciousness, all possibilities are lively in every point in creation. However, the all possibilities structure of the wave function of creation is collapsed by the crude perception of the knowers in the state of ignorance. The collapse of the wave function means that it can only be one thing: Then it loses its all possibilities structure. When many ignorant knowers come together and create a community, they mutually promote the solidity of the relative field, the collapsed, consolidated state of all possibilities, which we call "matter." By their faculty of attention, the knowers in the state of ignorance are literally turning heaven into solid earth.

Verse 25:

दृढभावानुसंधानाद्विमूढा अपि राघव
विषं नयन्त्यमृतताममृतं विषतामपि २५

O Rāghava, people are confounded more and more by investigating into the nature of existence of the [apparently solid] material world.

They are taking their attention to poison—that gives rise to the poisonous state of ignorance as surely as taking the attention to immortality gives rise to the state of immortality.

Analyzing darkness is not the means to bring light. Investigating into the causes of ignorance is of no use. The illusion of the world is brought into being by the mistaken intellect belonging to the ignorant level of consciousness. One can travel to the depths of the ocean, and to the heights of the mountains, one can use microscopes to examine the tiniest atoms, and telescopes to explore the worlds of distant galaxies, but such investigations are all confounding. They bring more and more ignorance. These investigations, Vasishtha says, are putting the attention on poison. Poison sustains ignorance. Better to put the attention on perfect health and immortality. How to do that? The practice of Yogic Flying is precisely that, it is a technique to put the awareness on perfect health, and to grow in immortality, instead of expanding the field of ignorance more and more.

Verse 26:

एवं यथा यदेवेह भाव्यते दृढभावनात्
भूयते हि तदेवाशु तदित्यालोकितं मुहुः २६

This is how one gains perfect health and immortality in this practice of Yogic Flying: One is putting the attention on what is eternal coming into Being here and now, through the process of manifestation of matter from consciousness.

Consciousness has become matter, because that which was on its own, the completely self-sufficient Being, quickly gets transformed into the body that is suddenly seen [rising up].

Verse 27:

सत्यभावनदृष्टोऽयं देहो देहो भवत्यलम्
दृष्टस्त्वसत्यभावेन व्योमतां याति देहकः २७

This body is seen as the manifesting of eternal truth, the body is made of consciousness.

But what is actually seen by the transformation of eternal truth into non-truth, into matter, is the physical body moving through space at will.

> The body is made of consciousness means that whatever one desires for the body, that the body will accomplish. The physical body which has the ability to fly through the air at will is not a bondage to the mind. The all possibilities structure of consciousness can be sustained even on the level of the physical body if the body can move

anywhere through the air at will. Then the body is made of consciousness, then the body has the freedom and all-possibilities-structure of consciousness. The body is not an outsider, it is not the lesha-avidyā, "remains of ignorance." The body is made of pure knowledge, "truth," and flows to support the "truth" of every impulse of the mind. The body is the image of truth, the image of perfection. This is the body in the state of perfect health.

Verse 28:

अणिमादिपदप्राप्तौ ज्ञानयुक्तिरिति श्रुता
भवता साधुना राम युक्तिमन्यामिमां शृणु २८

When there is the power of attaining anything at will by the mere impulse of consciousness, the first small hop of the body is very small and insignificant, but it is enough to demonstrate the [successful] application of total knowledge [to practical life].

By capturing the fort of Being, [one attains all objects] O Rāma! Listen to the procedure of harnessing unbounded awareness, the total potential of natural law, to fulfill your individual desires.

Vasishtha has explained the entire path to perfection of the flying Siddhi, culminating in the ability to fly through the air, and the acquisition of the eight Siddhis, *Aṇimā*, ability to make the body very small, etc. To reach that lofty height of perfection consisting of complete mastery of creation, complete mastery of all the laws of nature, no new technologies have been added, nothing more is needed beyond what was described in the previous chapter. Now Vasishtha returns to the theme of the liftoff, which was the central focus of the previous chapter. He emphasizes that the total knowledge of the path to enlightenment is already contained in the liftoff. Nothing else needs to be added, no further fertilizer is required. Only long and continued practice is needed. The efficiency of this program consists in going straight to the goal, and capturing the fort. The fort is that which guards and protects the entire territory. By capturing the fort, one gains access to all the territories that belong to the fort. By infusing *Ākāśa* into the physiology through the liftoff, one gains deeper and deeper levels of Being, finally reaching to the inner sanctum inside the nineteenth enclosure of Mother Divine. There is the fort which controls all the territories, all the jewels and riches, all the special abilities, total and complete fulfillment and liberation. The focus is always on capturing the fort. The "fort" of life is self-referral consciousness. In verses 29-30, the process of gaining pure consciousness through the technique of effortless transcending is described.

Verse 29:

रेचकाभ्यासयोगेन जीवः कुण्डलिनीगृहात्
उद्धृत्य योज्यते यावदामोदः पवनादिव २६

By the yogic practice of attention going to unmanifest Being, the individual soul comes into alignment with the home of all the laws of nature.

Raising individual awareness to cosmic status as the individual is united more and more with Being, the soul experiences increasing happiness through increasing purity.

Verse 30:

त्यज्यते विरतस्पन्दो देहोऽयं काष्ठलोष्टवत्
देहेऽपि जीवेऽपि मतावासेचक इवादरः ३०

Having let go the finest impulse of thought, the activity of the mind is reduced to nil; the body correspondingly gains deep rest.

Increased physiological activity in the body corresponds to increased mental activity; when there is a thought, there is increased blood flow and metabolic activity, corresponding to the increased mental activity.

Verse 31:

स्थावरे जंगमे वापि यथाभिमतयेच्छया
भोक्तुं तत्संपदं सम्यग्जीवोऽन्तर्विनिवेश्यते ३१

[Ordinarily] When the body is stationary, consciousness is Self-referral; when the body is active, consciousness desires objects, consciousness [loses Self-referral and] becomes object referral.

To fully enjoy life, that mind-body coordination must be perfect [so that infinite silence is maintained in the midst of infinite dynamism]. [Then] the awareness is permanently established in Self-referral consciousness, [and that inner Being is experienced as an all-time reality].

> In this verse, and the next two verses, the program of *Saṁyama* using the Siddhis of Patañjali in order to stabilize self-referral consciousness is being described. These are techniques to make mind-body coordination perfect.

> Perfect mind-body coordination will maintain infinite silence in the midst of unlimited dynamism.

Verse 32:

इति सिद्धिश्रियं भुक्त्वा स्थितं चेत्तद्वपुः पुनः
प्रविश्यते स्वमन्यद्वा यद्यत्तात विरोचते ३२

Thus [The goal of all Siddhi practice is achieved when Self-referral consciousness becomes permanent]: If the auspicious predicted result of the Siddhi has been enjoyed, the seed of perfect mind-body coordination is sown, and if the Siddhi is practiced repeatedly, that perfect mind-body coordination becomes lasting.

Having realized that the Self is truly a field of all possibilities, whatever one asks of it shines forth and becomes visible.

> The goal of the Siddhi practices is to capture the fort. The flavor of awareness that is generated is valuable, but the overriding purpose is to stabilize Self-referral consciousness. This has been the theme since verse 14, when he announced that now he would speak out "the greatest of all jewels of wisdom that can be heard through the ears." That greatest of all jewels is not the knowledge of how to perfect any particular Siddhi or channel of mind-body coordination: It is the knowledge of how to capture the fort and gain command over the entire territory of life.

Verse 33:

देहादयस्तथा बिम्बान्व्याप्तवत्याखिलानथ
संविदा जगदापूर्य संपूर्णं स्थीयतेऽथवा ३३

All the flavors of the Siddhis, lifting up of the body, etc., are images of the Self, wholenesses completely permeated by the total potential of natural law, precipitations of unbounded pure consciousness.

Having fulfilled all possible worldly desires by means of consciousness moving within itself, the individual is completely fulfilled, established in the state of enlightenment, as demonstrated by the mastery of the Siddhis.

Verse 34:

ज्ञात्वा सदाभ्युदितमुज्झितदोषमीशो
यद्यद्यथा समभिवाञ्छति चित्प्रकाशः
प्राप्नोति तत्तदचिरेण तथैव राम
सम्यक्पदं विदुरनावरणात्वमेव ३४

Having gained total knowledge of natural law, demonstrated by the ability to remain in the air continuously, [and move about at will] freed from the restrictions of gravity, he is the master of Yogic Flying.

Whatever object or experience he might long for, the light of consciousness attains [for him] that object or experience instantly, O Rāma.

Having gained perfect mind-body coordination and true wisdom, there is nothing whatsoever hidden or unattainable by him.

The mastery of Yogic Flying is the yardstick to measure the capturing of the fort of life. When the ability to remain up in the air and fly through the air at will has been attained, there is nothing that cannot be attained. This is the state of perfection, the goal of all search. Mastering Yogic Flying, one has captured the fort of life and gained access to all the territories that belong to the fort. This is the teaching of Vasishtha's Yoga.

Colophon:

इत्यार्षे श्रीवासिष्ठमहारामायणे वाल्मीकीये मोक्षोपायेषु निर्वाणप्रकरणे अणिमादिलाभयोगोपदेशो नाम द्व्यशीतितमः सर्गः ८२

Endnotes

1 Swami Vijnanananda, *Śrīmad Devī Bhāgavatam*, Oriental Books Reprint: New Delhi, 1977, 1192 pages. The nineteen enclosures of Mother Divine are described in Skanda 12, Chapters 10-12. These are reproduced in the Appendix.

Chapter 7: Third Stage of Yogic Flying

Verse 1:

वसिष्ठ उवाच
अणिमादिगुणैश्वर्ययुक्ता सा नृपभामिनी
एवं बभूव चूडाला घनाभ्यासवती सती १

Vasishtha said:

Putting to practical use the [eight] superhuman powers beginning with making the body as small as an atom, that are the qualifications [of the unbounded infinite Self,] she [became even more than before] the passionate loving companion of the king.

Cūḍālā, in this way became a Yogi of the highest degree, the complete master of the Siddhis, the perfect wife.

> Cūḍālā was searching for a way to convince her husband that she had attained enlightenment, so that she could guide him to perfection. Towards that end she learned the practice of Yogic Flying, and then sought to bring that practice to perfection. In perfecting the flying Siddhi, she gained something else that she had not sought for, namely mastery of total natural law, complete mastery over creation. And with complete mastery over creation, she was fully competent to fulfill her dharma as the wife of the king and bring complete fulfillment to that relationship. She was the ideal wife, full of youthful beauty and vitality, able to anticipate her husband's needs and desires and to fulfill them instantly. The idea of proving to him her high level of spiritual accomplishment fell by the wayside. Her newfound ability to bring success to every area of life brought perfection to their married life also. This is a common theme in the area of

spiritual quests: One is searching for the goal, but one doesn't really know what the goal is like. Ofttimes the goal is much greater and more valuable than the narrow boundaries of an imagined state of perfection which one was seeking. This conundrum, that one doesn't actually know what the goal is like and cannot imagine it from the lower level of consciousness from where one starts, and yet one must engage in searching in order to reach the goal, is the moral of the story of the miser that is told in the second half of this chapter. Both Cūḍālā and the miser were searching for something, with great persistence and devotion. Both found instead something much greater, the "philosopher's stone," the ability to fulfill all desires spontaneously. And both consequently let go of their original small desires and enjoyed life in fullness and abundance with their newfound riches.

We are certainly surprised by the turn of the story at this point: Cūḍālā becomes the complete master of creation, with unlimited authority over natural law, and she uses all these newfound abilities in her practical life. For what purpose? To be the perfect passionate and loving companion for her husband. Where is the sense of renunciation and turning away from the world? How can Cūḍālā maintain her responsibilities and duties as the mistress of her household now that she is enlightened? Will she not sense the evanescence of all worldly desires and renounce everything and go to live in the forest? No, instead she stays in her dharma, and uses her newfound abilities to bring complete success to every desire of the royal couple.

Kṛṣṇa says in the Bhagavad Gītā (4:1,2), that in the beginning this knowledge of enlightenment and mind-body integration was given to the kings, the rulers of the world. And Vasishtha also teaches that this knowledge was first given to the rulers of the world. There is a path to enlightenment through perfection of the Siddhis which is open to householders, and allows the householders to grow in the ability to fulfill all their desires. The path of renunciation is a different path, for a different section of society. Renunciation is not a prerequisite for enlightenment, nor a corequisite, nor even a consequence. If one can learn to use one's total brain potential, one can very well remain in one's current dharma, and do full justice to every impulse of life in the present dharma. Total brain potential is enough to bring complete fulfillment to any dharma; the performance of one's dharma is not an obstacle to enlightenment. Cūḍālā stayed in the comfort of the palace and enjoyed unlimited freedom, moving about at will, wherever and whenever she liked.

Verse 2:

जगामाकाशमार्गेण विवेशाम्बुधिकोटरम्
चचार वसुधापीठं गङ्गेवामलशीतला २

By moving through the *Ākāśa*, she entered into the oceans, exploring [even] its deepest trenches.

She visited the shrines and holy places where the gods bestow bounty on the earth, like the crystal pure headwaters of the river Gaṅgā, high in the snow-capped mountains [of the Himālayas].

Verse 3:

क्षणमप्यगता भर्तुर्वक्षसश्चेतसस्तथा
सर्वेषूवास राज्येषु लक्ष्मीरिव जगत्सु च ३

In the twinkling of an eye, not departing from the bosom of her lord, at will she went here and there,

Visiting every kingdom on every level of creation, bringing her blessings to all the worlds, like Lakṣmī.

> Cūḍālā visited kingdoms on every level of creation, and made friends everywhere, giving her enlightened blessings to peoples in all the different worlds. She did not travel by imagination, or by projecting her mind, but rather actually visited those places with her body, bringing blessings, sharing knowledge, making friends, and spreading joy everywhere.

Verse 4:

आकाशगामिनी श्यामा विद्युत्प्रारम्भभूषणा
बभ्राम मेघमालेव गिरिमाला महीतले ४

Able to go anywhere in space at will, the accomplished lady began to glow like a precious jewel.

She carried her radiant aura like a mountain graced with a necklace of clouds, or like a chain of mountains on the surface of the earth.

> Mastery of the Siddhis means that the *Soma*, the link between consciousness and physiology is on the highest level of perfection. Conjoined with the highly refined *Soma*, a related chemical called Ojas, is secreted on the

skin, and that Ojas gives rise to a profound radiance and glow. Cūḍālā was seen to have a very profound physical presence, even more radiant than before, as a result of her mastery of the Siddhis. That is why she looked like a mountain graced with a necklace of clouds.

Verse 5:

काष्ठं तृणोपलं भूतं खं वातमनलं जलम्
निर्विघ्नमविशत्सर्वं तन्तुर्मुक्ताफलं यथा ५

Wood, herbs, jewels, earth, space, wind, fire and water,

Without obstacles, she entered into all, one after the other, as the fruit of her liberated state.

Verse 6:

मेरोरुपरि शृङ्गाणि लोकपालपुराणि च
दिग्व्योमोदररन्ध्राणि विजहार यथासुखम् ६

[She went] Up to the summits of Mount Meru and other mountains, and [to] the cities of the regents of the quarters.

She explored according to her pleasure the high mountains and deep canyons in all the directions of space.

Verse 7:

तिर्यग्भूतपिशाचाद्यैः सहनागामरासुरैः
विद्याधराप्सरःसिद्धैर्व्यवहारं चकार सा ७

Exploring the inhabited regions, she had converse with the foremost demons and ogres, with serpent-demons, gods and *Asuras*, and with Siddhas, *Apsaras* and angels [on the topic of the knowledge of immortality of *Ātmā*].

> She explored all the different levels of creation. Vyāsa, in his commentary on the Yoga Sūtra, explains (III.26) that for complete enlightenment, the Yogi has to become familiar with every level of creation.

Verse 8:

यत्नेन तं च भर्तारमात्मज्ञानामृतं प्रति
बहुशो बोधयामास चूडाला न विवेद सः ८

Cūḍālā repeatedly made efforts to awaken her husband to the knowledge of the immortality of the Self, [but] he did not understand.

Verse 9:

कलाविदग्धा मुग्धा च बालेयं गृहिणी मम
इत्येवं केवलं राजा स चूडालां विवेद ताम् ९

[Cūḍālā thought:][He is] bound up in the parts, and completely ignorant of the reality [of the whole], [That is why he says:] "This mistress of my house is suited to caring for children [and nothing more]."

[Due to ignorance,] the king can only think in this way, that Cūḍālā is the mistress of his household [and nothing more].

> Cūḍālā laments her inability to teach her husband the knowledge of immortality which she has gained.

Verse 10:

एतावतापि कालेन तामेवं गुणशालिनीम्
बालो विद्यामिव नृपश्चूडालां न विवेद सः १०

"Moreover, the illusion has become so great, so deep, over time, through long habit of perceiving the world in this way, [that] the boundaries have made their home in his awareness.

"The king is a fool: Like someone under a spell he does not discern who Cūḍālā really is.

Verse 11:

साप्यलब्धात्मविश्रान्तेस्तां सिद्धिश्रियमात्मनः
दर्शयामास नो राज्ञः शूद्रस्येव मखक्रियाम् ११

"Moreover, because of not having become familiar with the Self through direct experience, he does not know that the glory of the outer expression of Siddhis comes from the Self.

"Demonstrating our abilities to the king [will be inappropriate, even damaging] like the presence of a *Śūdra* at a sacrificial rite."

The king does not know that gravity is the supreme natural law in the universe, and that mastery of gravity means complete mastery of total natural law has been gained. Nor does he realize that the ability to fly demonstrates the degree of stabilization of the Self. Demonstrating her Siddhis is more likely to confuse the king, rather than convince him of her competence to guide his path to enlightenment.

In the performance of Vedic sacrifices, only individuals who have been initiated into the study of the Veda are permitted onto the sacrificial ground. The influence of the uninitiated is considered detrimental to the success of the yagya, and so they are excluded. In some cases, there are expiatory rites that can be performed to restore order to a sacrifice that has been spoiled by the accidental entry of a Śūdra to the sacrificial hall. The attention of a Śudra on a sacrifice, and the attention of Śikhidhvaja on Cūḍālā's Siddhis will be incongruous and damaging, like a bull in a china shop, to use a modern analogy. So, she decides not to demonstrate to him her abilities.

Verse 12:

श्रीराम उवाच
महत्याः सिद्धयोगिन्यास्तस्या अपि शिखिध्वजः
यत्नेन प्राप नो बोधं बुध्यतेऽन्यः कथं प्रभो १२

The glorious Rāma said:

O Master, if even with effort the great perfected yogi (Cūḍālā) was not successful in awakening the consciousness of Śikhidhvaja, how indeed can [we, or] anyone else attain for ourselves the state of enlightenment?

Verse 13:

वसिष्ठ उवाच
उपदेशक्रमो राम व्यवस्थामात्रपालनम्
ज्ञप्तेस्तु कारणं शुद्धा शिष्यप्रज्ञैव राघव १३

Vasishtha said:

O Rāma, instruction is sequential; according to the degree of progress on the path to enlightenment, there is a corresponding [instruction] to nourish and promote progress on that level.

According to the clarity of consciousness and depth of knowledge of the disciple, by means of rational intellectual analysis, the [underlying] cause becomes clear, O descendant of the House of Raghu.

Knowledge is different in different states of consciousness, and the instruction must be matched to the level of accomplishment of the aspirant. This is a skill of the teacher, recognizing the level of attainment of the student, and providing the carefully crafted and appropriate instruction suitable for that level.

Verse 14:

न श्रुतेन न पुरायेन ज्ञायते ज्ञेयमात्मनः
जानात्यात्मानमात्मैव सर्पः सर्पपदानिव १४

Not by hearing [discourses] about it, nor by acquiring spiritual merit through virtuous actions, does that which can only be known by direct experience of the Self (*Ātmā*) become known.

Only the Self knows the Self, just as [only] a snake understands on what feet [or by what means] snakes move about.

The Self is not gained by listening to lectures, or by reading about it in books. It is only gained by direct experience, under the guidance of a trained teacher.

Verse 15:

श्रीराम उवाच
एवंस्थिते वाथ मुने कथमेतज्जगत्स्थिता
क्रमो गुरूपदेशाख्यः स्वात्मज्ञानस्य कारणम् १५

The glorious Rāma said:

O sage, when this is the unique status of Self-knowledge, how can this knowledge be established in the whole world in the present time?

What are all the instructions of the teacher, in sequence, that give rise to the complete knowledge of the Self?

Verse 16:

वसिष्ठ उवाच
अत्यन्तकृपणः कश्चित्किराटो धनधान्यवान्
अस्ति विन्ध्याटवीकक्षे कुटुम्बी ब्राह्मणो यथा १६

Vasishtha said:

Once upon a time there was an extraordinarily miserly merchant possessed of abundance of wealth and grains, living as a Brahmin with his family in a small clearing in the Vindhya forest.

> Vasishtha begins to answer *Rām's* question by telling a story about a merchant living in the forest with his family.

Verse 17:

तस्यैकदा निपतिता गच्छतो विन्ध्यजङ्गले
एका वराटिका राम तृणजालकसंवृते १७

Coming out of the Vindhya forest [one time] a small coin belonging to him was allowed to fall [from his purse] and was lost in the thick grass.

Verse 18:

कार्पण्यात्स प्रयत्नेन सर्वं तृणतुषादिकम्
कपर्दकार्थमभितो दुधाव दिवसत्रयम् १८

Out of desperation from that loss, he made effort to look under every blade of grass in the meadow.

For three days he combed through the grass, searching to find the missing coin.

Verse 19:

कपर्दकाः स्युर्भवता चत्वारोऽष्टौ च कालतः
ततः शतं सहस्रं च सहस्रे चेति चेतसा १९

He thought, "[Through business] the missing coin could become four coins and then eight. From the eight it could become a hundred and then a thousand, and then thousands upon thousands."

Verse 20:

कलयञ्जङ्गले दीनो रात्रिंदिवमतन्द्रितः
जनहाससहस्त्राणि बुबुधे न परं तु सः २०

Feeling miserable in the absence of those thousands, [he searched] night and day unwearyingly. Although [it is] laughable to search for one coin with the fervor appropriate to the loss of thousands, he was oblivious to everything else, and continued on searching [for that one lost coin].

Verse 21:

ततो दिनत्रयस्यान्ते तेन तस्माच्च जङ्गलात्
पूर्णेन्दुबिम्बप्रतिमो लब्धश्चिन्तामणिर्महान् २१

Then, at the end of the third day, he found by his search in that same forest, a fabulous jewel—the *Cintāmaṇi*, or philosopher's stone, capable of amplifying the power of thought to fulfill any desire—which shone as brightly as the disc of the full moon.

Verse 22:

तं प्राप्य तुष्टहृदयः समागम्य गृहं सुखम्
प्राप्ताखिलजगद्भूतिशान्तसर्वतया स्थितः २२

Having found that jewel, his heart felt peace, and he returned happily to his house.

Having attained unbroken worldly prosperity, he felt at home with everything, and he remained that way, [feeling at home with everything wherever he went].

Verse 23:

एवं यथा किराटेन कपर्दान्वेषणेन तत्
रत्नं लब्धं जगन्मूल्यमहोरात्रमखेदिना २३

In this way, whatever funds were needed by the merchant, they were immediately available to him. With the attainment of the jewel, he had money enough to buy anything in the world, [at any time] day or night, without his treasury ever becoming depleted.

Verse 24:

तथा श्रुतोपदेशेन स्वात्मज्ञानमवाप्यते
अन्यदन्विष्यते चान्यल्लभ्यते हि गुरुक्रमात् २४

Just like that, by the instruction being heard [by the disciple], the most excellent knowledge of the *Ātmā*, [which like the *Cintāmaṇi* of the merchant, is capable of bringing fulfillment to any desire and makes one feel at home with everything in creation, day and night] is attained.

What is being sought is [always] different from what one has, and what is attained is again different from what one is seeking [because in the absence of the experience of the goal, one does not really understand the nature of what one is searching for]; hence through a program of graded steps, the teacher [leads the disciple from ignorance to the goal of complete knowledge of the Self].

Now, in this verse, Vasishtha returns to *Rām's* question, and begins to explain the moral of his story. The aspirant does not understand the nature of the goal, but he cannot reach the goal without making earnest efforts to attain it. By graded steps, the teacher leads the disciple to that unimaginable great goal of complete mastery of total natural law.

Verse 25:

ब्रह्म सर्वेन्द्रियातीतं श्रुतादीन्द्रियसंविदः
तेनोपदेशादनघ नात्मतत्त्वमवाप्यते २५

Brahman is beyond all the sense faculties [yet] the initial instruction that one hears is in terms of searching and finding through the senses.

By a process of transcending the activity of the senses, through the instruction [of the teacher], that which is beyond the stain of relative boundaries, the [eternal unbounded unmanifest transcendental] reality of the Self is directly experienced.

Verse 26:

गुरूपदेशं च विना नात्मतत्त्वागमो भवेत्
केन चिन्तामणिर्लब्धः कपर्दान्वेषणं विना २६

Without the instruction of the teacher, there is no arrival at the goal of experiencing the reality of the *Ātmā*.

How can anyone find the *Cintāmaṇi* jewel [which bestows unlimited wealth], without seeking for wealth?

Verse 27:

तत्त्वस्यास्य महार्थस्य गुरूपकथनं गतम्
अकारणं कारणतां मणेरिव कपर्दकः २७

The great goal of realization of the transcendental reality of life is like this wish-fulfilling gem, and the instructions by the teacher [followed steadfastly by the disciple] disappear [into the transcendent] like the lost coin of the merchant.

There is [an indirect] causal relationship between the lost coin and the jewel, [and between the instructions of the teacher and the experience of the transcendent] [because the one cannot occur without the other][but it is] an unmanifest, implicit cause.

Verse 28:

पश्य राघव मायेयं मोहिनी महतामपि
अन्यदन्विष्यते यत्नादन्यदासाद्यते फलम् २८

Behold, O descendent of the house of Raghu, this illusion (Māyā), bewitching like a seductive woman and infinitely diverse.

Through effort, that which is other than this illusion is sought, and [yet] without effort, the fruit which is again different than what was sought, is attained.

Verse 29:

अन्यत्करोति पुरुषः फलमन्यदेव
प्राप्नोति यन्त्रिषु जगत्स्ववलोक्यते च ।
तस्मादनन्तरभवस्य जगद्भ्रमस्य
श्रेयोतिवाहनमसङ्गमनिच्छयैव २९

One does something in relative boundaries, but the fruit that one attains is seeing the Self (*Puruṣa*) [which is] beyond the limitations of the boundaries of the world.

Therefore, the best technique of bringing to awareness that unmanifest Being deep within [the mind], the best procedure of roaming through the boundaries of the world, can only be that which effortlessly conveys the awareness beyond boundaries, without attachment to anything in the relative.

> This is the brilliant conclusion, that the best technique of bringing unmanifest Being to the awareness must be effortless transcending which spontaneously takes the awareness beyond relative boundaries.

Colophon:

इत्यार्षे श्रीवासिष्ठमहारामायणे वल्मीकीये मोक्षोपायेषु निर्वाणप्रकरणे किराटोपाख्यानं नाम त्र्यशीतितमः सर्गः ८३

> This story of the merchant and his lost penny brings to a beautiful summation the entire discussion of Yogic Flying. One thing is sought after with great determination by the aspirant of unrefined consciousness. But what he

actually finds, what he attains or realizes is much greater than that for which he was seeking. From his low level of consciousness at the start, he could not foresee, could not dream of what could be accomplished, what could be attained. But possessed of passion to attain some little boundary, some trifling thing, he devotes himself to a search which unfolds for him the supreme attainment—the philosopher's stone, as it were.

The desire to fly and enjoy the freedom of the skies is natural and universal. And the experience of Yogic Flying, even in the first stage of hopping, brings great fulfillment to that desire for freedom. One has the sense of flying, the fulfillment of the bliss of flying, even though the body is only moving a comparably short distance. What one does not realize is that in the process of Yogic Flying, even at the outset, one is increasing the value of *Ākāśa* in the physiology. Thereby one grasps the central switchboard of the relationship of consciousness and physiology—the fort from which the entire territory of individual life is managed with perfection. Not only is this the fort from which all mind-body coordination is organized, it is the fort which commands perfect health of the body, it is the fort which commands the level of consciousness of individual awareness, and when many practice Yogic Flying together, it is the fort which commands the collective consciousness of society, and the fort which commands the entire near and far environment of the nation. The desire to fly through the air is completely insignificant measured against the possibility of governing entire nations in peace, prosperity and happiness. That huge accomplishment is simply attained by conquering the fort from which the whole nation is spontaneously and truthfully governed. And that fort is the *Ākāśa* which grows in the physiology through the practice of Yogic Flying. By the expansion of *Ākāśa* in the physiology, the expanded awareness naturally penetrates to deeper values of natural law, gaining greater and greater command over the more excited states of natural law, and passes through successively subtler and more powerful hidden enclosures of Mother Divine. Each successive enclosure has greater treasures and greater powers of action, but the inner sanctum, inside the nineteenth enclosure is the fort which commands the whole territory of life: Attaining that, capturing that fort, one gains mastery over nature, mastery over the total value of natural law.

The story of the merchant searching for his lost penny is like that. One wants to fly, and one devotes oneself day and night to the practice of Yogic Flying. On the individual level, one accomplishes the desire, but what is achieved in that stroke goes inestimably beyond the scope of some small individual desire to fly. In one stroke one solves all the problems of individual life, all the problems of society, makes the nation invincible to negative outside influences, brings support of nature and averts disasters and cataclysms for the whole nation, and creates peace in the family of nations.

This is the answer to *Rām's* question "How can this knowledge be established in the whole world in the present time?" By the application of the technologies of Yoga, world peace can be achieved, and all the problems of society can be eliminated. However, individuals will not join together in groups altruistically, at great personal cost and sacrifice, in order to bring peace and orderliness to the whole society. But everyone naturally wants to be free of gravity and to fly through the air. By searching for that goal which is, relatively speaking, as small as the merchant's lost penny, one creates automation in administration for the whole nation, and the whole society enjoys increasing success and rising collective consciousness.

Yogic Flying should be taught in every high school and every college around the world: This will bring fulfillment to every government, peace to the world, and enlightenment and perfect health to every student in each new and fortunate generation. The desire to fly is universal, common to people at every level of consciousness. Even youngsters are eager to fly, and they greatly enjoy Yogic Flying. Young students can be motivated by the bliss of flying, they don't need to be convinced that they should fly in order to fill the need to raise collective consciousness of society by group practice. That can be a side effect of their own individual desire for joy and freedom. What one seeks through the practice of Yoga will always be narrow and limited compared to the enlightenment which one gains. Yogic Flying capitalizes on everyone's innate desire for more and more happiness and freedom and delivers far more: It opens up to the individual the central switchboard of total natural law, giving mastery over the whole creation, coherence on the level of society, and enlightenment and perfect health in the life of the individual.

Vasishtha has placed in Rām's hands the technology for creating a perfect, orderly, progressive and peaceful society. Rām used this knowledge of Yogic Flying to create Rām Rāj, a time of peace characterized by perfect administration of society. Under the rule of Rām, noone suffered, everyone lived their full term of life, and there were no diseases or hardships of any kind. Rām's rule lasted for 11,000 years. Now, in this age, the knowledge of Yogic Flying has been revived in its completeness by Maharishi Mahesh Yogi. We have in hand the same technology, and we can create Rām Rāj now in this generation.

Capturing some isolated treasure, some gold mine or silver mine somewhere, could be very difficult. Much easier than going for isolated and limited treasures, is to capture the fort. The fort that governs the whole of life is Yogic Flying. The practice of Yogic Flying, infusing *Ākāśa* into the nature of the physiology, is the greatest blessing to man in all ages: It is the opportunity to capture the fort that governs all the individual and collective realities in society, and to live life on the level of perfection, to create Heavenly life on earth. Yogic Flying means capturing the fort of life. This is the supreme teaching of Vasishtha's Yoga. Thanks to Maharishi for reviving this knowledge and making it available throughout the world, and thanks to the Vedic Tradition of Masters for keeping this knowledge alive throughout the ages.

Nineteen Enclosures of Mother Divine from Devī Bhāgavatam Mahāpurāṇa

"Mother Divine, Parā Śakti, flashes forth and the body (the divine Vīṇā) rises up and moves in the air." (4.41) Vasishtha attributes a central role in the mechanics of Yogic Flying to Mother Divine. What exactly does he mean by Mother Divine, and how are we to understand it?

Mother Divine, Vasishtha explains, is made of the fluctuations of consciousness within the unboundedness of the Self. She resides in the infinite bliss of the Ānandamaya Kośa, the sheath made of bliss. (4.41) She is not something outside, she is the nature of one's own Self. We will see that "Mother Divine" is a technical term which describes specific structures, functions and phenomena with which we are already familiar through the investigations of modern science.

Modern science has brought us enormous knowledge of the structure and function of human physiology. A close study of this section, and the knowledge of Veda in Human Physiology brought out by Dr. Tony Nader, on which it is based, will reveal that there is a profound connection, even a one to one correspondence between the knowledge of the ancient Vedic Science and the discoveries of the modern physiological sciences. The descriptions of Mother Divine capture in simple language the complex architecture of the administration of order and intelligence in the physiology.

The role of Mother Divine in Yogic Flying is first described in Chapter 4 Section 3, verses 41 through 48, on "The Mechanics of Yogic Flying." Mother Divine is described as the supreme power within all living beings, the source of energy and intelligence for all the impulses of the mind: She is spoken of as that which unfolds "A," total Veda, the total potential of natural law, into "the circle of life." This first section, attributing the dynamics of the lift-off to Mother Divine, concludes with the statement that "She is the life-principle of every sentient being, verily she is declared to be the One who becomes the many."

In the next chapter, (Chapter 5) She is described as Lakṣmī, Mother Divine, sitting inside on her perpetual seat, "Remaining blocked, inaccessible and unable to function." She is "covered over and hidden from sight within her [nineteen layered] enclosure, like a fabulous treasure." (V.64)

In the sixth chapter, the expansion of the liftoff from small hops to long flights takes place by harnessing the power of Mother Divine to the physical body. She is hidden deep inside, and the infusion of Ākāśa into the physiology makes her increasingly accessible. Her infinite organizing power is harnessed more and more. Finally, when all the blocks are removed, the full value of the treasure of her organizing power is made available. Then, Vasishtha explains, "She [Mother Divine] coming to perception is the total disclosure of all knowledge, the supremely sweet nectar which is the source and goal of all search, and that alone moves the body up into the air according to the desires of the mind more and more as it unfolds." (VI.10)

The disclosure of all knowledge through the unfoldment of deeper and deeper levels of one's own Self is modeled on the one hand by the description of the nineteen enclosures of Mother Divine which protect and hide the infinite knowledge and organizing power at the basis of the whole creation. On the other hand, Dr. Nader shows that the structure and function of human physiology is a model in miniature of the layout of cosmic intelligence of the universe.[1] In the physiology also, the repository of total knowledge and organizing power is hidden deep within, behind nineteen enclosures, each one parallel in its characteristics and qualities to the enclosures ascribed to the Sarvaloka of Mother Divine. In the physiology, at the core, inside the nineteenth enclosure, there is the DNA, the blueprint for all cellular processes.

DNA has the same characteristics that were attributed to Mother Divine: DNA may be said to be the "One who becomes the many." (IV.48) The DNA dictates all the specific characteristics which make up each individual's own unique nature, so the DNA is the "nature of one's own Self." (IV.48) The DNA is understood to be the life principle, the core of biological existence of every intelligent species. (IV.48) Dr. Nader's conclusion is that the DNA is the physical counterpart, the manifest image of the cosmic reality of total knowledge of natural law embodied in Mother Divine.

Increasing the Ākāśa in the physiology through Yogic Flying is a procedure for making the unlimited knowledge and organizing power of Mother Divine, embodied in the DNA, accessible, and functional. That power is hidden from sight within these nineteen enclosures, but its full glory can be harnessed. Even in the first stage of Yogic Flying, health improves, IQ rises, and support of nature and success in activity is magnified. All of these dramatic results make sense in the context of accessing the comprehensive knowledge of total natural law imbibed in the DNA of every individual. The technology for harnessing that infinite intelligence and putting it to function in practical life is the program of Siddhis and Yogic Flying. It is worthwhile exploring the reality of "The total disclosure of all knowledge" in Mother Divine (VI.10), enlivened in the physiology through Yogic Flying.

In the following are presented the 19 enclosures of Mother Divine as described in the *Devī Bhāgavata Purāṇa*, in Sanskrit[2] and in English,[3] along with brief summaries of their correlates in human physiology, based on the research of Dr. Tony Nader.[4]

The abode of Devī in Maṇidvīpa (island of gems)

In the physiology, the head and the brain are superior to all other areas of the physiology. The brain ensures the safety, nourishment and enjoyment of all aspects of the physiology. Functioning in perfect health, it "destroys the pains and sufferings of this world." This is the location of Sarvaloka in the physiology.

श्रीमद्देवीभागवते महापुराणे द्वादशस्कन्धे
अध्यायः १०

अथ दशमोऽध्यायः
व्यास उवाच
ब्रह्मलोकादूर्ध्वभागे सर्वलोकोऽस्ति यः श्रुतः
मणिद्वीपः स एवास्ति यत्र देवी विराजते १
सर्वस्मादधिको यस्मात्सर्वलोकस्ततः स्मृतः
पुरा पराम्बयैवायं कल्पितो मानसेच्छया २
सर्वादौ निजवासार्थं प्रकृत्या मूलभूतया
कैलासादधिको लोको वैकुण्ठादपि चोत्तमः ३
गोलोकादपि सर्वस्मात्सर्वलोकोऽधिकः स्मृतः
नैतत्समं त्रिलोक्यां तु सुन्दरं विद्यते क्वचित् ४
छत्रीभूतं त्रिजगतो भवसन्तापनाशकम्
छायाभूतं तदेवास्ति ब्रह्माण्डानां तु सत्तमः ५
बहुयोजनविस्तीर्णो गम्भीरस्तावदेव हि
मणिद्वीपस्य परितो वर्तते तु सुधोदधिः ६
मरुत्संघट्टनोत्कीर्णतरङ्गशतसंकुलः
रत्नाच्छवालुकायुक्तो झषशङ्खसमाकुलः ७
वीचिसंघर्षसंजातलहरीकणशीतलः
नानाध्वजसमायुक्तनानापोतगतागतैः ८
विराजमानः परितस्तीररत्नद्रुमो महान्

Sarvaloka, the abode of Devī in Devī Bhāgavata:

Vyāsa said :-- O King Janamejaya! What is known in the Śrutis, in the Subāla Upaniṣad, as the Sarvaloka, located above the Brahmāloka, that is Maṇidvīpa (island of gems). Here the Devī resides. This region is superior to all the other regions. Hence it is named "Sarvaloka." The Devī built this place of yore according to Her will.

In the very beginning, the Devī Mūla Prakṛti Bhagavatī built this place for Her residence, superior to Kailāśa, Vaikuṇṭha and Goloka. Verily no other place in this universe can stand before it. Hence it is called Maṇidvīpa, or Sarvaloka, as superior to all other Lokas. This Maṇidvīpa is situated at the top of all the regions, and resembles an umbrella. Its shadow falls on the Brahmāṇḍa (universe) and destroys the pains and sufferings of this world. Surrounding this Maṇidvīpa exists an ocean called the Sudhā Samudra (ocean of nectar), many yojanas wide and many yojanas deep. Many waves arise in it due to winds. Various fishes and conches and other aquatic animals play here, and the beach is full of clear sand-like gems. The sea shores are always kept cool by the splashes of the waves of water striking the beach. Various ships decked with various nice flags are plying to and fro. Various trees bearing gems are adorning the beach.

First Enclosure, made of iron

In the physiology, according to Dr. Tony Nader, the first of the nineteen enclosures of Mother Divine is the outermost layer of the skin, called the epidermis. It is a thin protective layer from .5 to 2.3 mm. in depth.

तदुत्तरमयोधातुनिर्मितो गगने ततः ९
सप्तयोजनविस्तीर्णः प्राकारो वर्तते महान्
नानाशस्त्रप्रहरणा नानायुद्धविशारदाः १०
रक्षका निवसंत्यत्र मोदमानाः समंततः
चतुर्द्वारसमायुक्तो द्वारपालशतान्वितः ११
नानागणैः परिवृतो देवीभक्तियुतैर्नृप

दर्शनार्थं समायान्ति ये देवा जगदीशितुः १२
तेषां गणा वसन्त्यत्र वाहनानि च तत्र हि
विमानशतसंघर्षघण्टास्वनसमाकुलः १३
हयहेषाखुराघातबधिरीकृतदिङ्मुखः
गणैः किलकिलारावैर्वेत्रहस्तैश्च ताडिताः १४
सेवका देवसंघानां भ्राजन्ते तत्र भूमिप
तस्मिन्कोलाहले राजन्न शब्दः केनचित्क्वचित् १५
कस्यचिच्छ्रूयतेऽत्यन्तं नानाध्वनिसमाकुले
पदे पदे मिष्टवारिपरिपूर्णसरांसि च १६

First Enclosure in Devī Bhāgavata Purāṇa:

Across this ocean there is an iron enclosure, very long and seven yojanas wide, very high so as to block the Heavens. Within this enclosure wall the military guards skilled in war and furnished with various weapons are running gladly to and fro. There are four gateways or entrances; at every gate there are hundreds of guards and various hosts of the devotees of the Devī. Whenever any Deva comes to pay a visit to the Jagadīśvarī, their Vāhanas (carriers) and retinue are stopped here. O King! This place resounds with the chimings of the bells of hundreds of chariots of the Devas and the neighing of their horses and the sounds of their hoofs. The Devīs walk here and there with canes in their hands, chiding at intervals the attendants of the Devas. This place is so noisy that no one can hear clearly another's word. Here are seen thousands of houses adorned with trees of gems and jewels, and tanks filled with plenty of tasteful, good sweet waters.

Second Enclosure, made of white copper

In the physiology, the second enclosure is the dermis, the thickest layer of the skin, lying between the epidermis and the subcutaneous layer. It provides strength and flexibility to the skin.

वाटिका विविधा राजन् रत्नद्रुमविराजिताः
तदुत्तरं महासारधातुनिर्मितमण्डलः १७
शालोऽपरो महानस्ति गगनस्पर्शि यच्छिरः
तेजसा स्याच्छतगुणः पूर्वशालादयं परः १८
गोपुरद्वारसहितो बहुवृक्षसमन्वितः
या वृक्षजातयः सन्ति सर्वास्तास्तत्र सन्ति च १९
निरन्तरं पुष्पयुताः सदाफलसमन्विताः
नवपल्लवसंयुक्ताः परसौरभसंकुलाः २०
पनसा वकुला लोध्रा कर्णिकाराश्च शिंशपाः
देवदारुकाञ्चनारा आम्राश्चैव सुमेरवः २१
लिकुचा हिङ्गुलाश्चैला लवङ्गाः कट्फलास्तथा
पाटला मुचुकुन्दाश्च फलिन्यो जघनेफलाः २२
तालास्तमालाः सालाश्च कङ्कोला नागभद्रकाः
पुन्नागाः पीलवः साल्वका वै कर्पूरशाखिनः २३
अश्वकर्णा हस्तिकर्णास्तालपर्णाश्च दाडिमाः
गणिका बन्धुजीवाश्च जम्बीराश्च कुरण्डकाः २४
चाम्पेया बन्धुजीवाश्च तथा वै कनकद्रुमाः
कालागुरुद्रुमाश्चैव तथा चन्दनपादपाः २५
खर्जूरा यूथिकास्तालपर्ण्यश्चैव तथेक्षवः
क्षीरवृक्षाश्च खदिराश्चिञ्चाभल्लातकास्तथा २६
रुचकाः कुटजा वृक्षा बिल्ववृक्षास्तथैव च

तुलसीनां वनान्येवं मल्लिकानां तथैव च २७
इत्यादितरुजातीनां वनान्युपवनानि च
नानावापीशतैर्युक्तान्येवं सन्ति धराधिप २८
कोकिलारावसंयुक्ता गुञ्जद्भ्रमरभूषिताः
निर्यासस्राविणः सर्वे स्निग्धच्छायास्तरूत्तमाः २९
नानात्रृतुभवा वृक्षा नानापक्षिसमाकुलाः
नानारसस्राविणीभिर्नदीभिरतिशोभिताः ३०
पारावतशुकव्रातसारिकापक्षमारुतैः
हंसपक्षसमुद्भूतवातव्रातैश्चलद्द्रुमम् ३१
सुगंधग्राहिपवनपूरितं तद्वनोत्तमम्
सहितं हरिणीयूथैर्धावमानैरितस्ततः ३२
नृत्यद्बर्हिकदम्बस्य केकारावैः सुखप्रदैः
नादितं तद्वनं दिव्यं मधुस्राावि समन्ततः ३३

Second Enclosure in Devī Bhāgavata Purāṇa:

O King! After this there is a second enclosure wall, very big and built of white copper metal (an amalgam of zinc or tin, with copper); it is so very high that it almost touches the Heavens. It is a hundred times more brilliant than the preceding enclosure wall; there are many principal entrance gates and various trees here. What to speak of the trees there more than this, that all the trees that are found in this universe are found here and they bear always flowers, fruits and new leaves! All quarters are scented with their sweet fragrance! O King! Now hear, in brief, the names of some of the trees that are found in abundance there: Panasa, Vakula, Lodhra, Karṇikāra, Śinśapa, Deodāra, Kānchanāra, Mango,

Sumeru, Likucha, Hingula, Elā, Lavaṅga, Kaṭ fruit tree, Pāṭala, Muchukunda, Phalinī, Jaghanephala, Tāla, Tamāla, Sāla, Kaṅkola, Nāgabhadraka, Punnāga, Pīlu, Sālvaka, Karpūra, Aśvakarṇa, Hastikarṇa, Tālaparna, Pomegranate, Gaṇikā, Bandhujīva, Jambīra, Kuraṇḍaka, Chāmpeya, Bandhujīva, Kanakavṛkṣa, Kālāguru (usually coiled all over with black poisonous cobras), Sandaltree, Datetree, Yūthikā, Tālaparṇī, Sugarcane, Ksīra-tree, Khadira, Bhallātaka, Ruchaka, Kuṭaja, Bel tree and others, the Tulasī and Mallikā and other forest plants. The place is interspersed with various forests and gardens. At intervals there are wells and tanks, adding very much to the beauty of the place. The cuckoos are perching on every tree and they are cooing sweetly; the bees are drinking the honey and humming all around. The trees are emitting juices and sweet fragrance all around. The trees are casting nice cool shadows. The trees of all seasons are seen here; on the tops of these are sitting pigeons, parrots, female birds of the Mayanā species and other birds of various other species. There are rivers flowing at intervals carrying many juicy liquids. The flamingoes, swans, and other aquatic animals are playing in them. The breeze is stealing away the perfumes of flowers and carrying it all around. The deer are following this breeze, the wild, mad peacocks are dancing with madness, and the whole place looks very nice, lovely and charming.

Third Enclosure, made of copper

In the physiology, the third enclosure is the subcutaneous tissue lying below the dermis, called the hypodermis. It is the deepest layer of the skin.

कांस्यशालादुत्तरे तु ताम्रशालः प्रकीर्तितः
चतुरस्रसमाकार उन्नत्या सप्तयोजनः ३४
द्वयोस्तु शालयोर्मध्ये संप्रोक्ता कल्पवाटिका
येषां तरूणां पुष्पाणि काञ्चनाभानि भूमिप ३५
पत्राणि काञ्चनाभानि रत्नबीजफलानि च
दशयोजनगन्धो हि प्रसर्पति समन्ततः ३६
तद्वनं रक्षितं राजन्वसन्तेनर्तुनाऽनिशम्
पुष्पसिंहासनासीनः पुष्पच्छत्रविराजितः ३७
पुष्पभूषाभूषितश्च पुष्पासवविघूर्णितः
मधुश्रीर्माधवश्रीश्च द्वे भार्ये तस्य संमते ३८
क्रीडतः स्मेरवदने सुमस्तबककन्दुकैः
अतीव रम्यं विपिनं मधुस्रावि सन्ततः ३९
दशयोजनपर्यन्तं कुसुमामोदवायुना
पूरितं दिव्यगन्धर्वैः साङ्गनैर्गानलोलुपैः ४०
शोभितं तद्वनं दिव्यं मत्तकोकिलनादितम्
वसन्तलक्ष्मीसंयुक्तं कामिकामप्रवर्धनम् ४१

Third Enclosure in Devī Bhāgavata Purāṇa:

Next to this Kāmsya enclosure comes the third enclosure, a wall of copper. It is square-shaped and seven yojanas high. Within this are forests of Kalpavṛkṣas (wish fulfilling trees), bearing golden leaves and flowers and fruits like gems. Their perfumes spread ten yojanas and gladden things all around. The king of the seasons always preserves this place. The king's seat is made of flowers;

his umbrella is of flowers; his ornaments are made of flowers; he drinks the honey of the flowers; and, with rolling eyes, he lives here always with his two wives named Madhu Śrī and Mādhava Śrī. The two wives of Spring have their faces always smiling. They play with bunches of flowers. This forest is very pleasant. Oh! The honey of the flowers is seen here in abundance. The perfumes of the fully bloomed flowers spread to a distance of ten yojanas. The Gandharvans, the celestial musicians, live here with their wives. The places around this are filled with the beauties of the spring and with the cooing of cuckoos. No doubt this place intensifies the desires of the amorous persons!

Fourth Enclosure, made of lead

In the physiology, the fourth enclosure is the cranium, the part of the bony skeleton that houses and protects the brain.

ताम्रशालादुत्तरत्र सीसशालः प्रकीर्तितः
समुच्छ्रायः स्मृतोऽप्यस्य सप्तयोजनसंख्यया ४२
सन्तानवाटिकामध्ये शालयोस्तु द्वयोर्नृप
दशयोजनगन्धस्तु प्रसूनानां समन्ततः ४३
हिरण्याभानि कुसुमान्युत्फुल्लानि निरन्तरम्
अमृतद्रवसंयुक्तफलानि मधुराणि च ४४
ग्रीष्मर्तुर्नायकस्तस्या वाटिकाया नृपोत्तम
शुक्रश्रीश्च शुचिश्रीश्च द्वे भार्ये तस्य संमते ४५
संतापत्रस्तलोकास्तु वृक्षमूलेषु संस्थिताः
नाना सिद्धैः परिवृता नानादेवैः समन्विताः ४६

विलासिनीनां वृन्दैस्तु चन्दनद्रवपङ्किलैः
पुष्पमालाभूषितैस्तु तालवृन्तकराम्बुजैः ४७
प्राकारः शोभितो राजञ्छीतलाम्बुनिषेविभिः

Fourth Enclosure in Devī Bhāgavata Purāṇa:

O King! Next comes the enclosure wall made of lead. Its height is seven yojanas. Within this enclosure there is the garden of the Santānaka tree (a Kalpavṛkṣa tree), one of the five trees in Indra's Heaven. The fragrance of its flowers extends to ten yojanas. The flowers look like gold and are always in full bloom. Its fruits are very sweet; they seem to be imbued with nectar drops. In this garden resides the Summer Season with his two wives Śukra Śrī and Śuchi Śrī. The inhabitants of this place always remain under trees; otherwise they would be scorched by summer rays. Various Siddhas and Devas inhabit this place. The water here is very cool and refreshing. And owing to heat all the people here use this water.

Fifth Enclosure, built of brass

In the physiology, the fifth enclosure corresponds to the periosteal dura mater, the outermost layer of the membrane surrounding the brain, i.e., the part of the dura mater which adheres to the periosteum of the bones of the cranial vault.

सीसशालादुत्तरत्राप्यारकूटमयः शुभः ४८
प्राकारो वर्तते राजन्मुनियोजनदैर्घ्यवान्
हरिचन्दनवृक्षाणां वाटीमध्ये तयोः स्मृतः ४९
शालयोरधिनाथस्तु वर्षर्तुर्मेघवाहनः

विद्युत्पिङ्गलनेत्रश्च जीमूतकवचः स्मृतः ५०
वज्रनिर्घोषमुखरश्चेन्द्रधन्वा समन्ततः
सहस्रशो वारिधारा मुञ्चन्नास्ते गणावृतः ५१
नभःश्रीश्च नभस्यश्रीः स्वरस्वारस्यमालिनी
अंबा दुला निरत्निश्चाभ्रमन्ती मेघयन्तिका ५२
वर्षयन्ती चिबुणिका वारिधारा च संमताः
वर्षर्तोर्द्वादश प्रोक्ताः शक्तयो मदविह्वलाः ५३
नवपल्लववृक्षाश्च नवीनलतिकान्विताः
हरितानि तृणान्येव वेष्टिता यैर्धराऽखिला ५४
नदीनदप्रवाहाश्च प्रवहन्ति च वेगतः
सरांसि कलुषाम्बूनि रागिचित्तसमानि च ५५
वसन्ति देवा सिद्धाश्च ये देवीकर्मकारिणः
वापीकूपतडागाश्च ये देव्यर्थं समर्पिताः ५६
ते गणा निवसन्त्यत्र सविलासाश्च साङ्गनाः

Fifth Enclosure in Devī Bhāgavata Purāṇa:

Next to this lead enclosure comes the wall made of brass, the fifth enclosure wall. It is seven yojanas long. In the center is situated the garden of Harichandana trees. Its ruler is the Rainy Season. The lightnings are his auburn eyes, the clouds are his armor, the thunder is his voice, and the rainbow is his arrow. Surrounded by his hosts he rains incessantly. He has twelve wives : (1) Nabhaḥ Śrī, (2) Nabhasya Śrī, (3) Svarasya, (4) Rasyasālinī, (5) Ambā, (6) Dulā, (7) Niratni, (8) Abhramantī, (9) Megha Yantikā, (10) Varṣayantī, (11) Chivunikā, and (12) Vāridhārā (or Madamattā). All the trees here are always seen with new leaves and entwined with new creepers. The whole site is covered all over with fresh green leaves and twigs. The rivers here always flow full and the current is strong indeed! The tanks here are very dirty, like the minds of worldly persons attached to worldly things. The devotees of Devī, such as the Siddhas, the Devas, and those persons who have consecrated wells and reservoirs for the Devas, dwell here with their wives.

Sixth Enclosure, built of five-fold irons

In the physiology, the sixth enclosure is the inner layer of the dura mater, called the meningeal dura mater.

आरकूटमयादग्रे सप्तयोजनदैर्घ्यवान् ५७
पञ्चलोहात्मकः शालो मध्ये मन्दारवाटिका
नानापुष्पलताकीर्णा नानापल्लवशोभिता ५८
अधिष्ठाताऽत्र संप्रोक्तः शरदृतुरनामयः
इषुलक्ष्मीरूर्जलक्ष्मीर्द्वे भार्ये तस्य संमते ५९
नानासिद्धा वसन्त्यत्र साङ्गनाः सपरिच्छदाः

Sixth Enclosure in Devī Bhāgavata Purāṇa:

O King! Next to this brass enclosure comes the sixth enclosure wall, made of five-fold irons. It is seven yojanas long. In the center is situated the Garden of Mandāra trees. This garden is beautified by various creepers, flowers and leaves. The Autumn season lives here with his two wives Iśālaksmī and Ûrjalaksmī. Various Siddhas dwell here with their wives, well clothed.

Seventh Enclosure, built of silver

In the physiology, the seventh enclosure is the arachnoid, the middle layer of the meninges, the protective covering of the brain.

पञ्चलोहमयादग्रे सप्तयोजनदैर्घ्यवान् ६०
दीप्यमानो महाशृङ्गैर्वर्तते रौप्यशालकः
पारिजाताटवो मध्ये प्रसूनस्तबकान्विता ६१
दशयोजनगन्धीनि कुसुमानि समन्ततः
मोदयति गणान्सर्वान् ये देवीकर्मकारिणः ६२
तत्राधिनाथः संप्रोक्तो हेमन्तर्तुर्महोज्ज्वलः
सगणः सायुधः सर्वान् रागिणो रञ्जयन्नृपः ६३
सहश्रीश्च सहस्यश्रीर्द्वे भार्ये तस्य संमते
वसन्ति तत्र सिद्धाश्च ये देवीव्रतकारिणः ६४

Seventh Enclosure in Devī Bhāgavata Purāṇa:

O King! Next comes the seventh enclosure wall, seven yojanas long and built of silver. In the center is situated the garden of Pārijāta trees, which are filled with bunches of flowers. The fragrance of these Pārijātas extends up to ten Yojanas and gladdens all the things all around. Those who are the Devī Bhaktas and who do the work of the Devī are delighted with this fragrance. The Hemanta (dewy) season is the regent of this place. He lives here with his two wives Saha Śrī and Sahasya Śrī, and with his hosts. Those who are of a loving nature are pleased hereby. Those who have become perfect by performing vows to the Devī also live here.

Eighth Enclosure, made of molten gold

In the physiology, the eighth enclosure corresponds to the pia mater, the innermost layer of the covering of the brain. It is a thin fibrous tissue that is impermeable to fluid.

रौप्यशालमयादग्रे सप्तयोजनदैर्घ्यवान्
सौवर्णशालः संप्रोक्तस्तप्तहाटककल्पितः ६५
मध्ये कदम्बवाटी तु पुष्पपुल्लवशोभिता
कदम्बमदिराधाराः प्रवर्तन्ते सहस्रशः ६६
याभिर्निपीतपीताभिर्निजानन्दोऽनुभूयते
तत्राधिनाथः संप्रोक्तः शैशिरर्तुर्महोदयः ६७
तपःश्रीश्च तपस्यश्रीर्द्वे भार्ये तस्य संमते
मोदमानः सहैताभ्यां वर्तते शिशिराकृतिः ६८
नानाविलाससंयुक्तो नानागणसमावृतः
निवसन्ति महासिद्धा ये देवीदानकारिणः ६९
नानाभोगसमुत्पन्नमहानन्दसमन्विताः
सांगनाः परिवारैस्तु संघशः परिवारिताः ७०

Eighth Enclosure in Devī Bhāgavata Purāṇa:

O King! Next to this silver enclosure comes the eighth enclosure wall, built of molten gold. It is seven Yojanas long. In the center there is the garden of the Kadamba tree. The trees are always covered with fruits and flowers, and honey is always coming out of the trees from all sides. The devotees of the Devī always drink this honey and feel intense delight; the Dewy Season is the Regent of this place. He resides here with his two wives, Tapaḥ Śrī and Tapasyā Śrī, and his various hosts, and enjoys gladly the objects of enjoyments. Those who have made various gifts for the Devī's satisfaction, those great Siddha Puruṣas, live here with their wives and live very gladly with various enjoyment.

Ninth Enclosure, made of saffron-colored Puṣparāga gems (faceted yellow topaz or sapphire)

In the physiology, the ninth enclosure is cortex layer 1.

स्वर्णशालमयादग्रे मुनियोजनदैर्घ्यवान्
पुष्परागमयः शालः कुङ्कुमारुणविग्रहः ७१
पुष्परागमयी भूमिर्वनान्युपवनानि च
रत्नवृक्षालबालाश्च पुष्परागमयाः स्मृताः ७२
प्राकारो यस्य रत्नस्य तद्रत्नरचिता द्रुमाः
वनभूः पक्षिणश्चैव रत्नवर्णजलानि च ७३
मण्डपा मडपस्तम्भाः सरांसि कमलानि च
प्राकारे तत्र यद्यत्स्यात्तत्सर्वं तत्समं भवेत् ७४
परिभाषेयमुद्दिष्टा रत्नशालादिषु प्रभो
तेजसा स्याल्लक्षगुणः पूर्वशालात्परो नृप ७५
दिक्पाला निवसन्त्यत्र प्रतिब्रह्माण्डवर्तिनाम्
दिक्पालानां समष्ट्यात्मरूपाः स्फूर्जद्वरायुधाः ७६
पूर्वाशायां समुत्तुङ्गशृङ्गा पूरमरावती
नानोपवनसंयुक्ता महेन्द्रस्तत्र राजते ७७
स्वर्गशोभा च या स्वर्गे यावती स्यात्ततोऽधिका
समष्टिशतनेत्रस्य सहस्रगुणतः स्मृता ७८
ऐरावतसमारूढो वज्रहस्तः प्रतापवान्

देवसेनापरिवृतो राजतेऽत्र शतक्रतुः ७९
देवाङ्गनागणयुता शची तत्र विराजते
वह्निकोणे वह्निपुरी वह्निपूःसदृशी नृप ८०
स्वाहास्वधासमायुक्तो वह्निस्तत्र विराजते
निजवाहनभूषाढ्यो निजदेवगणैर्वृतः ८१
याम्याशायां यमपुरी तत्र दंडधरो महान्
स्वभटैर्वेष्टितो राजन् चित्रगुप्तपुरोगमैः ८२
निजशक्तियुतो भास्वत्तनयोऽस्ति यमो महान्
नैर्ऋत्यां दिशि राक्षस्यां राक्षसैः परिवारितः ८३
खड्गधारी स्फुरन्नास्ते निर्ऋतिनिजशक्तियुक्
वारुण्यां वरुणो राजा पाशधारी प्रतापवान् ८४
महाझषसमारूढो वारुणीमधुविह्वलः
निजशक्तिसमायुक्तो निजयादोगणान्वितः ८५
समास्ते वारुणे लोके वरुणानीरताकुलः
वायुकोणे वायुलोको वायुस्तत्राधितिष्ठति ८६
वायुसाधनसंसिद्धयोगिभिः परिवारितः
ध्वजहस्तो विशालाक्षो मृगवाहनसंस्थितः ८७
मरुद्गणैः परिवृतो निजशक्तिसमन्वितः
उत्तरस्यां दिशि महान्यक्षलोकोऽस्ति भूमिप ८८
यक्षाधिराजस्तत्रास्ते वृद्धि ऋद्ध्यादिशक्तिभिः
नवभिर्निधिभिर्युक्तस्तुन्दिलो धननायकः ८९
मणिभद्रः पूर्णभद्रो मणिमान्मणिकन्धरः
मणिभूषो मणिस्रग्वी मणिकार्मुकधारकः ९०
इत्यादियक्षसेनानीसहितो निजशक्तियुक्
ईशानकोणे संप्रोक्तो रुद्रलोको महत्तरः ९१

अनर्घ्यं रत्नखचितो यत्र रुद्रोऽधिदैवतम्
मन्युमान्दीप्तनयनो बद्धपृष्ठमहेषुधिः ९२
स्फूर्जद्धनुर्वामहस्तोऽधिज्यधन्वभिरावृतः
स्वसमानैरसंख्यातरुद्रैः शूलवरायुधैः ९३
विकृतास्यैः करालस्यैर्वमद्वह्निभिरास्यतः
दशहस्तैः शतकरैः सहस्त्रभुजसंयुतैः ९४
दशपादैर्दशग्रीवैस्त्रिनेत्रैरुग्रमूर्तिभिः
अन्तरिक्षचरा ये च ये च भूमिचराः स्मृताः ९५
रुद्राध्याये स्मृता रुद्रास्तैः सर्वैश्च समावृतः
रुद्राणीकोटिसहितो भद्रकाल्यादिमातृभिः ९६
नानाशक्तिसमाविष्टडामर्यादिगणावृतः
वीरभद्रादिसहितो रुद्रो राजन्विराजते ९७
मुण्डमालाधरो नागवलयो नागकन्धरः
व्याघ्रचर्मपरीधानो गजचर्मोत्तरीयकः ९८
चिताभस्माङ्गलिप्ताङ्गः प्रमथादिगणावृतः
निनदड्डमरुध्वानैर्बधिरीकृतदिङ्मुखः ९९
अट्टहासास्फोटशब्दैः संत्रासितनभस्तलः
भूतसंघसमाविष्टो भूतावासो महेश्वरः १००
ईशानदिक्पतिः सोऽयं नाम्ना चेशान एव च १०१
इति श्रीदेवीभागवते महापुराणे द्वादशस्कन्धे
दशमोऽध्यायः

Ninth Enclosure in Devī Bhāgavata Purāṇa:

O King! Next to the golden enclosure wall comes the ninth enclosure made of red Kuṅkuma-(saffron-)colored Puṣparāga gems. The ground inside this enclosure, the ditches and the basins for water dug round their roots, are all built of Puṣparāga gems. Next to this wall there are other enclosure walls built of various other gems and jewels. The sites, forests, trees, flowers, birds, rivers, tanks, lotuses, Maṇḍaps (halls) and their pillars are all built respectively of those gems. Only this is to be remembered—that those (gems) coming nearer and nearer to the center are one lakh times more brilliant than the ones receding from there. This is the general rule observed in the construction of these enclosures and the articles contained therein. Here the Regents of the several quarters, the Dikpāl reside, representing the sum total of the several Dikpālas of every Brahmāṇḍa and their guardians.

On the eastern quarter is situated the Amarāvatī city. Here the high-peaked mountains exist, and various trees are seen. Indra, the Lord of the Devas, dwells here. Whatever beauty exists in the separate Heavens, in the several places, one thousand times more than that is the beauty that exists in the Heaven of this cosmic Indra, the thousand-eyed Lord. Here Indra mounting on the elephant Airāvata with thunderbolt in his hand, lives with Śachī Devī and other immortal ladies, and with the hosts of the Deva forces.

On the Agni (southeastern) corner is the city of Agni. This represents the sum total of the several cities of Agni in different Brahmāṇḍas. Here resides the Agni Deva very gladly with his two wives, Svāhā and Svadhā, and with his Vāhana and the other Devas.

On the south is situated the city of Yama, the God of

death. Here lives Dharma Rāja with rod in his hand, and the Chitragupta, and several other hosts.

On the south-western corner is the place of the Rākṣasas. Here resides Nirṛti with his axe in his hand, and with his wife and other Rākṣasas.

On the west is the city of Varuṇa. Here Varuṇa Rāja, always intoxicated with the drink of Vāruṇi honey, resides with his wife Vāruṇī; his weapon is the noose, his Vāhana is the King of fishes, and his subjects are the aquatic animals.

On the north-western corner dwells Vāyu Deva. Here Pāvana Deva lives with his wife and with the Yogis, perfect in the practice of Prāṇāyāma. He holds a flag in his hand. His Vāhana is deer and his family consists of the forty-nine Vāyus.

In the north reside the Yakṣas. The corpulent King of the Yakṣas, Kubera, lives here with his Śaktis, Vṛddhi and Ṛiddhi, in possession of various gems and jewels. His generals Maṇibhadra, Purṇabhadra, Maṇimān, Maṇikandhara, Maṇibhūṣa, Maṇisragvī, Maṇikar-mukadhārī, etc., live here.

On the northeastern corner is situated the Rudra loka, decked with invaluable gems. Here dwells the Rudra Deva. On His back is kept the arrow-case, and he holds a bow in his left hand. He looks very angry and his eyes are red with anger. There are other Rudras like him with bows and spears and other weapons, surrounding him. The faces of some of them are distorted; some are very horrible with fire coming out of the mouths. Some have ten hands, some hundred hands, some a thousand. Some have ten feet; some have ten heads whereas some others have three eyes. Those who roam in the intermediate spaces between the Heaven and Earth, those who move on the Earth, or the Rudras mentioned in the Rudrādhyāya, all live here. O King! Īsāna, the Regent of the northeastern quarter lives here with Bhadrakālī and other Mātrigaṇas, with Kotis and Kotis of Rudrāṇīs and with Dāmarīs and Vīra Bhadras and various other Śaktis. On his neck there is a garland of skulls, on his hand there is a ring of snakes; he wears a tiger skin; his upper clothing is a tiger skin and his body is smeared with the ashes of the dead. He sounds his Damaru frequently; this sound reverberates on all sides. He makes big laughs called Attahāsya, reverberating through the heavens. He remains always surrounded with Pramathas and Bhūtas; they live here.

Here ends the Tenth Chapter of the Twelfth Book on the description of Maṇi Dvīpa in the Mahāpurānam Śrī Mad Devī Bhāgavatam of 18,000 verses by Maharshi Veda Vyāsa.

Tenth Enclosure, made of red Padmarāga jewels (rubies)

In the physiology, the tenth enclosure is cortex layer 2.

अथ एकादशोऽध्यायः

व्यास उवाच

पुष्परागमयादग्रे कुङ्कुमारुणविग्रहः
पद्मरागमयः शालो मध्ये भूश्चैव तादृशी १
दशयोजनवान्दैर्घ्ये गोपुरद्वारसंयुतः

तन्मणिस्तम्भसंयुक्ता मण्डपाः शतशो नृप २
मध्ये भुवि समासीनाश्चतुःषष्टिमिताः कलाः
नानायुधधरा वीरा रत्नभूषणभूषिताः ३
प्रत्येकलोकस्तासां तु तत्तल्लोकस्य नायकाः
समन्तात्पद्मरागस्य परिवार्य स्थिताः सदा ४
स्वस्वलोकजनैर्जुष्टाः स्वस्ववाहनहेतिभिः
तासां नामानि वक्ष्यामि शृणु त्वं जनमेजय ५
पिङ्गलाक्षी विशालाक्षी समृद्धिर्वृद्धिरेव च
श्रद्धा स्वाहा स्वधाभिख्या माया संज्ञा वसुन्धरा ६
त्रिलोकधात्री सावित्री गायत्री त्रिदशेश्वरी
सुरूपा बहुरूपा च स्कंदमाताऽच्युतप्रिया ७
विमला चामला तद्वदरुणी तुनरारुणी
प्रकृतिर्विकृतिः सृष्टिः स्थितिः संहृतिरेव च ८
संध्या माता सती हंसी मर्दिका वज्रिका परा
देवमाता भगवती देवकी कमलासना ९
त्रिमुखी सप्तमुख्यन्या सुरासुरविमर्दिनी
लम्बोष्ठी चोर्ध्वकेशी च बहुशीर्षा वृकोदरी १०
रथरेखाह्वया पश्चाच्छशिरेखा तथा परा
गगनवेगा पवनवेगा वेगा चैव ततः परम् ११
अग्रे भुवनपाला स्यात्तत्पश्चान्मदनातुरा
अनङ्गानङ्गमथना तथैवानङ्गमेखला १२
अनङ्गकुसुमा पश्चाद्विश्वरूपा सुरादिका
क्षयंकरी भवेच्छक्तिरक्षोभ्या च ततः परम् १३
सत्यवादिन्यथ प्रोक्ता बहुरूपा शुचिव्रता
उदाराख्या च वागीशा चतुःषष्टिमिताः स्मृताः १४

ज्वलज्जिह्वाननाः सर्वा वमंत्यो वह्निमुल्बणम्
जलं पिवामः सकलं संहरामो विभावसुम् १५
पवनं स्तम्भयामोऽद्य भक्षयामोऽखिल जगत्
इति वाचं संगिरन्ते क्रोधसंरक्तलोचनाः १६
चापबाणधराः सर्वा युद्धायैवोत्सुकाः सदा
दंष्ट्राकटकटारावैर्बधिरीकृतदिङ्मुखाः १७
पिङ्गोर्ध्वकेश्यः संप्रोक्ताश्चापबाणकराः सदा
शताक्षौहिणिका सेनाप्येकैकस्याः प्रकीर्तिता १८
एकैकशक्तेः सामर्थ्यं लक्षब्रह्माण्डनाशने
शताक्षौहिणीका सेना तादृशी नृपसत्तम १९
किं न कुर्याज्जगत्यस्मिन्नशक्यं वक्तुमेव तत्
सर्वापि युद्धसामग्री तस्मिन्शाले स्थिता मुने २०
रथानां गणना नास्ति हयानां करिणां तथा
शस्त्राणां गणना तद्वद्गणानां गणना तथा २१

Tenth Enclosure in Devī Bhāgavata Purāṇa:

Vyāsa said: O King Janamejaya! Next to this Puṣparāgamaṇi enclosure wall comes the tenth enclosure wall, made of Padmarāgamaṇi (ruby), red like the red Kuṅkuma and the rising Sun. It is ten yojanas high. All its ground, entrance gates, temples and arbors are made of Padmarāgamaṇi. Within this reside the sixty-four Kalās, or Sub-Śaktis, adorned with various ornaments, and holding weapons in their hands. Each of them has a separate Loka (region) allotted, and within this Loka each has his own formidable weapons, Vāhanas, families and their leaders or Governors. O King! Now hear the names of the sixty-four Kalās. They are: Pingalākṣī, Viśālākṣī,

Samṛddhi, Vṛddhi, Śraddhā, Svāhā, Svadhā, Māyā, Saṅgyā, Vasundharā, Trīlokadhātrī, Sāvitrī, Gāyatrī, Tridaśeśvarī, Surūpā, Bahurūpā, Skandamātā, Achyutapriyā, Vimalā, Amalā, Aruṇī, Āruṇī, Prakṛti, Vikṛti, Sṛṣṭi, Sthiti, Saṁhriti, Sandhyā, Mātā, Satī, Haṁsī, Mardikā, Vajrikā, Parā, Devamātā, Bhagavatī, Devakī, Kamalāsanā, Trimukhī, Saptamukhī, Surāsura vimardinī, Lambosthī, Ūrdhvakeśī, Bahusīrsā, Vrikodarī, Ratharekhāhvayā, Śaśirekā, Gaganavegā, Pavanavegā, Vegā, Bhuvanapālā, Madanāturā, Anaṅgā, Anaṅgamathanā, Anaṅgamekhalā, Anaṅgakusumā, Viśvarūpā, Surādikā, Kṣayaṁkarī, Akṣyobhyā, Satyavādinī, Bahurūpā, Śuchivratā, Udārā and Vāgiśī. These are the sixty-four Kalās. All of them have luminous faces and long rolling tongues. Fire is always coming out from their faces. Their eyes are red with anger. They are uttering : "We will drink all the water and thus dry the oceans; we will annihilate fire, we will stop the flow of air and control it. Today we will devour the whole universe," and so forth. All of them have bows and arrows in their hands; all are eager to fight. The four quarters are constantly reverberating with the clashing of their teeth. The hairs on their heads are all tawny and standing upright. Each of them has one hundred Akṣauhinī forces under them. O King! Each of them has the power to destroy one hundred thousand Brahmāṇḍas; and their one hundred Akṣauhinī forces also can do the same. There is nothing that is impracticable with them. What they cannot do cannot be conceived by the mind nor uttered in speech. All the war materials exist within their enclosures. Chariots, horses, elephants, weapons, and forces are all unlimited. All the war materials are ready at all times and in abundance.

Eleventh Enclosure, made of Gomeda gems (a gem associated with Rāhu)

In the physiology, the eleventh enclosure is cortex layer 3.

पद्मरागमयादग्रे गोमेदमणिनिर्मितः
दशयोजनदैर्घ्येण प्राकारो वर्तते महान् २२
भास्वज्जपाप्रसूनाभो मध्यभूतस्य तादृशी
गोमेदकल्पितान्येव तद्वासिसदना च सा २३
पक्षिणः स्तम्भवर्याश्च वृक्षा वाप्यः सरांसि च
गोमेदकल्पिता एव कुङ्कुमारुणविग्रहाः २४
तन्मध्यस्था महादेव्यो द्वात्रिंशच्छक्तयः स्मृताः
नानाशस्त्रप्रहरणा गोमेदमणिभूषिताः २५
प्रत्येकलोकवासिन्यः परिवार्य समन्ततः
गोमेदशाले सन्नद्धाः पिशाचवदना नृप २६
स्वर्लोकवासिभिर्नित्यं पूजिताश्चक्रबाहवः
क्रोधरक्तेक्षणा भिन्धि पच छिन्धि दहेति च २७
वदन्ति सततं वाचं युद्धोत्सुकहृदन्तराः
एकैकस्या महाशक्तेर्दशाक्षौहिणिका मता २८
सेना तत्राप्येकशक्तिर्लक्षब्रह्माण्डनाशिनी
तादृशीनां महासेना वर्णनीया कथं नृप २९
रथानां नैव गणना वाहनानां तथैव च
सर्वयुद्धसमारम्भस्तत्र देव्या विराजते ३०
तासां नामानि वक्ष्यामि पापनाशकराणि च

विद्या ह्री पुष्टयः प्रज्ञा सिनीवाली कुहूस्तथा ३१
रुद्रा वीर्या प्रभा नन्दा पोषिणी ऋद्धिदा शुभा
कालरात्रिर्महारात्रिर्भद्रकाली कपर्दिनी ३२
विकृतिर्दण्डिमुण्डिन्यौ सेन्दुखण्डा शिखण्डिनी
निशुम्भशुम्भमथिनी महिषासुरमर्दिनी ३३
इन्द्राणी चैव रुद्राणी शङ्करार्धशरीरिणी
नारी नारायणी चैव त्रिशूलिन्यपि पालिनी ३४
अम्बिका ह्लादिनी पश्चादित्येवं शक्तयः स्मृताः
यद्येताः कुपिता देव्यस्तदा ब्रह्माण्डनाशनम् ३५
पराजयो न चैतासां कदाचित्क्वचिदस्ति हि

Eleventh Enclosure in Devī Bhāgavata Purāṇa:

Next comes the eleventh enclosure wall built of Gomedamaṇi. It is ten Yojanas high. Its color is like the newly blossomed Javā flower. All the ground, trees, tanks, houses, pillars, birds and all other things are all red and built of Gomedamaṇi. Here dwell the thirty-two Mahā Śaktis adorned with various ornaments made of Gomedamaṇi and furnished with various weapons. They are always eager to fight. Their eyes are always red with anger; their faces are like Piśāchas and their hands are like Chakras (discs). "Pierce him," "Beat him," "Cut him," "Tear him asunder," "Burn him down," are the words constantly uttered by them. The inhabitants of the place worship them. Each of the 32 Śaktis has ten Akṣauhinī forces. These are inordinately powerful. It is impossible to describe it. It seems that each Śakti can easily destroy one hundred thousand Brahmāṇḍas.

Innumerable chariots, elephants, hordes, etc., and other Vāhanas are here. All the war materials of the Devī Bhagavatī are seen in this Gomedamaṇi enclosure. Now I am mentioning the auspicious, sin destroying names of these Śaktis: Vidyā, Hrī, Puṣṭi, Prajñā, Sinīvālī, Kuhū, Rudrā, Vīryā, Prabhā, Nandā, Poṣiṇī, Ṛiddhidā, Śubhā, Kālarātri, Mahārātri, Bhadrakālī, Kapardinī, Vikṛti, Daṇḍi, Muṇḍinī, Sendukhaṇḍā, Śikhaṇḍinī, Niśumbha, Śumbha, Mathinī, Mahiṣāsura, Mardinī, Indrāṇī, Rudrāṇī, Śankarārdha, Śarīrinī, Nārī, Nārāyaṇī Triśūlinī, Pālinī, Ambikā, and Hlādinī.

Never is there any chance that any of these Śaktis will be defeated anywhere. Hence if all those Śaktis become angry at any time, the universe will cease to exist.

Twelfth Enclosure, made of diamonds

In the physiology, the twelfth enclosure is cortex layer 4.

गोमेदकमयादग्रे सद्वज्रमणिनिर्मितः ३६

दशयोजनतुङ्गोऽसौ गोपुरद्वारसंयुतः
कपाटशृङ्खलाबद्धो नववृक्षसमुज्ज्वलः ३७
शालस्तन्मध्यभूम्यादि सर्वं हीरमयं स्मृतम्
गृहाणि वीथयो रथ्या महामार्गाङ्गणानि च ३८
वृक्षालवालतरवः सारङ्गा अपि तादृशाः
दीर्घिकाश्रेणयो वाप्यस्तडागाः कूपसंयुताः ३९
तत्र श्रीभुवनेश्वर्या वसन्ति परिचारिकाः
एकैका लक्षदासीभिः सेविता मदगर्विताः ४०

तालवृन्तधराः काश्चिच्चषकाढ्यकराम्बुजाः
काश्चित्ताम्बूलपात्राणि धारयन्त्योऽतिगर्विताः ४१
कश्चित्तच्छवधारिण्यश्चामराणां विधारिकाः
नानावस्त्रधराः काश्चित्काश्चित्पुष्पकराम्बुजाः ४२
नानादर्शकराः काश्चित्काश्चित्कुङ्कुमलेपनम्
धारयन्त्यः कज्जलं च सिन्दूरचषकं पराः ४३
काश्चिच्चित्रकनिर्मात्र्यः पादसंवाहने रताः
काश्चित्तु भूषाकारिण्यो नानाभूषाधराः पराः ४४
पुष्पभूषणनिर्मात्र्यः पुष्पशृङ्गारकारिकाः
नानाविलासचतुरा वह्न्य एवंविधाः परा ४५
निबद्धपरिधानीया युवत्यः सकला अपि
देवी कृपालेशवशात्तुच्छीकृतजगत्त्रयाः ४६
एता दूत्यः स्मृता देव्यः शृङ्गारमदगर्विताः
तासां नामानि वक्ष्यामि शृणु मे नृपसत्तम ४७
अनङ्गरूपा प्रथमाप्यनङ्गमदना परा
तृतीया तु ततः प्रोक्ता सुन्दरी मदनातुरा ४८
ततो भुवनवेगा स्यात्तथा भुवनपालिका
स्यात्सर्वशिशिरानङ्गवेदनाऽनङ्गमेखला ४९
विद्युद्दामसमानाङ्ग्यः क्वणत्काञ्चीगुणान्विताः
रणन्मञ्जीरचरणा बहिरन्तरितास्ततः ५०
धावमानास्तु शोभन्ते सर्वा विद्युल्लतोपमाः
कुशलाः सर्वकार्येषु वेत्रहस्ताः समन्ततः ५१
अष्टदिक्षु तथैतासां प्राकाराद्बहिरेव च
सदनानि विराजन्ते नानावाहनहेतिभिः ५२

Twelfth Enclosure in Devī Bhāgavata Purāṇa:

Next to this Gomedamaṇi enclosure comes the enclosure made of diamonds. It is ten yojanas high; on all sides there are entrance gates; the doors are hinged there with nice mechanisms. Nice new diamond trees exist here. All the royal roads, trees, and the spaces for watering their roots, tanks, wells, reservoirs, Sārangā and other musical instruments are all made of diamonds. Śrī Bhuvaneśvarī Devī dwells here with Her attendants. O King! Each attendant has a lakh (one hundred thousand) attendants, and all are proud of their beauty. Some are holding fans in their hands; some are holding cups for drinking water; some, betelnuts; some are holding umbrellas, some chowries, some various clothing, flowers, looking glasses, saffrons, collyrium; some are holding Sindūra (red lead). All are ready to attend the Devī in various ways. Some are ready to do the painting works; some are looking to shampoo the feet; some are eager to help Her wear ornaments; some want to put garlands of flowers on Her neck. All of them are skilled in various arts of enjoyments and all are young. To gain the Grace of the Devī, they all consider the universe as trifling. Now I shall mention to you the names of the attendants of the Devī, proud of possessing lots of amorous gestures and postures. Listen. They are: Anaṅgarūpā, Anaṅgamadanā, Madanāturā, Bhuvanavegā, Bhuvanapālikā, Sarvaśiśirā, Anaṅgavedanā, Anaṅgamekhalā, these are the eight attendants. Each of them is as fair as Vidyullatā. Each of the attendants is adorned with various ornaments and skilled in all actions. When they walk to and fro with canes and rods in their hands in the service of the Devī, they look as if the lightning flashes glimmer on all sides.

On the outer portion of this enclosure wall on the eight sides are situated the dwelling houses of these eight attendants and they are always full of various Vāhanas and weapons.

Thirteenth Enclosure, made of Vaidūrya gems (lapis lazuli)

In the physiology, the thirteenth enclosure is cortex layer 5.

वज्रशालादग्रभागे सालो वैदूर्यनिर्मितः
दशयोजनतुङ्गोऽसौ गोपुरद्वारभूषितः ५३
वैदूर्यभूमिः सर्वापि गृहाणि विविधानि च
वीथ्यो रथ्या महामार्गाः सर्वे वैदूर्यनिर्मिताः ५४
वापीकूपतडागाश्च स्रवन्तीना तटानि च
बालुका चैव सर्वाऽपि वैदूर्यमणिनिर्मिता ५५
तत्राष्टदिक्षु परितो ब्राह्म्यादीनां च मंडलम्
निजैर्गणैः परिवृतं भ्राजते नृपसत्तम ५६
प्रतिब्रह्माण्डमातॄणां ताः समष्टय ईरिताः
ब्राह्मी माहेश्वरी चैव कौमारी वैष्णवी तथा ५७
वाराही च तथेन्द्राणी चामुण्डाः सप्त मातरः
अष्टमी तु महालक्ष्मीर्नाम्ना प्रोक्तास्तु मातरः ५८
ब्रह्मरुद्रादिदेवानां समाकारास्तु ताः स्मृताः
जगत्कल्याणकारिण्यः स्वस्वसेनासमावृताः ५९
तच्छालस्य चतुर्द्वार्षु वाहनानि महेशितुः

सज्जानि नृपते सन्ति सालङ्काराणि नित्यशः ६०
दन्तिनः कोटिशो वाहाः कोटिशः शिबिकास्तथा
हंसा सिंहाश्च गरुडा मयूरा वृषभास्तथा ६१
तैर्युक्ताः स्यंदनास्तद्वत्कोटिशो नृपनन्दन
पार्ष्णिग्राहसमायुक्ता ध्वजैराकाशचुम्बिनः ६२
कोटिशस्तु विमानानि नानाचिह्नान्वितानि
नानावादित्रयुक्तानि महाध्वजयुतानि च ६३

Thirteenth Enclosure in Devī Bhāgavata Purāṇa:

Next to this enclosure of diamond comes the thirteenth enclosure wall made of Vaidūryamaṇi (lapis lazuli). Its height is ten yojanas. There are entrance gates and doorways on four sides. The court inside, the houses, the big roads, wells, tanks, ponds, rivers and even the sands, are all made of Vaiduryamaṇi. On the eight sides reside the eight Mātrikās Brāhmī, etc., with their hosts. These Mātrikās represent the sum-total of the individual Mātrikās in every Brahmāṇḍa. Now hear their names: (1) Brāhmī, (2) Māheśvarī, (3) Kaumārī, (4) Vaiṣnavī, (5) Vārāhī, (6) Indrāṇī, (7) Chāmuṇḍā, and (8) Mahā Lakṣmī. Their forms are like those of Brahmā and Rudra and others. They are always engaged in doing good to the universe and reside here with their own Vāhanas (vehicles) and weapons.

At the four gates, the various Vāhanas of Bhagavatī remain always fully equipped. Somewhere there are Kotis and Kotis of elephants. At some places there are Kotis and Kotis of horses; at others there are camps and houses; at others swans and lions; at others Garuḍas. At other places there are peacocks, bulls and various other beings all fully equipped and arranged in due order. Similarly, the above mentioned animals are yoked to Kotis and Kotis of chariots; there are coachmen, and at some places flags are fluttering high on the chariots so as to reach the Heavens, thus adding beauty. At other places the aerial cars are arranged in countless rows, with various-sounding instruments in them, with flags soaring high in the Heavens, and endowed with various ensigns and emblems.

Fourteenth Enclosure, built of Indranīlamaṇi (blue sapphire)

In the physiology, the fourteenth enclosure is cortex layer 6.

वैदूर्यमणिशालस्याप्यग्रे शालः परः स्मृतः
दशयोजनतुङ्गोऽसाविन्द्रनीलाश्मनिर्मितः ६४
तन्मध्यभूस्तथा वीथ्यो महामार्गा गृहाणि च
वापीकूपतडागाश्च सर्वे तन्मणिनिर्मिताः ६५
तत्र पद्मं तु संप्रोक्तं बहुयोजनविस्तृतम्
षोडशारं दीप्यमानं सुदर्शनमिवापरम् ६६
तत्र षोडशशक्तीणां स्थानानि विविधानि च
सर्वोपस्करयुक्तानि समृद्धानि वसन्ति हि ६७
तासां नामानि वक्ष्यामि शृणु मे नृपसत्तम
कराली विकराली च तथोमा च सरस्वती ६८
श्रीदुर्गोषा तथा लक्ष्मीः श्रुतिश्चैव स्मृतिर्धृतिः
श्रद्धा मेधा मतिः कान्तिरार्या षोडश शक्तयः ६९
नीलजीमूतसंकाशाः करवालकराम्बुजाः

समाः खेटकधारिरायो युद्धोपक्रान्तमानसाः ७०
सेनान्यः सकला एताः श्रीदेव्या जगदीशितुः
प्रतिब्रह्माराडसंस्थानां शक्तीनां नायिकाः स्मृताः ७१
ब्रह्माराडक्षोभकारिरायो देवीशक्त्युपबृंहिताः
नानारथसमारूढा नानाशक्तिभिरन्विताः ७२
एतत्पराक्रमं वक्तुं सहस्रास्योऽपि न क्षमः

Fourteenth Enclosure in Devī Bhāgavata Purāṇa:

O King! Next to this Vaidūrya enclosure wall, comes the fourteenth enclosure wall, built of Indranīlamaṇi (blue sapphire); its height is ten Yojanas. The court inside, houses, roads, wells, tanks and reservoirs, etc., all are built of Indranīlamaṇi. There is here a lotus consisting of sixteen petals, extending to many Yojanas in width, and shining like a second Sudarśana Chakra. On these sixteen petals reside the sixteen Śaktis of Bhagavatī, with their hosts. Now I am mentioning the names of these. Hear: Karālī, Vikarālī, Umā, Sarasvatī, Śrī, Durgā, Ûṣā, Lakṣmī, Śruti, Smṛti, Dhṛti, Śraddhā, Medhā, Mati, Kānti, and Āryā. These are the 16 Śaktis. They are a dark blue, like the color of the fresh rain-cloud; they wield in their hands axes and shields. They are ever eager to fight. O King! These Śaktis are the rulers of all the separate Śaktis of the other Brahmāṇḍas. These are the forces of Śrī Devī.

Being strengthened by the Devī's strength, they are always surrounded by various chariots and forces, and various other Śaktis follow them. If they like, they can cause great agitation in the whole universe. Had I a thousand faces, I would not have been able to describe what strength they wield.

Fifteenth Enclosure, made of pearls

In the physiology, the fifteenth enclosure is the white matter of the brain. The white matter consists of the interconnecting fibers which relay information throughout the nervous system. These interconnecting fibers are the axons of the cortical cells in the six layers of the cortex.

इन्द्रनीलमहाशालादग्रे तु बहुविस्तृतः ७३
मुक्ताप्राकार उदितो दशयोजनदैर्घ्यवान्
मध्यभूः पूर्ववत्प्रोक्ता तन्मध्येऽष्टदलाम्बुजम् ७४
मुक्तामणिगणाकीर्णं विस्तृतं तु सकेशरम्
तत्र देवीसमाकारा दिव्यायुधधराः सदा ७५
संप्रोक्ता अष्ट मन्त्रिण्यो जगद्वार्ताप्रबोधिकाः
देवीसमानभोगास्ता इङ्गितज्ञास्तु पण्डिताः ७६
कुशलाः सर्वकार्येषु स्वामिकार्यपरायणाः
देव्यभिप्रायबोध्यस्ताश्चतुरा अतिसुन्दराः ७७
नानाशक्तिसमायुक्ताः प्रतिब्रह्माण्डवर्तिनाम्
प्राणिनां ताः समाचारं ज्ञानशक्त्या विदन्ति च ७८
तासां नामानि वक्ष्यामि मत्त शृणु नृपोत्तम
अनङ्गकुसुमा प्रोक्ताऽप्यनङ्गकुसुमातुरा ७९
अनङ्गमदना तद्वदनङ्गमदनातुरा
भुवनपाला गगनवेगा चैव ततः परम् ८०
शशिरेखा च गगनरेखा चैव ततः परम्
पाशाङ्कुशवराभीतिधरा अरुणविग्रहाः ८१

विश्वसंबन्धिनी वार्तां बोधयन्ति प्रतिक्षणम्

Fifteenth Enclosure in Devī Bhāgavata Purāṇa:

Now I describe the fifteenth enclosure wall. Listen. Next to this Indranīlamaṇi enclosure, comes the enclosure made of pearls (Muktā), very wide and ten Yojanas high. The court inside, its space and its trees, all are built of pearls. Within this enclosure there is a lotus with eight petals, all of pearls. On these petals reside the eight Śaktis, the advisers and ministers of the Devī. Their appearances, weapons, dresses, enjoyments, and all are like those of Śrī Devī. Their duty is to inform the Devī of what is going on in the Brahmāṇḍas (other regions or universes). They are skilled in all sciences and arts and clever in all actions. They are very skillful in knowing beforehand all the desires and intentions of Śrī Devī, and they perform those things accordingly. Each one of them has many other Śaktis who also live here. By their Gyān Śakti they know all the news concerning the Jīvas in every Brahmāṇḍa. Now I mention the names of those eight Sakhīs. Listen. Anaṅgakusumā, Anaṅgakusumāturā, Anaṅgamadanā, Anaṅgamadanāturā, Bhuvanapālā, Gaganavegā, Śaśirekhā, and Gaganarekhā. These are the eight Sakhīs. They all look red like the rising Sun, and in their four hands they hold a noose, a mace, the signs of granting boons, and signs of "no fear." At every instant they inform Śrī Devī of the events of the universe.

Sixteenth Enclosure, made of emerald

In the physiology, the sixteenth enclosure is the inner brain grey matter of the deep seated basal ganglia located around the hollow ventricles at the center of the brain. This area of the brain contains administrative structures which control the activities of the whole physiology. This is the core intelligence of Natural Law in the nervous system.

मुक्ताशालादग्रभागे महामारकतोऽपरः ८२
शालोत्तमः समुद्दिष्टो दशयोजनदैर्घ्यवान्
नानासौभाग्यसंयुक्तो नानाभोगसमन्वितः ८३
मध्यभूस्तादृशी प्रोक्ता सदनानि तथैव च
षट्कोणमञ्चविस्तीर्णकोणस्था देवताः शृणु ८४
पूर्वकोणे चतुर्वक्त्रो गायत्रीसहितो वीथिः
कुण्डिकाक्षगुणाभीतिदण्डायुधधरः परः ८५
तदायुधधरा देवी गायत्री परदेवता
वेदाः सर्वे मूर्तिमन्तः शास्त्राणि विविधानि च ८६
स्मृतयश्च पुराणानि मूर्तिमन्ति वसन्ति हि
ये ब्रह्मविग्रहाः सन्ति गायत्रीविग्रहाश्च ये ८७
व्याहृतीनां विग्रहाश्च ते नित्यं तत्र सन्ति हि
रक्षाकोणे शङ्खचक्रगदाम्बुजकराम्बुजा ८८
सावित्री वर्तते तत्र महाविष्णुश्च तादृशः
ये विष्णुविग्रहाः सन्ति मत्स्यकूर्मादयोऽखिलाः ८९
सावित्रीविग्रहा ये च ते सर्वे तत्र सन्ति हि
वायुकोणे परश्वक्षमालाभयवरान्वितः ९०
महारुद्रो वर्ततेऽत्र सरस्वत्यपि तादृशी
ये ये तु रुद्रभेदाः स्युर्दक्षिणास्यादयो नृप ९१

गौरीभेदाश्च ये सर्वे ते तत्र निवसन्ति हि
चतुःषष्ट्यागमा ये च ये चान्येप्यागमाः स्मृताः ९२
ते सर्वे मूर्तिमन्तश्च तत्र वै निवसन्ति हि
अग्निकोणे रत्नकुम्भं तथा मणिकरण्डकम् ९३
दधानो निजहस्ताभ्यां कुबेरो धनदायकः
नानावीथीसमायुक्तो महालक्ष्मीसमन्वितः ९४
देव्या निधिपतिस्त्वास्ते स्वगुणैः परिवेष्टितः
वारुणे तु महाकोणे मदनो रतिसंयुतः ९५
पाशाङ्कुशधनुर्बाणधरो नित्यं विराजते
शृङ्गारा मूर्तिमन्तस्तु तत्र सन्निहिताः सदा ९६
ईशानकोणे विघ्नेशो नित्यं पुष्टिसमन्वितः
पाशाङ्कुशधरो वीरो विघ्नहर्ता विराजते ९७
विभूतयो गणेशस्य या याः सन्ति नृपोत्तम
ताः सर्वा निवसंत्यत्र महैश्वर्यसमन्विताः ९८
प्रतिब्रह्माण्डसंस्थानां ब्रह्मादीनां समष्टयः
एते ब्रह्मादयः प्रोक्ताः सेवन्ते जगदीश्वरीम् ९९

Sixteenth Enclosure in Devī Bhāgavata Purāṇa:

Next to this comes the sixteenth enclosure wall made of emerald (Marakata); it is ten Yojanas high; the court inside, its space, houses, and everything are built of emeralds (Marakatamaṇi). Here exist all the good objects of enjoyments. This is hexagonal, of the Yantra shape, and Devas reside at every corner. On the eastern corner resides the four-faced Brahmā with Gāyatrī Devī: both hold Kamaṇḍalu, rosary, signs indicating "no fear" and Daṇḍa (rod). Here are all the Vedas, Smṛtis, and Purāṇas, and various weapons in their incarnate forms.

All the Avatāras of Brahmā, Gāyatrī, and the Vyāhritis in this Brahmāṇḍa live here. On the south-west corner Mahā Vishnu lives with Sāvitrī; both hold conch shell, disc, club, and lotus. All the Avatāras of Vishnu and all the Avatāras of Sāvitrī that exist in every universe, all dwell in this place. On the north western corner is Mahā Rudra with Sarasvatī. Both of them hold in their hands Paraśu, rosary, signs granting boons and "no fear."

All the Avatārs of Rudra and Pārvatī (Gaurī, etc.) facing south that exist in the universe are found here. All the chief Āgamas, sixty-four in number and all the other Tantras reside here, incarnate in their due forms.

On the south-eastern corner is the Lord of Wealth, Kubera, surrounded by roads and shops, with Mahālakṣmī, holding a jar of jewels (Maṇikaraṇḍika). On the western corner is Madana with Rati, holding noose, goad, bow and arrow. All his amorous attendants always reside here, incarnate in their forms. On the north-eastern corner resides the great hero Ganeśa, the Remover of obstacles, holding noose and goad and with his Puṣṭi Devī. O King! All the Vibhūtis (manifestations) of Ganeśa that exist in all the universes reside here. What more to say than this, that Brahmā and the other Devas and Devīs here represent the sum-total of all the Brahmās and the Devas and the Devīs that exist in all the Brahmāṇḍas. These all worship Śrī Bhagavatī, remaining in their own spheres respectively. O King!

Seventeenth Enclosure, made of saffron-red coral

In the physiology, the seventeenth enclosure is the cell wall. The first sixteen enclosures have traversed the head, from the outermost layer of skin to the deepest nuclei at the center of the brain. Further enclosures take us deeper into the structure of every cell of the body, starting with the cell wall.

महामारकतस्याग्रे शतयोजनदैर्घ्यवान्
प्रबालशालोऽस्त्यपरः कुङ्कमारुणविग्रहः १००
मध्यभूस्तादृशी प्रोक्ता सदनानि च पूर्ववत्
तन्मध्ये पञ्चभूतानां स्वामिन्यः पञ्च सन्ति च १०१
हृल्लेखा गगना रक्ता चतुर्थी तु करालिका
महोच्छुष्मा पञ्चमी च पञ्चभूतसमप्रभा १०२
पाशाङ्कुशवराभीतिधारिण्योऽमितभूषणाः
देवीसमानवेषाढ्या नवयौवनगर्विताः १०३

Seventeenth Enclosure in Devī Bhāgavata Purāṇa:

Next comes the seventeenth enclosure wall made of Prabala (red coral). It is red like saffron and it is one hundred Yojanas high. As before, the court inside, the ground and the houses are all made of coral. The goddesses of the five elements, Hrillekhā, Gaganā, Raktā, Karālikā, and Mahochchhuṣmā reside here. The colors and lusters of the bodies of the goddesses resemble those of the elements over which they preside respectively. All of them are proud of their youth and hold in their four hands noose, goad and signs of granting boons and "no fear." They are dressed like Śrī Devī and reside here always.

Eighteenth Enclosure, built of Navaratna (the 9 jewels)

The eighteenth enclosure is the wall of the nucleus within the cell.

प्रबालशालादग्रे तु नवरत्नविनिर्मितः
बहुयोजनविस्तीर्णो महाशालोऽस्ति भूमिप १०४
तत्र चाम्नायदेवीनां सदनानि बहून्यपि
नवरत्नमयान्येव तडागाश्च सरांसि च १०५
श्रीदेव्या येऽवताराः स्युस्ते तत्र निवसन्ति हि
महाविद्या महाभेदाः सन्ति तत्रैव भूमिप १०६
निजावरणदेवीभिर्निजभूषणवाहनैः
सर्वदेव्यो विराजन्ते कोटिसूर्यसमप्रभाः १०७
सप्तकोटिमहामन्त्रदेवताः सन्ति तत्र हि

Eighteenth Enclosure in Devī Bhāgavata Purāṇa:

Next to this comes the eighteenth enclosure wall built of Navaratna (the nine jewels). It is many yojanas wide. This enclosure wall is superior to all others and it is higher also. On the four sides there exist innumerable houses, tanks, and reservoirs, all built of Navaratna; these belong to the Devīs, the presiding Deities of Āmnāyas (that which is to be studied or learnt by heart, the Vedas). The ten Mahāvidyās of Śrī Devī, Kālī, Tārā, etc., and all their Avatārs, dwell here with their respective Āvaraṇas (shields), Vāhanas (chariots) and ornaments. All the Avatārs of Śrī Devī, who kill the Daityas and show favor to the devotees, live here. They are Paśamkuśeśvarī, Bhuvaneśvarī, Bhairavī, Kapāla Bhuvaneśvarī,

Aṅkuśa Bhuvaneśvarī, Pramāda Bhuvaneśvarī, Śrī Krodha Bhuvaneśvarī, Triputāśvārūdhā, Nityaklinnā, Annapurṇā, Tvaritā, and the other Avatārs of Bhuvaneśvarī, and Kālī, Tārā and the other Mahāvidyās are known as Mahāvidyās. They live here with their Āvaraṇa (attendant) Devatās, Vāhanas, and ornaments respectively. Here live also the seven Kotis of Devīs presiding over the Mahāmantras, all brilliant and fair like one Koti of Suns.

Nineteenth Enclosure, built of Chintāmani gems

The nineteenth enclosure is the DNA within the cell nucleus. This final enclosure contains the intelligence which structures the individual physiology. It is made up of packages of knowledge in the form of sequences of nucleotides. It is the center of all the enclosures, the location of the creative force of Natural Law, the home of Mother Divine.

नवरत्नमयादग्रे चिन्तामणिगृहं महत् १०८
तत्रत्यं वस्तुमात्रं तु चिन्तामणिविनिर्मितम्
सूर्योद्गारोपलैस्तद्वच्चन्द्रोद्गारोपलैस्तथा १०९
विद्युत्प्रभोपलैः स्तम्भाः कल्पितास्तु सहस्रशः
येषां प्रभाभिरन्तःस्थं वस्तु किञ्चिन्न दृश्यते ११०

इति श्रीदेवीभागवतं महापुराणे द्वादशस्कन्धे
एकादशोऽध्यायः ११

अथ द्वादशोऽध्यायः

व्यास उवाच

तदेव देवीसदनं मध्यभागे विराजते

सहस्रस्तम्भसंयुक्ताश्चत्वारस्तेषु मराडपाः १
शृङ्गारमराडपश्चैको मुक्तिमराडप एव च
ज्ञानमराडपसंज्ञस्तु तृतीयः परिकीर्तितः २
एकान्तमराडपश्चैव चतुर्थः परिकीर्तितः
नानावितानसंयुक्ता नानाधूपैस्तु धूपिताः ३
कोटिसूर्यसमाः कान्त्या भ्राजन्ते मराडपाः शुभाः
तन्मराडपानां परितः काश्मीरवनिका स्मृता ४
मल्लिकाकुन्दवनिका यत्र पुष्कलकाः स्थिताः
असंख्याता मृगमदैः पूरितास्तत्स्रवा नृप ५
महापद्माटपी तद्वद्रत्नसोपाननिर्मिता
सुधारसेन सम्पूर्णा गुञ्जन्मत्तमधुव्रता ६
हंसकाररडवाकीर्णा गन्धपूरितदिक्तटा
वनिकानां सुगन्धैस्तु मणिद्वीपं सुवासितम् ७
शृङ्गारमराडपे देव्यो गायन्ति विविधैः स्वरैः
सभासदो देववरा मध्ये श्रीजगदम्बिका ८
मुक्तिमराडपमध्ये तु मोचयत्यनिशं शिवा
ज्ञानोपदेशं कुरुते तृतीये नृप मराडपे ९
चतुर्थमराडपे चैव जगद्रक्षाविचिन्तनम्
मन्त्रिणीसहिता नित्यं करोति जगदम्बिका १०
चिन्तामणिगृहे राजञ्छक्तितत्त्वात्मकैः परैः
सोपानैर्दशभिर्युक्तो मञ्चकोऽप्यधिराजते ११
ब्रह्मा विष्णुश्च रुद्रश्च ईश्वरश्च सदाशिवः
एते पञ्च खुराः प्रोक्ताः फलकस्तु सदाशिवः १२
तस्योपरि महादेवी भुवनेशी विराजते
या देवी निजलीलार्थं द्विधाभूता बभूव ह १३

सृष्ट्यादौ तु स एवायं तदर्धाङ्गो महेश्वरः
कन्दर्पदर्पनाशोद्यत्कोटिकन्दर्पसुन्दरः १४
पञ्चवक्त्रस्त्रिनेत्रश्च मणिभूषणभूषितः
हरिणाभीतिपरशून्वरं च निजबाहुभिः १५
दधानः षोडशाब्दोऽसौ देवः सर्वेश्वरो महान्
कोटिसूर्यपतीकाशश्चन्द्रकोटिसुशीतलः १६
शुद्धस्फटिकसंकाशस्त्रिनेत्रः शीतलद्युतिः
वामाङ्के सन्निषण्णाऽस्य देवी श्रीभुवनेश्वरी १७
नवरत्नगणाकीर्णकाञ्चीदामविराजिता
तप्तकाञ्चनसन्नद्धवैदूर्याङ्गदभूषणा १८
कनच्छ्रीचक्रताटङ्कविटकवदनाम्बुजा
ललाटकान्तिविभवविजितार्धसुधाकरा १९
बिम्बकान्तितिरस्कारिरदच्छदविराजिता
लसत्कुङ्कुमकस्तूरीतिलकोद्भासिताननना २०
दिव्यचूडामणिस्फारचञ्चच्चन्द्रकसूर्यका
उद्यत्कविसमस्वच्छनासाभरणभासुरा २१
चिन्ताकलम्बितस्वच्छमुक्तागुच्छविराजिता
पाटीरपंककर्पूरकुङ्कुमालङ्कृतस्तनी २२
विचित्रविविधाकल्पा कम्बुसंकाशकन्धरा
दाडिमीफलबीजाभदन्तपङ्क्तिविराजिता २३
अनर्घ्यरत्नघटितमुकुटाञ्चितमस्तका
मत्तालिमालाविलसदलकाढ्यमुखाम्बुजा २४
कलङ्ककार्श्यनिर्मुक्तशरच्चन्द्रनिभानना
जाह्नवीसलिलावर्तशोभिनाभिविभूषिता २५
माणिक्यशकलाबद्धमुद्रिकाङ्गुलिभूषिता

पुण्डरीकदलाकारनयनत्रयसुन्दरी २६
कल्पिताच्छमहारागपद्मरागोज्ज्वलप्रभा
रत्नकिङ्किणिकायुक्तरत्नकङ्कणशोभिता २७
मणिमुक्तासरापारलसत्पदकसन्ततिः
रत्नाङ्गुलिप्रविततप्रभाजाललसत्करा २८
कञ्चुकीगुम्फितापारनानारत्नततिद्युतिः
मल्लिकामोदिधम्मिल्लमल्लिकालिसरावृता २९
सुवृत्तनिविडोत्तुङ्गकुचभारालसा शिवा
वरपाशाङ्कुशाभीतिलसद्बाहुचतुष्टया ३०
सर्वशृङ्गारवेषाढ्या सुकुमाराङ्गवल्लरी
सौन्दर्यधारासर्वस्वा निर्व्याजकरुणामयी ३१
निजसंलापमाधुर्यविनिर्भर्त्सितकच्छपी
कोटिकोटिरवींदूनां कान्तिं या बिभ्रती परा ३२
नानासखीभिर्दासीभिस्तथा देवाङ्गनादिभिः
सर्वाभिर्देवताभिस्तु समन्तात्परिवेष्टिता ३३
इच्छाशक्त्या ज्ञानशक्त्या क्रियाशक्त्या समन्विता
लज्जा तुष्टिस्तथा पुष्टिः कीर्तिः कान्ति क्षमा दया ३४
बुद्धिर्मेधा स्मृतिर्लक्ष्मीमूर्तिमत्योऽङ्गनाः स्मृताः
जया च विजया चैवाप्यजिता चापराजिता ३५
नित्या विलासिनी दोग्ध्री त्वघोरा मङ्गला नवा
पीठशक्तय एतास्तु सेवन्ते यां पराम्बिकाम् ३६
यस्यास्तु पार्श्वभागे स्तो निधी तौ शङ्खपद्मकौ
नवरत्नवहा नद्यस्तथा वै काञ्चनस्रवाः ३७
सप्तधातुवहा नद्यो निधिभ्यां तु विनिर्गताः
सुधासिन्ध्वन्तगामिन्यस्ताः सर्वा नृपसत्तम ३८

सा देवी भुवनेशानी तद्वामाङ्के विराजते
सर्वेशत्वं महेशस्य यत्संगादेव नान्यथा ३९
चिन्तामणिगृहस्यास्य प्रमाणं शृणु भूमिप
सहस्रयोजनायामं महान्तस्तत्प्रचक्षते ४०
तदुत्तरे महाशालाः पूर्वस्माद्द्विगुणाः स्मृताः
अन्तरिक्षगतं त्वेतन्निराधारं विराजते ४१
संकोचश्च विकासश्च जायतेऽस्य निरन्तरम्
पटवत्कार्यवशतः प्रलये सर्जने तथा ४२
शालानां चैव सर्वेषां सर्वकान्तिपरावधि
चिन्तामणिगृहं प्रोक्तं यत्र देवी महोमयी ४३
ये ये उपासकाः सन्ति प्रतिब्रह्माण्डवर्तिनः
देवेषु नागलोकेषु मनुष्येष्वितरेषु च ४४
श्रीदेव्यास्ते च सर्वेऽपि व्रजंत्यत्रैव भूमिप
देवीक्षेत्रे ये त्यजन्ति प्राणान्देव्यर्चने रताः ४५
ते सर्वे यान्ति तत्रैव यत्र देवी महोत्सवा
घृतकुल्या दुग्धकुल्या दधिकुल्या मधुस्रवाः ४६
स्यन्दन्ति सरितः सर्वास्तथामृतवहाः पराः
द्राक्षारसवहाः काश्चिज्जम्बूरसवहाः पराः ४७
आम्रेक्षुरसवाहिन्यो नद्यस्तास्तु सहस्रशः
मनोरथफला वृक्षा वाप्यः कूपास्तथैव च ४८
यथेष्टपानफलदा न न्यूनं किंचिदस्ति हि
न रोगपलितं वापि जरा वापि कदाचन ४९
न चिन्ता न च मात्सर्यं कामक्रोधादिकं तथा
सर्वे युवानः सस्त्रीकाः सहस्रादित्यवर्चसः ५०
भजन्ति सततं देवीं तत्र श्रीभुवनेश्वरीम्

केचित्सलोकतापन्नाः केचित्सामीप्यतां गताः ५१
सरूपतां गताः केचित्साष्टिं तां च परे गताः
या यास्तु देवतास्तत्र प्रतिब्रह्माण्डवर्तिनाम् ५२
समष्टयः स्थितास्तास्तु देवन्ते जगदीश्वरीम्
सप्तकोटिमहामन्त्रा मूर्तिमन्त उपासते ५३
महाविद्याश्च सकलाः साम्यावस्थात्मिकां शिवाम्
कारणब्रह्मरूपां तां मायाशबलविग्रहाम् ५४
इत्थं राजन्मया प्रोक्तं मणिद्वीपं महत्तरम्
न सूर्यचन्द्रौ नो विद्युत्कोटयोऽग्निस्तथैव च ५५
एतस्य भासा कोट्यंशकोट्यंशेनापि ते समाः
क्वचिद्विद्रुमसंकाशं क्वचिन्मरकतच्छवि ५६
विद्युद्भानुसमच्छायं मध्यसूर्यसमं क्वचित्
विद्युत्कोटिमहाधारा सारकान्तिततं क्वचित् ५७
क्वचित्सिन्दूरनीलेन्द्रमाणिक्यसदृशच्छवि
हीरसारमहागर्भधगद्धगितदिक्तटम् ५८
कान्त्या दावानलसमं तप्तकाञ्चनसन्निभम्
क्वचिच्चन्द्रोपलोद्गारं सूर्योद्गारं च कुत्रचित् ५९
रत्नशृङ्गिसमायुक्तं रत्नप्राकारगोपुरम्
रत्नपत्रै रत्नफलैर्वृक्षैश्च परिमण्डितम् ६०
नृत्यन्मयूरसङ्घैश्च कपोतरणितोज्ज्वलम्
कोकिलाकाकलीलापैः शुकलापैश्च शोभितम् ६१
सुरम्यरमणीयाम्बुलक्षावधिसरोवृतम्
तन्मध्यभागविलसद्विकचद्रत्नपङ्कजैः ६२
सुगन्धिभिः समन्तात्तु वासितं शतयोजनम्
मन्दमारुतसम्भिन्नचलद्द्रुमसमाकुलम् ६३

चिन्तामणिसमूहानां ज्योतिषा वितताम्बरम्
रत्नप्रभाभिरभितो धगद्धगितदिक्तटम् ६४
वृक्षव्रातमहागन्धवातव्रातसुपूरितम्
धूपधूपायितं राजन्मणिदीपायुतोज्ज्वलम् ६५
मणिजालकसच्छिद्रतरलोदरकान्तिभिः
दिङ्मोहजनकं चैतद्दर्पणोदरसंयुतम् ६६
ऐश्वर्यस्य समग्रस्य शृङ्गारस्याखिलस्य च
सर्वज्ञतायाः सर्वायास्तेजसश्चाखिलस्य च ६७
पराक्रमस्य सर्वस्य सर्वोत्तमगुणस्य च
सकलाया दयायाश्च समाप्तिरिह भूपते ६८
राज्ञ आनन्दमारभ्य ब्रह्मलोकान्तभूमिषु
आनन्दा ये स्थिताः सर्वे तेऽत्रैवान्तर्भवन्ति हि ६९
इति ते वर्णितं राजन्मणिद्वीपं महत्तरम्
महादेव्याः परं स्थानं सर्वलोकोत्तमोत्तमम् ७०
एतस्य स्मरणात्सद्यः सर्वपापं विनश्यति
प्राणोत्क्रमणसन्धौ तु स्मृत्वा तत्रैव गच्छति ७१
अध्यायपञ्चकं त्वेतत्पठेन्नित्यं समाहितः
भूतप्रेतपिशाचादिबाधा तत्र भवेन्न हि ७२
नवीनगृहनिर्माणे वास्तुयोगे तथैव च
पठितव्यं प्रयत्नेन कल्याणं तेन जायते ७३
इति श्रीदेवीभागवते महापुराणे द्वादशस्कन्धे
द्वादशोऽध्यायः १२

Nineteenth Enclosure in Devī Bhāgavata Purāṇa:

O King! Next to this enclosure wall comes the chief and crowning palace of Śrī Devī, built of Chintāmani gems. All the articles within this enclosure are built of

Chintāmani gems. Within this palace are seen hundreds and thousands of pillars built of Sūryakāntamaṇi, Chandrakāntamaṇi, and Vidyutkāntamaṇi. O King! The luster and brilliance of these pillars is so strong that no articles within this palace are visible to the eye.

Here ends the Eleventh Chapter on the description of the enclosure walls built of Padmarāgamaṇi, etc., of the Maṇi Dvīpa in the Mahāpurāṇam Śrīmad Devī Bhāgavatam of 18,000 verses by Maharṣi Veda Vyāsa.

Chapter XII On the description of Maṇidvīpa

Vyāsa said: O King Janamejaya! The Ratnagṛha, above mentioned, is the Central, the Chief and the Crowning Place of Mūla Prakṛti. [The nine jewels are: (1) Muktā, (2) Mānikya, (3) Vaidūrya, (4) Gomeda, (5) Vajra, (6) Vidruma, (7) Padmarāga, (8) Marakata, and (9) Nīla.] This is in the center of all the enclosures. Within this there are the four Maṇḍaps, halls built of one thousand (*i.e.*, innumerable) pillars. These are the Śringāra Maṇḍap, Mukti Maṇḍap, Gyān Maṇḍap and Ekānta Maṇḍap. On top of these are canopies of various colors; within are many scented articles scented by the Dhūpas. The brilliance of these is like that of one Koti Suns. On all sides of these four Maṇḍaps there are nice groups of gardens of Kaśmīra, Mallikā, and Kunda flowers. Various scents, and scented articles, for example, of musk, etc., are fully arranged in due order. There is a very big lotus pond here; the steps leading to it are built of jewels. Its water is nectar, and on it are innumerable fully bloomed lotuses with bees always humming over them. Many birds, swans, Kāraṇḍavas, etc., are swimming to and fro. The sweet scents of lotuses are playing all round.

In fact, the whole Maṇidvīpa is perfumed with various scented things. Within the Śringāra Maṇḍap, the Devī Bhagavatī is situated in the center on an Āsana (seat) and She hears the songs sung in tune by the other Devīs along with the other Devas. Similarly, sitting on the Mukti Maṇḍap, She frees the Jīvas from the bondages of the world. Sitting on the Gyān Maṇḍap, She gives instructions on Gyān, and sitting on the fourth, the Ekānta Maṇḍap, She consults with Her ministers, the Sakhīs, Anaṅga Kusuma, etc., on the creation, preservation, and destruction of the universe.

O King! Now I shall describe about the main Khās room of Śrī Devī. Listen. The Khās Mahāl palace of the Devī Bhagavatī is named Śrī Chintāmaṇi Gṛha. Within this is placed a raised platform, the dais and sofa whereon the Devī taketh Her honorable seat. The ten Śakti-tattvas form the staircases. The four legs are (1) Brahmā, (2) Viṣṇu, (3) Rudra, and (4) Maheśvara. Sadāśiva forms the upper covering plank. Over this Śrī Bhuvaneśvara Mahā Deva or the Supreme Architect of the Universe is reigning.

Now hear something about this Bhuvaneśvara. Before creation while intending to sport, the Devī Bhagavatī divided Her Body into two parts and from the right part created Bhuvaneśvara. He has five faces and each face has three eyes. He has four hands and He is holding in each hand spear, signs indicating do not fear, axe, and signs granting boons. He looks sixteen years old. The luster of His Body is more beautiful than Koti Kandarpas and more fiery than a thousand Suns; and at the same time cool like Koti Suns. His color is crystal white, and on His left lap Śrī Bhuvaneśvarī Devī is always sitting. On the hip of Śrī Bhuvaneśvarī, is shining the girdle with small tinkling bells, built of various jewels; the ornaments on the arms are made of burnished gold studded with Vaidūryamaṇis; the Tātanka ornaments on Her ears are very beautiful like Śrīchakra and they enhance very much the beauty of Her lotus face. The beauty of Her forehead vies with, or defies the Moon of the eighth bright lunar day. Her lips challenge the fully ripened Bimba fruits. Her face is shining with the Tilaka mark made of musk and saffron. The divine crown on Her head is beautified with the Sun and Moon made of jewels; the nose ornaments are like the star Venus and built of transparent gems, looking exceedingly beautiful and shedding charming luster all around. The neck is decorated with necklaces built of gems and jewels. Her breasts are nicely decorated with camphor and saffron. Her neck is shining like a conchshell decorated with artistic designs. Her teeth look like fully ripe pomegranate fruits. On Her head is shining the jewel crown. Her lotus face is beautified with Alakā as if these are mad bees. Her navel is beautiful like the whirls in the river Bhāgirathī; Her fingers are decorated with jewel rings; She has three eyes like lotus leaves; the luster of Her body is bright like Padmarāgamaṇi cut and carved and sharpened on stone. The bracelets are adorned with jewel tinkling bells; Her neck ornaments and medals are studded with gems and jewels. Her hands are resplendent with the luster of the jewels on the fingers; the braid of hair on Her head is wreathed with a garland of Mallikā flowers; Her bodice (short jacket) is studded with various jewels. O King! Śrī Devī is slightly bent down with the weight of Her very high hard breasts. She has four hands and She is holding noose, goad and signs granting boons and "do not fear." The all beautiful all merciful Devī is full of love gestures and beauties. Her voice is sweeter than that of lute; the luster of Her body is like Kotis and Kotis of Suns and Moons rising simultaneously on the sky. The Sakhīs, attendants, the Devas and the Devīs surround Her on all sides. Ichchā Śakti, Gyān Śakti, and Kriyā Śakti all are always present before the Devī. Lajjā, Tuṣṭi, Puṣṭi, Kīrti, Kānti, Kṣamā, Dayā, Buddhi, Medhā, Smṛti, and Laksmī are always seen here incarnate in their due Forms. The nine Pītha Śaktis, Jayā, Vijayā, Ajitā, Aparājitā, Nityā, Vilāsinī, Dogdhrī, Aghorā, and Mangalā reside here always and are in the service of the Devī Bhuvaneśvarī. On the side of the Devī are the two oceans of treasures; from these streams of Navaratna, gold, and seven Dhātus (elements) go out and assume the forms of rivers and fall into the ocean Sudhā Sindhu. Because such a Devī Bhuvaneśvarī, resplendent with all powers and prosperities, sits on the left lap of Bhuvaneśvara, thus He has, no doubt acquired His omnipotence.

O King! Now I will describe the dimensions of the Chintāmaṇi Gṛha. Listen. It is one thousand Yojanas wide; its center is very big; the rooms situated further and further are twice those preceding them. It lies in Antarīksa (the intervening space) without any support. At the times of dissolution and creation it contracts and expands like a cloth. The luster of this Chintāmani Griha is comparatively far more bright and beautiful than that of other enclosure walls. Śrī Devī Bhagavatī dwells always in this place. O King! All the great Bhaktas of the Devī in every Brahmāṇḍa, in the Devaloka, in Nāgaloka, in the world of men or in any other loka, all those who were engaged in meditation on the Devī in the sacred places of the Devī and died there, all come here and reside with the Devī in great joy and festivity.

On all sides rivers are flowing; some of ghee, some of milk, curd, honey, nectar, pomegranate juice, jambu juice; and some of mango juice and sugarcane juice are flowing on all sides. The trees here yield fruits according to one's desires, and the wells and tanks yield water also as people desire. Never is there any want felt here for anything. Never are seen here diseases, sorrow, old age, decrepitude, anxiety, anger, jealousy, envy or other lower emotions. All the inhabitants of this place are full of youth and look like one thousand Suns. All enjoy with their wives and they worship Śrī Bhuvaneśvarī. Some have attained Sālokya, some Sāmīpya, some Sārūpya and some have attained Sārsti and pass their days in highest comfort. The Devas that are in every Brahmāṇḍa all live here and worship Śrī Devī. The seven Koti Mahāmantras and Mahāvidyās here assume forms and worship the Mahā Māyā Śrī Bhagavatī, who is of the nature of Brahmā.

O King! Thus I have described to you all about this Maṇidvīpa. The luster of Sun, Moon and Kotis and Kotis of lightnings cannot be one Kotieth of one Koti part of Its luster. At some places the luster is like Vidrumamaṇi;

some places are illumined like the luster of Marakata Maṇi; some, like Sūrya Kāntamaṇi and some places are rendered brilliant like Kotis and Kotis of lightnings. The light at some places is like Sindūra; at some places like Indranīlamaṇi; at some places, like Mānikya, and at some places like diamond. Some places are blazing like the conflagration of fire; and some places look like molten gold; some places seem filled with the luster of Chandrakāntamaṇi, and some places look brilliant like Sūryakāntamaṇi. The mountains here are all built of gems and jewels; the entrance gates and enclosures are built of gems and jewels; the trees and their leaves are all of gems; in fact all that exists here is made of gems and jewels. At some places numbers of peacocks are dancing; at some places cuckoos are captivating the minds of persons by cooing in the fifth tune and at others doves and pigeons and parrots are making sweet cackling sounds. Lakhs and lakhs of tanks are there with their pure crystal-like waters. The red lotuses have blossomed fully and enhanced the beauty of the place. The captivating scents of these lotuses extend to a distance of one hundred Yojanas all around and gladden the minds of people. The leaves are rustling with gentle breeze. The whole sky overhead is radiant with the luster of Chintāmaṇi gems and jewels. All the sides are illuminated with the brilliancy of the gems and jewels. O King! These jewels act like lamps. And the sweet scented trees emit their fragrance and it is transmitted by breezes all around. Thus these trees serve the purpose of dhūp (scent). The rays of these gems pierce through the openings of the jewel screens on the houses and fall on the mirrors inside, thus causing a nice brilliant appearance that captivates the mind and causes confusion. O King! What shall I say of this place, more than this, that all the powers, and wealth, all the love sentiments, all the dress suited to amorous interviews, all the splendors, fire, energy, beauty and brilliance, the omniscience, the indomitable strength, all the excellent qualities and all mercy and kindness are present here! The All Comprehending Bliss and the Brahmānanda can always be witnessed here! O King! Thus I have described to you about the Maṇidvīpa, the most exalted place of the Devī Bhagavatī. At Her remembrance all the sins are instantly destroyed. The more so, if a man remembers the Devī and this place at the time of death. He surely goes there. O King! He who daily reads the five Chapters, *i.e.*, from the eighth to this twelfth chapter, is surely untouched by any obstacles due to the Bhūtas, Pretas and Piśāchas. Especially the recitation of this at the time of building a new house and at the time of Vāstuyāga ensures all good and auspiciousness.

Here ends the Twelfth Chapter of the Twelfth Book on the description of Maṇidvīpa in the Mahāpurānam Śrī Mad Devī Bhāgavatam of 18,000 verses by Maharṣi Veda Vyāsa.

Conclusion

Why does Vasishtha use the expression, "Mother Divine," to explain what lifts the body up in the air? Mother Divine is the embodiment of total knowledge and total organizing power. She is the nature of Puruṣa, the Nature of one's own Self.

Traversing from the outer surface of the skin, to the deep set basal ganglia in the center of the brain, there are 16 steps, sixteen layers, sixteen enclosures. Then entering onto the cellular level, there are three more layers to arrive at the fundamental basis of intelligence in human physiology, the DNA within every cell. There are nineteen layers, nineteen distinct enclosures between the surface level of the skin and the treasure of infinite intelligence and organizing power deep within, at the core of the whole physiology, in the DNA.

This whole range, from the outside surface to the central core—the territory of the island of gems, *Maṇidvīpa*—is called Sarvaloka in the language of the *Devī Bhāgavatam*. "Sarvaloka" means literally all the worlds. Sarvaloka, with its nineteen different enclosures, encompasses all the worlds, all the lokas. All the trees and plants and fruits that exist anywhere in the universe are in Sarvaloka. All the levels of creation, from the minute to the cosmic in scale, all the places of abode of the regents of the quarters, the abodes of Indra, Yama, Varuṇa and Kubera; the abodes of all the Devas, the abode of the Gandharvans and the abode of the Rākṣasas—all the lokas are there in Sarvaloka. That means all the organizing power to accomplish anything whatsoever, creative or destructive, is available in Sarvaloka; all the treasures of gems of all kinds, the riches of the whole creation are available in Sarvaloka in unlimited abundance.

Sarvaloka, the abode of Mother Divine, is there in every human physiology, between the surface of the skin, on the outside, to the strands of DNA deep within the nucleus of the cell, on the inside. All knowledge and organizing power, all bliss and fulfillment, and all the treasures of the whole creation, are there in every human physiology. Every human being is born with this unlimited inexhaustible treasure within.

Yogic Flying, as Vasishtha teaches, is the science and technology of locating and harnessing the power of Devī, the power of Mother Divine within everyone. It is a completely natural and innocent process of unfolding one's own unbounded potential, discovering the infinite, and making it function in every channel of human endeavor. Yogic Flying according to Yoga Vasishtha is the fastest path to gaining total enlightenment, Brahman Consciousness, and living life here and now in affluence and fulfillment.

Endnotes

1 Nader, Tony, *Human Physiology, Expression of Veda and Vedic Literature*, Maharishi University of Management Press: Fairfield, Iowa, 2014, 388-419.

2 Pāṇḍeya, Rāmateja, *Śrīmaddevībhāgavatam Mahāpurāṇam*,-CaukhambāVidyābhavana: Varanasi, 1986.pp. 813-823.

3 Swami Vijnanananda, *The Śrīmad Devī Bhāgawatam*, Parts I and II, Oriental Books Reprint Corporation: New Delhi, 1986.

4 Nader, Tony, *Human Physiology*, 388-419.

EPILOG

Everyone longs to fly. Everyone naturally desires to soar through the air, free from the binding influence of gravity. Everyone wishes to be able to go anywhere at will, instantly.

Thousands of years ago, in the age of Rām, there was already an established tradition of Yogic Flying, upheld by the masters of the Vedic tradition. The technique is described in the Yoga Sūtras of Patañjali, and it is a practice which develops supreme mind-body coordination. This ancient practice, taught by Vasishtha to Rām, has many beneficial side effects for the individual and for the whole society. Rām established groups of Yogic Flyers and created a golden age of human civilization, in which no one suffered, there were no diseases anywhere, and everyone lived their full span of years. Yogic Flying, according to Vasishtha, is an essential and intrinsic part of human life, which brings complete fulfillment and total perfection to every avenue of human endeavor. Heavenly life can be lived on earth through Yogic Flying.

In this scientific age, the techniques of automatic self-transcending and Yogic Flying have been revived by Maharishi Mahesh Yogi in their full purity and effectiveness. At the moment of lift-off in Maharishi's technique of Yogic Flying, scientific research has shown that there is maximum coherence in brain functioning: Coherence in all frequency ranges spreads throughout the cortex. This is the physiological basis of the dramatic benefits of the liftoff described by Vasishtha as perfect health, enlightenment, and alliance with total natural law. This dramatic and powerful technology of the ancient Vedic civilization is available in the world today in centers teaching the Transcendental Meditation program.

Everyone in the world should practice this program of Yogic Flying, for their personal evolution and growing fulfillment in life, and to contribute to the creation of an ideal society in which everyone lives together in peace and harmony, the society prospers, and the civilization as a whole rises to higher and higher levels of collective consciousness.

There are thousands of techniques of meditation available in the world today, but only one has this special badge of authenticity. Only one, Maharishi's Transcendental Meditation program, is always taught in the name of the great holy sage Vasishtha and the great sages of the Vedic Tradition of Masters. Teachers of Maharishi's Transcendental Meditation program always teach in the name of the great holy sage Vasishtha, the same Vasishtha, Maharishi says, who wrote the Yoga Vasishtha. Hearing his name invoked in a short ceremony of gratitude performed at the time of personal instruction enlivens the teacher's connection with this ancient tradition, and verifies for the student that he is receiving the wisdom of Vasishtha and the great teachers of the Vedic tradition in its perfect purity.

Maharishi's Transcendental Meditation program is taught all over the world. Find the center nearest you on TM.org, and learn these technologies of consciousness: Become a siddha man or woman as quickly as possible, and take Vasishtha's advice to rise to higher states of consciousness. There are seven states of consciousness open to man. Don't be satisfied with waking, dreaming and sleeping states. There is so much more to be explored: Consciousness is a field of all possibilities.

Perfect health, infinite freedom and fulfillment are beckoning. Together, let us create world peace and bring perfection to life everywhere. Let's make the world golden. Yogic Flying is the greatest gift of God to mankind. This treasure is for you to enjoy!

Made in United States
Orlando, FL
13 January 2023

28626937R00272